AF413341

TOO GOOD TO
GET MARRIED

Miss Alice Austen

TOO GOOD TO GET MARRIED

THE LIFE AND PHOTOGRAPHS OF MISS ALICE AUSTEN

BONNIE YOCHELSON

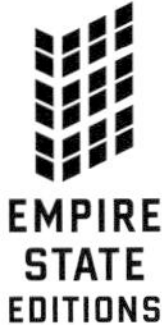

EMPIRE
STATE
EDITIONS

AN IMPRINT OF FORDHAM UNIVERSITY PRESS   NEW YORK 2025

Fordham University Press gratefully acknowledges financial assistance and support provided for the publication of this book by Historic Richmond Town.

Visit us online at www.fordhampress.com/empire-state-editions.

For EU safety / GPSR concerns: Mare Nostrum Group B.V., Mauritskade 21D, 1091 GC Amsterdam, The Netherlands, gpsr@mare-nostrum.co.uk

Library of Congress Cataloging-in-Publication Data available online at https://catalog.loc.gov.

Printed in Canada

27 26 25   5 4 3 2 1

First edition

CONTENTS

FOREWORD

In 2013, Historic Richmond Town completed a seven-year project establishing digital access and preservation of the Alice Austen Photograph Collection. Acquired in 1950, the Collection comprises over 7,800 pieces, including glass plate and film negatives and various types of prints. With this collection fully researched and digitized, Historic Richmond Town was eager to produce a book that would illuminate the life and work of Alice Austen.

Soon thereafter, Bonnie Yochelson contacted Historic Richmond Town to write a fresh assessment of Alice Austen based on the newly accessible collection. A well-known art historian and curator, Bonnie had written authoritative books and organized international exhibitions on many New York photographers, including Jacob A. Riis and Berenice Abbott. Historic Richmond Town was pleased to work with Bonnie on the creation of a modern history of Alice Austen that would feature a large selection of her photographs, beautifully printed.

Alice Austen was a major supporter of Historic Richmond Town (then known as the Staten Island Historical Society) during her lifetime. It has been our honor to steward Alice Austen's body of work over the decades. In 2023, Historic Richmond Town shared the full collection of digitized images with the Alice Austen House. We are hopeful for a boundless reach of the Austen Collection through this book and through the work of the Alice Austen House.

JESSICA B. PHILLIPS
Chief Executive Officer
Historic Richmond Town

FOREWORD

Alice Austen's life story and photographic legacy continue to inspire new generations of artists, activists, and scholars. Her home and studio—now the Alice Austen House and Park—serve as a platform for contemporary artists to explore connections between their work and this nationally recognized LGBTQ+ landmark, as well as the broader contexts of photographic and queer history.

With her camera, Austen shattered the confines of Victorian societal norms for women. She fearlessly ventured into both the natural world and urban landscapes, creating an extensive photographic collection that showcases not only her surroundings but also the profound connections she shared with her intimate circle of female friends.

It is a great honor to help preserve Austen's legacy and collaborate with the larger archive held at Historic Richmond Town, ensuring open and free access to her archives. This enables important projects, such as the creation of this illuminating book, to come to life.

VICTORIA MUNRO
Executive Director,
Alice Austen House

TOO GOOD TO
GET MARRIED

INTRODUCTION

In 1951, while researching an illustrated history of American women, Oliver Jensen stumbled upon Alice Austen's photographs at the Staten Island Historical Society. Soon he met the eighty-five-year-old photographer and arranged for *LIFE* magazine, his former employer, to run a feature story about her. Interviewing Alice for the article, he asked her why she never married, and she replied, "I guess I was too good to get married."[1] In his 1952 book, *The Revolt of American Women*, Jensen remarked on Alice's skills at social activities like tennis and photography and reinterpreted her comment: "But she never married. 'She was too good for the men,' friends said; that is, she could do everything better."[2] In his research notes, Jensen speculated in yet another direction. Alice was distrustful of marriage because she and her mother had been abandoned by her father, Edward Munn: "[If] mother and daughter [had] kindlier memories of Edward Munn . . . perhaps the course of Alice's life would have been different."[3] Jensen greatly respected Alice; he developed a warm relationship with Alice's partner, Gertrude Tate; and he likely knew that they were a lesbian couple. The product of a Freudian era, however, he believed that heterosexual marriage was the norm (he married five times), and he understood lesbianism as an illness rooted in childhood trauma. In *LIFE* and in his book, he sought to protect Alice and Gertrude from censure by referring to Gertrude as Alice's "life-long friend."[4] Alice may, though, have simply given Jensen a forthright answer: in her youth, she had engaged in the courtship rituals of her social set, but she then rejected marriage and its strictures and realized that she loved women. Alice's response to Jensen was characteristically candid and covert, at once honest and discreet.

The 1951 article in *LIFE* presented Alice Austen—an amateur photographer who brilliantly captured the relaxed luxury of Gilded Age high society and depicted the working classes of Manhattan's crowded streets—to the American public for the first time. Twenty-five years later in 1976, Ann Novotny wrote *Alice's World, The Life and Photography of an American Original, 1866–1952*, the first and only prior monograph on Alice Austen. Writing a commercial book for a general audience, Novotny, like Jensen, described Alice and Gertrude as friends, not partners or lovers. Novotny adhered to Jensen's explanation for Alice not marrying: "From her earliest child-hood memories of her mother's betrayal by Edward Munn, she undoubtedly retained some mistrust of men as husbands, even though she enjoyed their companionship."[5] At the time, Novotny was herself coming out as a lesbian, and she subsequently wrote articles for small feminist and lesbian magazines presenting Alice as a lesbian artist.

In 1983, the Alice Austen House became a public museum, and its staff and support-ers, relying on the authority of *Alice's World*, chose not to acknowledge Alice's sexual identity. At the same time, women's studies scholars and lesbian activists, relying on Novotny's articles, celebrated Alice's photographs as evidence of lesbian art before the gay rights movement. Thus, two separate stories took hold, ironically both initiated by the same author. In 1994, the Lesbian Avengers disrupted an annual festival at the Alice Austen House and distributed a "Guide to the Alice Austen and Gertrude Tate House, a National Historic Lesbian Landmark."[6] When a defensive museum volunteer accused the protesters of knowing nothing about Alice Austen, they retorted, "We know her from her pictures."[7] Among those pictures was "Trude & I Masked, Short Skirts" (Figure i.1), in which the protesters recognized kindred spirits: two women in a bedroom posing in their undergarments with their hair down, "smoking" ciga-rettes, and wearing masks to hide their identities. The "was-she-or-wasn't-she" dis-pute plagued the Alice Austen House until 2017, when it was designated a national site of LGBTQ history. The 1994 pronouncement of the Lesbian Avengers, seemingly quixotic at the time, became a reality.

In 1891, a century before the Lesbian Avengers, when Alice took the photograph "Trude and I Masked," the term "lesbian" might conjure in the American imagination foreign women of ill repute, perhaps an idea in Alice's mind as well.[8] But her photo-graphs reveal that in the early 1890s, she was exploring what being a woman meant to her. She and her friends posed as prostitutes, drunkards, men, fashion plates, and femmes fatales. The photographs that resonate today offer glimpses of Alice coming to know herself. As art historian Richard Meyer has evocatively observed, "These images stand on the threshold of queer visibility."[9]

A glaring weakness of Novotny's 1976 book is the concealment of Alice's sexual identity. Less glaring but also problematic is its lack of attention to chronology. Be-cause Novotny surveyed the photographs thematically—friends and family, Staten Is-land, Manhattan, travel—she did not address how Alice and her photography evolved within a changing world, especially one of changing gender roles. Prioritizing chronol-ogy shows how Alice's friendships, ambitions, and photographs were shaped by a shifting cultural landscape.

There is considerable evidence at hand to describe Alice's life and the role photog-

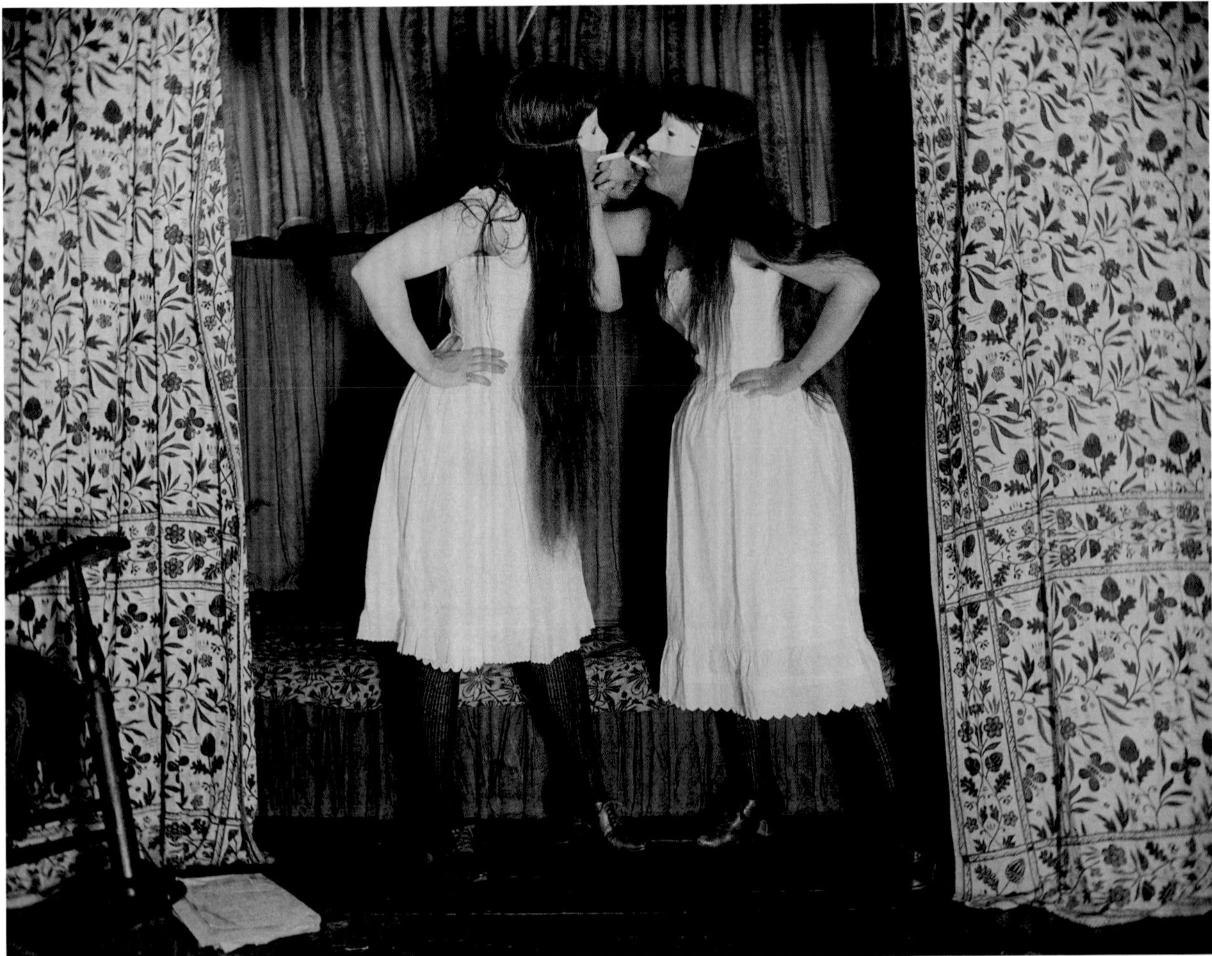

Figure i.1   Trude & I Masked, Short Skirts

raphy played in it: over 7,800 negatives and vintage prints—recently digitized and cataloged—and a treasure trove of family memorabilia, including photo albums, scrapbooks, oil portraits, and ephemera such as dance cards filled in by her partners, the pencils still attached. There are three scrapbooks in which she carefully documented her social activities between 1882 and 1892, and 700 letters written to her from friends and family between 1883 and 1898. But Alice's thoughts and motives remain elusive. There are no diaries; her side of the correspondence is missing; and the photographs, even those identified by subject and date, retain their secrets.

Despite the absence of her voice, a rich portrait of Alice's temperament and values emerges. She was an independent and strong-willed woman who nonetheless remained steadfastly loyal to her family heritage. In each chapter of her life, her rebellious impulses were held in check by an insular world defined by affluence and whiteness. A descendant of English colonists who had amassed great wealth, she lived most of her life at Clear Comfort, the Staten Island home that her grandparents had built, which was filled with family furniture and memorabilia. In the post-Reconstruction era of her youth, theories of racial hierarchy were prevalent, and Americans of "Knickerbocker stock" assumed that their class status reflected their innate superiority. Alice's society was filled with prejudice that she would not have recognized as such. As their letters attest, she accepted the casual racism of her friends. Arriving at an Adirondack resort, one friend wrote: "The people are all very nice, no Jews or invalids."[10] Alice loved popular culture, including minstrelsy, a form of "subversive" humor that offered white audiences a "playful" release by mocking the disempowered. John A. Morton Jr., a close friend and admirer, waxed lyrical about Alice's *noblesse oblige*:

> Alice Austen was a lady, an aristocrat in the best sense of that word. . . . She was charitable, kind, understanding and dignified, she was never a snob, never in any pose, never forgetful of her duties as a lady and never undemocratic. (Ask her garage man . . . hear it from her ex-servants!)[11]

Alice's family presented her with an unorthodox model of Victorian domesticity. Taking over his father's auction business, Alice's grandfather suffered several financial reversals but maintained his family's financial security until his death in 1894 at age 83. Alice's grandmother, a devoted wife and mother, provided the family ballast. But neither Alice's mother nor her aunt conformed to the conventional ideal of feminine devotion and sound household management. Her mother, also named Alice, returned home after a brief failed marriage, and her Aunt Min and Min's second husband, Oswald Muller, traveled the world before retiring to Clear Comfort when Alice was in her teens. The family encouraged Alice's passions for shopping, scrapbooking, and athletics, supported her desire to travel, and did not pressure her to marry.

Alice entered society in 1883, engaging in a whirlwind of leisure activities, which she dubbed "the larky life."[12] She was devoted to tennis, a new sport open to women as well as men, which offered myriad opportunities for intimacy and independence among young people. A competitor in all things, she was a local tennis champion and was popular with men as well as women. The numerous letters of the 1880s from her women friends express the excitement that these relatively unchaperoned events—tennis tournaments, boating competitions, amateur theatricals, and dances—inspired among them. The more formal, flirtatious letters from men and the many dance cards that she saved indicate Alice's interest in courting men's affection.

In the mid-1880s, Alice took up photography, a fashionable and expensive hobby, at which she excelled. Once introduced to the camera by her Uncle Oswald, she perfected her skill on her own, specializing in portraits and landscapes that documented her Staten Island circle and their pastimes and her visits to resorts and the lavish homes of family members and friends. In group portraits and tableaux orchestrated for the camera, Alice included herself within the frame, creating a kind of visual diary of her coming of age. Garnering great praise for her superior craftsmanship and giving photographs as gifts, she used photography to enhance her social persona. She had neither the need nor the time to participate in the activities of the burgeoning photography clubs of the day, nor was she interested in the artistic effects, idealized subjects, and debates about art that preoccupied her contemporaries who fell under the spell of pictorialism.

Although Alice's equipment was up-to-date, her aesthetic belonged to an earlier era, and her visual imagination was stimulated by popular culture—trade cards, magazines, calendars, postcards, stereographs—rather than the fine arts.

By 1891, when Alice and her friends faced the prospect of matrimony, the underlying risks of the larky life emerged. She came to realize the emotional costs of flirtatious behavior, including her own, and to understand that the social power of a popular girl crumbled in the face of marital obligation. Although she celebrated the marriages of several friends by photographing their new homes, she also used the camera to explore her feelings about women's social roles. This moment of reckoning inspired Alice's now-famous photographs of her and her friends clowning before the camera. Both transgressive and humorous, the photographs reveal her skeptical view of the mating rituals and gender roles that had preoccupied her for many years. When Jensen showed Alice a modern print of her 1891 photograph of Julia Martin, Julia Bredt, and herself dressed in men's clothing, she remarked: "Maybe we looked better as men than women." (Figure i.2).[13]

In the mid-1890s, the concept of the "New Woman" was coined to describe women of Alice's generation who challenged Victorian norms and asserted their independence by attending college, pursuing careers, eschewing marriage, and exploring their sexuality. Alice did not pursue a career, but she challenged Victorian norms in her own way. Her former tennis partner Violet Ward, who had not been among her "larky life" companions, played a major role in encouraging Alice to strike out in new directions. Alice collaborated with Violet on two photography projects, including Violet's popular book, *Bicycling for Ladies*, and she produced a photographic portfolio of

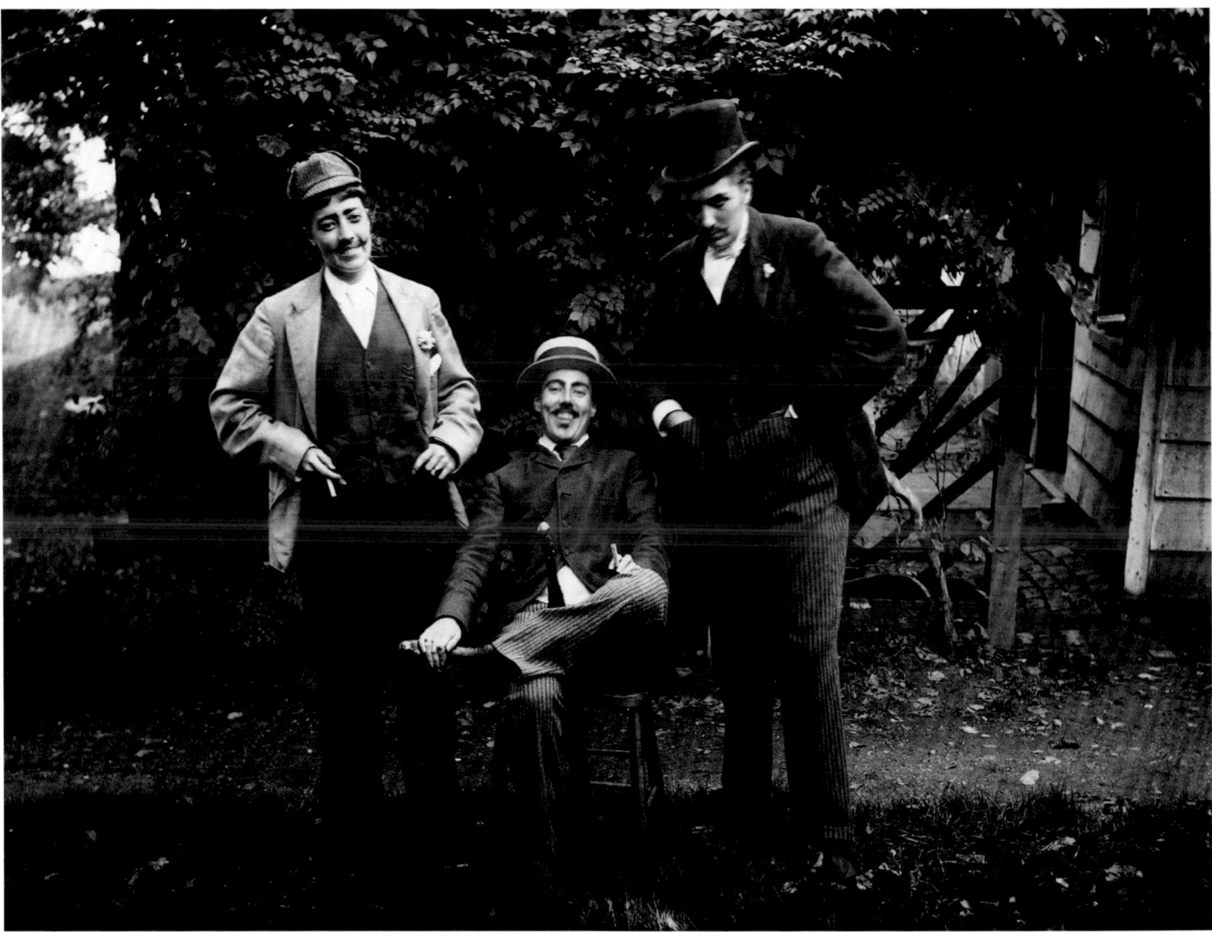

Figure i.2   Julia Martin, Julia Bredt & Self, Dressed Up

"New York Street Types," for which she violated the norms of feminine behavior by traveling throughout Manhattan in search of working-class subjects. Violet also introduced Alice to Daisy Elliott, a somewhat older woman who became romantically involved with Violet and Alice for several years.

Alice's allegiance to her class, however, limited her horizons. As a woman of means, she was wary of commercial exchange; when she sent prints to friends and family, she ignored their requests to compensate her. In the 1890s, when many women amateurs became professional photographers, she produced historically important and commercially viable photographs but failed to identify an audience for them and was left with dozens of unsold prints.

Alice met Gertrude Tate in 1897, and their partnership defined the rest of Alice's life. Although Gertrude lived in Brooklyn with her family until 1917 when she moved to Clear Comfort, she spent much of her time on Staten Island with Alice's family and friends. Prior to World War I, the two women traveled extensively, spending numerous summers in Europe.

In the course of their lives together, public attitudes toward women's sexuality radically changed. The Victorian concept of "romantic friendship," which presumed that women who loved women were chaste, gave way to the authority of "sexologists," who described same-sex love as a mental illness and a threat to the social fabric. Women exhibiting so-called male behaviors, including "mannish" dress and sexual desire for other women, were labeled "sexual inverts" or, lesbians. Protected by class privilege, Alice and Gertrude successfully navigated a heterosexual culture in which the belief that lesbians were deviant was commonplace. Their activities and associations were exclusive: Alice maintained memberships in private clubs on Staten Island and in Manhattan and founded the Staten Island Garden Club, and Gertrude taught dance and deportment to the children of the wealthy and briefly ran a fashionable tearoom. They were staunch Republicans, which in New York signified anti-Tammany Hall and anti-immigrant sentiments. Neither of them showed any interest in the women's suffrage movement, although when women's suffrage was won, they registered to vote.

Once Alice met Gertrude, her photography languished. In the 1880s and 1890s, she had been an accomplished craftsman, and her beautiful or humorous photographs enhanced her reputation. After 1900, she used her darkroom only occasionally and sent out her negatives to be commercially developed and printed. She was content to record the incidents of daily life, and she experimented with various new gadgets, including a motion picture camera. She became an amateur photographer in the pejorative sense of the word.

When Alice lost all her money in the stock market crash of 1929, she hoped in vain that class status would protect her and Gertrude. Their last twenty years together were grim. They clung to Clear Comfort, which fell into disrepair as Alice succumbed to crippling arthritis. When Gertrude could no longer care for her ailing partner, Alice relinquished her remaining possessions to Gertrude and was admitted to the Staten Island Farm Colony as a pauper. In her final year, Oliver Jensen, the writer from Manhattan, introduced Alice and her photographs to the American public, thereby raising enough money to rescue her from penury and launch her on the path to fame.

1   CLEAR COMFORT

In one of her few extant letters, Alice wrote to her grandfather, John Haggerty Austen, when she and her mother were visiting their cousins in Fishkill, New York, in 1892:[1]

> My dear Grandpa / It is raining hard today & puts a stop to my photographing, I have taken several pretty pictures but the Mts. have been so hazy that I have not as many as I intended. . . . The other day we drove about twenty miles to Wappinger Falls, it is a beautiful drive over the old front-road, we go somewhere every afternoon & almost all the drives are pretty—I have been over a rubber factory where they make toys & the whole process was most interesting. . . . As I want to put this in the early mail I must close with much love to you all / as ever your affect[ionate] Granddaughter / Alice Austen.[2]

Although a routine missive, the letter reveals much about Alice and her way of life as a young woman. Then twenty-six years old, she lived with her extended family and regularly visited friends and relatives, where she indulged her passion for photography. The letter expresses her genuine love for her grandfather, who at eighty-one, although formally retired, still commuted to his Manhattan office and regularly tended his garden (Figure 1.1).

Alice photographed the house and grounds of Clear Comfort, her family's Staten Island home, from the first day that she picked up a camera to the last, sixty years later. Living in a home created by her grandparents, who were among the first New Yorkers to settle on Staten Island, distinguished Alice from many of her friends, whose parents moved there after the Civil War and built large country villas which reflected the tastes and aspirations of the Gilded Age. Clear Comfort formed the backbone of Alice's life, inspired her art, and created in her a deep attachment to the past.

"How Lovely the Old Cottage Looked"

Alice's cherished family heritage was built upon the wealth accumulated by David Embree Austen, her paternal great-grandfather. David and his brother-in-law John

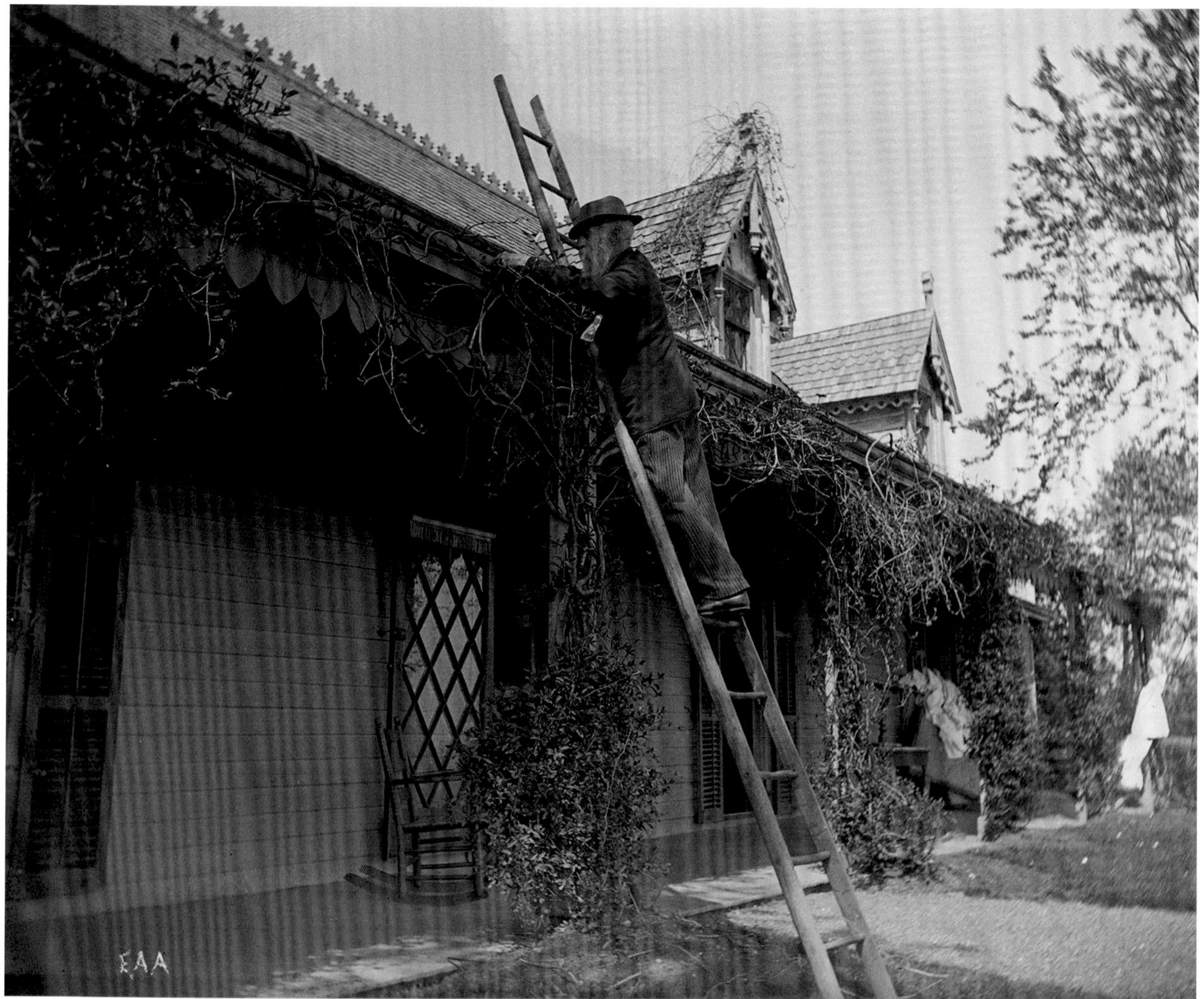

Figure 1.1   Alice's grandfather, age eighty, prunes the vines climbing the Austen House piazza.

Haggerty owned the Manhattan auction firm of Haggerty, Austen & Co., with offices near the East River docks. In the wake of the War of 1812, foreign imports of textiles and other household goods came to dominate American trade, and European manufacturers preferred selling their wares to auctioneers, who guaranteed them fixed prices in an unfamiliar market. Regulated and supported by state law, the auction system helped establish New York as the nation's leading port.[3] In 1827, at the height of the system, more than half of New York imports were sold at auction, and Haggerty, Austen & Co. sold $6 million of goods, equivalent to $156 million today.[4] In 1834, the two men parted ways, and David partnered with William E. Wilmerding, opening offices at William Street and Exchange Place, in the heart of the financial district, where they worked together for a decade. In Moses Beach's *Wealth and Biography of the Wealthy Citizens of New York City*, published in 1845, David's net worth is listed as $400,000, the same as Cornelius Vanderbilt's and equivalent to $14 million today. The book described David as "an excellent business man and a most esteemed citizen."[5]

David Austen's lasting civic contribution was spearheading the move of Grace Church from Broadway and Rector Street uptown to Broadway and 10th Street, where its marble, Gothic Revival edifice remains one of the city's treasured landmarks. As cochair of the finance committee, David arranged to purchase the land and hired the twenty-five-year-old architect James Renwick Jr., to design the church.[6] When the initial phase of construction was completed in 1846, David's newest firm, Austens & Spicer, auctioned off the pews and set the church on a sound financial and social footing. The *New York Courier and Enquirer* related the story:

> The pews in this really magnificent church were put up at auction yesterday by Messrs. Austen [sic] and Spicer, and the hundred and fifty that were sold out of the two hundred and twelve in the church, brought a larger amount of premiums than was ever before known. . . . The purchasers were among the wealthiest and most respectable of our citizens, and Grace Church will doubtless henceforth be *the* church of the city.[7]

By mid-century, wholesalers had edged out auctioneers in the sale of imported and domestic goods, and even the most established auction firms faltered. The business community was shocked when in March 1851 Austens & Spicer went bankrupt. *The Commercial* reported that the failure of the firm "will cast a gloom over many of our citizens," and that "no man in this community has earned a more honorable reputation than David Austen."[8]

In the wake of his bankruptcy, David retired at the age of sixty-seven. By then, his eldest son, John Haggerty Austen, had entered the auction business with every advantage. In his early twenties, John partnered for two years with an auctioneer of his father's generation and then spent eighteen months in Europe to meet clients and gain familiarity with European culture, a prerequisite for handling luxury imports.[9] When his father retired, John and his brother David Austen Jr. immediately reopened the business under their names at the address of their father's firm.

The following year, the Austen brothers handled one of the year's most newsworthy cultural events, the auction of the American Art Union's art collection. Founded by a group of prominent New York business and cultural leaders, the Union promoted living American artists by purchasing artworks and holding exhibitions. As it grew in stature and size—there were almost 19,000 subscribers in 1849—the Union fell into debt.[10] John, a member of its management committee, cleared its debts by auctioning off its assets.

A "Notes on New York" newspaper column featured a lively description of a typical Austen auction, which John clipped for his scrapbook:

> Mr. Austen's large auction room, hung with carpets, forms a fine picture gallery. . . . Those velvet tapestries—what colors—what shadings—what flowers—what figures! . . . Before the hour of the sale, you will find a hundred men gathered in the hall. . . . They are no triflers—no loungers—no blunderers—they are at home among carpets. . . . The hour has come for the sale, and the clerks are all at their gas-lighted desk. . . . "This way gentlemen," says the auctioneer, . . . Lot No. 1 in your catalogues, gentlemen, what is it worth, what do I hear? . . . To the honor of our leading auctioneers be it said that their honesty is evident. . . . Under such management, the auction room is a place worthy of a true merchant.[11]

Although John was an effective auctioneer, the auction business was high-stakes and high-risk. In 1856, John and David stopped working together, and John partnered briefly with his brother George to market kerosene, a new fuel based on the extraction of oil from coal or petroleum. In 1857, John traveled to Europe in hope of marketing kerosene to the Belgian railroads but soon gave up the enterprise.[12] Instead of forming another firm, he became a freelance auctioneer, selling not only works of art and luxury goods but everything, from raw materials to real estate. From 1857 to 1883, when he retired at the age of seventy-two, he was listed as an auctioneer in more than 400 newspaper advertisements. The Civil War years were lean, but his business subsequently picked up enough to allow him to indulge in several trips to Europe, mixing business with pleasure.[13] Between 1867 and 1872 he traveled abroad each summer,[14] missing only 1868, when he filed for bankruptcy.[15] Unlike his father's, John's bankruptcy appears to have been more a financial maneuver than a life-changing event.

John Austen married Elizabeth Alice Townsend in 1836 when he was twenty-five and she was twenty-three. Elizabeth was the daughter of Alice Cornell and Peter Townsend Jr., prominent New Yorkers with landholdings and business interests extending from Albany to Long Island. Their family's prominence dated back further than the Austens' to Elizabeth's grandfather, a businessman-hero of the Revolutionary War. Owner of the Sterling Iron Works, Peter Townsend Sr., famously forged a giant chain, 1,500 feet long and weighing more than fifty tons, which spanned the Hudson River at West Point and succeeded in keeping the British fleet from reaching Albany.[16]

The Austen and Townsend families were remarkably intertwined: two of John's siblings married two of Elizabeth's siblings.[17] John and Elizabeth first lived in Manhattan,[18] where Elizabeth gave birth to four children: Alice Cornell, called Ally (b. 1837); Mary Haggerty, called Minn (b. 1840); John David (b. 1843); and John Herbert (b. 1849). John David died at age four, and John Herbert at age one, both of respiratory illnesses. In 1844, the family bought a 140-year-old Staten Island farmhouse on the waterfront of New York Harbor, first as a summer home and by 1852, when their son Peter Townsend Austen was born, as a year-round residence.[19] The move to Staten Island appears to have been inspired in part by the fear of disease in Manhattan, where the dramatic rise in population—from 30,000 to 800,000 between 1790 and 1860—created unprecedented public health crises.[20] For the rest of her life, Elizabeth wore a mourning ring for her lost sons, and it was she who named their rural home "Clear Comfort."[21]

The Austen family belonged to the generation of city dwellers who established Staten Island as one of New York's earliest suburbs. With the introduction in 1817 of steam-powered ferries between Staten Island and Manhattan, the five-mile trip took a mere thirty minutes. By the 1830s, investors purchased farms, laid out villages with urban street grids, and sold lots to wealthy Manhattan residents in search of rural retreats. In 1835, the Staten Island Association purchased numerous farms on the northeastern part of the island, dividing the properties into lots for sale and establishing the neighborhood of Clifton. That same year, members of the Townsend family purchased a tract of land in and around Clifton that was later referred to as the Townsend "compound," and Townsend Avenue remains today.[22]

The Austen house had been part of a 120-acre farm dating back to the late seventeenth century. The half-acre lot was one of the smallest offered, but the harbor view was unsurpassed. In his 1842 report on Richmond County to the New York State Agricultural Society, Samuel Akerly captured the special allure of the Austen property:

> In looking to the south, we observe the Atlantic, from which a constant succession of vessels of all classes and sizes are coming in and passing up the river and bay to New-York, while others are leaving that emporium of commerce, bound outward. . . . If we cast our eyes across the bay and river eastward, Long-Island meets the view, and we see a rich and well cultivated part of Kings county, thickly settled, having numerous and elegant habitations along its shore, extending northward until the eye rests upon the city of Brooklyn. By a slight movement of the visual organ, the harbor and city of New-York are embraced within the panorama, which also takes in the distant hills of New-Jersey to the northward, and the vessels which crowd the Hudson river and disappear in the distance.[23]

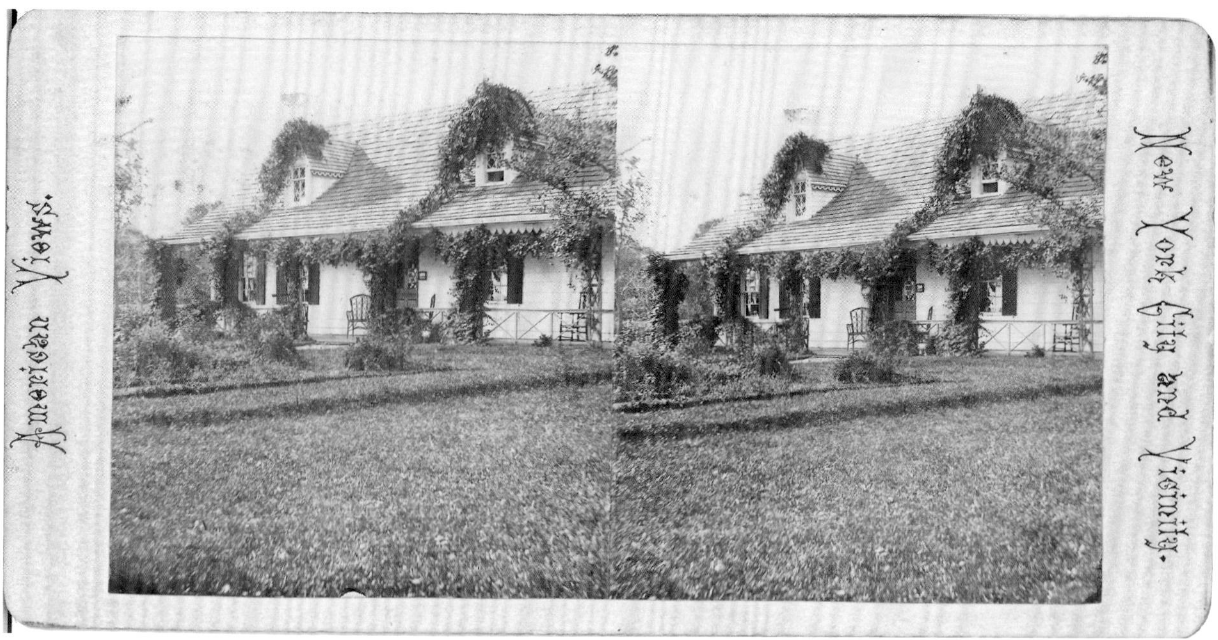

Figure 1.2   Photographer Herman Hoyer included the Austen House in an 1859 set of stereographs, "Illustrations of Staten Island."

The Austen farmhouse consisted of two rooms with a central hall facing the water (east) and a kitchen at the rear (west). When John and Elizabeth were renovating in the 1850s, the family consisted of their two adolescent daughters Ally and Minn, baby Peter, and John's elderly parents. To meet their needs, they added dormers to the upper story for bedrooms; enlarged the ground floor with another bedroom and a room next to the kitchen; and raised the roof over the kitchen for servants' quarters. A long porch, called the piazza, spanned the front of the house, providing a shaded area to enjoy the harbor view.[24] A stereograph of "The Old Austen House," by Herman Hoyer, ca. 1859, shows the house with these improvements (Figure 1.2).[25] The property ended abruptly on the north side of the house, a shortcoming that Elizabeth, who had family money of her own, remedied by purchasing a group of nine, small adjacent lots. The first were acquired in 1851, with the aid of architect James Renwick, who had business dealings with both the Austen and Townsend families.[26] Five more lots were added in 1859.[27] The purchases doubled the size of the property and placed the house in the middle of a lot that bordered Pennsylvania Avenue and extended to the shoreline.

In the 1860s, the family further transformed their home from a Colonial Dutch-American farmhouse into a Carpenter Gothic cottage, with bargeboard eaves, fanciful chimney pots, and elongated windows opening onto the piazza. The expansive lawn was transected with winding paths and dotted with plantings, forming a picturesque vista. An aficionado of European Gothic architecture and a knowledgeable gardener, John Austen was probably the initiator of the fashionable updates of the house and the design of the grounds.[28] Although Renwick, a Gothic Revival proponent, may have offered casual advice, Clear Comfort seems to have been inspired more directly by the writings of Alexander Jackson Downing, a trendsetting author and landscape designer.[29]

Converting a Colonial Dutch farmhouse with a few multipurpose rooms into a Victorian home, in which rooms were differentiated for specific uses, required improvisation. The first floor of the house included a formal parlor with a conservatory, a central hall, a middle parlor, a dining room, a kitchen, and a bedroom with a sunroom. A comparison of the floor plan with Downing's floor plan for a "Cottage in the English or Rural Gothic Style" shows that the Austen house had more rooms than Downing recommended and lacked the spatial coherence of a planned building (Figures 1.3 and 1.4). The rooms were smaller, and the ceilings, which were punctuated by huge, seventeenth-century oak beams, were lower than in a Victorian home. Floral wallpapers, framed pictures, and mirrors decorated the walls; patterned carpets

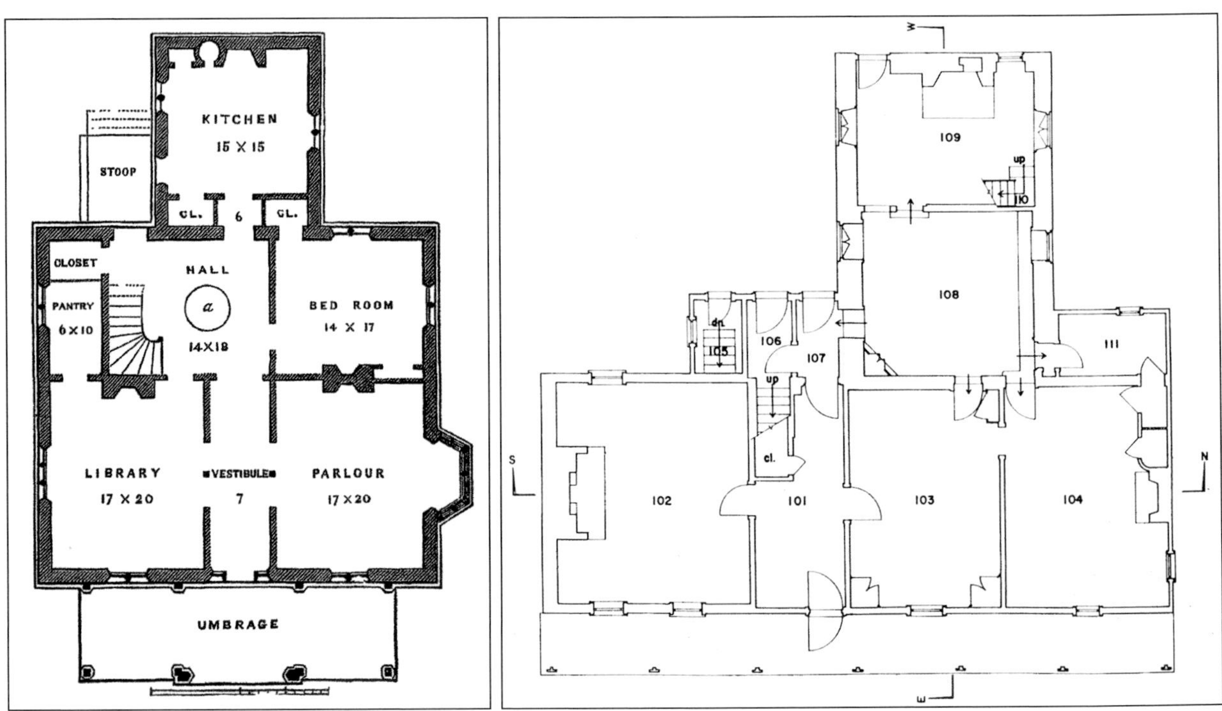

Figures 1.3 and 1.4   The centralized design of A. J. Downing's *Cottage Residences* (left) was nothing like the warren of small rooms resulting from the Downing-inspired renovation of the Austen farmhouse (right).

and oriental area rugs covered the floors; and every surface was adorned with objects of interest, thus taking the Victorian taste for exuberant decorating to an extreme.

Like the house itself, the objects inside it mixed the old and the new, due to John's appreciation of European objets d'art and the couple's pride in their family heritage. At the entrance, an enormous wrought iron knocker from a Rouen chateau, which John had purchased in France, was mounted on a Dutch door with diamond-shaped windowpanes. In the parlor, the fireplace retained the farmhouse's original Dutch tiles, while nearby was a ladies' slipper chair, a fashionable sideboard, and a suite of elaborately carved chairs, which were upholstered in velvet with heavy fringe. The house was filled with family heirlooms, creating a heterodox mixture of historical styles. An eighteenth-century wing chair, which had belonged to Elizabeth's grandparents, held center stage in the parlor (Figure 1.5).[30] An enormous iron link from the giant chain fabricated by Elizabeth's grandfather sat in front of the fireplace, and a bronze oil lamp in the form of an eagle, given to John by the French government, rested on the mantel (Figure 1.6). On either side of the fireplace were oil portraits of Elizabeth's parents in heavy gilt frames, and on the opposite wall hung an oil portrait of John's father, David (Figure 1.7). In the hallway was a Duncan Phyfe sofa and a Federal style mirror, and in the dining room stood a marble bust of David, which once adorned the vestibule of Grace Church.[31]

The product of the Austens' idiosyncratic tastes, the Old Austen House, as it was sometimes called, struck a chord with many Americans who yearned to connect to the nation's past, especially after the 1876 Centennial Exhibition in Philadelphia. A description of the Austen house in an article about historic Staten Island in the September 1878 issue of *Harper's New Monthly Magazine* captures this patriotic nostalgia:

> A short distance from the Quarantine station[32] stands a very old house, which was a home when Washington had scarcely reached the dignity of manhood, which has outlasted revolution and the storms of nearly two centuries, sheltering the British redcoats and the patriots against whom the redcoats fought, looking out through its quaint dormer windows on the thousand changes that have been wrought during its existence, and remaining to this very day a secure and hospitable dwelling.[33]

Reproducing sketches of the grounds and the parlor, the article told the story of Peter Townsend's great chain across the Hudson, along with folktales, like that of a ghost who supposedly haunted the house: "A King George's man fell in love with a maiden who lived in it, and being rejected, desperately hanged himself from a beam in the ceiling."[34] Feature stories about the house appeared in syndicated newspaper columns and national magazines for fifty years into the 1930s.[35]

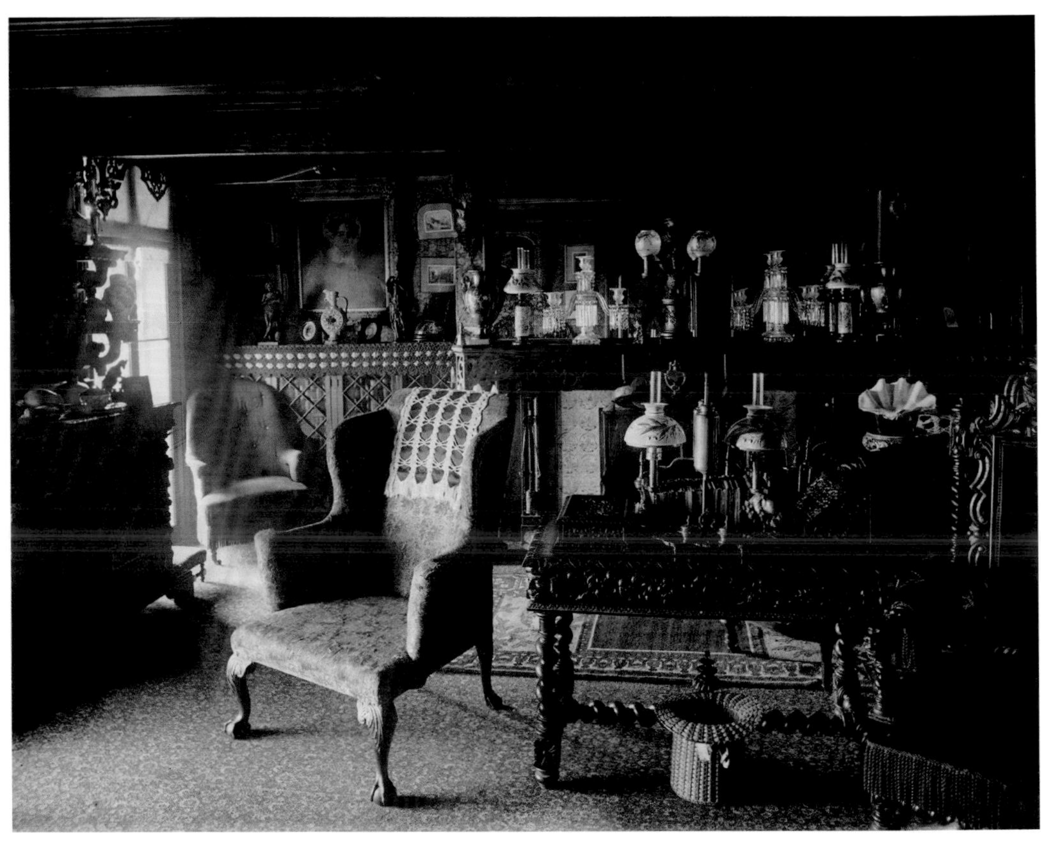

Figure 1.5　An eighteenth-century wing chair that belonged to Alice's maternal great-great-grandparents held pride of place in the parlor.

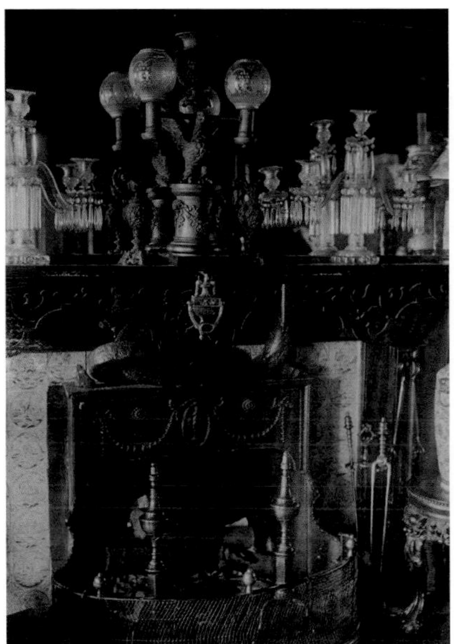

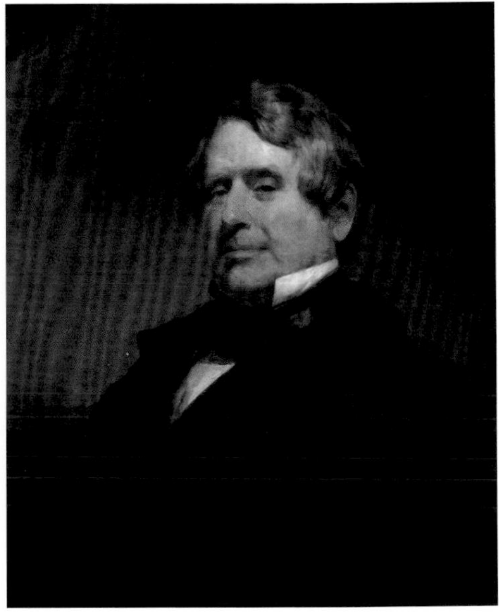

Figure 1.6　On the fireplace mantel was a link from a great iron chain manufactured by Peter Townsend, Alice's great-grandfather. A famous American Revolution relic, the chain had spanned the Hudson River at West Point, preventing English ships from reaching Albany.

Figure 1.7　Alice's great-grandfather David Embree Austen founded the family auction business. This 1846 oil portrait hung in the parlor.

In a conversation with a journalist, John Austen added a charming tale to these accounts. As he told it, he once asked Cornelius Vanderbilt, a Staten Island native who had by then amassed a legendary fortune in shipping and railroads, if he knew the house, to which Vanderbilt replied: "Well, I ought to know that place, if anybody does. It was right there that I courted one of the prettiest girls on the Island before you were born." Vanderbilt reported that the girl, Sally Lake, had beckoned him from the dock and invited him to stay for dinner at the house, which then belonged to her father. Vanderbilt wooed Sally for a few months until her mother ended the relationship, telling him that she did not want her daughter "to marry any poor devil like me." John then asked Vanderbilt about a windowpane in the house that was inscribed, "Sall Lake," with a big "C" next to the date "1812." "That was the identical gal," Vanderbilt answered, "and the big 'C' stands for 'Corneel,' and I put it there myself after Sall had scratched her own name on the window."[36]

John was exceedingly proud of his hybrid house, which was both venerable and fashionable. Writing to Elizabeth from London in 1867, he exclaimed, "I shall never forget the day I passed out of the narrows how lovely the old cottage looked, it was much admired by the passengers who stood near me."[37] On his return, he devised an "official" acknowledgment for his family as he sailed into the harbor, a ritual he repeated on subsequent trips: "I will be as near the stern as I can get & will if the Captain consents lower the flag of France to you the salute to be returned by Peter with his flag on the house & perhaps I may manage to get the guns fired at about the same time."[38]

Although John celebrated the Austen house, he was often away on business, and responsibility for running the household—and perhaps for renovating and decorating the house—fell to Elizabeth. John's European letters to her reveal her capabilities, including paying taxes and handling legal matters,[39] "[M]y dear Elizabeth," he wrote in one letter, "I must say adieu with ten thousand thanks for your great kindness & being so willing to let me go off & leave you alone to make this to me a most delightfull [sic] visit to Europe."[40]

An oil portrait of Elizabeth that hung at Clear Comfort depicts a young Quaker matron who eschewed adornment and whose determined expression suggests a woman who managed her property and her family well (Figure 1.8). Elizabeth exemplified the wife and mother about whom Catharine E. Beecher and her sister Harriet Beecher Stowe wrote in their popular how-to guide, *The American Woman's Home*. The book's goal was to "render each department of woman's true profession as much desired and respected as are the most honored professions of men."[41] As her will reveals, Elizabeth owned Clear Comfort outright and was deeply invested in its future. The will stipulated that the house could not be sold if any family members wished to live there, and it provided up to $1,000 per year for taxes, insurance, and repairs.[42]

John's letters to Elizabeth shine a light on their different temperaments and prior-

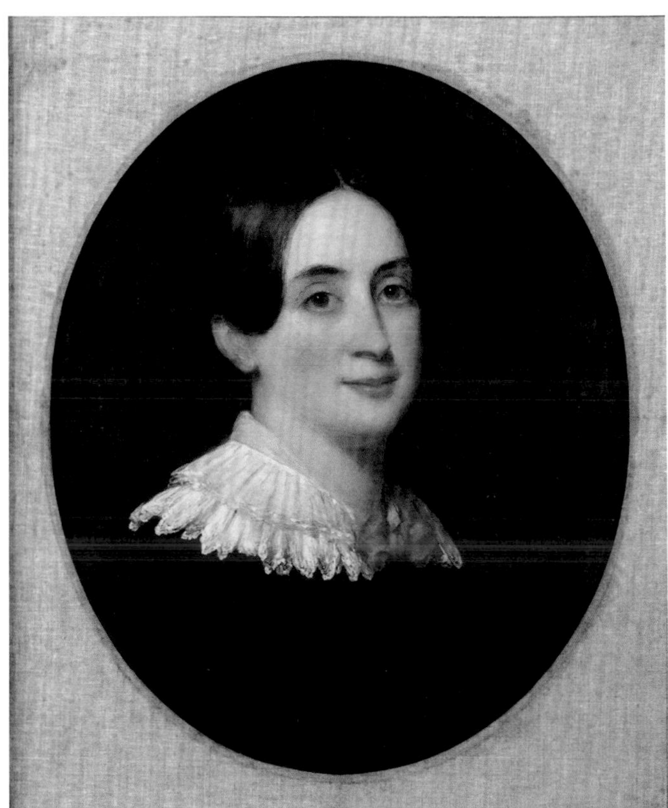

Figure 1.8   Alice was named for her grandmother, Elizabeth Alice Townsend Austen. This oil portrait was painted in the 1840s, when the family lived in Manhattan.

ities. For John, his European vacations were the dividend for his years of hard work. He was wealthy, his children were grown, his health was sound, and while retracing the steps of his formative years, he marveled at a Europe remade by industry and empire. He hoped Elizabeth would share this adventure, and his letters are filled with extravagant exhortations: "If I could bring you out just to see London & Paris I would be the happiest man alive."[43] Elizabeth, however, never traveled to Europe, and she viewed their family's circumstances differently. Their son Peter was still an adolescent, and both daughters, Ally and Minn, were in troubled marriages. Perhaps most important, there was a granddaughter at home. Elizabeth Alice Austen Munn— our Alice—named after her grandmother, was sixteen months old in June 1867 when John took his first summer trip to Europe.

Elizabeth Alice Austen Munn

When she was twenty-six, the Austens' older daughter Ally married Edward Stopford Munn, a thirty-five-year-old stockbroker. In 1851, Edward, along with his parents and five siblings, had emigrated from England to New York, and then twenty-three, he set out on his own.[44] In 1860, he cofounded the brokerage firm of Munn & Stewart,[45] and in June 1863, he and Ally married in Clifton.[46] After the wedding, the newlyweds took up residence at Woodbine Cottage, a small house near Clear Comfort that John and Elizabeth had purchased for them.[47] The 1865 New York State census lists Edward as a "broker" living with his wife and a servant on Staten Island.[48] Their only child, Elizabeth Alice Austen Munn—called Lolla, Loll, or Lollie as a small child and then Alice—was born on March 17, 1866. Soon after her birth, Ally and Edward separated, and mother and child moved home to Clear Comfort.[49] By 1870, Edward was living with his father in Brooklyn.[50]

Although Ally and Edward never divorced, Ally bound herself permanently to Clear Comfort. She discarded the name "Munn" and retook her maiden name, leaving her and her daughter in legal limbo.[51] At some point, the Austen family invented a fictional account of the failed marriage. In 1951, Alice reported to the writer Oliver Jensen that Edward had abandoned her and her mother and returned to his native England.[52] Edward, however, lived in Brooklyn with his parents until his death in 1879 at fifty-two. His failed career, his return to his parents' home, and his premature death suggests prolonged disability, perhaps due to alcoholism. He was buried in his family's plot in Greenwood Cemetery.[53]

Edward's family remained on cordial terms with Ally, as indicated in an 1881 letter addressed to "Mrs. Edward Munn, c/o John H. Austen Esq.," from Edward's sister, Ellen. The letter informed Ally of a bequest for "little Alice" from her paternal grandfather, whose will was in probate in London. Sharing news of other family matters, Ellen beseeched Ally to visit: "Come and see me but please send me word in case I might be out, any day but Monday will suit me."[54]

The letter only adds to the mystery of Edward Munn. If Ally did not divorce and remained in touch with Edward's family, why did she return to her maiden name, creating the possible impression that she had given birth to a child out of wedlock? Why was a story of abandonment preferable to one of incompatibility? Was the abandonment story fabricated for Alice's benefit? When did Alice, who retained Ellen's letter, learn the truth? And did she know her father's family? There are no ready answers to these questions.

Having escaped her marital difficulties, Ally succeeded in providing a loving and secure childhood for Alice at Clear Comfort (Figure 1.9). Ally's mother ran the household, while "Mamma," as Alice called Ally, shared a bedroom with her on the first floor of the house, and their relationship was as close as their small, crowded room would suggest. Alice's photographs of the room show two beds side by side with the walls and every surface covered with cherished objects (Figure 1.10).[55] Mamma's later letters to Alice are filled with local gossip, shopping reports, and maternal fretting—"You poor child to go in for rowing and tennis at once, please don't work too hard"—and boundless

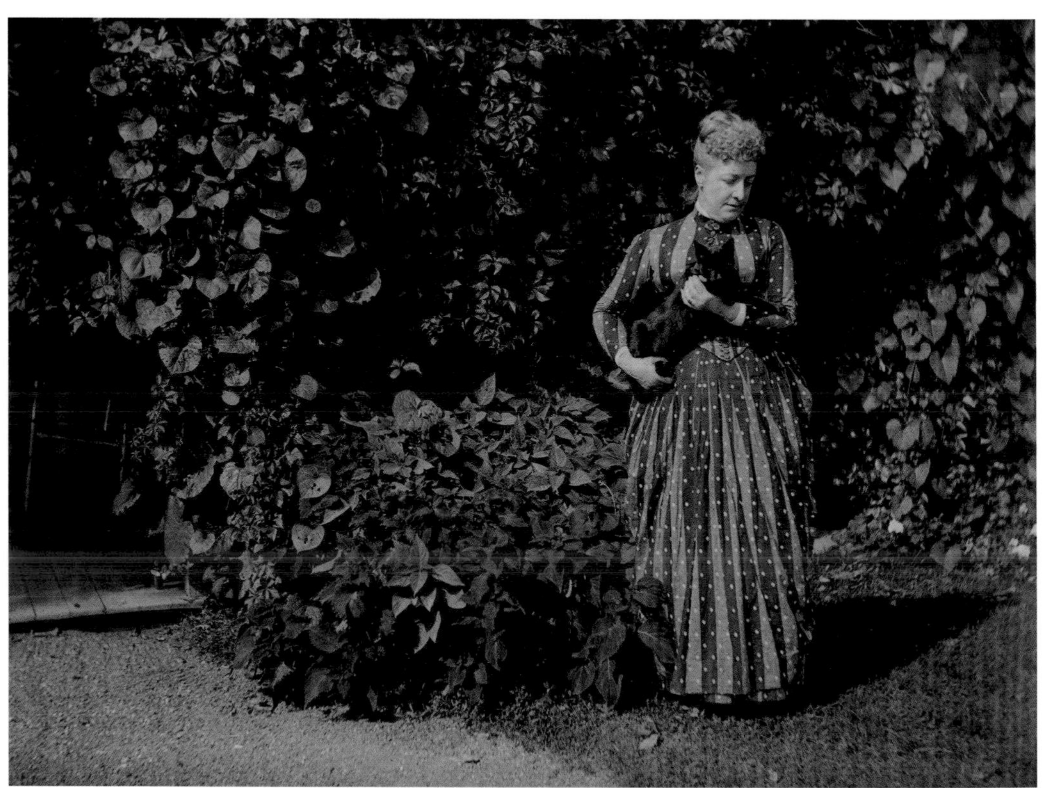

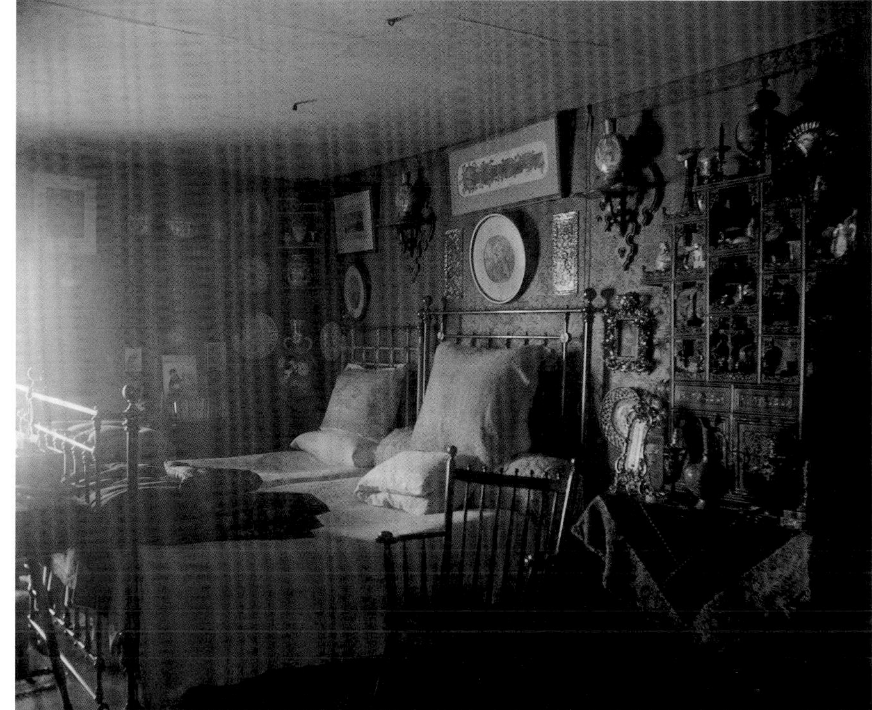

Figure 1.9   Alice's mother was also named Alice—Alice Cornell Austen. After she separated from her husband Edward Stopford Munn, she returned to Clear Comfort and resumed using her maiden name.

Figure 1.10   Alice and her mother shared a bedroom on the first floor of the house.

encouragement—"You certainly have accomplished a great deal . . . surely you are intended to succeed in life, and see the world."[56] An enthusiast of European culture and history, Ally was eager to accompany her father on one of his trips, but Alice's birth barred her way.[57] Perhaps Ally hoped that her daughter would fulfill her ambitions to travel widely. There is no hint in her letters that Ally encouraged Alice to marry.

The year before Ally's wedding, John and Elizabeth's younger daughter Minn married Samuel Hicks, the eldest son of a wealthy family that had recently moved from Manhattan to Clifton. By June 1865, however, they had separated; Sam was living with his widowed mother and younger siblings, and Minn was at Clear Comfort.[58] The problem may have been Sam's drinking. John wrote to Elizabeth, "I wish Sam could do without that one glass of wine there is great danger in that one glass."[59] In 1869, Minn and Sam, who was in poor health, embarked on a sea voyage on the merchant ship *Agra* to Australia, a destination recommended at the time for a therapeutic "change of air."[60] On the arduous journey home, Sam died of consumption at age thirty-eight.[61] Amid misfortune, Minn and the captain of the *Agra*, Oswald Muller, fell in love, and in March 1871, four months after Sam's funeral, they were married in Clifton.

A Danish-born seaman, Oswald came to the United States in his teens and earned the rank of commander in 1867, when he was twenty-eight. After their marriage, Minn accompanied Oswald at sea. According to a syndicated article, "an American upright piano was placed in the cabin of the good ship *Agra* by her captain, for the use of his wife, [an accomplished pianist,] to beguile the tediousness of the long sea voyages."[62] Their "honeymoon" voyage to Australia, China, Japan, and India lasted fifteen months, and their next voyage, in which they circled the globe, took almost two and a half years. The childless couple enjoyed each other immensely. On a trip to San Francisco in 1874, John wrote to Elizabeth:

> I do really think that Minnie & the Captain are just the happiest married couple that I ever saw. The charming manner with which Minnie greets the Captain when he comes on board . . . seems to fascinate him completely . . . I have slept on board in the room . . . [next to theirs and] I hear them begin to talk and laugh at about 5 o'clock [before breakfast].[63]

When Alice was a child, she knew Minn and Oswald only through sporadic letters and occasional visits. There were also newspaper accounts about Captain Muller's ships—the *Agra* (1867–1875) and then the *Samar* (1875–1884)—including a false report on Minn's honeymoon voyage that their ship had been lost at sea.[64] Perhaps appealing most to a child's imagination were the exotic souvenirs from around the world that adorned every room in the Austen house. In 1884 when Alice was eighteen,

Oswald retired as sea captain, became a naturalized US citizen, and opened a business as a stevedore on the East River docks. He and Minn, both forty-four years old, moved into the upstairs northern bedroom at Clear Comfort, enlarging and enclosing their porch and adding an exterior staircase to create an apartment—which they called "the quarterdeck"—crammed with Japanese fans, Asian porcelain, wicker furniture, and other mementos from their travels (Figure 1.11).[65] The Mullers were fun-loving and irreverent, even a bit scandalous. At the base of the stairs, a ship bell was mounted with a sign that read, "Ring the bell and ring like hell!"[66] In the house's only bathroom, Aunt Minn displayed her collection of more than 200 Victorian ceramic figurines of

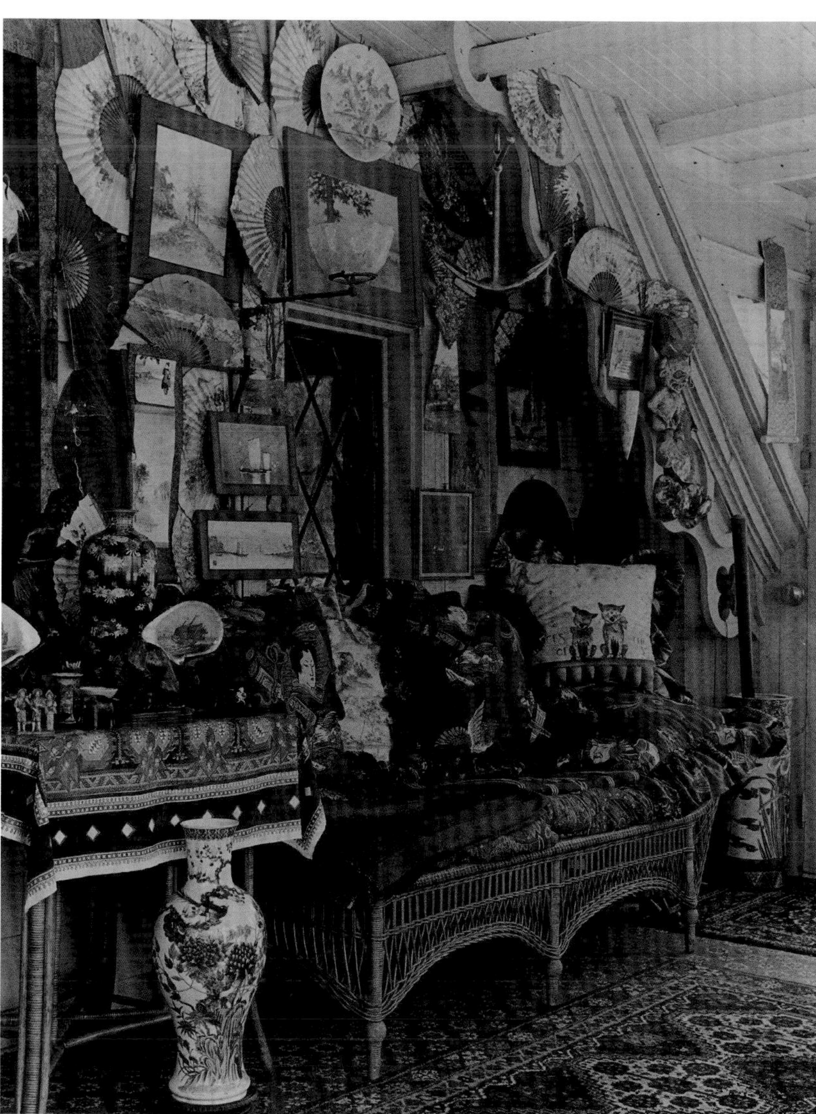

Figure 1.11 Alice's Aunt Minn and Uncle Oswald lived in "the quarterdeck," an apartment on the second floor, which they filled with souvenirs of their travels.

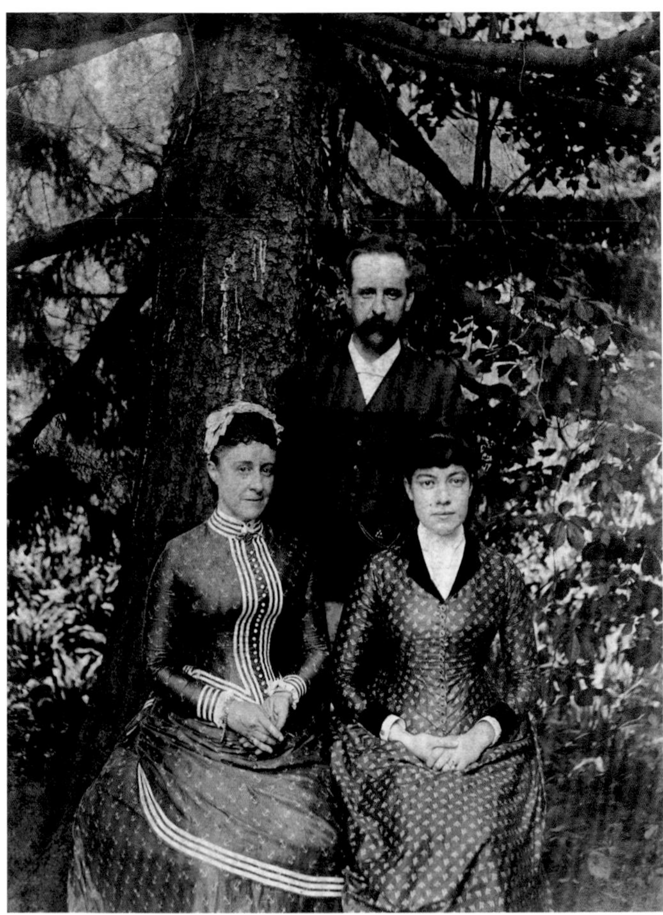

Figure 1.12   Uncle Oswald probably took this photograph of Aunt Minn, Uncle Peter, and Alice in 1885.

animals and humans on chamber pots. She named the profane collection "The Potter Family," in honor of Henry C. Potter, her friend who was the Episcopal bishop of New York.[67] It was also said that Oswald collected erotic literature.[68]

John and Elizabeth's youngest child Peter was fourteen years older than his niece Alice. In 1870, when Alice was four, Peter left home to attend Columbia College's School of Mines, a new program in applied science, and then spent three years in Europe earning a PhD in chemistry. When he returned to the United States in 1876, he taught for a year at Dartmouth College before moving to New Brunswick, New Jersey, to teach at Rutgers College, where he remained for fourteen years. Both of Alice's uncles, Peter and Oswald, were amateur photographers; a photograph of young Alice in her teens with Minn and Peter was probably taken by Oswald (Figure 1.12).

The Austen household also included two or three women servants, usually Irish immigrants, who slept in two small attic rooms (Figure 1.13). Relying on a wood-burning stove, oil and gas lamps, and well water, they cooked, did laundry, and

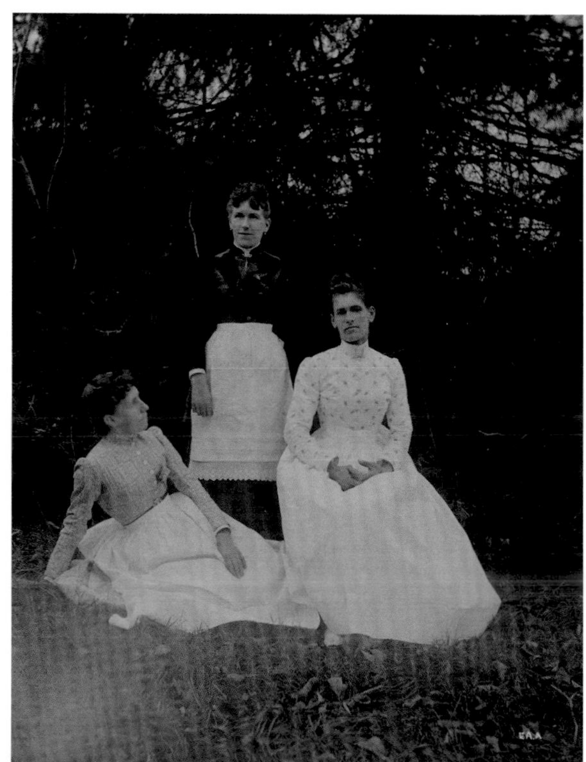

Figure 1.13   Katie, who lived with the Austen family for at least a decade, is one of the three servants pictured here.

Figure 1.14   A pug named Punch and a chihuahua named Chico were beloved members of the Austen family and appear in many of Alice's photographs.

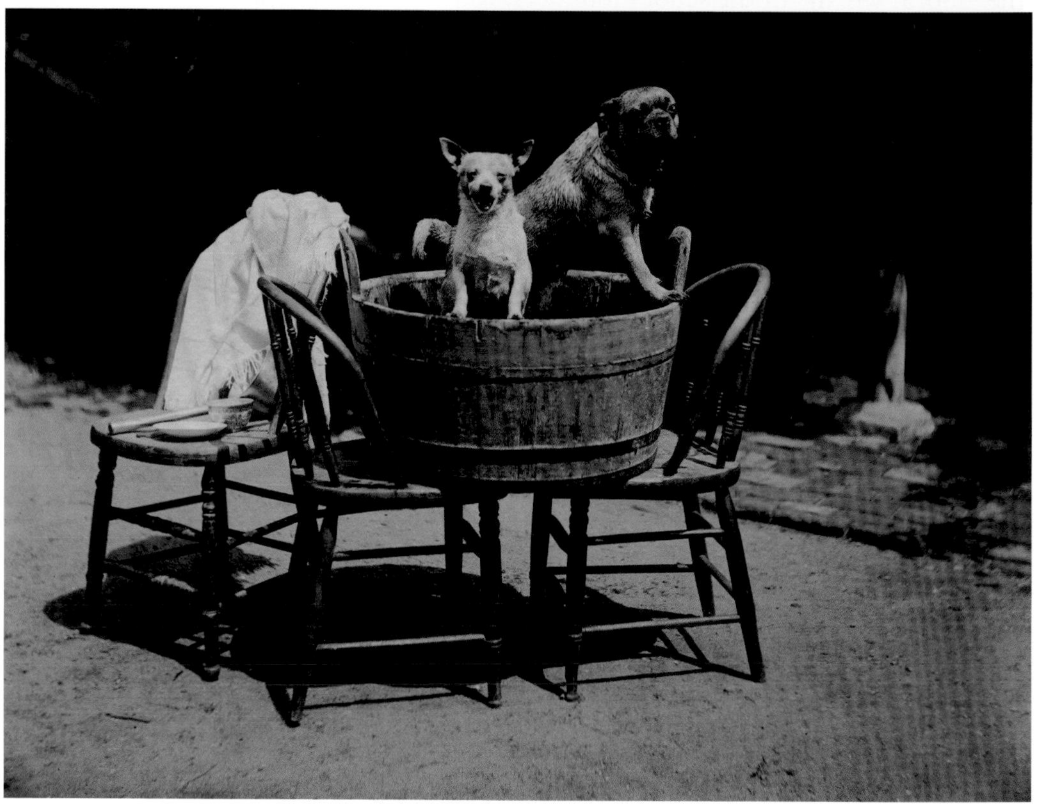

cleaned the house filled chockablock with dust-gathering objects. They also cared for the family's beloved dogs and cats and helped with the garden. Punch, a pug, and Chico, a chihuahua, figure prominently in Mamma's letters and Alice's photographs (Figure 1.14). On February 14, 1892, Mamma wrote:

> Tom [a stray] has not returned, he left a week ago today, I scarcely dare hope he has departed for good. Katie waters the plants, and the dogs are well. Punch burst through one of the middle room panes, shivering it to pieces, the piazza was covered with glass, he strolled out unhurt.[69]

In the 1880s and 1890s, as many as nine people lived in close proximity in the Austen house, a warren of eleven small rooms. Under these snug circumstances, the Austen family maintained cordial relationships with their servants, some of whom stayed with the family for decades.

Outside the home, Alice's childhood revolved around the Errington School for Young Ladies, which she attended from age eight or nine until fifteen or sixteen. Founded by Harriet and Georgiana Errington, the school occupied a large Gothic Revival building less than a mile from Clear Comfort. An early advertisement touted the "moral worth" of the school founders, which, for the parents of well-to-do girls, may have taken priority over academic credentials.[70] The curriculum consisted of subjects deemed essential for a woman's education—English, French, music, and the arts—and because Harriet Errington was an amateur botanist and paleontologist, perhaps the sciences as well.[71] The school did not assign grades or offer diplomas. The Errington sisters were much loved by their pupils, including Alice, who pasted Georgiana's 1881 obituary in a scrapbook[72] and sent Christmas cards to Harriet until her death in 1896.[73]

An 1877 autograph book belonging to Alice's classmate Grace Simonson provides a glimpse of the strong bonds that formed among the ten- and eleven-year-old girls. Most personal and heartfelt among the small poems in the book is Alice's, which appears on the first page:

> To Grace.
> Loves best greeting to you I send
> And remain forever,
> Your loving friend
> *E. Alice Austen / Feb 20, 1877 / Clifton. S.I.*[74]

Grace and her family moved from Clifton to Harlem in 1881 when she was sixteen, but she and Alice corresponded for more than ten years, despite the distance between them. They may have shared what Victorians called a "romantic friendship." Because men and women were educated separately and socialized differently, women were understandably more spontaneous and intimate with each other than with men, who were trained to treat women with chivalrous formality. Passionate feelings between young women, it was assumed, posed no threat to the ultimate goals of marriage and domesticity.[75] The contrast of the unconstrained language in the letters from Alice's female friends with the formal language of those from young men confirm that she grew up in a world that allowed her to express her feelings freely with women. Whether she understood the nature of those feelings, Alice did not need to restrain them with friends like Grace.

Unlike Alice, Grace pursued her studies, attending Cooper Union to prepare for a career. In August 1885, she wrote to Alice:

> I worked hard at Cooper all winter and was all tired out by summer. I am just beginning to feel myself again. Did you know that I took one of the first prizes in the school? It rather repaid me for working so hard.[76]

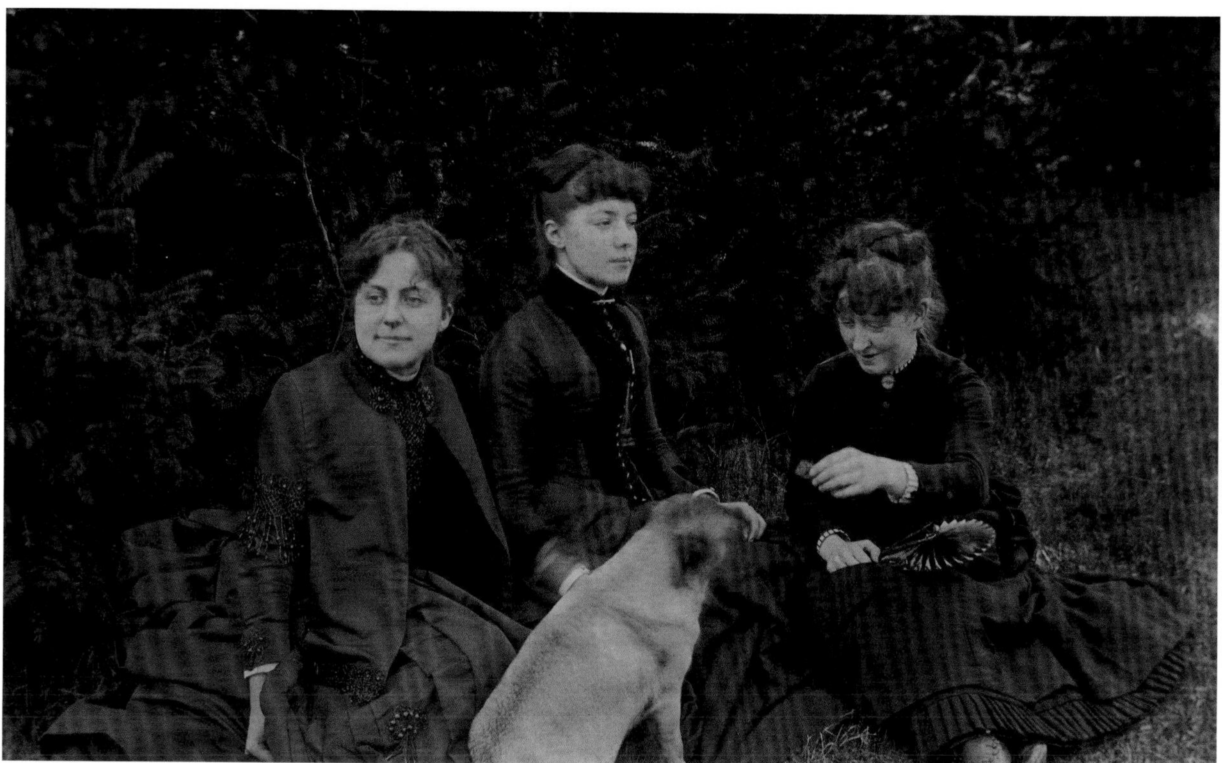

Figure 1.15 Although Grace Simonson (left) moved to Harlem in 1881, she and Alice remained close friends. They may have shared a "romantic friendship" from childhood through their teen years.

How often Grace and Alice saw each other is unknown, but at least once, in April 1886, Alice photographed them lounging together on the lawn at Clear Comfort with Alice's dog Punch and a friend (Figure 1.15). A successful textile designer, Grace never married.

Alice's privileged but unusual childhood set the stage for a life bounded by conservative tradition with the leeway to experiment and explore within those bounds. Her grandparents provided the financial security, domestic tranquility, and family pride that was expected of parents. The affection Alice's grandmother had for Alice was especially strong, as reflected in her will, which bequeathed to Alice, only eighteen when it was written, "free from the interference and control of any husband, all moneys which I may have or deposit on any savings Banks anywhere."[77]

A letter Alice wrote in 1933 to a curator at the Metropolitan Museum of Art, when the Museum acquired her great-great-grandparents' wing chair, shows her lifelong association of her home with her grandmother:

> Dear Mr. Downs, / In answer to your request in your very nice letter about the chair's history, I find your date is correct, the chair is entirely American made & has been in the family many years. . . . I will just copy my grandmother's descent from a book "Memorial of the Townsend Brothers." [*generations recorded*] . . . Peter Townsend married Hannah Hawxhurst whose chair you saw marked "H.H. 1750". My grandparents . . . moved to Staten Island . . . [and] their furniture came with them, handed down from their parents. My grandmother was a first cousin of the Albany Solomon Townsend, & told me she visited her relations in Albany as a girl & they came to see her in New York. Hoping this data will be of use to you & you will stop in again if on Staten Island./ I remain / Very sincerely / E Alice Austen[78]

As revealed in Alice's photographs, Clear Comfort remained largely unchanged from the 1880s until the 1930s, when Alice was forced to sell family heirlooms to remain there.

The unconventional lives of her mother—who was more like an older sister—and her Aunt Minn—who traveled the world and bore no children—allowed Alice to wear the mantle of Victorian womanhood lightly, and the ever-present servants spared her the burden of domestic work. Her education at the Errington School cemented relationships with some of Clifton's leading families. When she finished school, Alice was full of energy and ambition, which she directed toward two passionate hobbies, tennis and photography. Lacking socially prominent parents, she was determined to establish herself as a popular and respected member of what was referred to as Staten Island's "sporting society set."

2   THE SPORTING SOCIETY SET

Alice regarded her family's past with reverence, but she was also a modern girl with a strong sense of style and a penchant for spotting fashionable trends. The term "teen-ager" was not invented until the post-World War II era, but wealthy adolescents of the post–Civil War era were their natural predecessors. They took for granted all things modern, from the endless array of mass-produced goods to mass transit and train travel. Although Alice was not especially interested in literature or the fine arts, she could be counted on to take up the latest craze, be it tennis, photography, or bicycling.

New forms of mass media—syndicated newspapers and illustrated national magazines—introduced an unprecedented amount of information into the Austen home, and Alice's mother instilled in her daughter a taste for the popular press. Among Alice's surviving memorabilia is a selection of illustrated magazines—signed by Alice and sometimes inscribed from Mamma—that offer short stories, poems, puzzles, and sheet music for children. Alice's copies of *Chatterbox*, *Little Folks*, and *Wide Awake* date from 1877 to 1881, when she was eleven to fifteen.[1] In particular, *Wide Awake* wished to deal with the genuine concerns of children rather than rely upon formulaic narratives. The first issue of July 1875 announced: "Magazines like *Wide Awake* . . . contain nothing of the 'run-away-to-sea' style for boys, or the 'elope-and-be-happy' incentive for girls, which are greatly cried against by parents now-a-days."[2]

Alice's magazines were filled with brightly colored illustrations made possible through the invention of chromolithography, a new form of inexpensive color printing, which many considered gaudy and vulgar, but which strongly appealed to the young. Chromolithography also facilitated the explosive growth of trade cards, small eye-catching advertisements for products and merchants, which could be picked up in stores or found in mail-order packages. Alice became a passionate collector of trade cards beginning in 1880 at the start of a national craze that lasted a decade.[3] She filled three scrapbooks with them, combining the latest trend with a family tradition. Scrapbooks belonging to Alice's grandfather, grandmother, mother, and Uncle Peter were among the items salvaged from the Austen House in 1945.[4]

Trade cards provide an anthology of popular commercial imagery, from prosaic product displays to still lifes and landscapes, from fashion plates to comic or romantic narratives. A typical page from Alice's third scrapbook offers a cross section of her taste in cards: at center is a Christmas greeting for the toy store FAO Schwarz on Union Square; above it is a romantic picnic scene advertising thread (enlarged as fishing line) manufactured by the J. & P. Coats Company; flanking the picnic scene are two celebrity portraits from Thomas H. Hall Tobacco's "actress series"; below is a crudely drawn comic for waterproof "celluloid collars, cuffs & bosoms," in which a disgruntled Chinese laundryman scowls at the threat to his business; and on either side of the comic are die-cuts of thread spools, bearing the manufacturer's instructions on how to exchange an empty wooden spool for a pin cushion (Figure 2.1).[5] Alice's card collection was strong on fashion and humor, often of a racist character. Notably absent were cards that combined religious maxims with commercial advertising, which were a mainstay of other girls' collections.[6]

Alice measured her collection quantitatively, noting on the inside cover of each scrapbook the date it was finished and the number of cards it contained. For a brief period, she was obsessed: the three scrapbooks, which were filled in twenty-two months, contain 1,000 trade cards. In the first two scrapbooks, Alice experimented with the spelling of her name—"Alice Austyn"—as young girls contemplating their evolving identities often do.

Full of Manhattan addresses, Alice's trade cards reveal her love of shopping, an activity which grew in importance as she matured. Mamma's letters substantiate that she regularly went clothes shopping with Alice—"I saw the fall fashion plates in the windows, no change apparently, same skirt, round waists, materials in wool pretty, and within effect"[7]—and that she fussed over Alice's appearance—"I meant you to take the pink fan with gold sticks to wear with the pink sateen, I hope your dresses were not very badly creased."[8] Although mother and daughter purchased ready-to-wear clothing, they regularly hired dressmakers to adjust the fit and sew outfits for special occasions. A good dressmaker was a highly valued asset, as Mamma explained:

> Trudie [Eccleston] came Tuesday morning to ask the name of your new dressmaker, said she had forgotten [her] name and address. . . . I am afraid you were a little rash in mentioning [her]. . . . If [she] suits, I want her to do something for me too, and I don't care for the Ecclestons to take her off.[9]

Alice loved displaying her fashionable wardrobe in photographs, as seen in a portrait taken by her Uncle Oswald, which looks like a fashion plate from a magazine (Figure 2.2).[10]

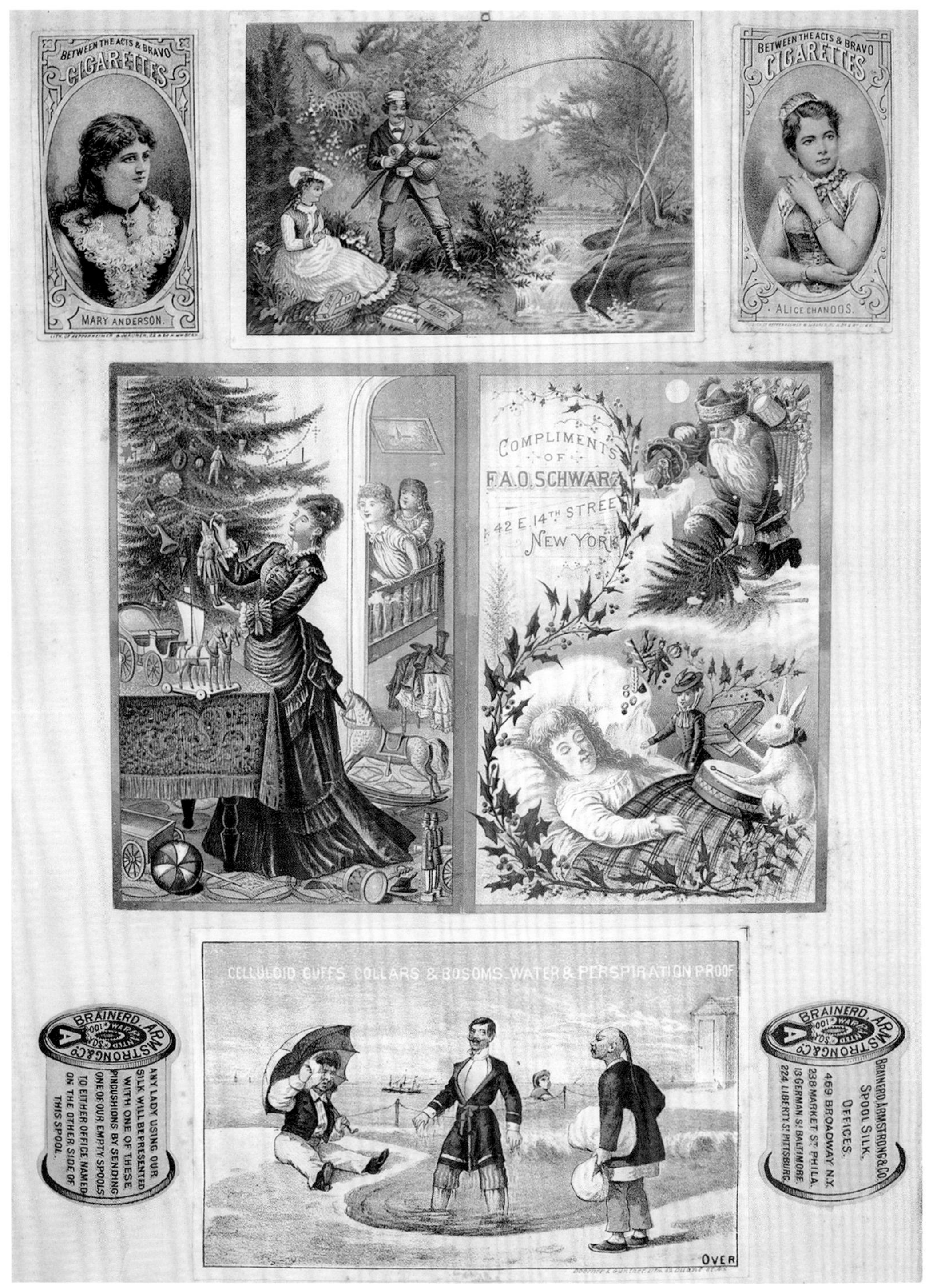

Figure 2.1   A typical page of one of Alice's trade card scrapbooks illustrates her love of commercial imagery: celebrity actresses smoking cigarettes, a toy store promoting Christmas gifts, and a cartoon lampooning Chinese laundrymen.

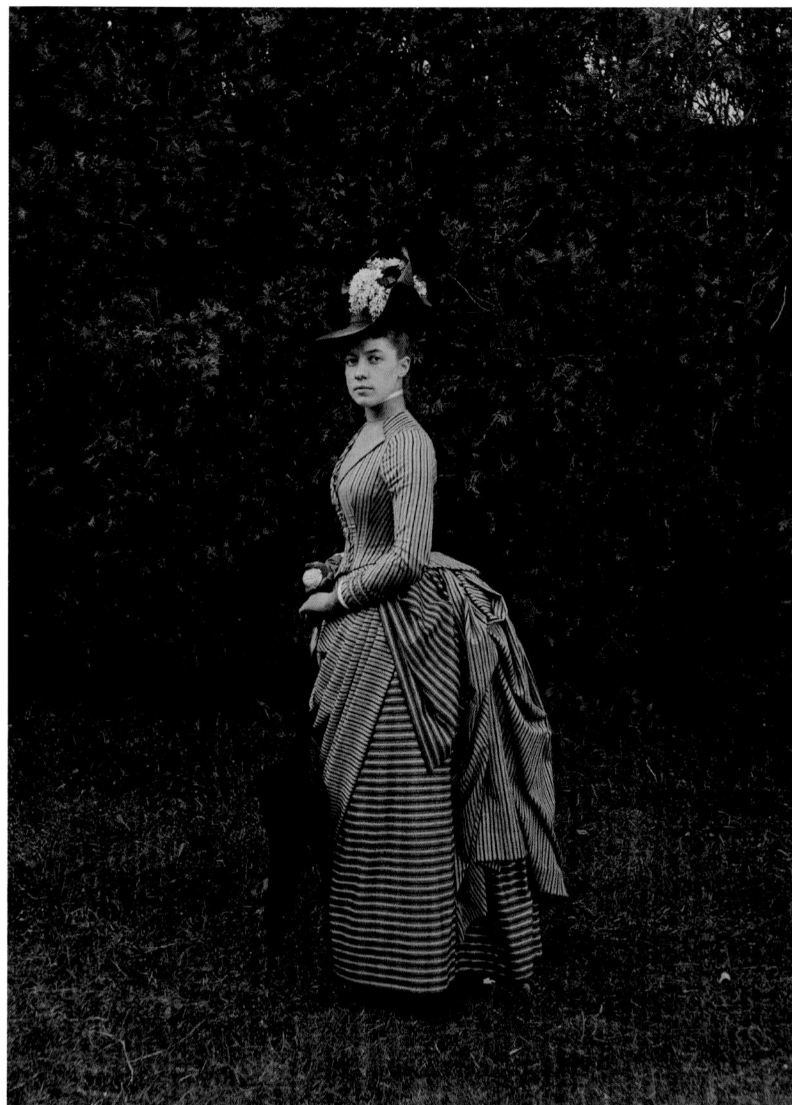

Figure 2.2 At twenty-two, Alice poses as a fashion plate for Uncle Oswald's camera.

In 1880, Alice began spending a week every June with her uncle Peter and his family in New Brunswick to attend the Rutgers College commencement. Shortly before he started teaching there, Peter married Ellen Middleton Munroe, called Nellie, a Clifton neighbor. Alice grew very close to Peter and Nellie; indeed, Peter doted on Alice, who was in her teens when his three children were born in the 1880s.[11] Under Peter's watchful eye, Alice enjoyed the three-day commencement celebration which included dinners, exhibitions, and musical performances, absorbing the rituals of all-male college culture. She attended for seven years, at first giving the exercises her full attention, annotating her programs with the dollar amount of academic prizes and assessing speeches with "good," "long," or "lisped," but eventually just doodling on

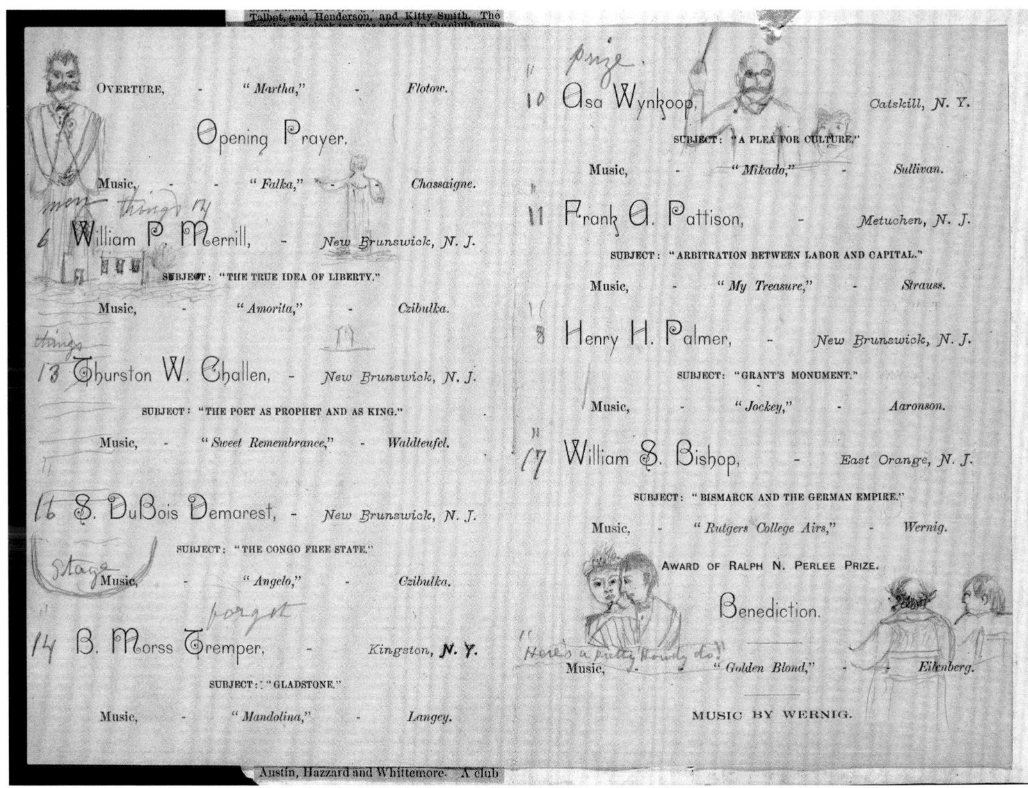

Figure 2.3   Alice sketched this picture of herself and a hapless suitor (lower right) in the margin of a Rutgers College graduation program.

them. Next to the "Benediction" at the end of the 1886 "junior exhibition" program is a little sketch of a young man trying (and apparently failing) to woo Alice. She added the sarcastic caption, "Here's a pretty howdy do." (Figure 2.3).[12]

Alice was joined at these festivities by Elisabeth Briand Strong, called Bessie, who was Alice's age and whose parents were friends with Peter and Nellie. The two young women shared many interests, including tennis, photography, and music. Studying music was mandatory for Victorian girls, and Bessie was especially talented, singing in public and teaching piano. Alice played piano and the banjo, an instrument derived from minstrelsy, which was especially suited to popular tunes. A photograph shows Alice holding her banjo and Bessie holding her guitar on the piazza of Clear Comfort (Figure 2.4). Alice's taste for popular entertainment is also reflected in the many programs she saved, including a production of Gilbert & Sullivan's *H.M.S. Pinafore* with John Philip Sousa conducting the orchestra.[13]

When she was seventeen, Alice began attending society events that were chronicled in New York and Brooklyn newspapers as well as on Staten Island. Although she never

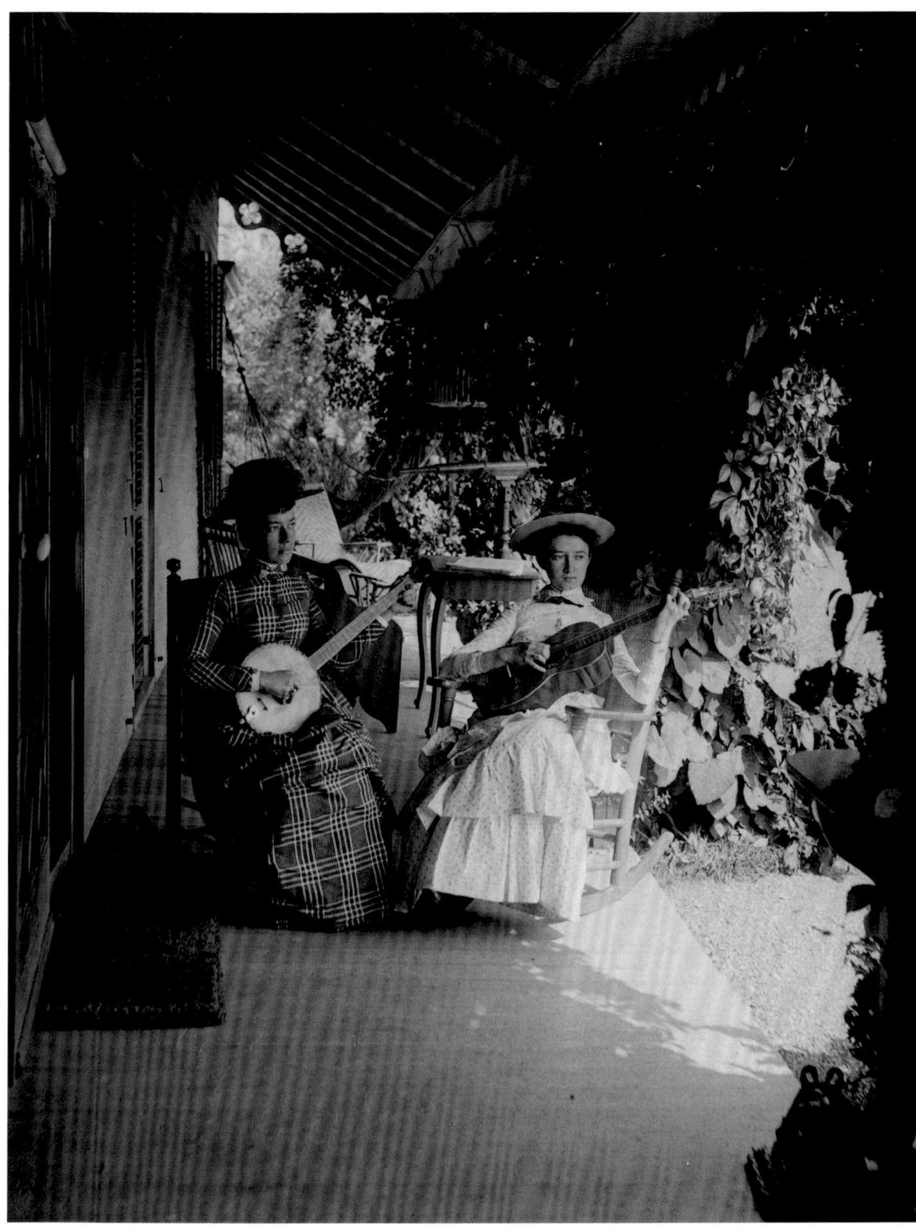

Figure 2.4   Alice and Bessie Strong pose with banjo and guitar on the piazza. Alice played the banjo, an instrument made popular by minstrel shows.

kept a diary, she assembled scrapbooks of newspaper clippings, invitations, tickets, and programs that documented her burgeoning social life.[14] The exhaustive, chronological record of tournaments, regattas, amateur theatricals, charity fairs, dances, and weddings demarcated her coming of age.[15] She completed two of these scrapbooks, the first from August 1883 to January 1887 and the second from February 1887 to August 1889; a third scrapbook was left unfinished.[16]

Alice's first passion was lawn tennis, a new sport open to women and men, and the recognition she gained as a competitive player launched her into society. Pasted on the first page of her first scrapbook was a magazine engraving titled, "A Modern Tournament," which showed women and men playing tennis together. Alice recalled that as a child, she was inclined to be fat, but added, "I ran it off."[17] Her interest in tennis became sufficiently strong that the family laid out a court for her and her friends on the grounds of Clear Comfort. The grass court was made possible by the recent invention of the residential lawn mower and the rubber-core tennis ball, which bounced when it hit the grass.

Tennis had come to Staten Island in 1874, when Mary Ewing Outerbridge brought home a tennis set from a vacation in Bermuda and convinced her brothers, founding members of the Staten Island Cricket and Baseball Club, to let her erect a net on the club grounds.[18] From the start, the game attracted women as well as men, and in 1877, the women players founded the Staten Island Ladies' Club for Outdoor-Sports (S.I.L.C.), which was given access to the club grounds on Fridays.[19] The clubs were exclusive: applicants had to be nominated by a member, and dues were steep. Run entirely by women, the S.I.L.C. stirred up interest in the community by sponsoring stylish fundraisers. One commentator noted that if the S.I.L.C. had not been established, "there seemed to be some probability of the men's club falling to pieces owing to lack of interest taken in its maintenance by its members."[20]

At the June opening of each season, the women organized a party with live music, and at the October closing, they held a "German," a dance party with games, at the Pavilion Hotel in nearby New Brighton. The events garnered national press. A syndicated article, "Ladies as Athletes, The Latest Sweet Thing Among Eastern Fashionables," reported on the 1880 opening:

No less than eight courts for lawn tennis occupied the space nearest to the spectators, while beyond were numerous croquet sets and a dozen targets for archery. . . . The members of the club were early on the grounds . . . [and] by five o'clock all the guests had arrived. Coming by carriage and afoot, or by the boats from New York, no less than three hundred persons had gathered to encourage and envy the fair athletes. . . . Over it all from time to time was heard the music of the band of the Third Artillery. . . . Tea was served in the club house . . . and dancing was on the programme for the later hour.[21]

Alice began competing in the S.I.L.C. tournament in 1881, when she was fifteen. The two best women players at the club were Adeline King Robinson and Violet Ward, both slightly older than her, but Alice soon rose in the ranks, winning the women's doubles with Violet in 1886 and playing Adeline in the tournament finals in 1888. The

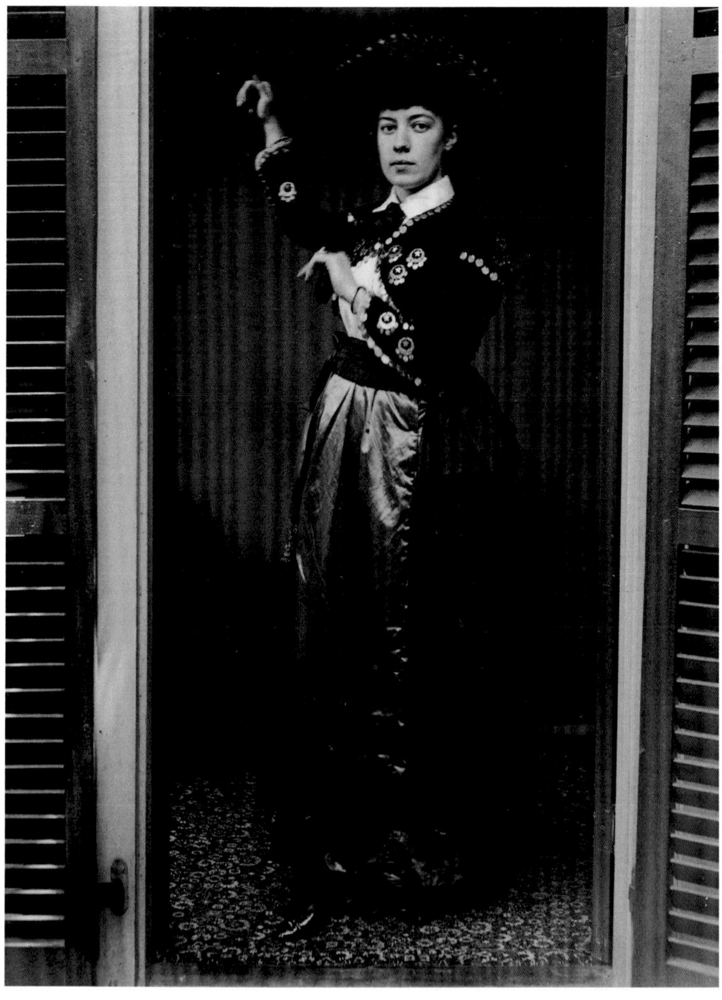

Figure 2.5   Alice was cast in the Spanish dance for an 1886 Staten Island Ladies' Club fundraiser. Before leaving home, she took this self-portrait.

press described Alice as a "new, promising player," who with "a little more experience in 'placing' her balls . . . will prove a player of much skill and nerve."[22]

In 1886, the Cricket & Baseball Club moved from Camp Washington (near present day St. George) to Bard Avenue in New Brighton.[23] Although the men raised the funds to purchase property and build two clubhouses—one for men, the other for women—the women pulled their weight by paying rent and supporting operating expenses for both clubs with special events, the most ambitious a carnival called a "Kirmess" that netted $715 (approximately $22,000 today). The highlight of the carnival was a series of specially choreographed dances that enlisted one hundred young people of Staten Island society, including Alice, who photographed "Myself in Spanish Costume" (Figure 2.5).[24] The women spared no cost in decorating their clubhouse, assuring that it was both feminine and fashionable, which was noticed in the press: "The club house is beautifully furnished in rattan, the painting inside being white and gold, the walls hung in pink and white cretonne, and the furniture in blue and white chintz—a very French effect."[25]

By 1888, the S.I.L.C. was the largest club of its kind in the country with 200 members, and that year the nation's most important tournament, the US National Lawn Tennis Association, was moved from Newport, Rhode Island to Staten Island. The local press crowed, "This will guarantee more spectators but will rob Newport of one of its summer highlights. The Staten Island club is jubilant."[26] Playing on her home court, Adeline Robinson won the women's singles, conferring on her the honor of US women's lawn tennis champion.[27]

Events like the women's tennis tournament were at odds with the commonly held Victorian view that physical and mental exertion risked young women's fertility and mental health. In his 1875 best-selling book, *Sex in Education, or, A Fair Chance for Girls*, Dr. Edward M. Clarke brought the authority of medical science to justify limiting girls' potential to learn and play. Between the ages of fourteen and eighteen, he argued, a girl must give priority to the development of her "reproductive apparatus" lest she "los[e] her feminine attractions, and probably also her chief feminine functions."[28] S.I.L.C. events where wellborn women were athletic, healthy, and feminine, would not have pleased Dr. Clarke, but they received breathless praise. Typical is "Beauty on the Green," a newspaper report on the opening festivities of the 1888 women's tournament:

> No artists could accurately produce on canvas the pretty picture at the grounds by the harmonious blending of the various colored tennis dresses and the rosy faces of the wearers offset by the broad expanse of greensward.[29]

Tennis expanded the boundaries of respectable courtship between young men and women, a purpose that croquet had served for an earlier generation, and it allowed women to flirt *and* compete. But how could women look their best in corsets and still move freely on the court? The answer was a tame version of tennis called "pat ball," as historian Patricia Campbell Warner explains:

> Not only were women stuffed into encasing sleeves, corsets, and bodices, but they were also bound by yards of draperies swathed around their knees and drawn up in the back to form the most protuberant bustle ever to confound fashion. Hats perched firmly in place, gloves covered the hands clutching the racquets (to say nothing of the trains of the gowns held in the other hand), and shoes as often as not had heels. Never mind: the women were not expected to actually run for the ball.[30]

"Pat ball," however, was not for the top women players. In "How a Girl Plays Tennis," Violet's no-nonsense approach was singled out: in plain, white flannel and a straw hat, she wore spectacles "and never smile[d] even when her friends applaud[ed] her."[31] In 1888, the year she won the US Championship, Adeline addressed the issue of tennis clothing in "Lawn Tennis Hints for Girls," published in the national magazine, *Harper's Young People*:

> In order to be a good tennis-player, one must dress for the *game* and not for the *people*. It is not only injurious but ridiculous to attempt playing in a tight waist and long skirts. They both interfere with your running, and your arms *must* have full swing. . . . Do not be afraid to run. If your dress is short and you wear a good pair of tennis shoes, there is no excuse for standing still and thinking, "Oh, I cannot get that ball, there is no use in running for it."[32]

Adeline and Violet played tennis not pat ball, discarding their corsets and dressing to win.

As in her later photographs, Alice used humor to address issues of gender. In her scrapbook she pasted a two-part cartoon called "Lawn Tennis," which lampoons women's tennis clothes. The first frame shows women wearing long dresses, hats, and heels and men wearing jerseys and knickers, and reads: "In this deservedly popular game, when the gentlemen are playing against the ladies, is it fair that the ladies should be hampered and held back by their dress while the gentlemen are allowed to wear a costume the convenience of which gives them an undeniable advantage?" The second frame proposes an equitable, if preposterous, "solution": "But as the ladies cannot very well adopt the easier costume of the other sex, would it not be simple justice to compel the gentlemen, when playing against the ladies, to wear the ladies' inconvenient style of dress?" (Figure 2.6). Despite her willingness to poke fun at tennis fashion, Alice wore a corset, a formfitting jacket, and voluminous skirts on the court. Eschewing Adeline's advice, she persisted in dressing for the game *and* for the people watching.

Alice reconnected with Violet and Adeline in the 1890s, but they were not among her intimate friends in the 1880s. Her attention was taken up with a close-knit group of young women and men in Clifton, who kept a jam-packed social calendar.

In 1880, the women of Clifton established their own Ladies' Club for Outdoor-Sports within walking distance of Clear Comfort. From 1884 to 1889, the club was permitted to play on the parade grounds at nearby Fort Wadsworth, where, on at least one occasion, Alice brought her camera (Figure 2.7).[33] In 1888, the club admitted male members and changed its name to the Clifton Tennis Club, and in 1890, it purchased

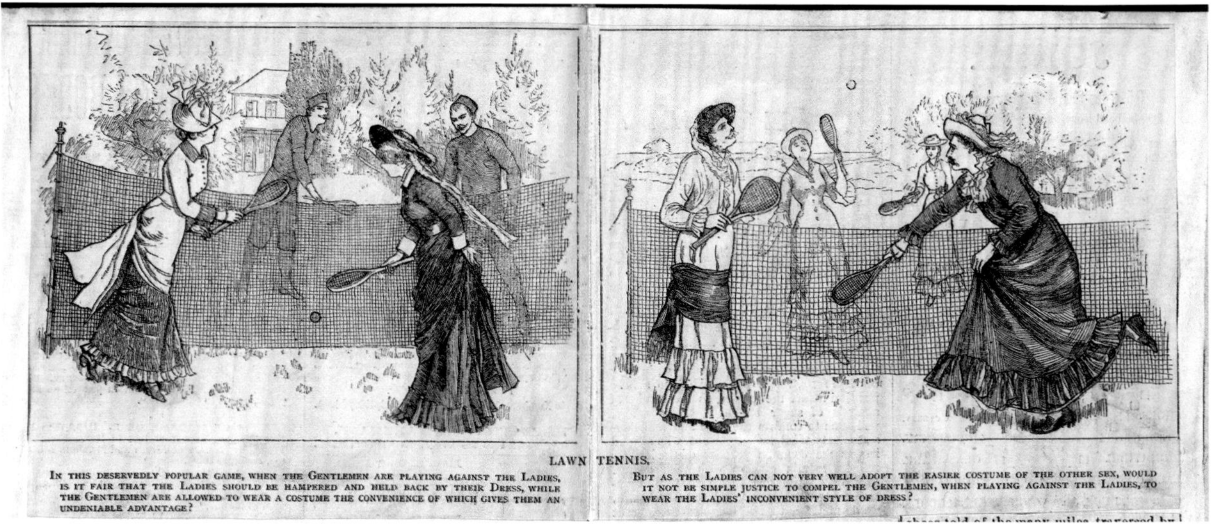

Figure 2.6   Alice pasted this "battle-of-the-sexes" cartoon in her scrapbook. It proposes a solution to the disadvantage of women's tennis garb: "As the ladies can not very well adopt the easier costume of the other sex, is it not simple justice to compel the Gentlemen, when playing against the Ladies, to wear the Ladies' inconvenient style of dress?"

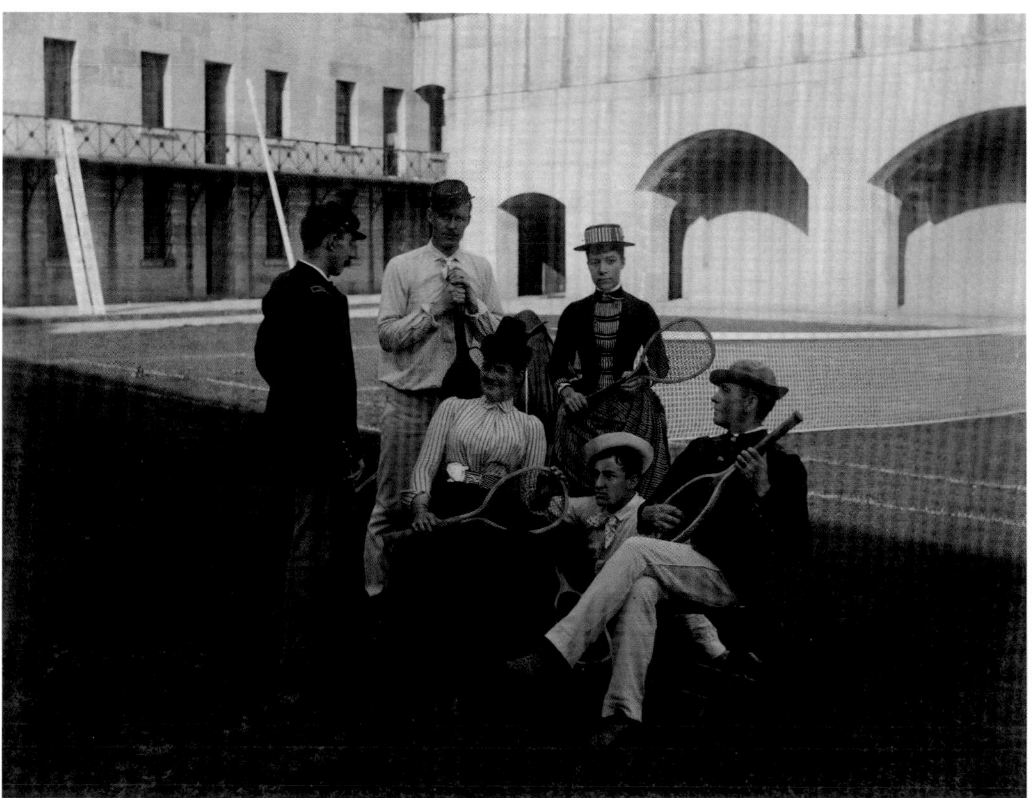

Figure 2.7   Trude Eccleston and Alice (standing) played tennis with soldiers at Fort Wadsworth, which was within walking distance of Clear Comfort.

property, built a clubhouse, and relinquished management of the club to the men.[34] At times, friendship overwhelmed the competitive spirit, as revealed in a charming press report on Alice's win over her close friend Julie Marsh: "It was pleasant to witness the rare good will exhibited between the contestants, and the pretty way in which Miss Marsh applauded a lucky turn of Miss Austin's [sic] wrist and finally insisted on clasping the pin on her friend herself."[35] Within this smaller circle of competitors, Alice was the reigning champion for years. In an 1893 article on the Clifton Tennis Club, the *New York Times* declared, "Of the women players, Miss Alice Austin [sic] is conceded to be the best."[36]

Alice was also a member of the Clifton Boat Club, which was founded in 1881 to provide a landing for boating parties and shelter for boats. In 1883, the club, which was within sight of Clear Comfort, began sponsoring an annual regatta with many of the boats "manned by young ladies."[37] The club was the work of Alice's crowd, who competed in the races, performed in its amateur theatricals (including a minstrel show in 1885), attended its dances, and organized its fundraisers.[38] Although she did not compete in the boat races, Alice was an attentive spectator, annotating the regatta programs with weather conditions, correcting the names of crew members, and noting the winners and their prizes from silver cups to cuff buttons initialed "C.B.C."

The photographs that Alice took of her friends lounging on the clubhouse porch suggest the casual ease of summer days spent swimming and boating (Figure 2.8). Like tennis, swimming gave men and women novel opportunities for unchaperoned socializing, but it posed yet another daunting fashion challenge. Men wore one-piece outfits of knit jersey, but to maintain their modesty and protect their skin from the sun, women were covered from head to toe in cotton twill or wool garments with high necks and long sleeves, stockings, shoes, and hats. As Warner explains, it was a losing battle: "The trouble was that when the body got wet, no matter how voluminous the drapery around it, it had a tendency to reveal itself under the sodden and clinging layers that were meant to hide it."[39] Wool presumably maximized movement and modesty but still left women unable to swim. Instead, they were expected to bathe, that is, to get wet. An 1890 photograph of Alice and the sisters Carrie and Violet Ward at Clear Comfort shows them dressed in stylish ensembles of blouses, trousers, skirts, stockings, shoes, and head coverings (Figure 2.9). Alice's short, puffed sleeves—the latest trend—afforded her more freedom of movement, but she seems lightly corseted to maintain her waistline and uplifted bosom.

Staten Island was truly gripped by club fever, from the stately Richmond County Country Club—founded in 1888 and one of the first of its kind in the country—to short-lived, informal clubs organized by groups of close friends.[40] Among the latter was the Young Ladies' Cooking Club of Clifton, whose members, including Alice,

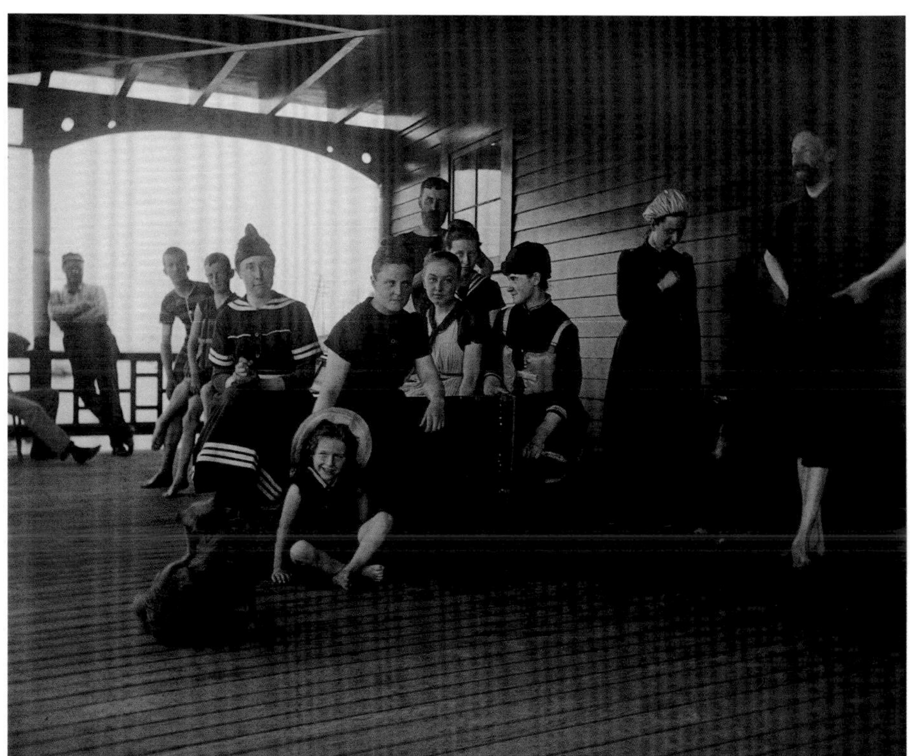

Figure 2.8   Alice's friends lounge on the porch of the Clifton Boat House, a short walk from Clear Comfort. Seated are Julie Marsh (center) and Violet and Carrie Ward (on either side of Julie).

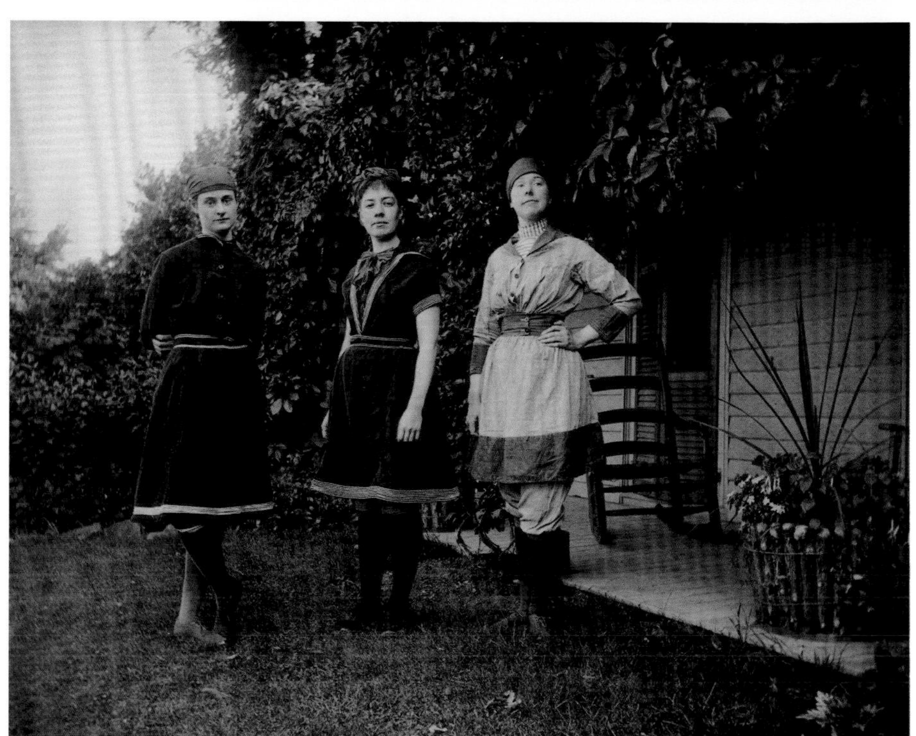

Figure 2.9   Carrie and Violet Ward (on either side of Alice) stand ready to go swimming at Clear Comfort.

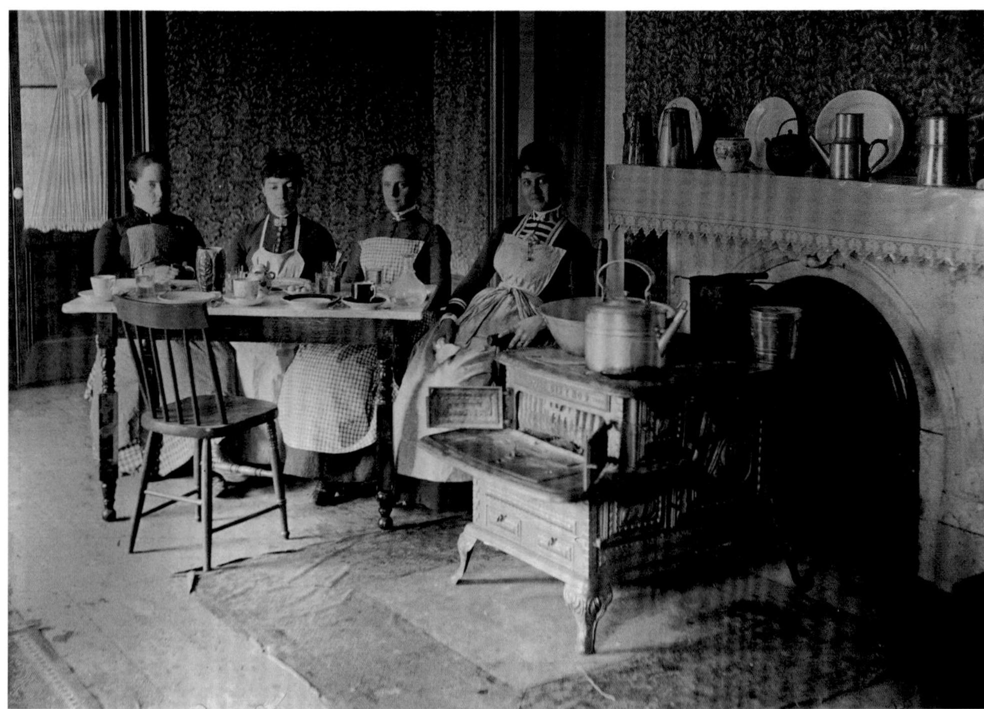

Figure 2.10   The Young Ladies' Cooking Club of Clifton experimented with their grandmothers' recipes in a vacant house owned by the Marsh family. From left to right are (possibly)
Sue Ripley, Alice, Julie Marsh, and Trude Eccleston.

Julie Marsh, and Trude Eccleston, experimented with their grandmothers' recipes in
a vacant house belonging to Julie's family (Figure 2.10).[41] A tongue-in-cheek article
suggested that the young ladies put their matrimonial chances at risk by serving high
tea to a group of young men. "We were glad to learn," the writer concluded, "that the
cooking was excellent, and that as a consequence, no engagements were broken off."[42]

In 1888, the young men of Alice's set, led by Trude Eccleston's brother Jack, formed
the mysterious "B.S. Club," whose sole purpose was to host "invitation-only" parties
chaperoned by Trude and Jack's mother. Alice was among those invited. A year later,
the club's full, meaningless name—Bean Soup Club—was revealed, perhaps an ironic
send-up of the club fad. Its parties were no joke: they were expensive and magical.
On July 26, 1889, for example, the B.S. Club chartered a large tug for a thirty-mile
cruise up the Hudson River, in which sixty-five guests enjoyed a catered dinner and
harmonized familiar tunes on their moonlit return to Staten Island.[43]

The increasingly ambitious event schedule of Staten Island society, which crowded
calendars and strained pocketbooks, bore comparison to Mrs. Astor's "Four Hundred" and soon spawned one-upmanship between Staten Island factions.[44] According

to the *New York World*, a "social war in the suburbs" broke out between the North Shore (New Brighton) and the East Shore (Clifton).[45] The subtext of the dispute was the growing rift between the nouveau riche newcomers to the North Shore, who were sponsoring increasingly lavish events, and the East Shore's older families, who were regarded as "rather select and recherché."[46] Alice received a cascade of invitations from both sides, all of which she dutifully pasted in her scrapbooks and annotated, lest she forget the minutiae of these extravaganzas.

During the winter social season, it was not unusual for Alice to attend a formal public event each week, interspersed with private parties. On Thursday, February 25, 1886, for example, she attended the Bal Poudré ("powdered ball") at the Pavilion Hotel in New Brighton, returning home at 2:30 a.m. The following Wednesday, she returned to the Pavilion for the Charity Ball, an annual benefit for the S. R. Smith Infirmary, a hospital for the poor. On the menu for a "supper by Mazzotti" served from 11 p.m. to 1 a.m., Alice jotted down the names of her six tablemates, and in her program, her partners had filled in their names next to every dance. She arrived home from the Charity Ball at 4 a.m. That same week, she attended a dinner party for eighteen at the home of Julie Marsh, and slipped into her invitation was a poem from an aggressive admirer:

> Miss Austin [sic]
> "Be plain in dress, and
> Sober in your diet.
> In short my deary, kiss
> Me and be quiet."[47]

For Alice and her friends, the goal of these social events was to attract men, and Alice was quite good at it. Bessie Strong relates a crush that one of her friends had on Alice:

> We told Mr. Beebe's fortune here on Friday evening and we found that he was to marry you. . . . He wished me to tell you that his moustache is getting on nicely. . . . You may see Harry Beebe before long, for when a young gentleman gets to that point where he wants the postage stamp from a young lady's letter, the next thing will be his calling on her quite often, even though she may live at some distance.[48]

Alice could be quite forward with men and, on at least one occasion, inspired nasty gossip. After a bowling party, her friend Trude Eccleston chided her: "Lena Dix told me privately that 'you had gone a <u>mashing</u>'—nice rep. you have these days."[49]

STATEN ISLAND LADIES' CLUB
LAWN TENNIS SCORE.

Scorer, _C. E. Eldridge_   Date, _Aug 3rd /87_

SETS WON.

Names of Players.

A vs. _Miss Austen_   6–0   6–0
B   _Miss Gallagher_

Entered according to Act of Congress, in the year 1886, by PECK & SNYDER, in the office of the Librarian of Congress, at Washington, D. C.

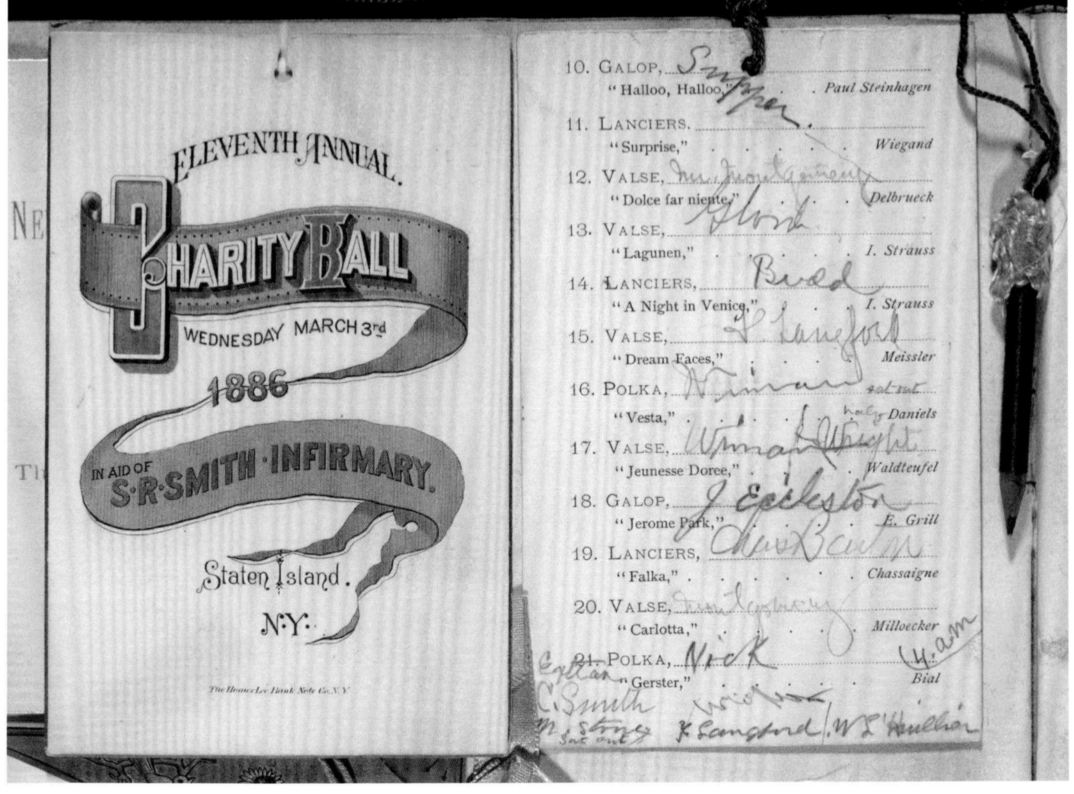

("Mashing" was slang for aggressive flirting, usually used to describe men's unwanted advances toward women.) Friends assumed that Alice would marry. In 1887, Grace Simonson wrote, "Are there any more people engaged or married. . . . I suppose you will be the next one, I hope you will find a splendid man."[50]

How Alice understood her sexual identity in the 1880s is hard to determine. She no doubt enjoyed her heterosexual adventures, but she does not seem to have been thinking of marriage. There is no indication that she was performing heterosexuality for fear that her feelings for women would be discovered. She wanted to have fun and wield social power. With their tennis tournaments, bathing parties, and moonlit boat rides, Alice's social set pushed against the boundaries of propriety, and Alice eagerly placed herself in its vanguard.

Thorstein Veblen's famous book, *The Theory of the Leisure Class*, scandalous when it appeared in 1899, accurately describes the Staten Island society that Alice inhabited, in which productive labor was the task of the "inferior pecuniary classes," and leisure was the task of the "superior pecuniary classes."[51] Alice worked hard at her life of leisure, striving for excellence, as her full dance cards and winning score cards make plain (Figures 2.11 and 2.12).

3 MAKESHIFT PHOTOGRAPHY

Alice Austen grew up in a house full of photographers and photographs. In 1951, she recalled that when she was a little girl, Oswald Muller, Aunt Minn's seafaring second husband, allowed her to play with his "bulky, old camera."[1] In addition to "the Captain," there was Uncle Peter and his close friend and neighbor Ralph Middleton Munroe, both amateur photographers who took up the craft as teenagers.

Alice's grandfather, John Haggerty Austen, was an avid photography collector who introduced the Austen family to his passion for the new technology before Alice was born. In the middle parlor of the Staten Island house was a large tabletop stereoscope for viewing stereographs, commercially produced photographs mounted on cards, which when viewed through a twin-lens viewer, appeared three-dimensional.[2] In his letters home from Europe, John often mentioned photographs in the family's collection, images that enhanced his experiences of sites he encountered abroad. Describing a stroll through the Latin Quarter in Paris in June 1869, he wrote:

> Then walked up a very fine old street that I had never seen before & found myself standing on a square with the most noble Pantheon on one side & the church of St. Etienne de Monte on the other. Entered this last first, admired the unmistakable winding stone staircases that we have photos of, also the beautiful carved pulpit, they are so familiar by their pictures that it appears to me that I must have seen them only yesterday.[3]

John often scoured the photography shops for finds: "I have not told you how much pleasure is afforded me by the photographic shops they see on every block & they make such a great display in their windows that I always have to stop & admire. . . . These stores attract more people than any others, and the photos are so cheap that one is tempted to buy continually."[4]

John valued photographs not only as aide-memoires, but as fine art. Framed photographs hung on the walls of the Austen house along with family portraits and prints after famous paintings.[5] A regular museum visitor, John expressed an aesthetic preference for photographs over paintings. Disappointed by an acclaimed painting collection at London's Royal Academy, he remarked, "I began to think that the wonderful trunk of photographs & stereoscopes [that I have bought] has caused me to find less interest in pictures painted by mortal hands."[6]

In 1867, John considered buying a camera "so that Peter & I can take pictures when we so are so inclined."[7] At the Exposition Universelle in Paris, he investigated the Dubroni, a camera "for taking photographs without a dark chamber intended mainly for amateurs."[8] He decided not to buy a camera in Paris but announced that "[s]ome day I may get a first rate apparatus in N[ew] York."[9]

Before the 1880s, few amateurs were willing to master the rigors of the wet plate process, which required the photographer to have a darkroom available to apply chemicals and develop a glass plate negative at the time of exposure. Easier but still arduous and expensive was dry plate photography, in which negatives were prepared in advance and could be developed later. Commercially available in the late 1870s, dry plate negatives stimulated a photography boom, and by the late 1880s, amateur clubs, print exchanges, and publications abounded. It appears that the Austen men were wielding cameras in the late 1870s and using the dry plate process before amateur photography became a full-blown fad among wealthy Americans.

John probably never took up the camera—in 1880 he was sixty-nine years old—but he encouraged his son Peter to do so. A scrapbook that Peter began in 1869 when he was sixteen reveals a precocious interest in chemistry and mechanics, the twin properties of photography. Filled with clippings from scientific journals, the scrapbook includes articles on the chemistry of tobacco, laughing gas as an anesthetic, and a demonstration of an early telephone.[10] Few of Peter's photographs survive, but his sustained interest is well documented.[11] In 1886, he founded the New Brunswick Camerads—later the New Brunswick Camera Club—which he led for many years, and in 1888, he began teaching "Photography Applied to Scientific Work" to his Rutgers seniors. The club and the class met at the Chemistry Rooms at Rutgers.[12] In a letter to Alice, Aunt Nellie attested to Peter's zeal, reporting what happened when he ignited flash powder to illuminate an event in a crowded church:

> I went to Middlebush with your uncle and attended the lecture. Seemed to me his special form of amusement was setting off flash lights and I kept bobbing behind people to get away from them. Filled the church with smoke and then froze the people by opening the windows.[13]

Before he left home in 1870 for graduate study in Europe, Peter shared his hobby with his neighbor Ralph Middleton Munroe, his future wife's brother.[14] In his autobiography, Ralph noted that "[p]hotography had early interested me, many years before the 'Kodak,' when amateur photographers were few indeed...."[15] "'Pete' Austen," he recalled, "proved to be my particular chum, and his home, the old Lake-Austen house . . . became mine as well."[16] Ralph briefly attended the Columbia College School of Mines, where Peter studied, but yearned for a life at sea. His passion led him to befriend Peter's brother-in-law Oswald Muller, who tried to lure Ralph to sea as a photographer:

> "Ralph," he said, "I'll tell you what we'll do. You come a voyage with me and bring your camera. . . . When we get settled in port we'll just slip off . . . and *see things*. We'll cruise the nooks and corners of the East Indies, and you'll make pictures that will be 'way ahead of anything we've ever had of the East—the first photographs ever taken. What do you say?"[17]

To his lifelong regret, Ralph declined the offer because "[t]here were my parents to consider and a world to conquer here at home."[18]

When he asked Ralph to join him at sea—sometime between 1876, when he took command of the *Samar*, and 1879, when Ralph married and built a home on Staten Island—Oswald was not yet photographing.[19] But by 1884, when he retired and moved to Clear Comfort, he was adept enough to give Alice her start.[20] Photography was an everyday occurrence at the house, and a tiny darkroom was installed on the second floor.[21] Letters to Alice from Mamma attest to the camera work going on around her. In June 1885, she mentioned that "Ralph Munroe has been photographing the house," and in 1891, she wrote, "The Captain was kept busy photographing of course."[22] Oswald did not leave a collection of his photographs, but some of his negatives can be found among Alice's.[23] Most notable is a group of twenty-five full plate photographs depicting ships anchored in the East River and at the piers near his office at 26 South Street in Manhattan (Figure 3.1).[24]

Alice's grandmother and mother were adept at the feminine art of painting, but she took up the hobby of the men in her midst.[25] In 1951, Oliver Jensen noted that "Miss Austen states firmly that in photography she was self-taught, once her uncle had shown her how the camera operated."[26] She may have oversimplified. An amateur but no dilettante, Alice reaped the benefits of having skilled photographers, including a teacher of the craft, in her family. At the precise moment that she was taking up photography, amateur clubs were sprouting up in Brooklyn, Manhattan, and New Jersey. Yet Alice was not an active member of any of them.[27] She had no need for their darkroom facilities and group excursions, nor did she have the time, since her calendar was already crowded with tennis tournaments and society events. Some clubs opposed women's membership altogether, a fight she had no interest in joining.[28]

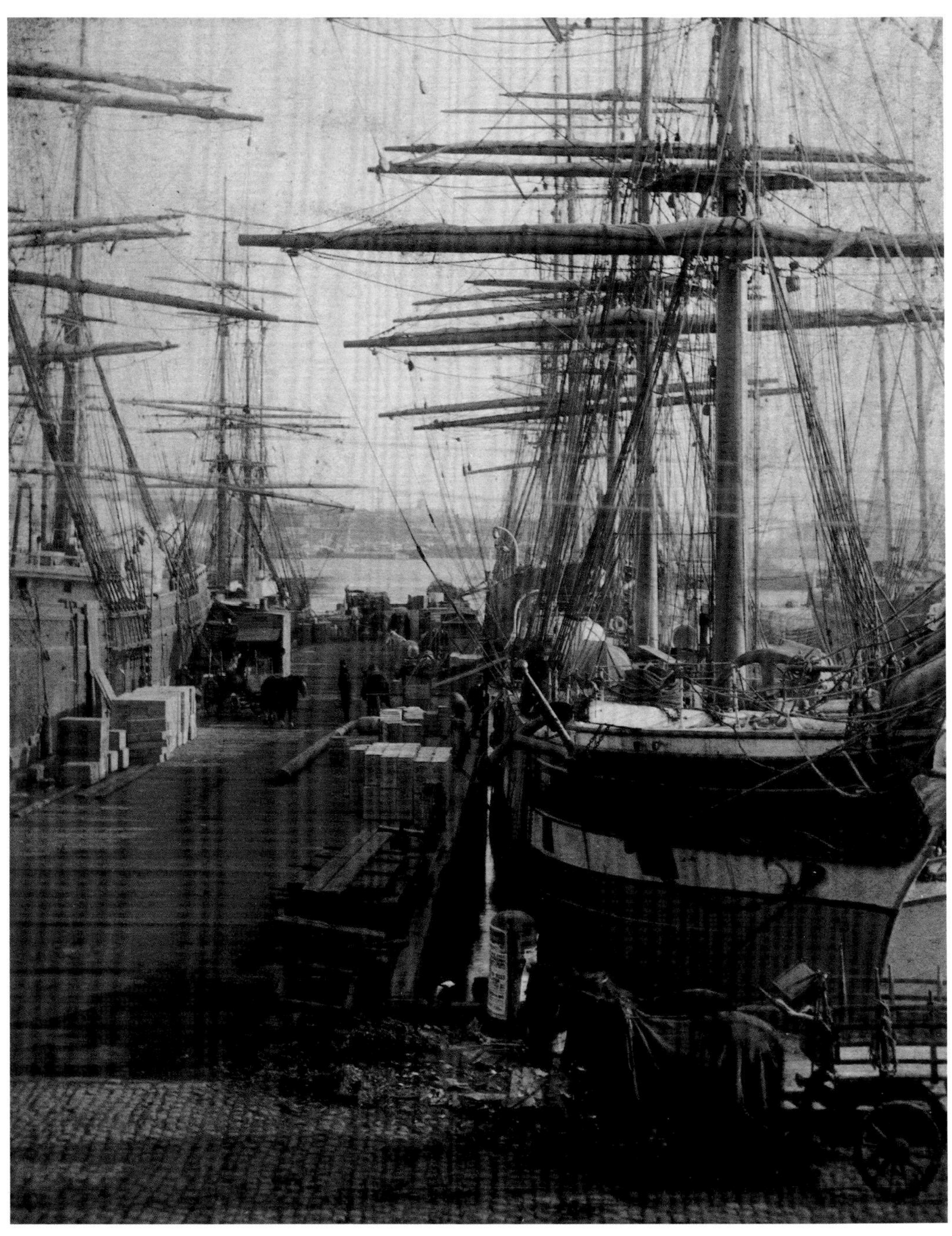

Figure 3.1 When Alice's Uncle Oswald retired as a sea captain, he opened a stevedore business on South Street in Manhattan. He took this photograph from his office window.

A handful of portraits of family members on the grounds of Clear Comfort are likely the product of Oswald's initial demonstrations for Alice.[29] His "bulky, old camera" consisted of a wooden box with a lens in front and a negative holder in back that held "full plate" (6 ½ by 8 ½ inch) glass negatives coated with light-sensitive, silver emulsion. Because exposure times could be seconds long, the camera was secured to a tripod for stability. To compose an image, Oswald placed his head under a focusing cloth, where he could see the scene on a ground glass, albeit upside down. Typical of these portraits is one of Oswald, Minn, Alice, and the family's pug Punch standing at the corner of the tennis court against a backdrop of shrubbery (Figure 3.2). Oswald posed the family and then took his place between Minn and Alice, squeezing the rubber shutter release in his right hand. The rubber tube leading from the release to the camera can be seen in the picture.[30]

These group portraits, in which family members pose in carefully chosen outfits against a background of shrubbery, are a rough-and-ready version of the popular cabinet card portraits of the day. By the early 1880s, it was commonplace for a broad

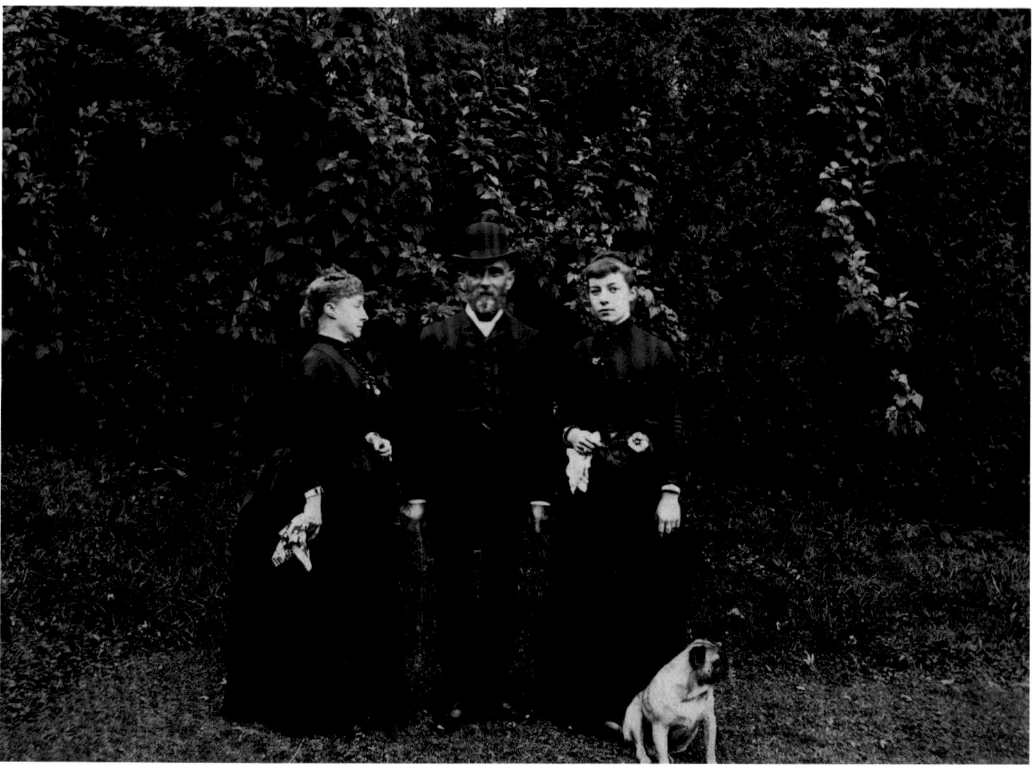

Figure 3.2   Uncle Oswald taught Alice how to use the camera by taking a series of family portraits on the lawn at Clear Comfort. This one shows Aunt Minn, Uncle Oswald (holding a shutter release in his right hand), Alice, and Punch.

swath of Americans to visit a professional photographer's studio and pose against a painted backdrop, which typically depicted a landscape.[31] By working outdoors on sunny days, Oswald did not have to worry about the longer exposures that studio photography required, and Clear Comfort provided a multitude of verdant backgrounds. Oswald's prints and Alice's earliest ones were mounted, like studio portraits, on gilt-edged cardboard.

Alice took her first photographs with a 5-by-8 inch camera. This camera was usually fitted with twin lenses to take two side by side photographs for stereo viewing, but Alice's camera had one lens to create a single, 5-by-8 inch photograph.[32] The earliest dated photograph in Alice's collection depicts her sitting on a wicker chair with Punch in her lap (Figure 3.3). Written in her hand on the back of the mounted print is the date, "1884." The photograph could have been composed by Alice, who may have set up the camera and asked Oswald to make the exposure. Another 5-by-8 inch photograph, also dated 1884, was clearly Alice's own. It depicts a tennis match at the Ladies' Tennis Club of Clifton, a few blocks from Clear Comfort (Figure 3.4). Because the camera was too slow to stop motion, the players are standing still, although a person at center moved slightly, creating a "ghost" image. With the camera placed at one corner of the court, its lines recede in two-point perspective, and tree

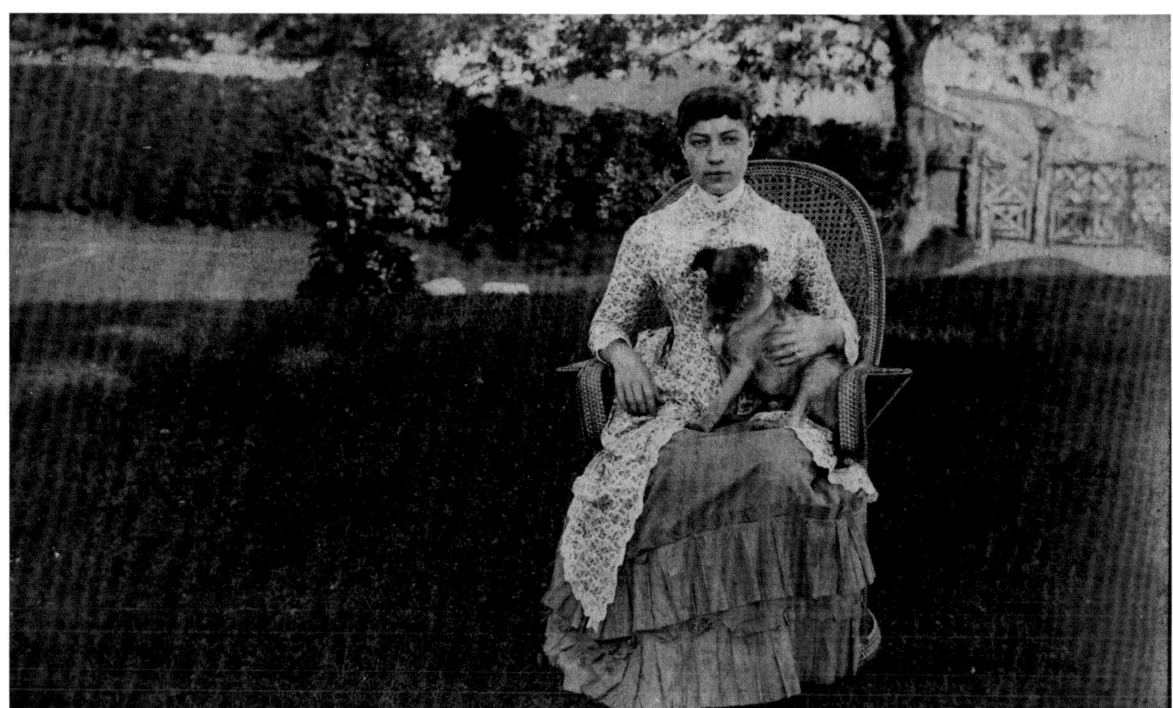

Figure 3.3   This 1884 self-portrait with Punch is Alice's earliest dated photograph.

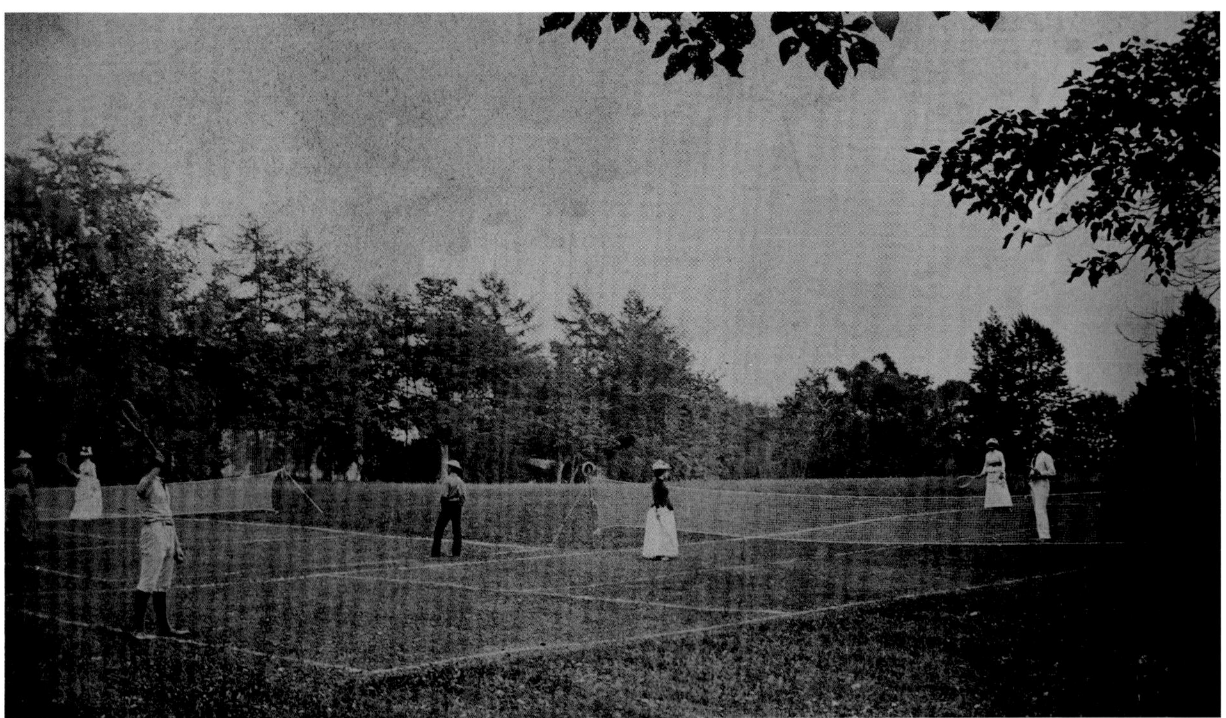

Figure 3.4   Throughout her life, Alice tried to photograph the game of tennis. Her first attempt was this 1884 view of play at the Clifton Ladies' Tennis Club.

limbs frame the image to establish the foreground. Every time Alice acquired a new camera or a new lens, she attempted to photograph tennis matches, despite the limits of nineteenth-century technology.

By September 1885, Alice began her self-education in earnest, numbering her negatives and annotating the sleeves with subject, date, time of day, lighting conditions, and exposure time. Alice's Number 7, for example, shows her posing with four other girls—including Trude Eccleston and Julie Marsh—ready to head down to the shore to swim (Figure 3.5). The negative sleeve reads, "Group in bathing costumes, Thursday, Sept. 17th, 1885. 12:30 p.m. Instantaneous." In the following months, Alice experimented with horizontal and vertical formats, exploring the themes that preoccupied her throughout her life: portrait groups, distant ships in the harbor, and the house and grounds of Clear Comfort from many points of view in all types of weather (Figure 3.6).[33] In April 1886, when Alice set aside the 5 by 8 for the full plate camera, her negative sleeves had reached Number 41.

Between the spring of 1886 and 1890, Alice used the full plate camera exclusively, averaging one hundred new negatives a year. On the full plate negative sleeves, she

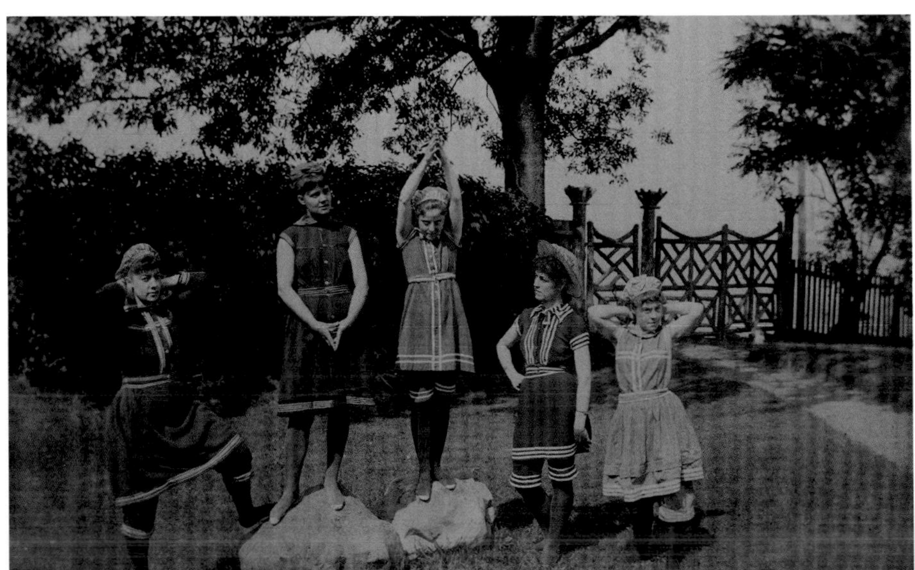

Figure 3.5 This September 1885 photograph of Alice, Trude Eccleston, Julie Marsh, and two other friends was one of the first that documents Alice's approach to mastering the camera. The negative sleeve is annotated with subject, date, time of day, lighting conditions, and exposure time.

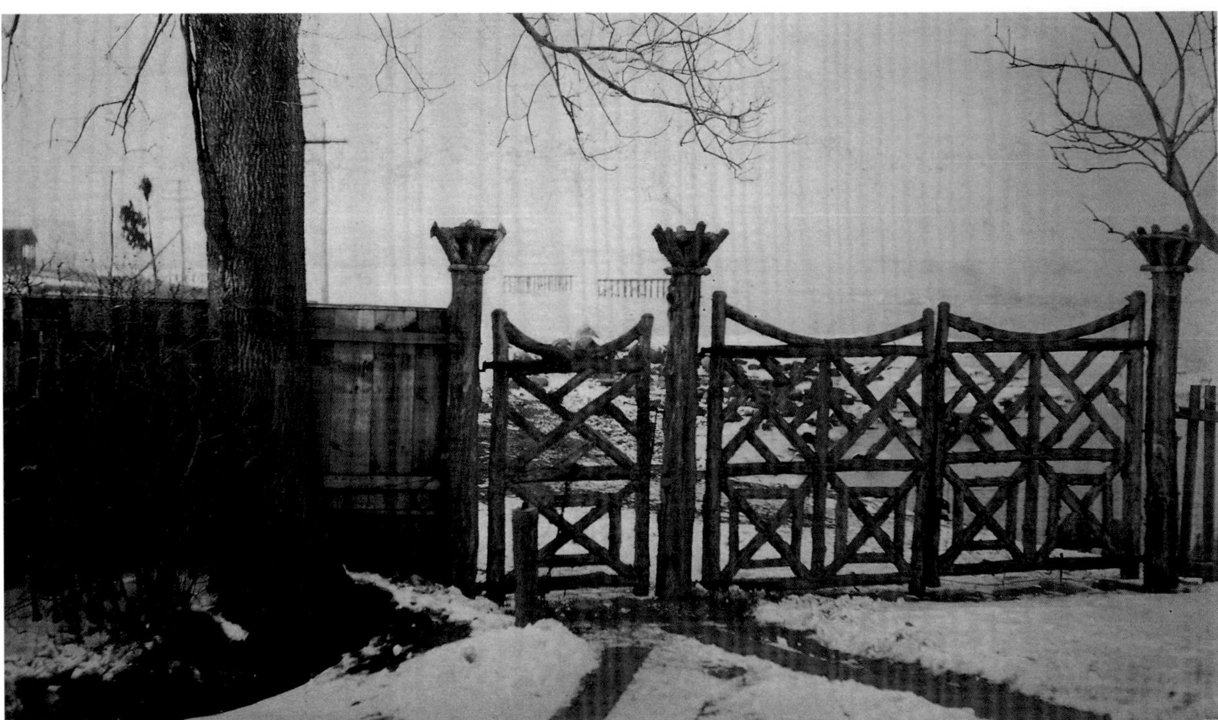

Figure 3.6 Clear Comfort gate in winter, 1886

added to her annotations the lens manufacturer, the glass plate brand, and the lens "stop" (opening), indicating her mastery of additional variables affecting exposure time and negative development.[34] She likely discarded her failed negatives but kept a few that were less than perfect. Two photographs of an August 1886 tennis party at home illustrate Alice's learning process (Figures 3.7 and 3.8). As the sleeves indicate,

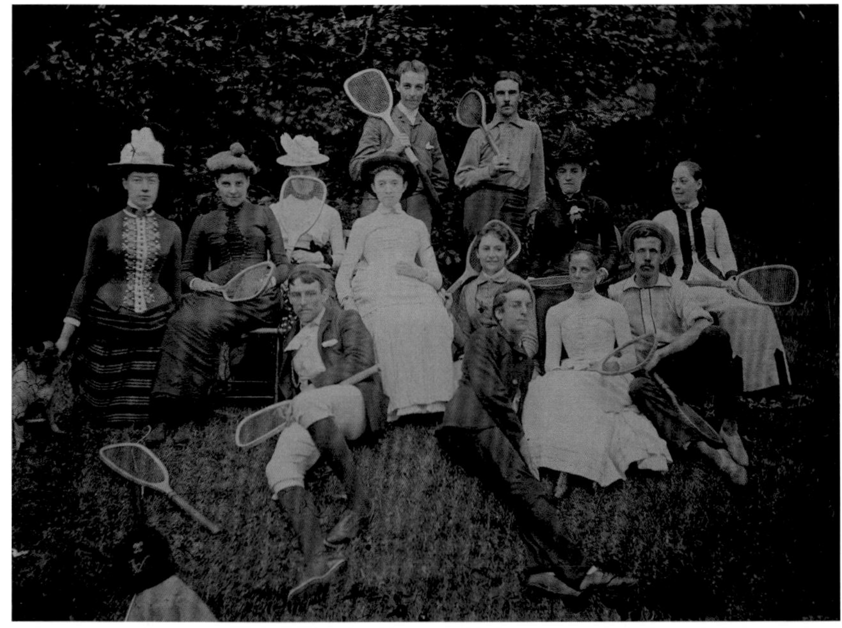

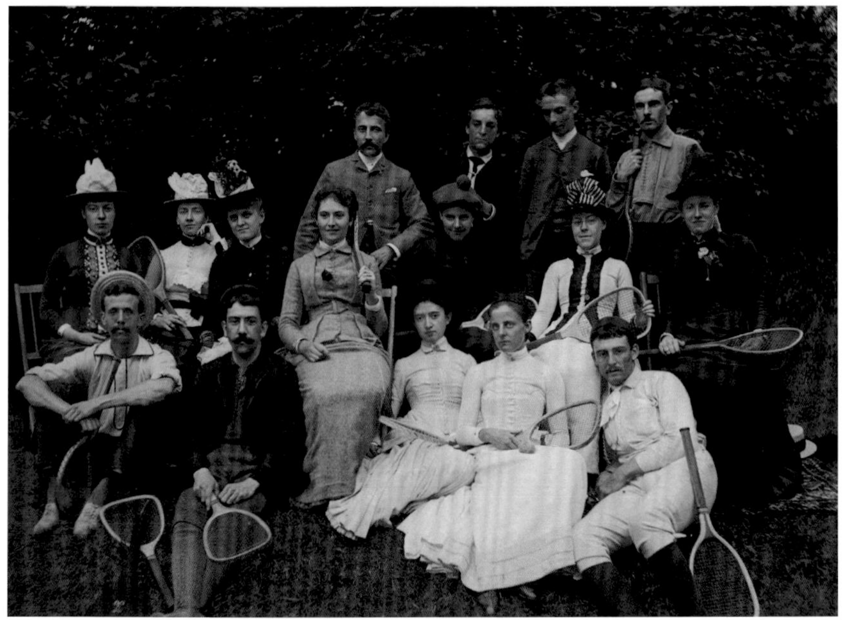

Figures 3.7 and 3.8   Alice kept both exposures of this Clear Comfort tennis party. The first was underexposed but captured the spontaneity of the moment. The second was a better exposure, but the group had stiffened up.

the weather was poor—"threatening rain, no sun"—and Alice must have feared that the first negative—taken at 5 p.m. with an exposure time of "about 1 sec"—was underexposed. She tried a second negative at 5:15 p.m. with an exposure time of "about 1½ sec." The second was technically better than the first, but her friends had stiffened up in the fifteen minutes between the two, and the spontaneity of the first was lost.

By August 1887, Alice was confident enough with the camera to undertake a comprehensive documentation of Clear Comfort, exposing twenty-eight negatives in less than two weeks. In the series, she recorded the picturesque gardens planned by her grandfather, which had been her childhood playground, using her intimate knowledge of the one-acre site and a lifetime of living in a house filled with prints and photographs, to compose a series of landscape views. "View from front door, tree & schooner" (Fine clear day, some wind / 12:45 P.M. / Stop 0 / Instantaneous / Dalh lense / Monday Aug 8th 1887) features the central axis of the property along a wide path that starts at the piazza and leads to the water, where two schooners were passing by (Figure 3.9).

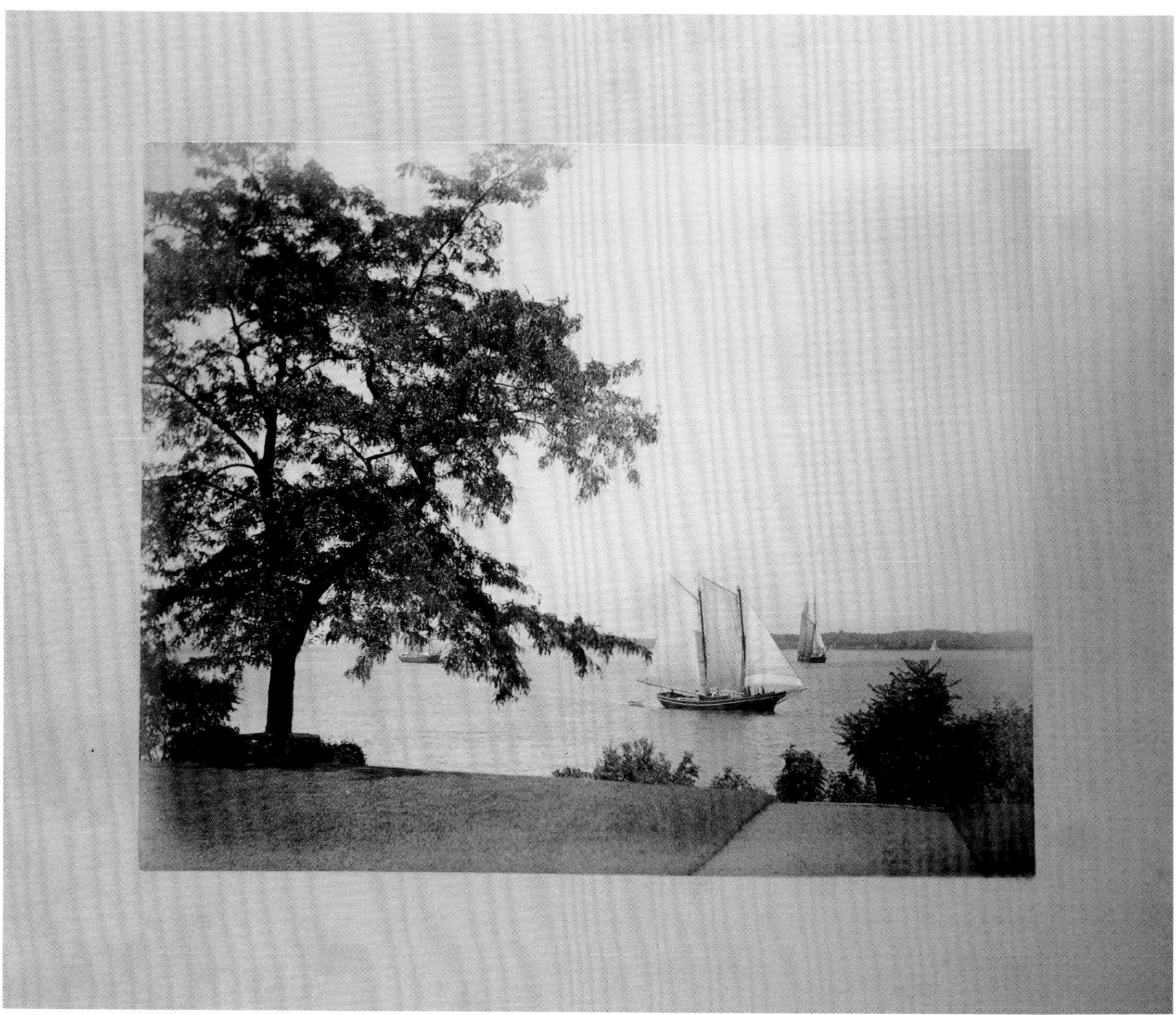

Figures 3.9 and 3.10   In the late summer of 1887, Alice intensively photographed Clear Comfort to create a photo album of exquisite prints mounted on 8-by-10 inch boards.

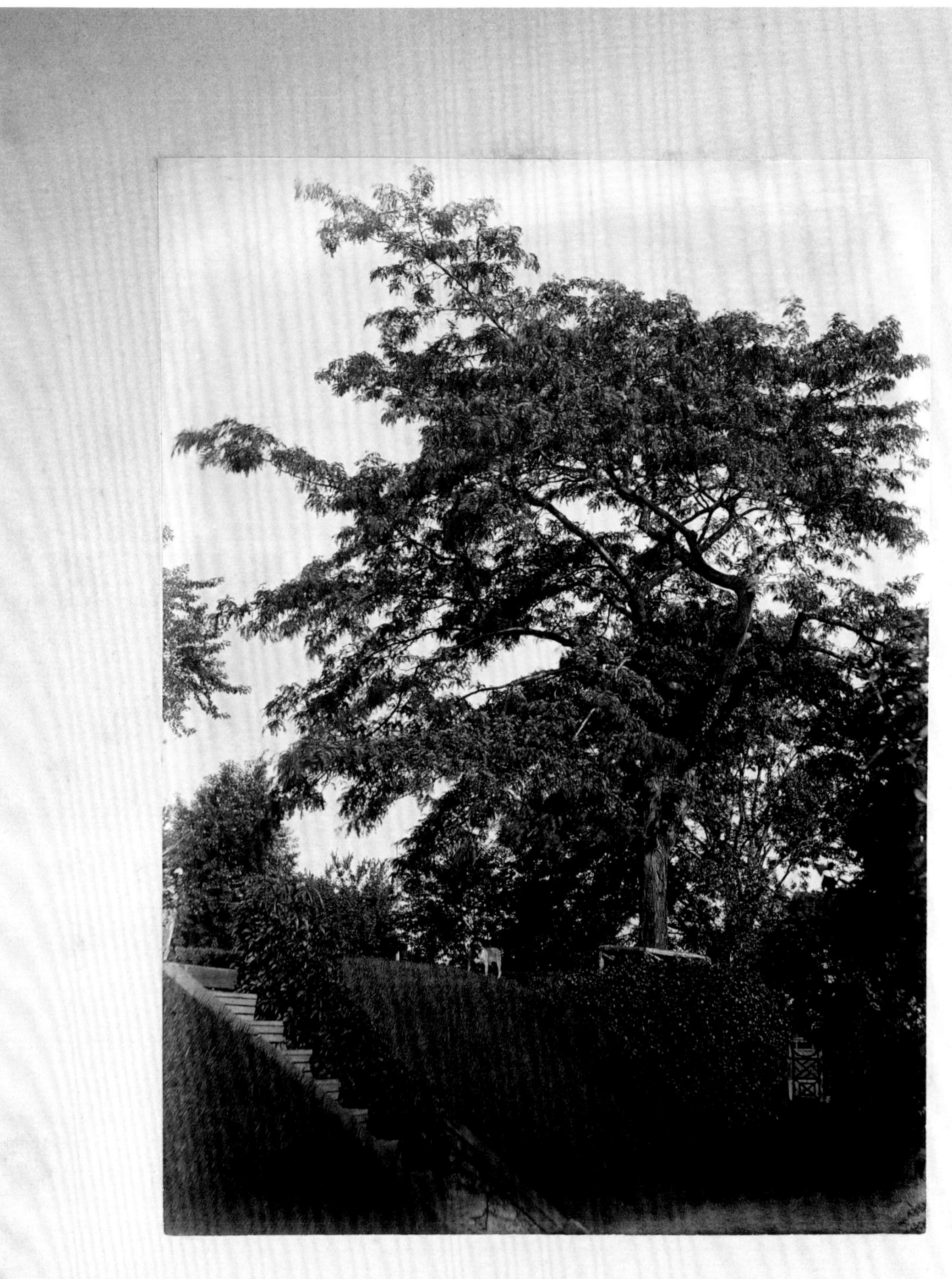

The central path occupies the right side of the composition, balanced by a majestic honey locust tree. The piazza and the tree, with a circular bench surrounding its trunk, were prime spots for viewing the harbor. Alice devised a traditional seascape, with a low horizon and framing landscape elements—familiar to her from the tourist views in the family's stereograph collection—and brought it to life by capturing the precise moment when the passing schooners aligned with the path leading from the house to the shore.

Alice's desire to capture the nooks and crannies of the property often led her to invent novel compositions. A walk down the path from the piazza to the edge of the terrace and down the terrace steps took her to the site of "Tree on Terrace, steps & Punch" (Fine bright day some wind / 8 a.m. / Stop 4 / Quick snaps / Dalh lense / Friday August 6th, 1887) (Figure 3.10). Turning her back to the water, she looked up at the terrace and the honey locust from below. Within this eccentric space between the steps and the rusticated entrance gate, the edge of the terrace served as an ad hoc "horizon," which led from the steps to the circular bench around the tree trunk. Punch "posed" on this "horizon" at the center of the picture.

That fall, Alice produced seven views of the interior of the Austen House, its small rooms brimming with family heirlooms but leaving little space for a tripod. She illuminated the views by manipulating reflected light from mirrors, opening and closing curtains, and lighting oil lamps. The negative sleeve for "Interior of Mamma's room" describes her method: "Fine sunny day, flashed light with looking glass / 9:40 a.m. Stop 5 / 7 ½ min / Dalh lense / Tuesday Sept 6, 1887" (Figure 3.11). Alice tried with little success to include family members in this series. In "Hall and Grandpa," John Austen sat in the front hall with the door wide open on a sunny day. The excess light at the doorway created an undesirable fogginess on the left side of the plate, and John's image blurred slightly due to the two-minute exposure time (Figure 3.12).

Alice's photographic practice was described in an article entitled, "Makeshift Photography," which appeared in a syndicated column called "A Page for Misses." Although the text is unattributed, the article is illustrated with four of Alice's photographs and is based entirely on her idiosyncratic methods.[35] The text emphasized that a thorough-going technical knowledge could help achieve "sometimes astounding" results with an inexpensive camera:

> The experience of judging light, the length of time for interiors and the speed to set the shutter for instantaneous work . . .—all this can only really be understood by remembering the conditions under which the pictures are taken and by afterward developing the plates.[36]

It discouraged the use of expensive equipment in favor of the simplest of household items, describing Alice's darkroom, which consisted of a windowless closet, where she mixed chemicals with well water carried upstairs in a pail. To stop the development of her negatives, she placed them directly under the well pump and let water wash over them for up to fifteen minutes, holding a piece of flannel over the faucet to strain out impurities. She printed her negatives in direct sunlight, a negative and sheet of light-sensitive paper coated with a silver solution held in place by a wooden frame. To stop the sun's action on the prints, they were placed in old china basins and washed at the well.

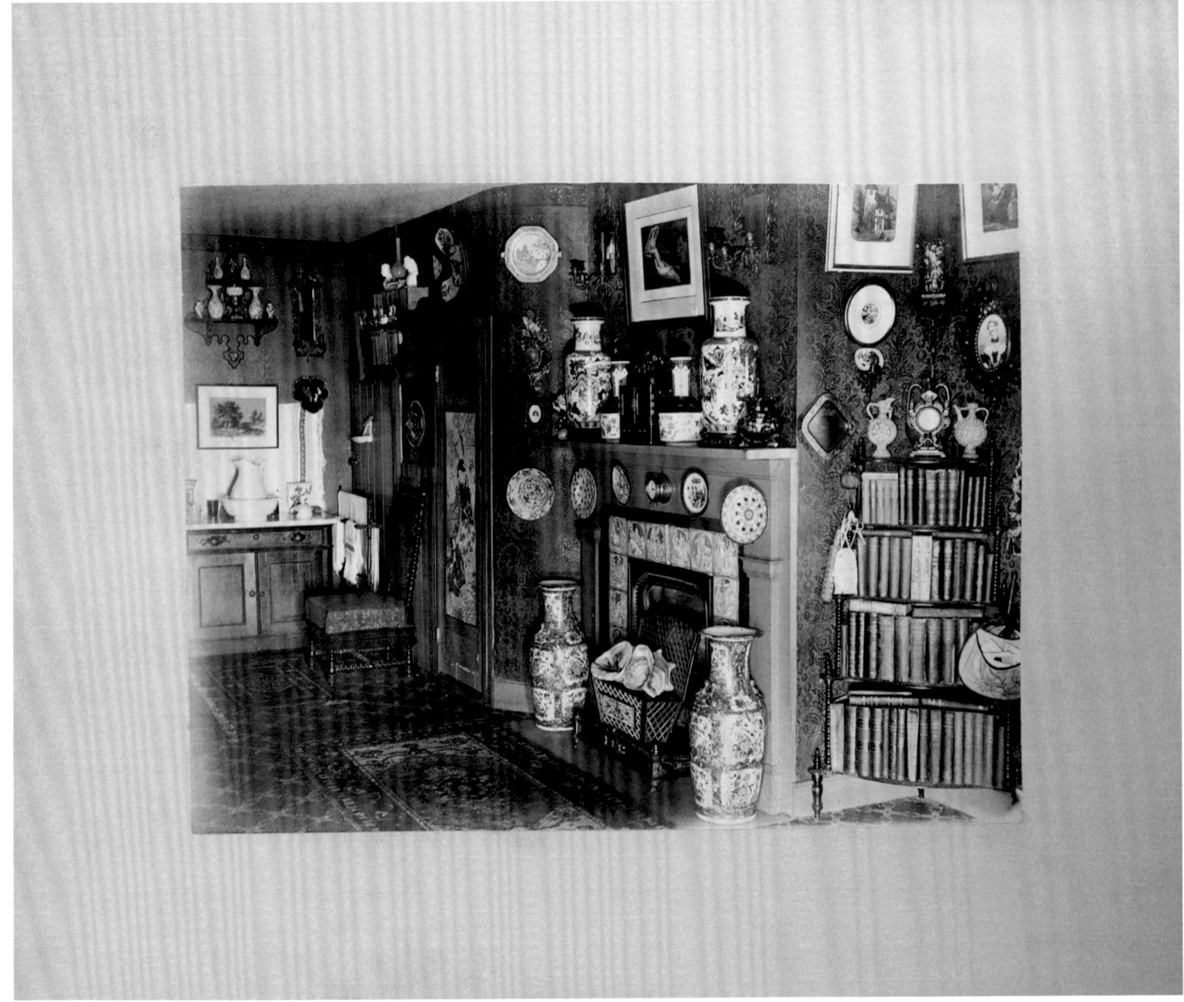

Figure 3.11 To capture the profusion of precious objects in the room she and Mamma shared, Alice manipulated several light sources and may not have had enough floor space to set up a tripod.

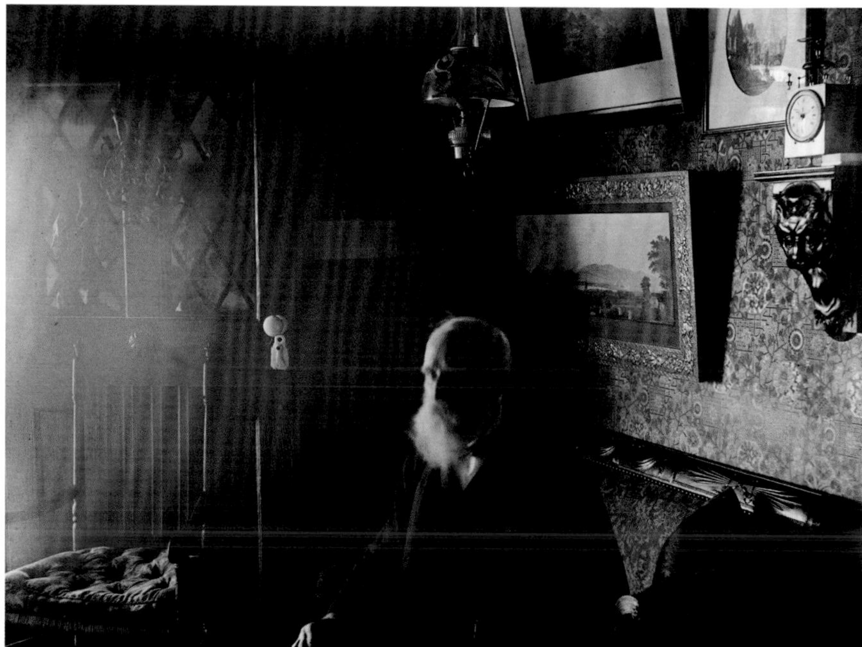

Figure 3.12 In the entrance hall, Alice's grandfather sits on a Duncan Phyfe sofa, one of the family's prized possessions. The old Dutch door is open to let in natural light and display the ornate, wrought iron door knocker, which he had acquired from a French chateau. The knocker is obscured here, but Alice later photographed it successfully with reflected light from a mirror.

In 1888, Alice assembled prints of Clear Comfort into what may have been the first of her many albums.[37] She purchased commercial albums consisting of black cardboard covers with cardboard inserts that served as mounts for her single-weight, gelatin silver prints which tended to curl if left unmounted. She gave her albums as gifts and did not keep many, but the few remaining large albums with full plate prints demonstrate her mastery of printmaking.[38]

Despite the bulk of the full plate camera and the fragility of glass plates, Alice began early on to take her camera with her away from home, which required the assistance of a friend or servant. Just as she aimed to photograph tennis matches, she pushed the limits of her equipment to photograph beach scenes. In September 1886, she ventured onto the sand at South Beach and miraculously came away with a technically sound negative. Her group portrait of friends piled together on the sand (with Julie Marsh at left and Alice holding the shutter release at right) captured the casual spirit of a beach day as successfully as "You-push-the-button-we-do-the-rest" Kodak snapshots of a decade later (Figure 3.13).

In August 1888, Alice packed her camera equipment in a separate trunk for a vacation to Lake Mahopac, fifty miles north of New York City. Visiting the Eccleston family there, she exposed twenty negatives, carrying her camera to the tennis court, into the woods, and across the lake by rowboat. On the island of Petra, she captured

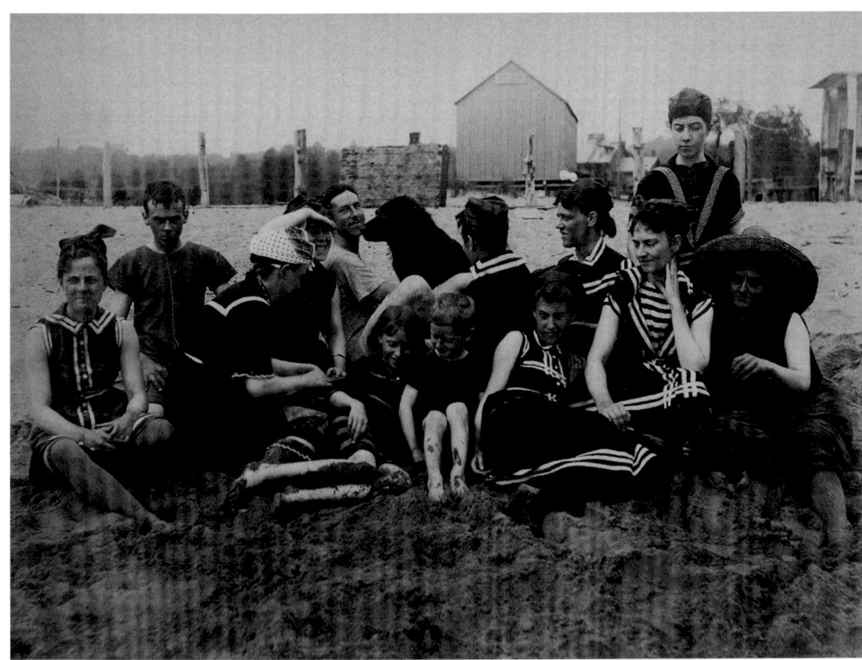

Figure 3.13   When Alice took this photograph in 1886, South Beach was already a well-known amusement area with a board-walk, carousel, and games of chance.

the magical light of a late summer afternoon, photographing Trude, Trude's future husband Charles Barton, and Alice's tennis partner Harry Wright resting on the shore before heading back to their hotel for dinner (Figure 3.14). "Makeshift Photography," described how Alice avoided taking a tripod on hikes: "Stones may be securely piled on some large stone near the wayside until the desired height for the tripod is reached."[39]

In June 1890, Alice began using a smaller, lighter camera, perhaps a gift from a cousin.[40] The 4-by-5 camera allowed for shorter exposure times, eliminating the need for a tripod in many instances. Alice also began using flash powder to permit instantaneous exposures indoors. Flash was a dangerous business at the time: an explosive powder was placed in pans and lit on fire to create a burst of light at the moment of exposure. Recalling the experience, Alice boasted to Oliver Jensen, "I never burned myself."[41]

The flexibility of the 4-by-5 camera inspired an outpouring of new work. Alice started a second negative numbering system for the smaller negatives, and within six months, her tally had reached 104. The next two years were her most active: by the end of 1893, she had amassed 676, 4-by-5 negatives and 542, full plate negatives. In 1892, she traveled for two-to-four-week stints, often taking both cameras and pho-tographing at each location: in February, to Bethlehem, Pennsylvania; in March, to

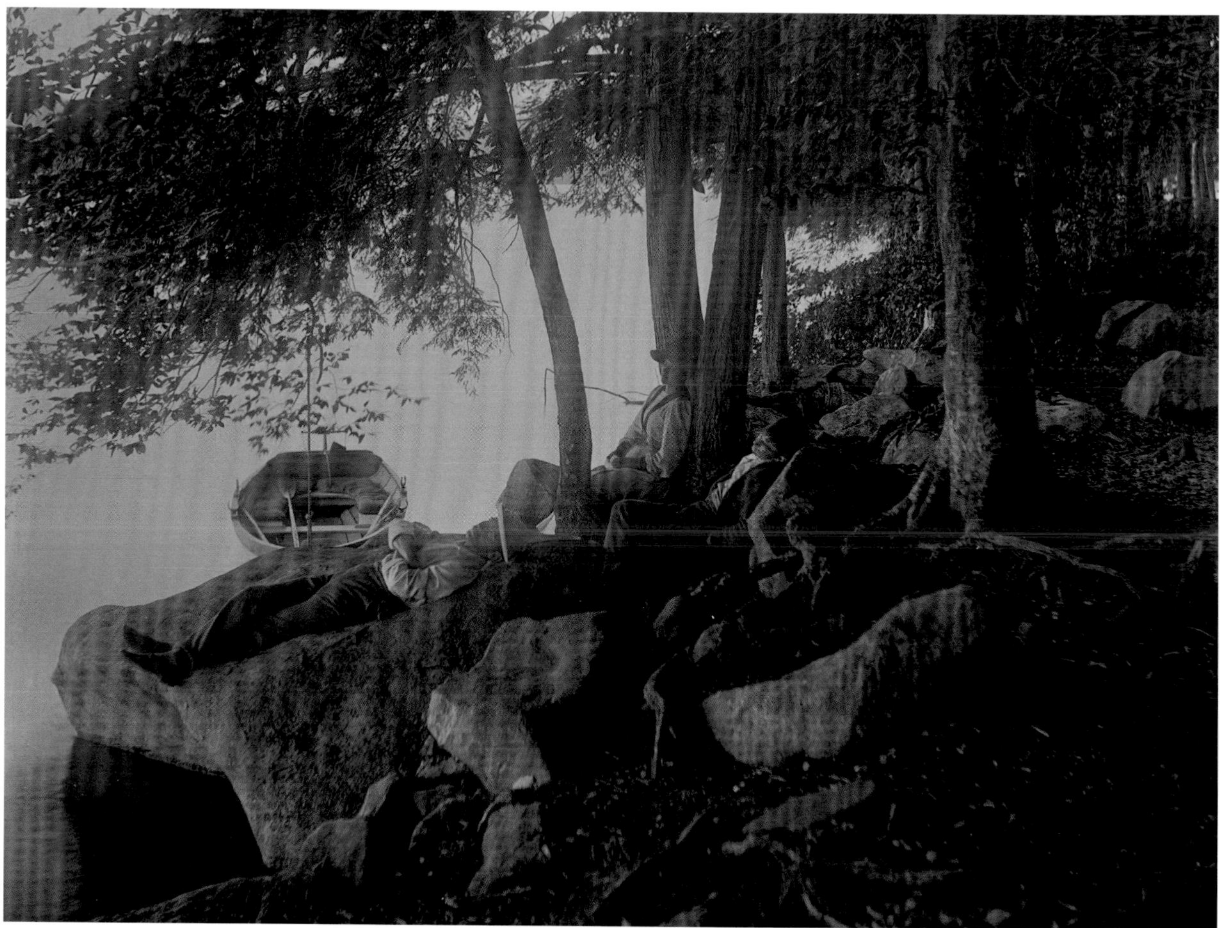

Figure 3.14 Alice captured the magical light of a late summer afternoon in this photograph of her friends lounging on the rocks of Petra, a tiny island in Lake Mahopac, where they were vacationing with the Eccleston family.

New Brunswick, New Jersey; in June, to Cambridge, Boston, and Concord; in July, to Watkins Glen, New York; in August, to Fishkill, New York; and in October, with her Aunt Nellie and Ralph Munroe, to Annapolis, Maryland on a ten-day canal trip. The frequency of these trips suggests that Alice was driven by the photographic opportunities they provided.

Most of Alice's excursions were to well-known tourist destinations, but the canal trip with Nellie and Ralph was anything but conventional. In 1886, after his wife and baby fell ill and tragically died, Ralph left Staten Island and moved to Coconut Grove, Florida, where he joined a small community of northeastern adventurers who helped found the city of Miami.[42] An amateur ship designer, Ralph teamed with a Staten Island shipbuilder to construct small yachts that could traverse the open waters of the

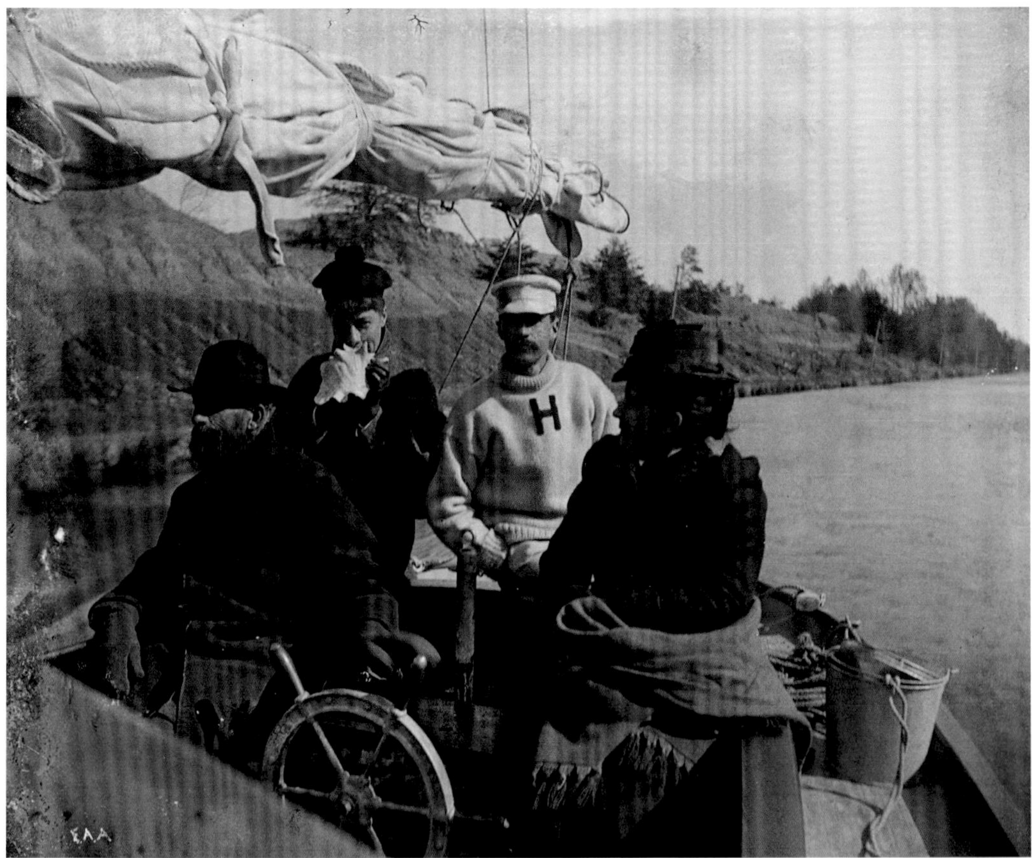

Figure 3.15   It was quite cold when Alice took this photograph of the *Wabun* party. Ralph Munroe wears heavy mittens, Aunt Nellie wraps her hands in her shawl, Tom Browne puts his hands in his pockets, and Alice, who bared her hands to set up the camera, is warming them with her breath as she squeezes the shutter release.

Atlantic Ocean and the shallow waterways at the mouth of the Miami River. When one of the yachts, the *Wabun*, was ready to launch, Ralph invited Nellie and Alice to accompany him on its maiden voyage. He and his first mate, Tom "Butterball" Browne, picked up their passengers in New Brunswick and sailed through a series of canals to the Chesapeake Bay as far as Annapolis, where the women disembarked. Some of Alice's fifty-one negatives from the trip were taken from atop the roof or inside the boat's small cabin. In a photograph of their party in the stern of the *Wabun*, she secured the camera to the roof and sat behind Ralph and Nellie and next to Browne, who wore his Harvard crew sweater (Figure 3.15).

Browne, too, was an amateur photographer, but his photographs of the canal trip came out poorly. When he received Alice's prints, he graciously thanked her—"The photographs are all so good that it would be an injustice to the others, if I mentioned any one in particular"—but complained—"I feel inclined to throw my Kodak away, whenever I look at them."[43] Alice also received hearty praise from Ralph, a seasoned photographer: "What a stunning success your shots on the trip are, I carried them in my pocket half the week so as to be sure that everyone of consequence in the settlement should see them."[44]

In June 1892, Alice and Nellie visited Nellie's uncle, Alfred Munroe, in Concord, Massachusetts. During the 1870s, Alfred lived in Clifton and knew Alice as a little girl. In 1877 when he turned sixty, he moved back to his family's home in Concord to live with his sister Mary. Taking up photography in his retirement, Alfred lovingly documented the cultural heritage and natural beauties of his hometown.[45] During their visit, Alice and Alfred photographed together and exchanged pictures. Alfred made a flattering portrait of Alice in his garden, and she made an idyllic portrait of Alfred and Nellie rowing on the Assabet River, which recalled Alfred's own river views (Figures 3.16 and 3.17). After the visit, Mary wrote Alice an appreciative note: "I trust our views of Concord scenes have come out well, and you are often led to think of us as you look at them."[46] Proud of her daughter for making a fine impression, Mamma boasted: "I expect Alfred Monroe [sic] is mourning over your departure. I knew he would take a fancy to you."[47]

In August 1892, on a visit to distant cousins in Fishkill, New York, Alice met John C. Browne, a founder of the Photographic Society of Philadelphia.[48] Browne became a mentor, and when she returned home, Alice sent him photographs, to which he responded with lengthy, technical advice:

> My dear Miss Austin [sic], Thank you ever so much for the two photos you sent me. Both are excellent, and show that you know how to handle your sights, lens, developer, printing &c. Blisters on albumen paper are very annoying. Some years ago I used to put my toned prints into salt & water and after fixing at once in to a bath of alcohol & water equal parts that seemed to stop the trouble. If I do any more printing I think I shall use platinum cold process. The results are fine particularly so far as 6 ½ × 8 ½ & 8 × 10 work. It is my judgment the best print process I ever used.[49]

Isaac Almstaedt, Staten Island's leading professional photographer, also mentored Alice.[50] In 1887, Alice watched Almstaedt work as he documented the Staten Island Cricket and Baseball Club for a feature article in *Outing Magazine*, which she pasted into her scrapbook.[51] She appeared in two of his photographs, and a print of his portrait of women tennis players was displayed in the Austen family's middle parlor.[52] In September 1892, Alice, Trude, and Julia Bredt sat for a portrait in Almstaedt's studio.[53]

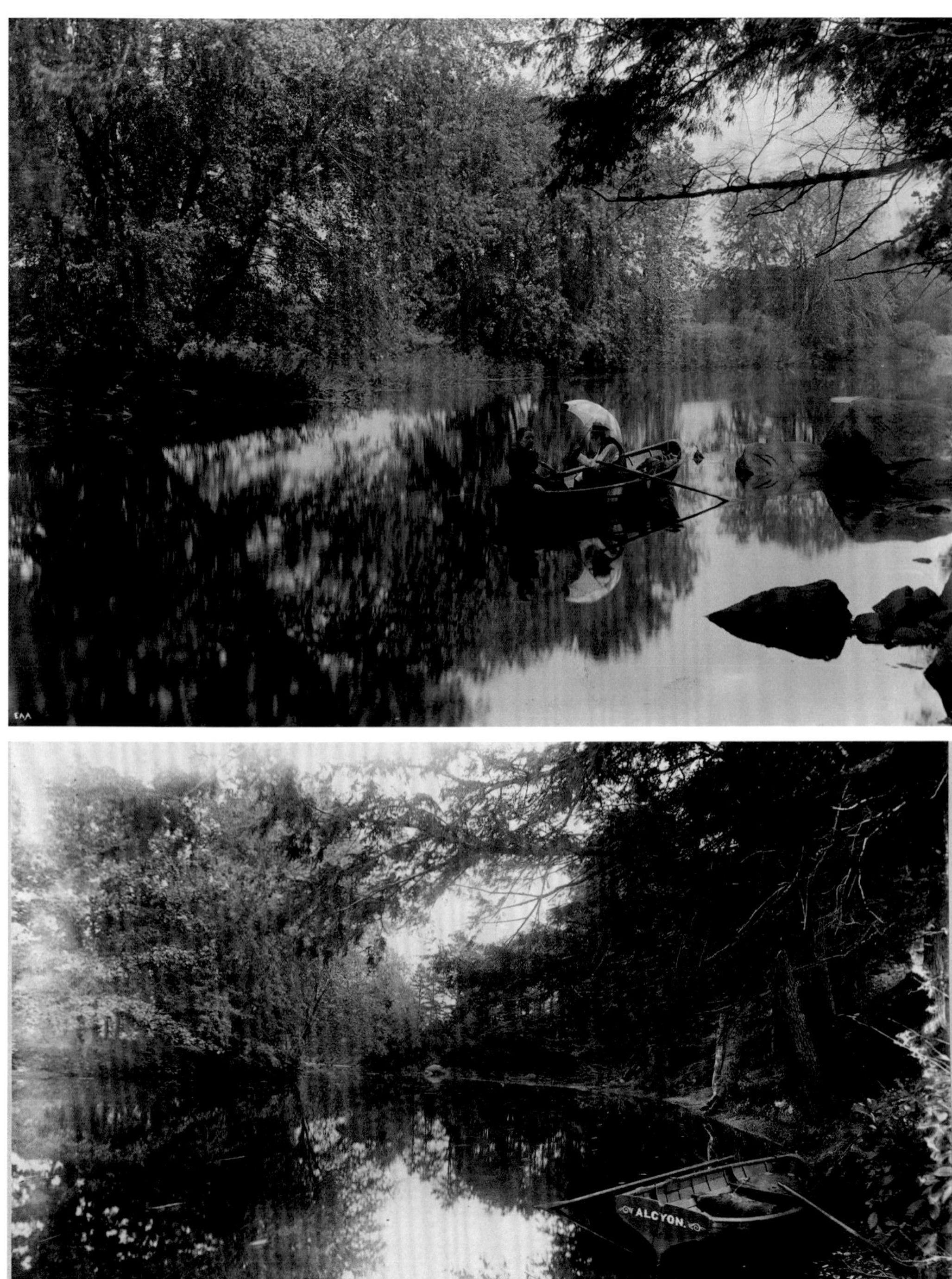

Figures 3.16 and 3.17   Alice's photograph (top) of Alfred Munroe and her Aunt Nellie was perhaps inspired by Alfred's own photographs of his Concord home and surroundings (bottom).

It may have been then that Alice and Almstaedt devised a plan to photograph together. Standing in front of St. John's Episcopal Church in Clifton, they set up their cameras side by side, Alice using a 4 by 5 and Almstaedt a 5 by 7. Their identical views show the church buildings in the distance with the steeple dominating a sky that occupies most of the frame. [54]

Alice's superior skill among her peers, many of whom tried their hands at photography, was widely acknowledged. Trude's sister Edith Blunt and Julia Bredt sent their photographs to Alice for comment. Intimidated, Edith wrote, "Remember, I have only just started photography. . . . So don't be too critical!!!"[55] Bessie Strong was Alice's only close friend with a serious commitment to photography. Like Alice, she was mentored by a family member—her cousin John C. Van Dyke, who taught fine art at Rutgers—but unlike Alice, Bessie was drawn to the camaraderie of the amateur clubs and most likely was a member of Uncle Peter's New Brunswick club.[56] Writing in December 1890, she asked Alice, "Have you had letters from photographic 'cranks' in the west and south asking you to exchange pictures?" Later she reported that she was "having a very interesting correspondence with my photographic friends south & west."[57]

In November 1890, Alice entered a contest sponsored by the popular biweekly newspaper, *Frank Leslie's Illustrated*, one of the few times she joined in an amateur photographers' event.[58] Six mounted, signed prints, mostly picturesque country scenes selected from her travel photographs, were likely her submission.[59] There were more than 500 entrants, and Alice was not singled out for recognition. An intense competitor, she never participated in contests again.[60] The winning photographs, which were published as wood engravings, show the nascent influence of pictorialism, a vogue that swept through the amateur photographic clubs in the 1890s. Advocates of pictorialism wished to integrate the aesthetics and appearance of modern European art into photography by encouraging a variety of technical and compositional experiments. One of the prize winners was Alfred Stieglitz, a gifted photographer and fierce advocate of pictorialism.

Alice was aware of the pictorial movement; she subscribed to *Sun & Shade, An Artistic Periodical*, a monthly journal devoted to artistic photography. In 1892, Bessie wrote Alice that she had received a gift of photographs that "are all this new kind of photograph and look so much like the engraving."[61] But the aspiration to make "Art" held no appeal for Alice, nor was she drawn to the "artistic" photographs of idealized Victorian womanhood, which were a specialty of women pictorialists. Alice's mentors were photographers of an older generation, and her taste was conditioned by the stereographs and framed landscape photographs from the 1860s and 1870s that were displayed in her home. Eschewing the clubs, she isolated herself from

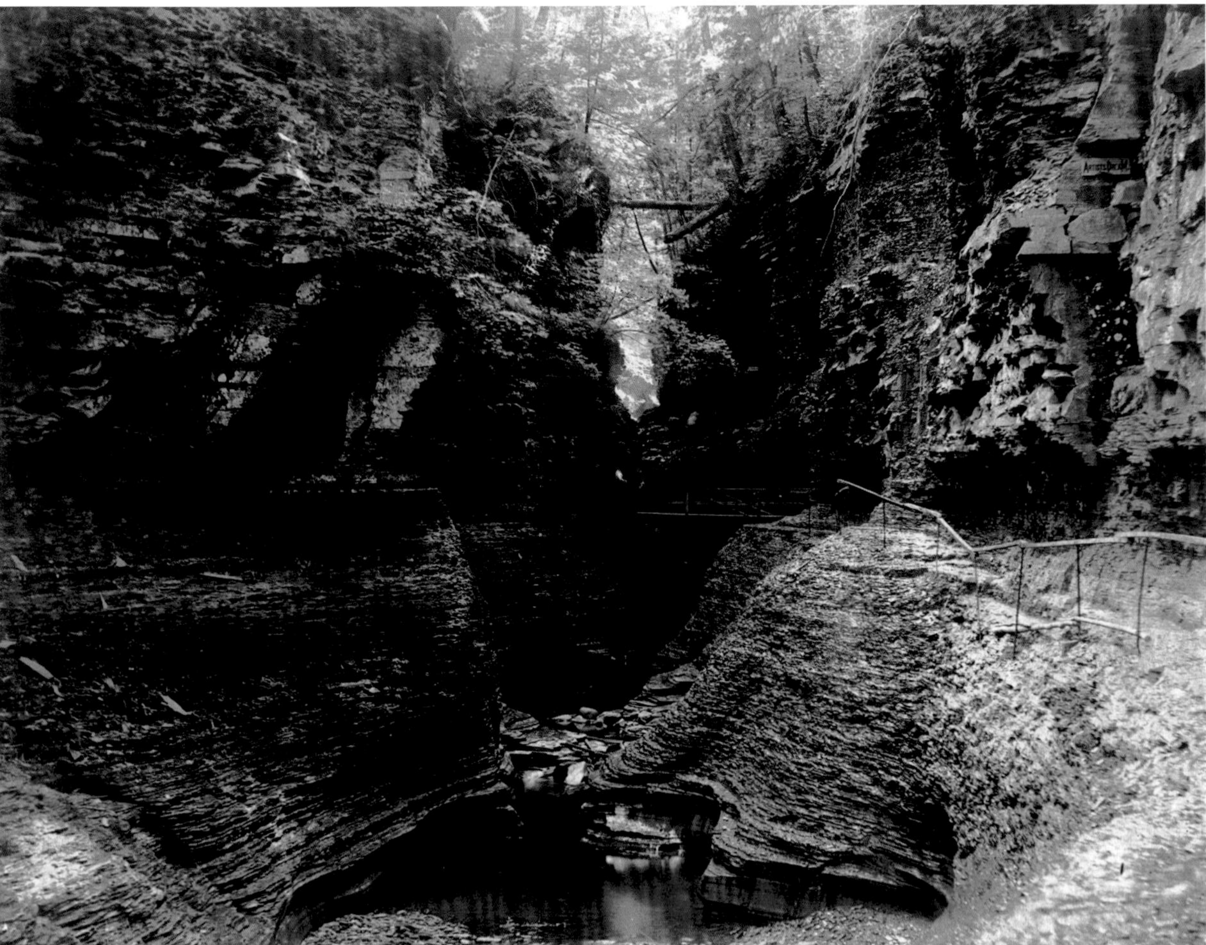

Figure 3.18   This grand vista of a gorge at Watkins Glen is also a portrait. At the left side of the bridge in the distance are Trude and her brother Sam.

the latest trends and from pictorialist photographers, like Stieglitz, who were her own age.

A photograph of the famous gorge at Watkins Glen, which she took on vacation in 1892, illustrates Alice's ambition as a photographer and her indifference to the fashion for "art photography" (Figure 3.18). Alice climbed up the gorge to this over-look wearing an ankle-length dress and delicate shoes while carrying a wooden box camera, tripod, and glass plates—not a feat for the faint of heart. Although Alice rarely titled her photographs, she called this one "Artist's Dream," which suggests she associated it with the sublime landscapes of Hudson River School painters. On the cliff at right, however, is a sign that reads, "Artist's Dream." Alice's title was literal, not aspirational.

Alice's conservative aesthetics yielded a collection of exquisite, if old-fashioned, landscape photographs. Her portraits, especially her group portraits, revitalized another conventional genre by providing an intimate view of the social rituals and gender politics of the Gilded Age. The group portraits were a visual diary, a natural extension of the scrapbooks that she had filled with newspaper clippings and ephemera documenting her social calendar. She had started a third scrapbook in 1889, collecting dozens of items but never pasting them in, as photography took over. That she often photographed herself dressed for a specific event—in Spanish costume for the 1886 Kirmess (Figure 2.5), for example—underscores the continuity between her scrapbooks and photographs. Significantly, Alice appears in almost all the group portraits; they chronicled her social life.

Although she was not a classic Victorian beauty, Alice appears self-assured in her photographs, her face serious but relaxed. Here, too, Bessie Strong, who fretted about her appearance in photographs, provides a contrast: "I have been trying in vain to get a decent photograph of myself, and have posed no less than five times within the last three weeks; but each picture has turned out with some marked peculiarity."[62] Alice's fashion sense and athleticism buoyed her self-confidence, and the very act of photographing added to it. Attending to the myriad decisions required of her behind the camera, she could not allow a stray hair or a pinching corset to distract her. And repeatedly seeing herself in photographs gave her a better sense of her appearance than women who relied solely on the mirror.

While Alice's scrapbooks were private, her photographs were shared. She frequently gave framed self-portraits to friends and family as Christmas or birthday presents. According to the practice of the day, she exchanged portraits with her suitors, an exchange she often initiated.[63] Photographs were expensive and time-consuming gifts, and Alice enjoyed giving them not only for special occasions. When she returned from a trip, she would send photographs to her hosts in lieu of a thank you note; when she photographed a tennis match, she sent prints to the players; and when she photographed her friends' homes (a form of family portraiture), she sent photographs to their parents. Beginning in 1886, she wrote her initials, "AA," or "EAA" on some of her negatives, which may indicate those she gave as presents.[64]

Alice saved more than fifty thank you letters from family, friends, and acquaintances. After receiving a portrait with her children, Alice's neighbor Hetty Furniss wrote:

> My dear Alice, Words are poor things in which to express my gratification and appreciation of your kindness in regard to the photographs. They are truly artistic both in

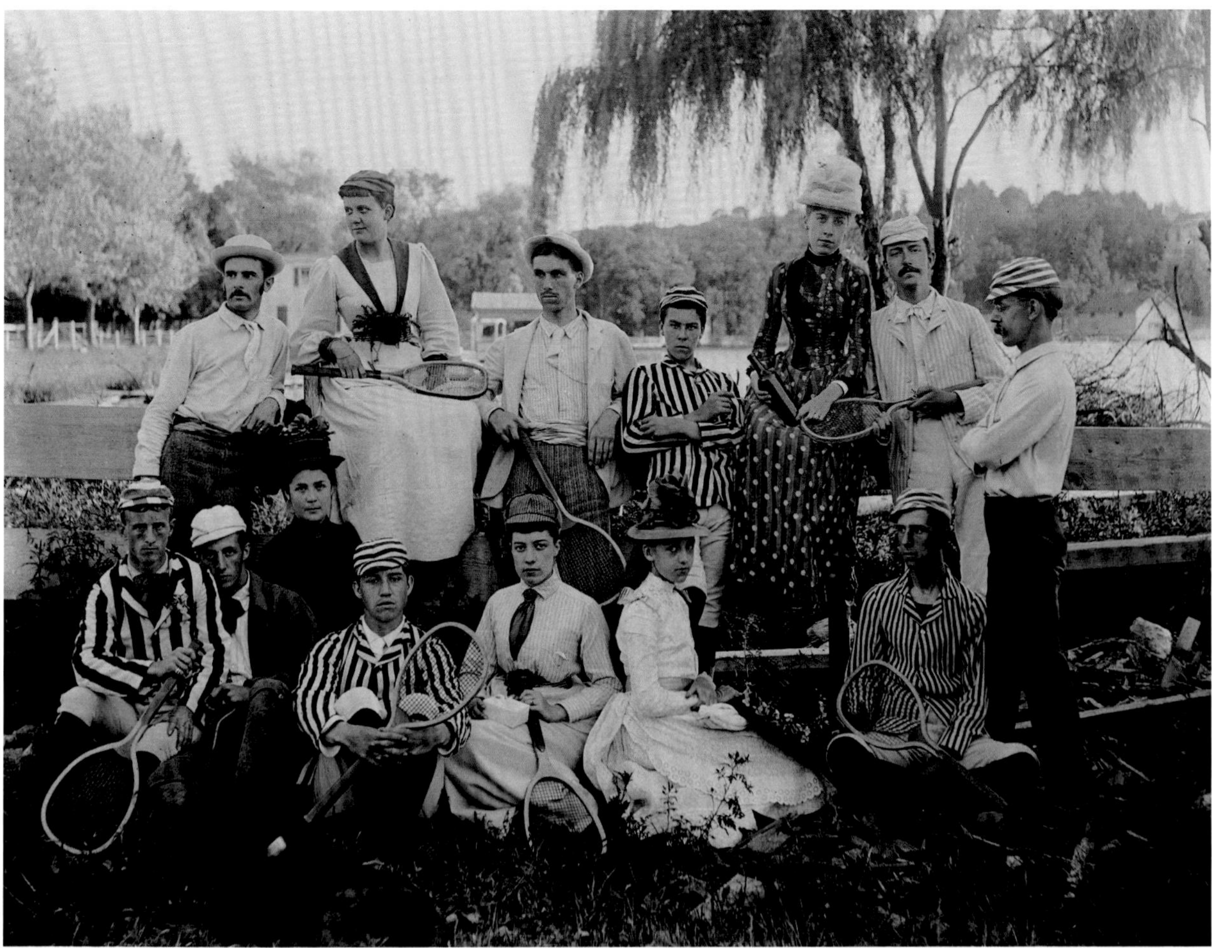

Figure 3.19   Alice (seated, center) and Trude (on the fence) are the only women with tennis racquets in this group portrait taken at Lake Mahopac.

arrangement and workmanship aside from their being most excellent likenesses. You are very generous with your talents and give a great deal of pleasure.[65]

Alice's friend Maud Wright was more direct: "Dear Alice, You are a duck! The photo is fine. Thank you ever so much."[66] Clifford R. Chapman, whom Alice met in Bethlehem, wrote: "My Dear Miss Austen, On returning home this morning I was very much surprised and delighted to find the five beautiful pictures you so kindly sent me. They will remind me—during many a long evening—of a delightfully spent day."[67]

Alice's photographs were not only souvenirs of shared experiences but group activities that she orchestrated. On vacation in 1888 with the Ecclestons at Lake Mahopac, for example, Alice skillfully posed fourteen tennis players so that everyone could be seen (Figure 3.19). The patterns of their clothing were artfully arranged, meaningful relationships were established, and Alice, appropriately, sat at the center of it all. Returning home from Mahopac, she developed her negatives and sent prints to Trude, who reported the excitement they caused:

> I think the pictures you sent me to look at splendid. . . . Mr. Manner saw the tennis group and wanted me to ask you if you could allow him to pay for one he thought is so good of himself & the others. . . . The Collinses think the pictures splendid, and they each want one of the group."[68]

Photography was a powerful tool for Alice in her bid for popularity. That began to change in 1891, when she started using the camera not only to gain social success but to satirize the rituals she lived by.

4 THE PASSING OF THE LARKY LIFE

As the years progressed, Alice's scrapbooks included a growing number of engagement announcements and wedding invitations, and the giddy gossip in her friends' letters gave way to the uncertainties they faced in their transition from girlhood to womanhood. When she reached her mid-twenties, Alice learned that the "larky life" was more than a game; it was a pathway to marriage that could be harrowing. Between 1890 and 1893, Julie Marsh married and had her first child; Trude Eccleston endured a humiliating broken engagement; Jule Martin, exiled by her family, confronted the social precariousness of not marrying; and Julia Bredt, although younger than Alice, encouraged her to flirt aggressively, even manipulatively.

As these events unfolded, Alice used the camera to reflect on the freedom lost in marriage, the shallowness of courtship rituals, and the artificiality of Victorian ideals of womanhood. Within a two-month period in the fall of 1891, she enlisted Trude and the three Julias—Marsh, Martin, and Bredt—to take her now-famous photographs "The Darned Club," "Trude & I Masked, Short Skirts," and Julia Martin, Julia Bredt, and Alice dressed in men's clothes. Growing up in a pre-Freudian era in which heterosexual mating was the norm and "romantic friendships" between women were permitted, Alice and her friends may not have thought critically about gender roles or sexual orientation. The photographs suggest that by the time they confronted the prospect of marriage, they had begun to do so.

The Darned Club

Trude Eccleston and Julie Marsh, daughters of two of Clifton's most respected families, lived across New York Avenue (now Bay Street) from each other and two blocks from Clear Comfort. From childhood, all three girls loved tennis, swimming, and boating, and Alice's friendships with Trude and Julie assured her a place in the spotlight of Staten Island society. Trude's and Julie's mothers were leading hostesses in Clifton, and several of their children became leaders of Clifton's younger set.

Trude's father, John C. Eccleston, was the rector of St. John's Episcopal Church. An erudite, worldly man with degrees in medicine and theology, Reverend Eccleston was a pillar of the Clifton community who commissioned its rough-hewn granite, neo-Gothic church and Queen Anne style rectory, which still stand today.[1] Trude had three siblings, and Alice was embraced by the entire Eccleston clan. She accompanied them on summer vacations and regularly photographed the church, the rectory, and the family. In a formal portrait taken in the rectory parlor, Trude holds center stage (Figure 4.1). On the left stand her brothers Jack and Sam, and seated, from left to right, is her sister Edith Blunt, Edith's two sons, Jack's wife, and Trude's mother.[2] An album of the church and rectory that Alice kept—she probably gave a similar one to the family—includes a view of Trude's room showing a photograph of Alice on the mantel (Figure 4.2).[3]

Julie's father, Nathaniel Marsh, died when she was a baby, but had been president of the New York and Erie Railroad. Her mother, a Townsend distantly related to Alice, was Nathaniel's second wife, and they had four children.[4] Mrs. Marsh loved entertaining at their home, which had its own bowling alley and was the site of bowling parties, dinners, and dances. Especially popular was the "German," a rowdy dance in which a man who failed to find a partner had to hop on one leg while fanning a dancing couple.

The letters that Julie and Trude sent to Alice when they were on vacation illuminate their relaxed intimacy with each other and their pride in the athletic prowess of Staten Island's young women. In one letter to Alice, Julie wrote:

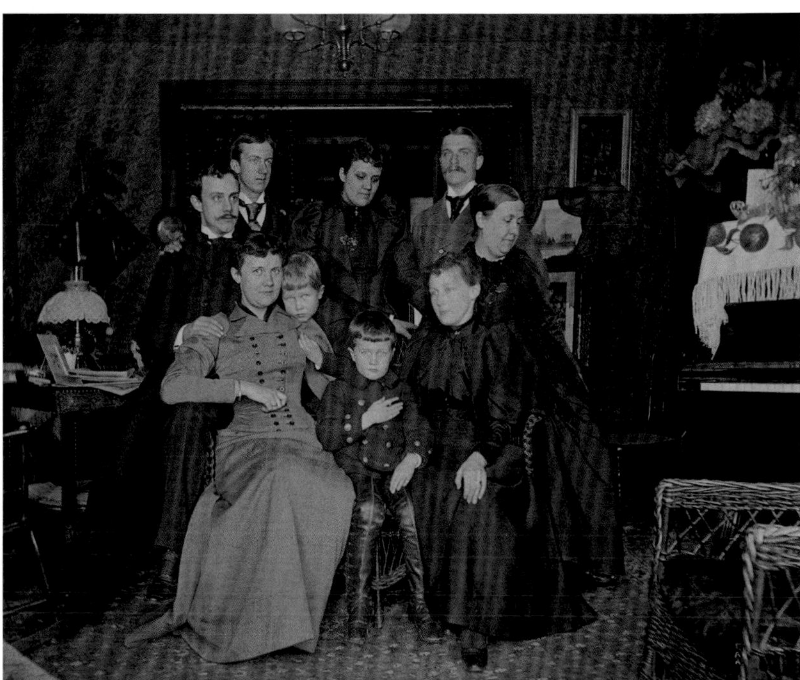

Figure 4.1   Missing from this formal group portrait are the Eccleston family patriarchs: Reverend John Eccleston and Colonel Albert Blunt, husband of Trude's sister Edith.

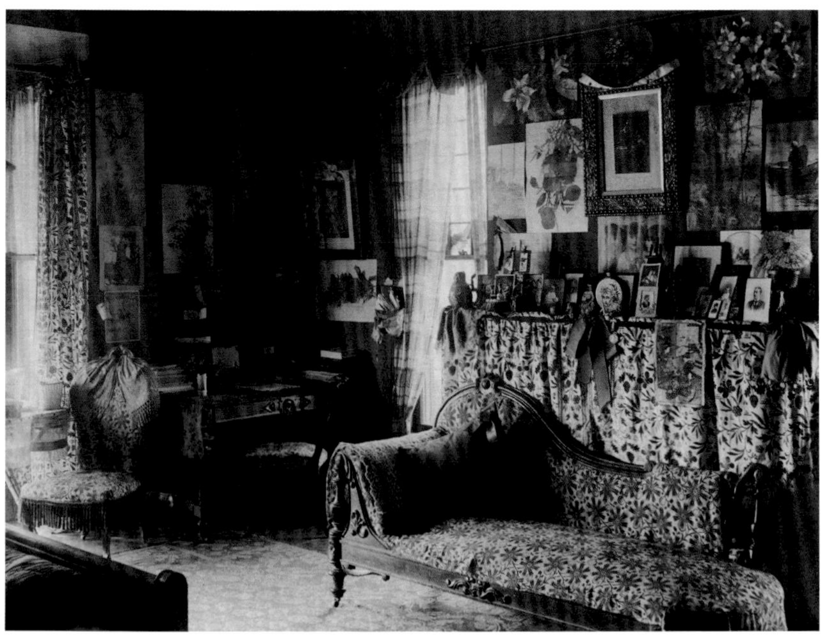

Figure 4.2   Alice took her now-famous photograph of "Trude and I Masked, Short Skirts" in Trude's bedroom in the rectory of St. John's Episcopal Church.

We amuse ourselves princibly [sic] by fishing, rowing and playing Tennis. The court is a very good dirt one but I do not like it nearly so well as I do turf. . . . I wish you could see the way the girls play; it makes me tired to look at them much more to play <u>with</u> them. There is one fat boy a Johnnie Freiland who plays very well indeed and I have had some very nice games with him. . . . Are you going bathing much now? I miss it ever so much for no one, but some of the boys, bathe here as the water is very cold.[5]

Trude, too, disparaged the unathletic women whom she met on vacation. Anticipating Alice's arrival at Lake Mahopac, she exclaimed that she was "in a fair way to get fat much to my disgust, so you must hurry up and come and we will play tennis and row until we are skeletons."[6] Like Julie, Trude encountered the taboo against women swimming. Writing Alice, she complained, "Oh how I envy you bathing, bring your bathing suit & we will find some place to go in, the boys bathe every day and say it is delicious."[7]

Trude and Alice both enjoyed the spotlight, and Alice's camera provided social opportunities for them. In numerous group photographs, Trude placed herself in the center and posed charmingly, which came naturally to her (Figure 2.7). A talented singer, she could be counted on to perform for friends and family and occasionally in public, sometimes to rave reviews. In 1888, the local press singled out her performance in a popular operetta: "Miss Eccleston was a vision of beauty with the merit that visions rarely possess . . . she interpreted her part with rare intelligence and grace."[8]

Trude's letters to Alice are filled with references to flirting with men, a pastime that they approached as sport. From Lake Mahopac, Trude wrote:

> There is a great dearth of men up here and although every place is full of people they all seem to be old people or very young girls. The most people are at Deans the other side of the lake, we must go over there to a hop [a dance].[9]

A minister's daughter, Trude perhaps talked about flirting more than she acted on it. On a trip to see her sister in Utah, she wrote, "The girls who are visiting here now I do not like very much, they are too free & easy for my style, decidedly fast."[10]

Unlike Alice and Trude, Julie was not especially interested in flirting and was the first of their set to get married. In December 1888, Reverend Eccleston officiated at her wedding ceremony to George Osgood Lord, another Clifton neighbor who worked for the Morgan Steamship Company. Trude and Alice were bridesmaids, and Alice pressed her flowers between the pages of her scrapbook. The wedding was the event of the social season, with a thousand invitations sent out and guests arriving from Manhattan as well as Staten Island.[11] The newlyweds built a new house so close to Clear Comfort that Alice's mother complained: "Julie's stable is very near indeed, and we see it plainly from the dining room, I am sorry to say."[12] When the Lords moved into their home, Alice photographed it, establishing a precedent; when each of her close friends married, she commemorated their new lives by photographing their new homes.[13]

Julie was also the first of Alice's friends to have a child, a cause of much excitement. A friend who had recently left Staten Island exclaimed in a letter to Alice, "Please go easy the next time you tell me such news as of Julia Lord. My breath was clean knocked out of my body."[14] Julie comfortably assumed the roles of wife and mother, albeit made easier by her reliance on household staff to relieve her of domestic duties. In a letter to Alice, she wrote about a wealthy young woman from New Orleans whom she met on vacation:

> Alice! think of it; she get[s] up at six in the morning & does all the marketing herself. You bet! I [w]ould have the butcher, baker and candlestick maker come to me, but I guess that in New Orleans they do not have things arranged as comfortably as we do on S.I.[15]

Ever the athlete, Julie balked at Victorian norms of confinement, which required her to remain inactive for one to two months before and after giving birth. Shortly after Gladys was born, Trude wrote Alice: "I don't believe they will be able to keep her in bed much longer she is so lively."[16] In a photograph taken at the Lords' Fourth of July

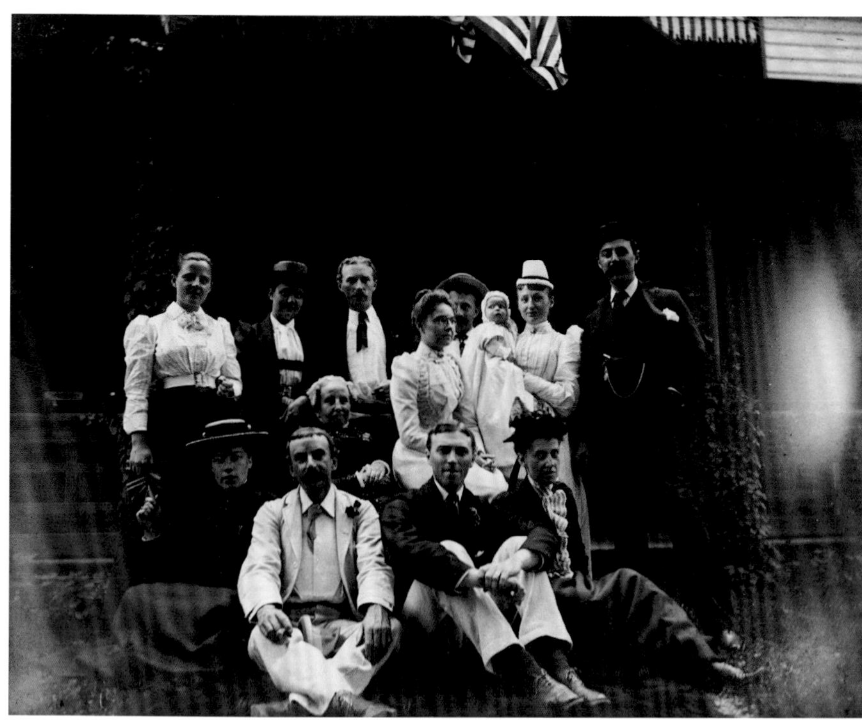

Figure 4.3   Louise Scofield, a fifteen-year-old aspiring photographer, took this group portrait at George and Julie Lord's July 4th party using Alice's camera. Alice (seated, left) waves a small American flag.

party, Julie stands at left, displaying her restored waistline, with Trude by her side and Alice at her feet; Julie's husband stands at right next to their nanny, who holds Gladys in her arms (Figure 4.3).[17]

Alice took "The Darned Club" on the grounds of Clear Comfort on October 29, 1891, when Julie was five months pregnant with Gladys. She made two exposures to commemorate the club, whose members were Alice, Trude, Julie, and Sue Ripley, Julie's first cousin. In one version, the group is seated against a background of tall grasses with Trude, Alice, and Julie gathered tightly around Sue, who sits on a low chair and looks out at the harbor (Figure 4.4). In the more well-known version, the women stand on high ground in back-to-back pairs, their merged silhouettes creating a rhythmic design against the sky and harbor in the background. Trude and Alice hug with their arms around each other, and Julie and Sue smile at each other as they place their hands on each other's waists (Figure 4.5). On the negative, Alice wrote in ink, "The Darned Club."

The arrangement of the women in the two pictures—seated in a tight cluster and standing with hands on hips—derived from conventional photographs of women friends or relatives. When the now-famous version was first published in *LIFE* magazine in 1951, a reader sent the editor a photograph showing four young women standing in the same formation (Figure 4.6). Juxtaposing her photograph with Alice's, she wrote:

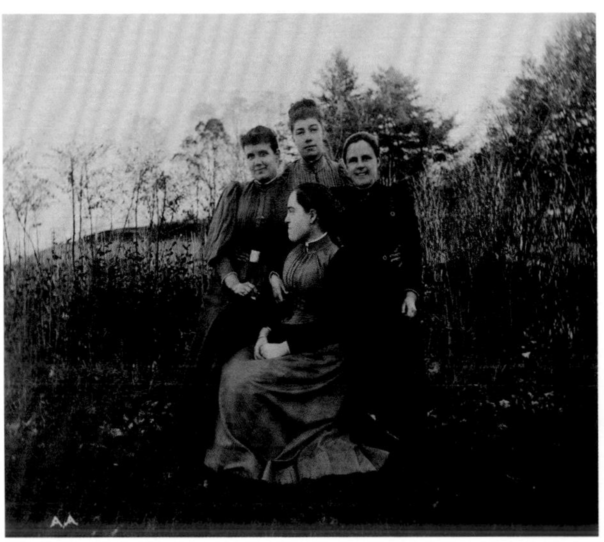 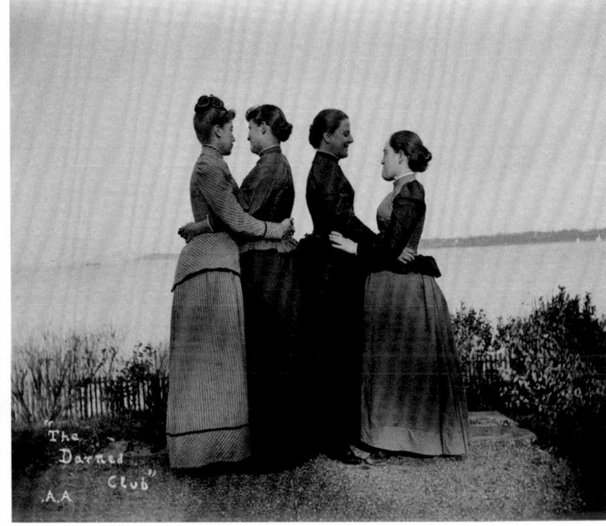

Figures 4.4 and 4.5   "The Darned Club," seated and standing, October 29, 1891

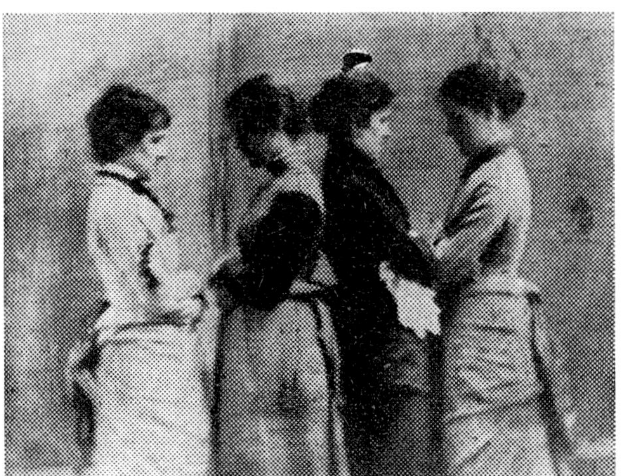 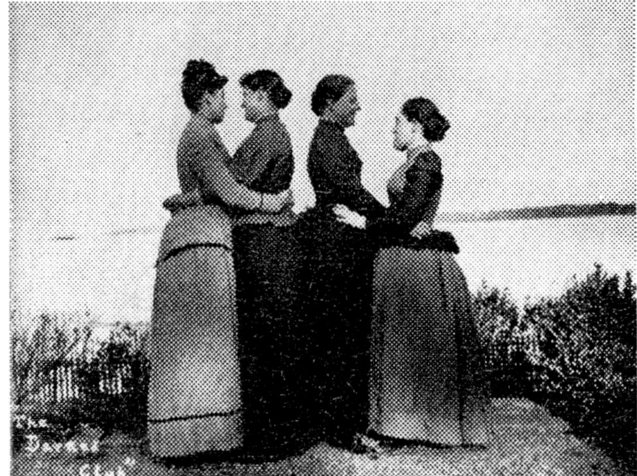

Figure 4.6   Letter to the Editor, *LIFE* magazine, October 15, 1952

Sirs: Compare this photograph with that on page 141 taken by Alice Austen. The pose must have been popular. This one was taken about 1875 and is of four of the 10 children of Julian S. Ramsey, Civil War mayor of Chicago.[18]

The name "The Darned Club" was a pun. In a June 21, 1891 letter to Alice, her mother wrote: "Sue Ripley came here to say that the darning Club would be put off until Tuesday and would take the form of Tennis."[19] The club was devoted less to darning and tennis than to keeping the women's friendships active, which for Julie—

recently married and expecting a baby—may have felt especially urgent. Miffed at being left out, the men invented the nickname, but the women welcomed it.[20] The Darned Club succeeded a club that the women had established five years earlier—the Young Ladies Cooking Club of Clifton—which sometimes prepared food for male guests.[21] The Cooking Club aimed to appeal to men while The Darned Club purposely excluded them.

Alice's rebellious spirit surfaced again on November 2, 1891, three days after photographing "The Darned Club." Violet and Carrie Ward invited Alice and Trude for a picnic in the Richmond Valley woods. As the horses grazed, the women spread out food and drink on the back of the Wards' elegant carriage, and Alice set up her camera and made three exposures. Two simply record a fall outing on a sunny day, but in the third, the women hammed it up for the camera, feigning drunkenness (Figure 4.7). Stretched out on the ground, Miss Jenkins pours from a bottle; Trude swigs from another; Violet, leaning against the carriage, looks quizzically at the camera; and Carrie stands on a wagon wheel drinking from a glass. The late afternoon light records Alice's shadow in the lower right corner.

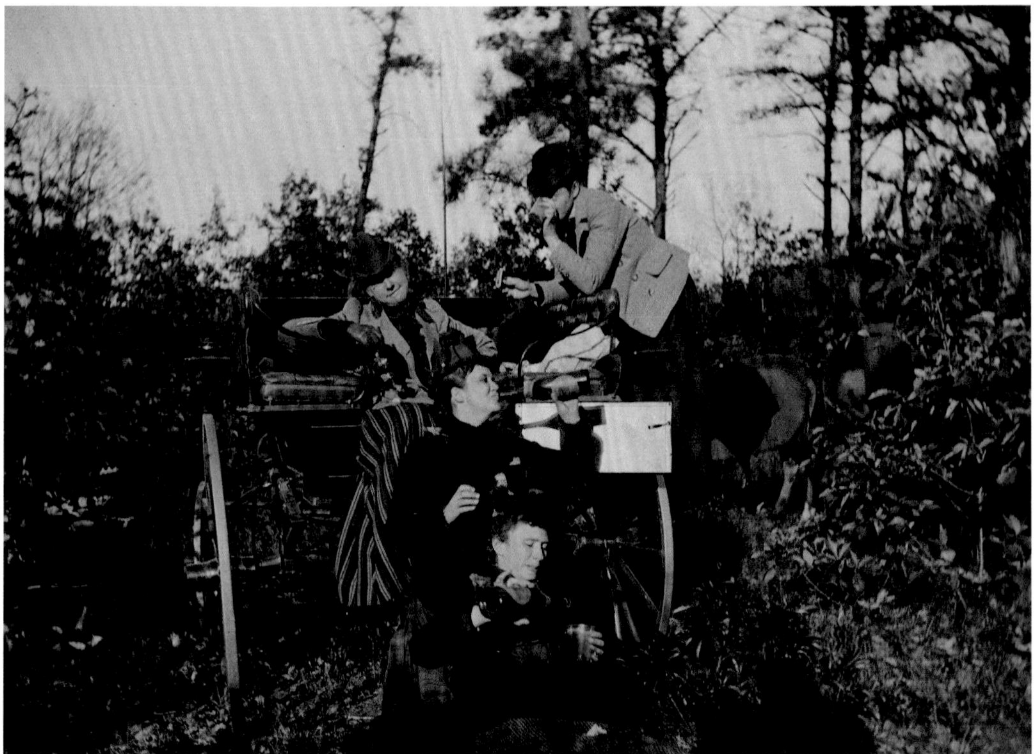

Figure 4.7   Three days after "The Darned Club," Alice, the Ward sisters, Trude, and another friend caroused for the camera while picnicking in the Richmond Valley woods.

Trude & I Masked, Short Skirts

In May 1890, while visiting her sister at Fort Douglas in Utah, Trude was introduced to Lieutenant John C. Gregg, a strikingly handsome officer who met Trude's amorous expectations:

> This morn. I went for a little stroll with him out to see target practice[. H]e wanted me to fire off one of the guns but they kick so hard that I could not & finally consented pulling the trigger if he held the gun & took aim, this necessitated my embracing him somewhat, well the thing went off and kicked so hard his shoulder hit my cheek & nearly upset me in the arms of another officer. I wish you could have seen the performance, it was great.[22]

In July 1891, Gregg visited Staten Island to propose marriage.[23] He and Trude spent many happy summer days together, and Alice was often there with her camera. On a day trip to the Jersey Shore on August 8th, she captured a group of swimmers holding onto a float, their heads emerging from the water, as Gregg placed his arm around a beaming Trude (Figure 4.8). The following day at Clear Comfort, Alice made a formal portrait of the couple, an engagement ring visible on Trude's left hand (Figure 4.9).

Alice and Trude posed together in several photographs that suggest their excitement and ambivalence about the engagement, a watershed event that presaged a radical change in their relationship. In one photograph taken from a floating dock, they mug for the camera as they straddle washtubs in wet bathing suits, gleefully defying "ladylike" propriety (Figure 4.10). Alice wrote on the negative, "Tweedledum and Tweedledee," a reference to the celebrated nonsense characters from Lewis Carroll's *Alice's Adventures in Wonderland*.

On August 6, 1891, Alice spent the night at the rectory and took two photographs in Trude's bedroom. The images required flash and technical ingenuity. In a totally darkened room, Alice removed the camera's lens cap, set a flash timer, assumed her position in the scene, and waited for the flash to go off. In "Trude & I Masked, Short Skirts" Alice and Trude brazenly pose as prostitutes. They face each other in their undergarments and stockings with their hair unbound and pretend to smoke cigarettes (Figure 4.11). Their masks and mirrored gestures make it difficult to tell them apart, except for one detail: Trude, at right, is wearing her engagement ring.

The second photograph taken that night was "Trude & I in Bed at Rectory" (Figure 4.12). Wearing nightgowns and tucked under the covers, they reveal their unsmiling faces for the camera and make hand signals: Alice holds up her open right

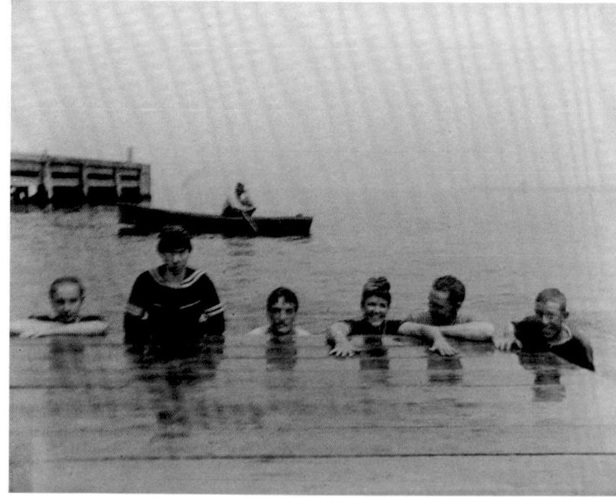

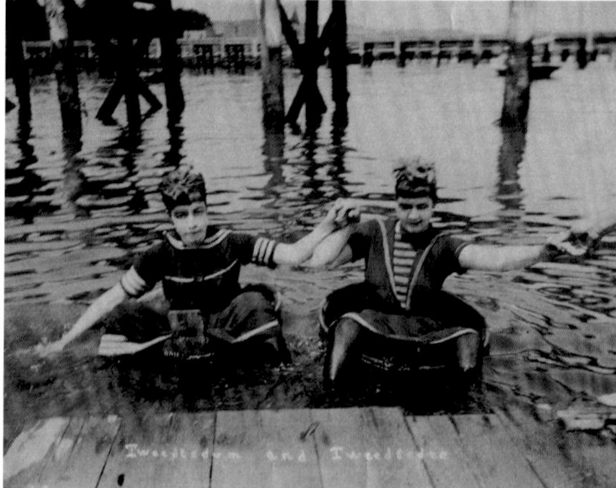

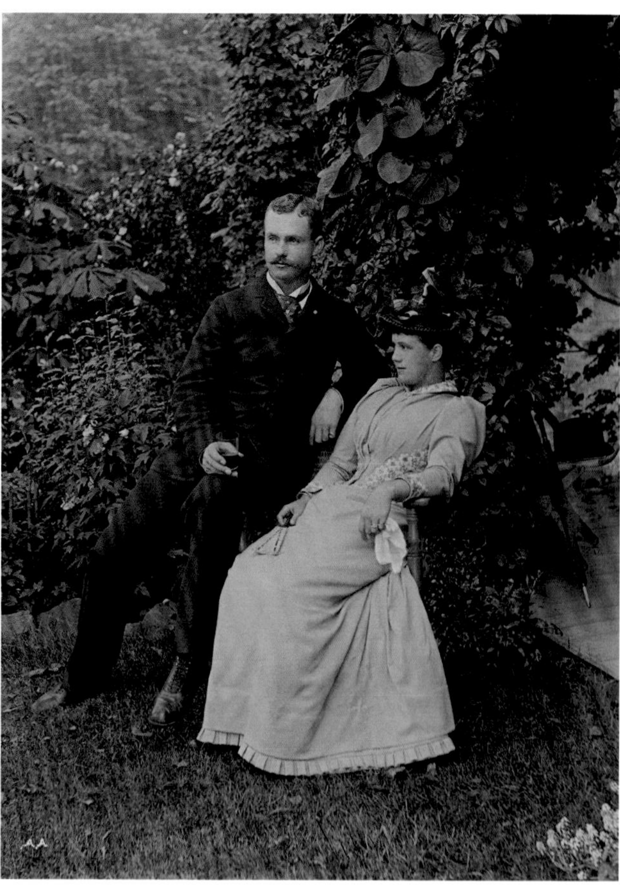

Figure 4.8 (top left)   Alice summoned her friends to the edge of a float to photograph them swimming. The dour expression of Violet Ward (second from left) contrasts with the relaxed happiness of Trude and her beau Lt. John C. Gregg (second and third from right).

Figure 4.9 (right)   The next day, Alice celebrated the engagement of Trude and Lt. Gregg with a formal portrait taken at Clear Comfort.

Figure 4.10 (bottom left)   Alice inscribed humorous titles in quotation marks on only two photographs: "The Darned Club" and "Tweedledum and Tweedledee." Although the latter is undated, it was probably also taken in 1891.

hand, and Trude holds up her open left hand (again displaying her engagement ring) and two fingers of her right hand in a "V." The contrast of the grave quiet of Trude and Alice in bed with the defiant posturing of Trude and Alice masked adds to the mystery of the photographs. Trude and Alice seem to be sharing secrets in these pictures, perhaps commemorating their intimacy in anticipation of Trude's marriage that would disrupt it.

Trude's engagement to Gregg lasted a year, but they did not marry. A week after Alice made their formal portrait at Clear Comfort, Gregg left for Europe for several

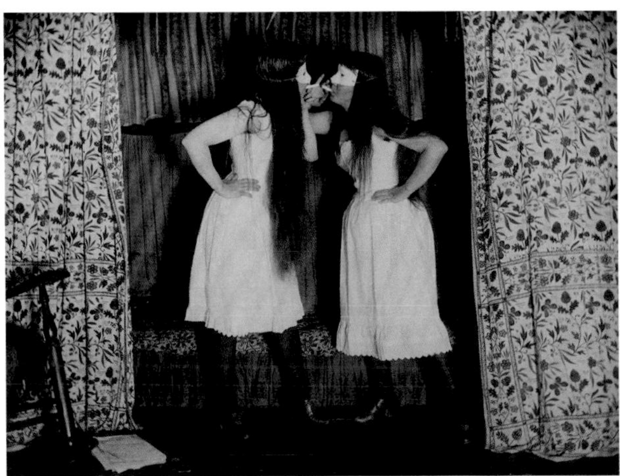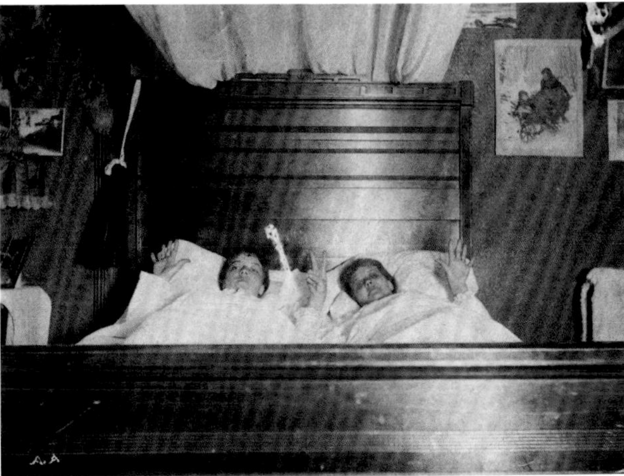

Figures 4.11 and 4.12   Alice took these two photographs of herself and Trude in Trude's bedroom three days before the engagement portrait of Trude and Lt. Gregg.

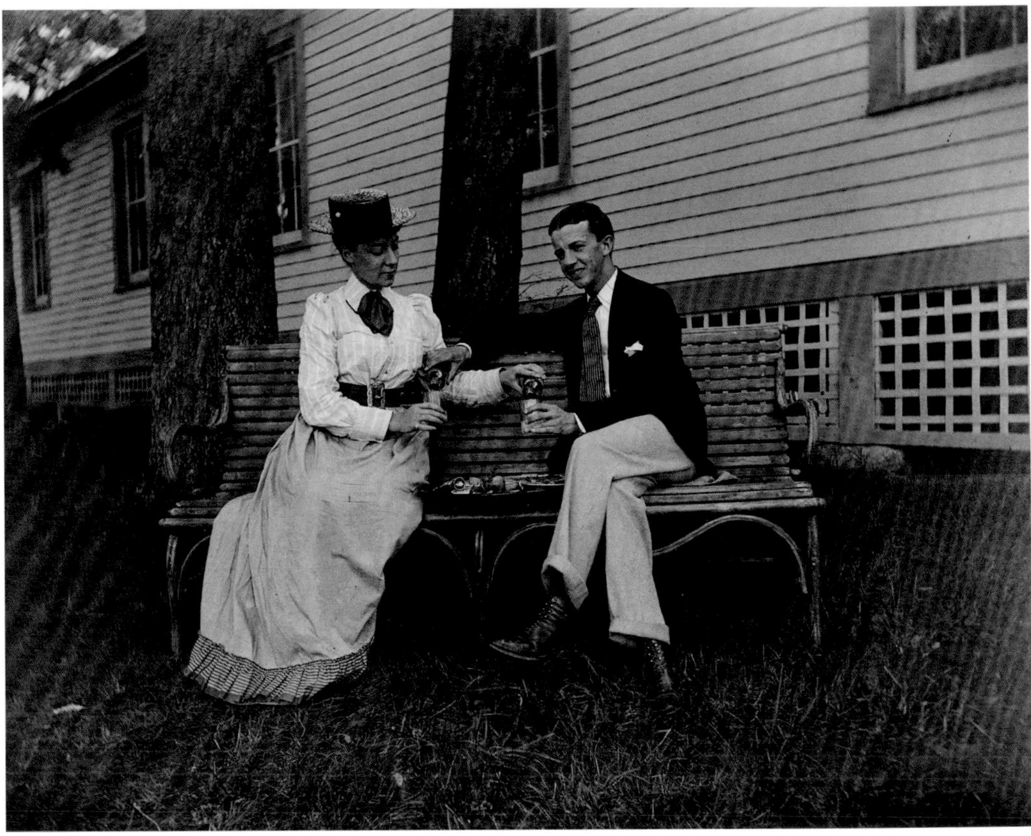

Figure 4.13   Shortly after Trude and Lt. Gregg broke up in 1892, Alice went on vacation with Trude to Watkins Glen, where the two young women aggressively flirted with Willie Hopper, an eighteen-year-old amateur photographer.

months before returning to New York to begin a nine-month course in torpedo training. In March 1892, Trude reported to Alice that "Mr. Gregg was here Thurs. evening
& we decided [to] stay quietly at home in front of a big wood fire."[24] By June, however, their relationship had foundered, and friends gathered around Trude to comfort
her.[25] Angry and hurt, she wrote condescendingly about Charles Barton, a longtime
suitor, who escorted her to a dance: "I just made up my mind that if he wished to be
useful I would use him, he was very nice & presented me with a beautiful Japanese
tea cup & a big bunch of roses."[26] By the fall when Lt. Gregg left New York for Fort
Douglas, their engagement was formally broken off.

In August when Trude was still fuming, Alice joined the Eccleston family on a trip
to a resort in Watkins Glen, New York. There Alice and Trude encountered Augustine Hopper (called Willie), an amateur photographer from Baltimore. The women
were in their mid-twenties and Willie only eighteen, but they toyed with his affections unabashedly. Alice used her camera to charm Willie, sharing lunch tête-à-têtes
(Figure 4.13), and Trude took him for a late-night stroll.[27]

The threesome also spent a day at the village cemetery, cleverly using a tombstone
inscribed with the family name "Noyes" to play out a six-part pantomime parodying
the perils of courtship (Figures 4.14–4.19). In Scene 1, Willie and Alice, posing as
lovers strolling in a cemetery, stand in front of the "Noyes" monument; in Scene 2, the
couple is seated as Willie proposes, and Alice—shielding "NO" from the camera—
says "YES." In Scene 3, Willie and Trude approach the tombstone; in Scene 4, Trude—
shielding "YES" from the camera—says, "NO" to Willie; but in Scene 5, Willie persists
and convinces her to say "YES." In each "YES" scene, the woman opens a parasol,
which helps shield the letters "NO" on the tombstone. Scene 6 delivers the punchline:
when the two women realize that Willie has wooed them both, they reject him, his
body shielding "YES" to reveal a final "NO." Ever the actress, Trude buries her face
in a handkerchief: having initially hesitated, she feels especially betrayed.

Serial narratives with humorous punchlines were commonplace in Victorian popular illustration, and Willie encouraged Alice to submit her photographs to *Life*,
a popular humor magazine that routinely featured cartoons poking fun at courtship
rituals.[28] Indeed, in July 1891, *Life* ran a five-part cartoon that may have inspired
the NOYES series. It portrayed a couple sitting on a large stone shielding themselves
with parasols to kiss in private.[29] Alice's series, however, did not end happily, perhaps
one reason *Life* did not publish it.

Although flirting with men was a constant preoccupation for Alice and Trude,
their devotion to one another was ardent and perhaps sexually charged. A study in
contrasts—Trude was voluptuous and vivacious, Alice stylish and self-possessed—
they enjoyed twinning, as in "Tweedledum and Tweedledee," and "Trude & I Masked,

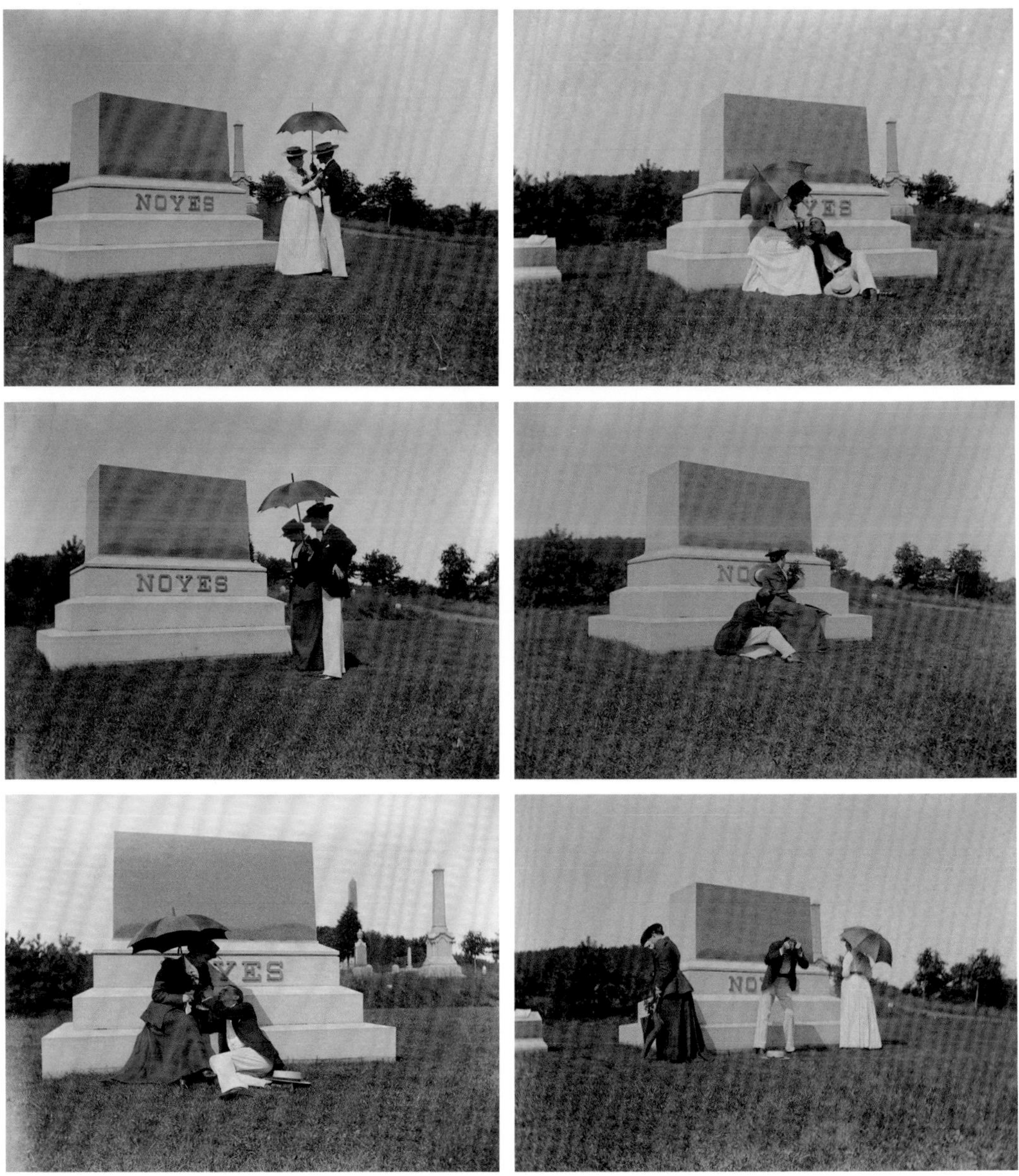

Figures 4.14–4.19 Trude, Alice, and Willie act out a six-part pantomime for the camera, in which Willie plays a suitor who courts two women, is found out, and loses them both. The story may have been inspired by Trude's failed romance with Lt. Gregg.

Short Skirts." These identity games may have titillated them and others. Alice was undoubtedly shaken by Trude's humiliation at the hands of Lt. Gregg and remained loyal to her throughout the 1890s, but Trude's spirit seems to have broken. By 1896, she began to rely on the affections of Charles Barton, a man who had always been there for her but whom she never loved.

Julia Martin, Julia Bredt & Self Dressed Up

The second of four children of Ira Kingsley Martin and his first wife Clementine Walton Martin, Julia Martin, called Jule, grew up in a large mansion on a twenty-five-acre estate overlooking the harbor about two miles from Clear Comfort. One of Alice's earliest portraits, taken in July 1885, shows her and Jule sitting on a bench built into the branches of a sumac tree and holding the Austen dogs, Chico and Punch (Figure 4.20). In 1886, Jule and Trude Eccleston spent a year together studying music in Dresden, Germany, a highlight of their young lives.[30] But Jule's life was less than idyllic. When she was eleven, her mother died of consumption.[31] Five years later, her father married Sarah Schuyler, a wealthy woman from an eminent Albany family, and they soon had a son of their own.

In August 1890, Alice accompanied Jule and her stepmother on a three-week vacation to Bennington, Vermont, where they stayed with Jule's stepmother's cousin, Mrs. Angelica Cooper, and her daughter, Mrs. Eliza Snively. Alice exposed more than fifty negatives during their visit, recording the natural beauty and historic monuments of the area. She placed many of these images in a large photograph album, which has survived.[32] A few days before leaving Bennington, Alice took photographs of her hosts, which she sent to them as a thank you gift. Mrs. Snively was delighted, "They are certainly lovely & I cannot tell you how much pleasure they have given me." She was especially pleased with a picture of herself with her dog Laddie and one of her mother, Mrs. Cooper, claiming it was "a great thing to have her just as I see her every day."

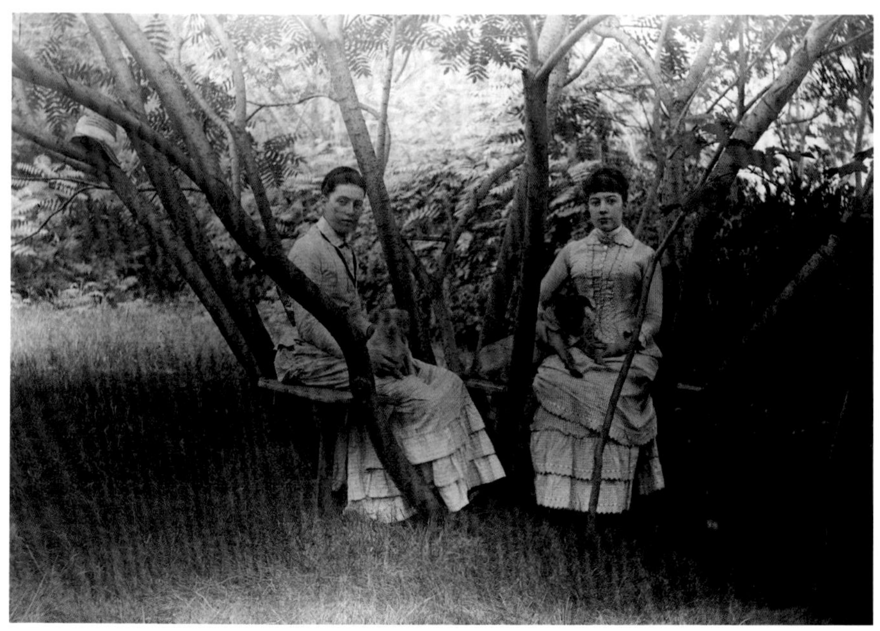

Figure 4.20   Jule Martin came from a socially prominent Clifton family, but in 1891, her father became embroiled in a financial scandal, and she was sent away to live in Albany. Alice remained loyal to Jule, whose letters reveal that they shared similar feelings of love for women and perhaps each other.

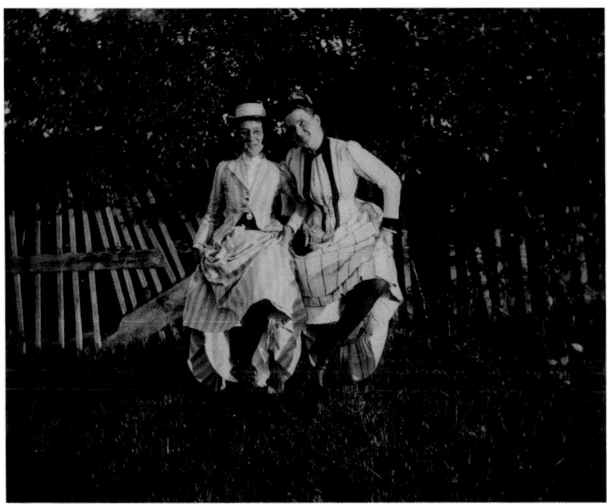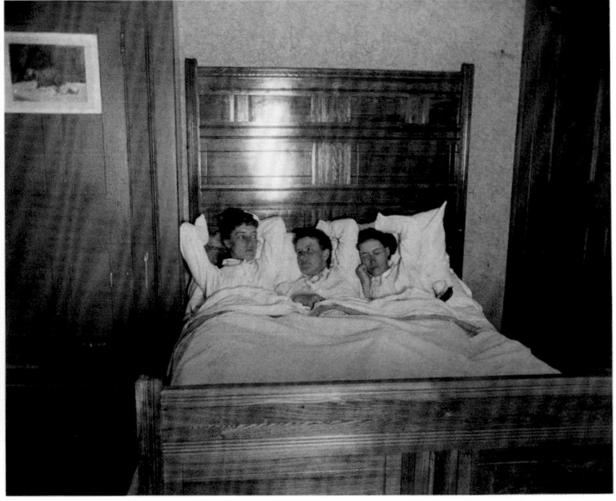

Figures 4.21 and 4.22   While vacationing in Vermont in 1890, Alice and Jule enjoyed the company of Mrs. Eliza Snively, Jule's stepcousin, whom Jule idolized and in later years turned to for financial help.

Mrs. Snively also singled out three of Alice's humorous photographs for special praise: "The Simpkins Family," which shows Mrs. Snively and three friends placing their faces in holes cut in a painted panel at a country fair; "Miss [Mary] Sanford & Mrs. Snively," which shows the two friends doing a jig (Figure 4.21); and "Mrs. Snively, Jule & I in bed," which Mrs. Snively dubbed, "Sleep babies sleep" (Figure 4.22).[33] At the time of the visit, Mrs. Snively, who had two young children of her own, was struggling with a discordant marriage (she would soon sue for divorce), and Alice and Jule's visit was a welcome respite. She concluded her letter to Alice, "I can't tell you how I missed you girls, I have been as blue as possible ever since you left."[34]

From Bennington, Jule returned to Albany with her relatives and wrote Alice to keep her up to date on the two men who were courting her: "Indeed my heart is quite cracked in two places the right side with Herr Docteur, the other with Mr Durant. . . . I think of the two he would be the best investment, as he has horses & money etc." In the same letter, Jule confessed that she had a crush on Mrs. Snively. She saw no conflict between the need for marriage, which provided security, and her passionate feelings for a woman.

> Woe be, I have not been to see my "Idol" as you call her . . . so I have to content myself with looking at her photograph for which I am greatly obliged to you. . . . I suppose Mrs. S. has written thanking you for the pictures, & I am overcome with jealousy.[35]

Jule's expectation of a propitious marriage, however, was about to drastically change. In May 1891, her father was accused of stealing $150,000 from his insurance broker-

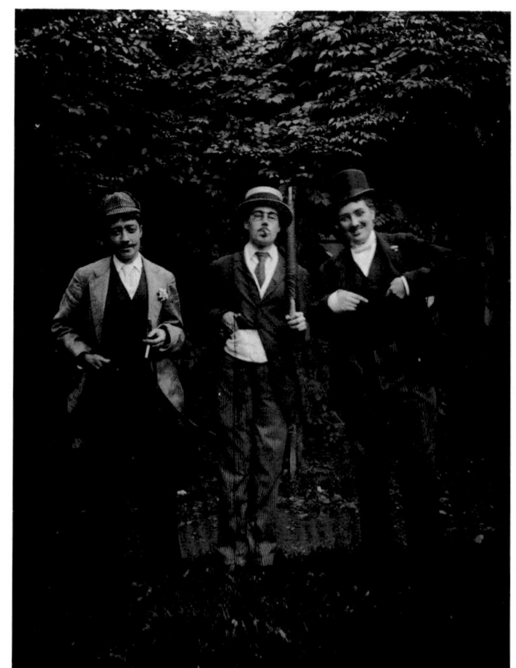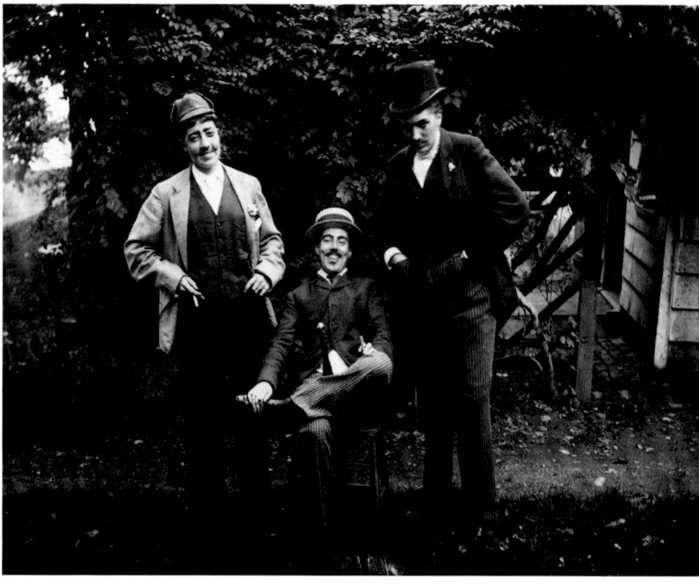

Figures 4.23 and 4.24   Alice photographed Jule Martin, Julia Bredt, and herself dressed in men's clothes twice, standing and seated.

age firm and fled to Canada to avoid arrest. Jule's stepmother also fled Staten Island and instructed Jule to close up the family's home and move to Albany to live with Mrs. Cooper as her companion.

On October 15, 1891 (two weeks before she photographed "The Darned Club"), Alice posed with Jule and Julia Bredt dressed in men's clothes. She took two photographs; in one, the three women are standing, and in the other, Jule is seated (Figures 4.23 and 4.24).[36] They wear trousers, shirts, vests, jackets, and shoes, and they have fake mustaches and darkened eyebrows. Alice, at left, dons a deerstalker hat and holds a fake cigarette; Julia Bredt, at right, wears a high crown derby; and Jule, at center, sports a straw boater while holding a fake cigarette and an umbrella. It was not uncommon for women to dress as men in Victorian amateur theatricals (the March sisters' Christmas play in Louisa May Alcott's *Little Women* is a prime example), but the seated version of Alice's photograph exceeded the bounds of respectability. Jule makes a mockery of male power by placing one foot on her knee and an umbrella between her thighs to suggest a giant erection.

Five days after Alice took these photographs, Jule left Staten Island for good. She and Alice exchanged letters every other week, which became Jule's only link to her childhood home. Jule assumed that Mrs. Cooper would consider her a guest, as she had the previous year, but after a few months, it was understood that she was to be a servant, dependent on Mrs. Cooper for money and without time to call her own. Jule's letters bear witness to her bewilderment and despondency. At the start of her

Albany stay in November, she urged Alice to send her the dress-up photographs: "Why don't you finish up & send me the photo of those three men. I have been looking for them for a long time."[37] By the time the photographs arrived in January, Jule had lost interest in them: "The photographs came all right & many many thanks to you for sending them, and humble apologies for not acknowledging them before."[38]

Unmarried and stripped of wealth and family, Jule was no longer a desirable mate. In a letter to Alice, she shared, with some bitterness, her meager matrimonial options: "I have a widower on the string now. . . . The only trouble is he doesn't seem much smitten & if he did, it would do little good, as I believe he did not treat his wife well—so no. 2 will have to look out."[39] Jule found herself dependent for friendship and support on women who did not judge her. She earned spending money by sewing and embroidering and accepted hand-me-downs from friends, who just months earlier had been her social equals.[40] Among her new friends were "the two Marys," about whom she wrote excitedly to Alice:

> I must tell of these friends. Miss Tibbits & Miss Richards, age questionable, commonly known as "The Two Marys." They met a good many years back, & took the greatest fancy to one and another, so decided to try living together & it met with so much success that they have lived with each other ever since. Both have a little money & they keep house in a most delightful way. I have been to one or two of their small lunches, which are always most pleasant. They are always together & I believe sleep in each others arms—and both are great friends of Mrs. Cooper's. Perhaps you and I might sometime set up such an establishment.*[41]

The asterisk at the end of the passage led to this caveat: "only I speak for a bed for myself." Was the caveat meant to set limits to Jule's love for women? Her love for Alice? What seems clear is that Jule had never met women like the two Marys who loved each other and lived together. That she shared her observations with Alice suggests that they both may have found the arrangement appealing.

By 1894, Jule felt imprisoned by Mrs. Cooper and sought a way out of Albany.[42] "Life to me is one great misery of uncertainty," she wrote Alice.[43] In May, she accepted Mrs. Cooper's invitation to join her in Santa Barbara, California, where she hatched a plan for independence which required her to discard all pretense of class privilege. With Mrs. Snively's help, Jule succeeded in establishing a boarding house for wealthy Easterners who were beginning to winter there. "You really would not know me," she wrote Alice, "I can hold my own so well."[44]

Alice remained Jule's loyal correspondent, although she resisted Jule's invitations

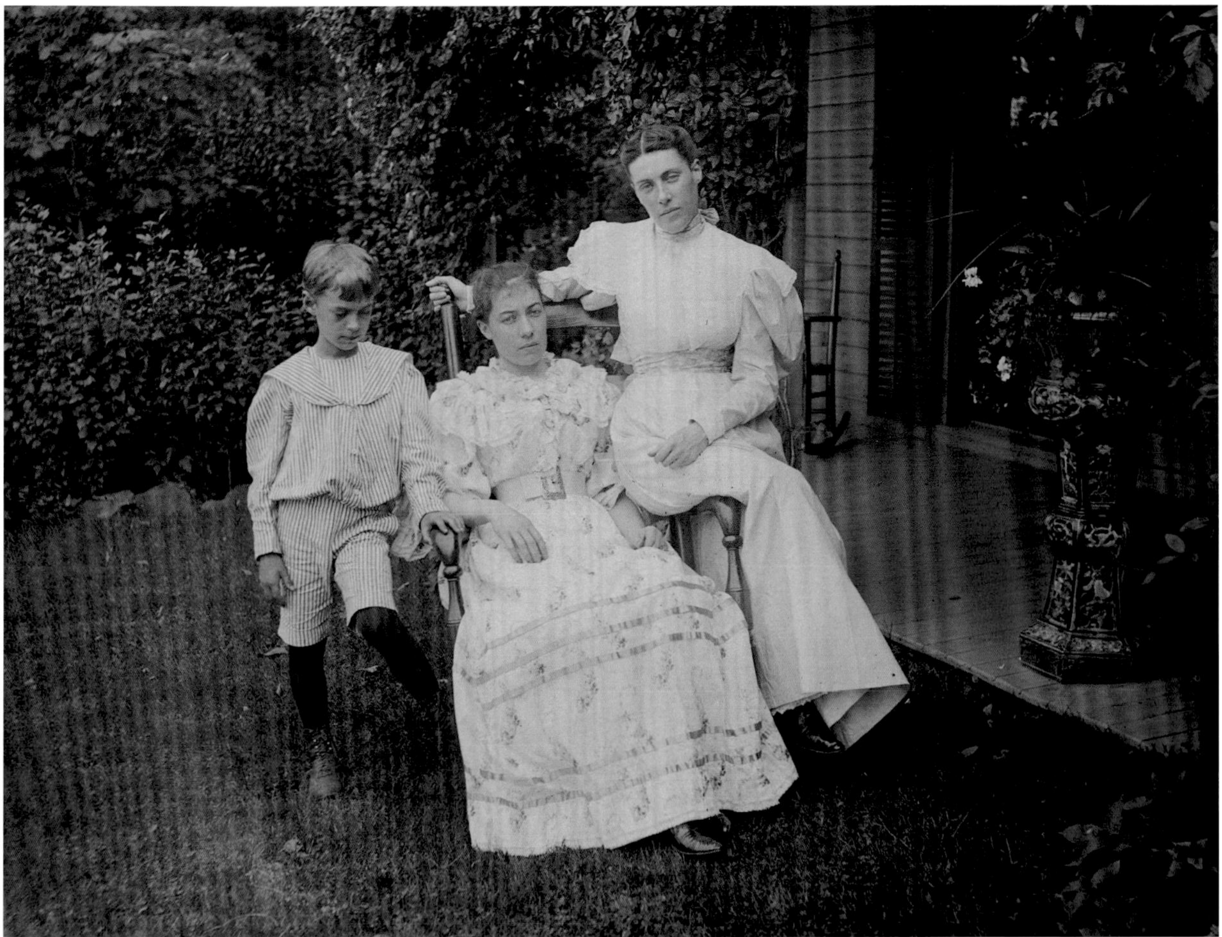

Figure 4.25   Jule and her nephew Kingsley Martin, whose family lived with Jule in Santa Barbara, visited Alice in 1896.

to visit. Perhaps she felt awkward confronting Jule's fall in class status. Not until 1896 was Jule's business secure enough for her to visit Staten Island, and Alice photographed them with Jule's nephew at Clear Comfort. It was their last time together (Figure 4.25).

Poker Game

As a child, Julia Bredt lived across Pennsylvania Avenue from Alice in a mansion called Beach Lawn.[45] Her father, Frederick Bredt, was a German-born merchant. In 1882, when Julia was thirteen, her parents separated, and her mother took the five Bredt children to Bethlehem, Pennsylvania, where she rented a large, elegant

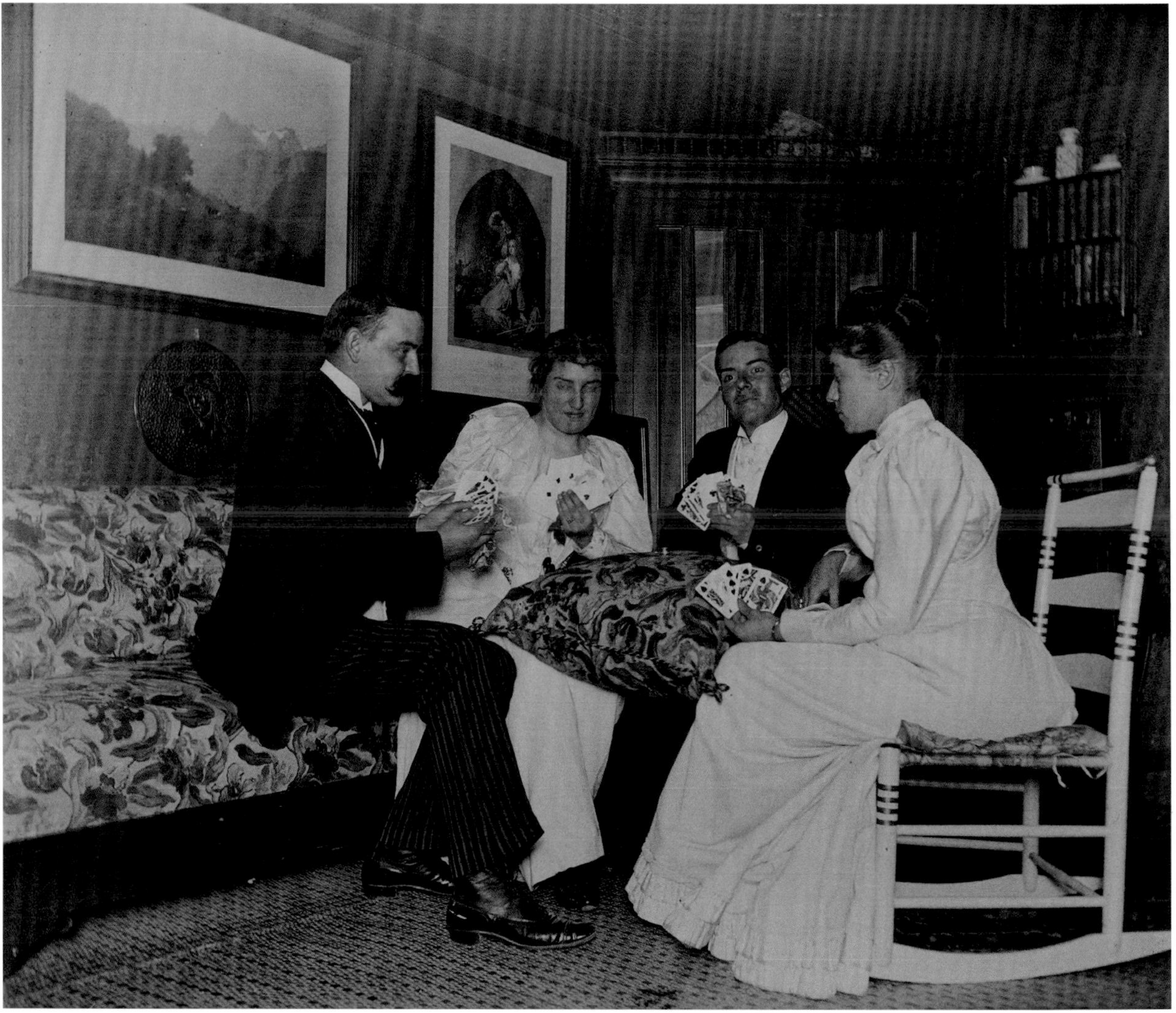

Figure 4.26 When Julia Bredt visited Alice in September 1892, Alice invited two gentlemen to Clear Comfort. At left is Henry Gilman, then Alice's suitor who died in an apparent suicide in 1893.

home near the Lehigh University campus.[46] Julia was three years younger than Alice and looked up to her like an older sister. After Julia's father died in 1889, Julia and Alice exchanged two or three visits a year for several years. Like Alice and Trude, Julia was preoccupied with socializing with young men, as this characteristic letter indicates:

I have been having a most hard question to decide, it is whether to have a pale pink mull or a white and green for a ball dress. I have two whites so I rather think it will end in me getting the pink, which would you, if you were me. Just think there are 160 freshmen, I have met a few and they seem rather nice.[47]

On each visit, either at Clear Comfort or in Bethlehem, Alice took photographs of her and Julia entertaining gentlemen. Typical is "Poker Game," in which Alice orchestrated a humorous, if hackneyed, tableau: the men and Alice each hold a royal flush, but Julia "wins" with five aces (Figure 4.26).[48]

In January 1892, when Julia received her prints of the three women wearing men's clothes, her family opened the package while she was out. Her alarm quickly passed when she realized that everyone thought the photographs great fun: "When I came in . . . the children had opened them & there they were out in full view. Of course everyone caught on, I was wild. . . . [T]he girls who saw them thought you the best."[49]

On a visit to Bethlehem in February 1892, Alice used her camera to stir up excitement at a series of soirees at Julia's house. On six different evenings, she stage-managed scenes of Julia's friends clowning for her camera. In one photograph of a tea party gone awry, Julia serves tea at a small table to Alice and four men, all seemingly oblivious to the anarchic display at their feet: two men lying on the floor, a tangle of limbs and pillows (Figure 4.27). In another, Julia holds court amid indecorous chaos: two men sit at her feet; two couples assume amorous poses; and a man poses as a lamp base, his face and body obscured by a length of fabric and a lamp shade seeming to rise from his head. Alice, at right, surveys it all (Figure 4.28). Creating these scenes was itself a racy party game: Alice opened the lens in the darkened room, set the flash timer, and took her place, undoubtedly urging the group to improvise while they waited for the flash to go off. When Julia finally received her prints, her response was more breathless than usual: "O! Lollie the pictures . . . are really the best I have ever seen, now Look here I want them all & O! the men are perfectly wild about them every time they come they sit & beg me and say tell Miss Austen to send the plates up they will settle the rest."[50]

Alice pursued extended flirtations with two of Julia's friends. One was Percy Drayton, a Lehigh senior and tennis player. He and four other men who appear in the Bethlehem photographs were members of the Mustard and Cheese Drama Society, which made them natural performers for Alice's camera.[51] When Alice sent Drayton prints, she enclosed her portrait and some lines of poetry.[52] Alice was also seeing George Rodney Booth, another of Julia's friends. A twenty-seven-year-old lawyer and amateur photographer, Booth had a sustained interest in Alice. In 1890, Julia reported, "I saw G. Booth. He is very anxious (as usual) to hear how you are. You will see him as soon as he goes to N.Y."[53] During Alice's February 1892 visit to Bethlehem,

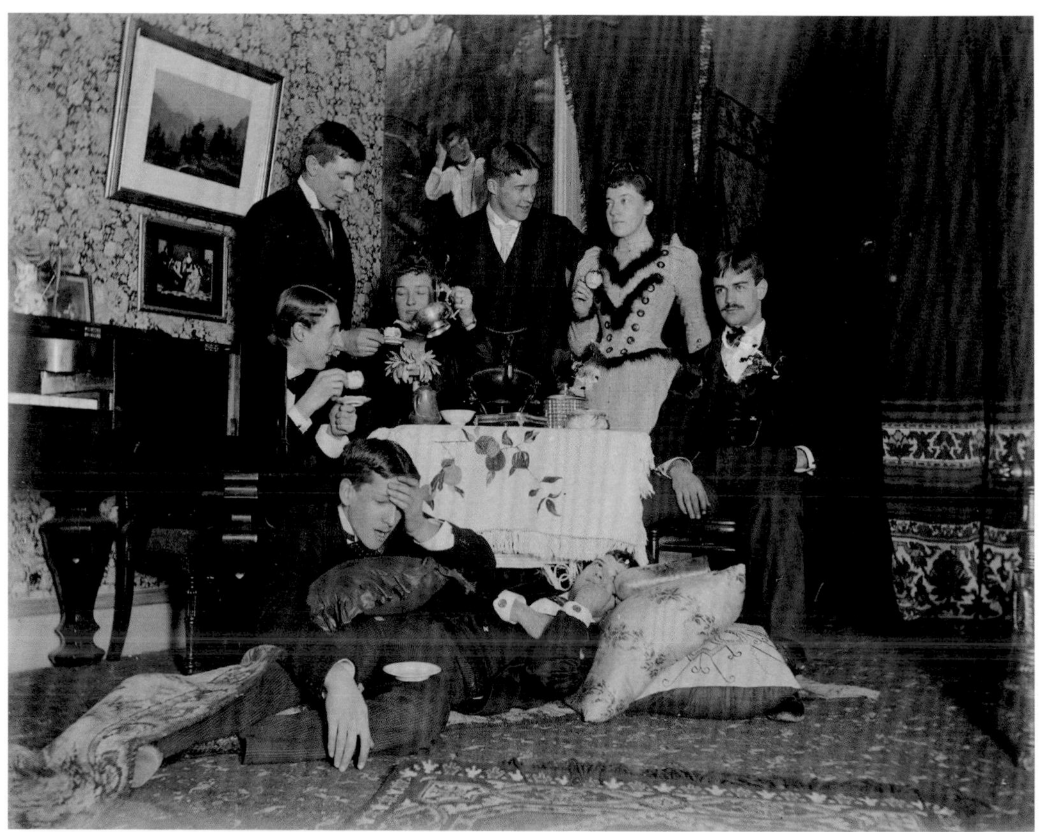

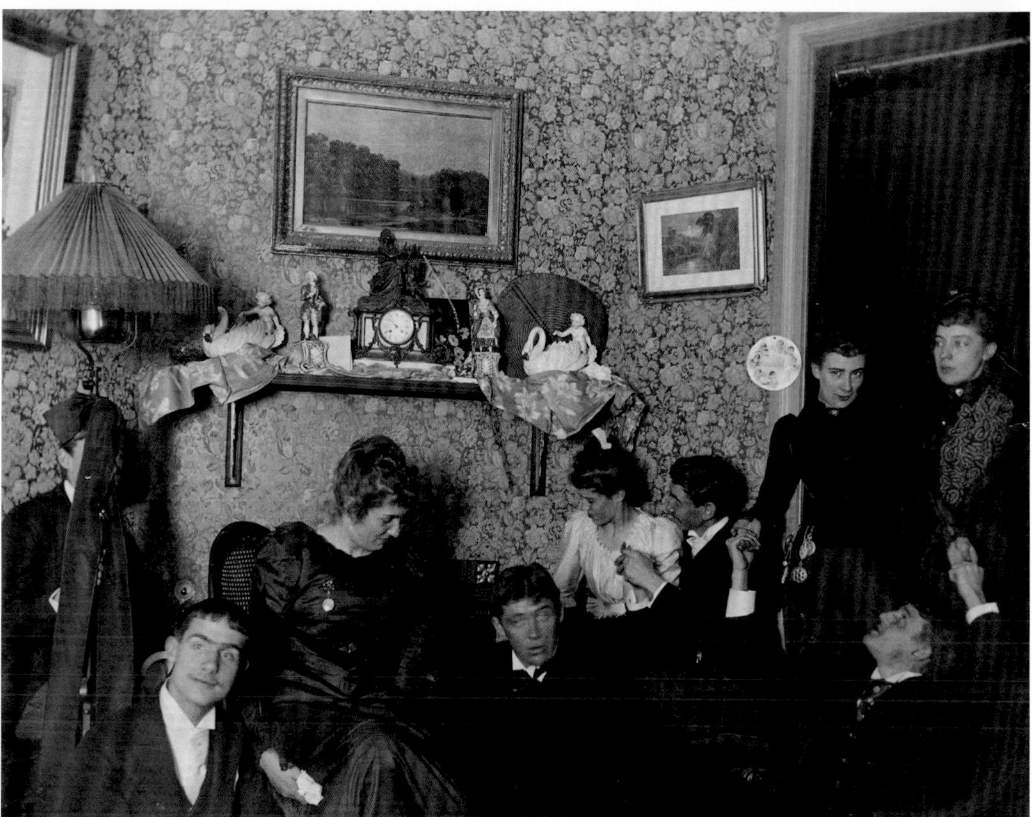

Figures 4.27 and 4.28   Many of the guests at Julia Bredt's evening soirees were members of Lehigh University's drama club, who enjoyed clowning for Alice's camera.

Booth gave her a tour of the city, and Julia wrote Alice to report on her subsequent conversation with him:

> [W]hat do you think he said to me now don't you tell him he said, "Miss Bredt did you & Miss Austen ever talk about me?" think of it I said, "no," then he said, ["]did you ever tell her anything about me," I said "mercy no." why. "[W]ell, I wondered, for she read me pretty well for a person who knows not much about me" . . . [D]on't you ever mention a thing to him, for he will tell, now be careful, for it would be awful if it got out.[54]

Alice was clearly toying with both Drayton and Booth, and Julia was egging her on. As was true for Alice and Trude, Alice and Julia's "boy-crazy" antics brought them closer together. Because her emotions were not seriously engaged, Alice had a distinct advantage over suitors like Booth, who could be genuinely hurt by her.

At the same time that she was encouraging Drayton and Booth, Alice was being courted at home by Henry K. Gilman, who appears in the photograph of the poker game, sitting on the sofa next to Julia. An apartment house manager in Manhattan, Gilman first met Alice in the summer of 1889 in Bay Head, New Jersey, when she was visiting Peter Austen's family at a beach house they had rented. The two did not see each other again for two years, and the Gilman family suffered scandal and tragedy in the interim. Gilman's older brother committed suicide after a business partner discovered that he had embezzled $220,000, and the story made the front page of the *New York Times*.[55]

Once they reunited, Gilman pursued Alice ardently. When she visited Bethlehem, he wrote her:

> It looks as though you might be getting some good skating these lovely moonlight nights—Don't let any of the Freshies trifle with your young affections under the plea of the moonlight. I hope to have the pleasure of meeting you on your return if you will let me know what train you are coming by, so I can escort you across the river—will you—please? Don't stay too long.[56]

During 1892, Alice was traveling frenetically (to Bethlehem, New Brunswick, Cambridge, Boston, Concord, Fishkill, and the *Wabun* canal trip), tending to Trude, and plotting mischief with Julia Bredt. She nevertheless encouraged Gilman's interest, asking him to have a portrait taken for her, accepting small gifts from him, and inviting him to visit on several occasions. Perhaps due to his family's scandal, Mamma was against him. When Alice told Mamma that Gilman wished to visit Clear Comfort when Alice was away, Mamma scoffed: "You were right to discourage H.G.

from coming to see me, what an idea."[57] Her friends were less dismissive. In September 1893, Bessie Strong inquired, "How is Mr. Gilman? I hear he is all devotion still."[58]

Gilman, however, sank into depression, and his behavior became increasingly erratic, and his mood swings intense. In desperation, he reached out to Alice for help:

> I think a sight of you would help me to shake off a desperate attack of the blues which seems to have fastened their demoralizing clutches up on me, and I wish you would drop me a line to say which evening this week I shall find you disengaged—either Wednesday, Thursday or Friday. . . . So do take pity on a poor, grubbing, desolate soul, and lay up for yourself treasures in Heaven, by a charitable action.[59]

On December 27, 1893, Gilman died of asphyxiation in his bedroom at the building where he worked, a suspected suicide. His obituary recapitulated the story of his brother's theft and suicide.[60]

Gilman's death, no doubt, shocked Alice. She had not shunned him, as her mother would have preferred, but she did not open her heart to fully appreciate his distress and need for her affection. After his death, Alice's flirtations with men ended, and her collecting of newspaper articles about her "larky life" waned.

Although each of Alice's irreverent photographs arose from a specific event, they illustrate her growing impatience with the expectation that women should comport themselves modestly and obediently. Alice's interest in gender roles and their disruption was not new. It was nurtured by a steady diet of popular visual culture—trade cards, stereographs, humor magazines, fashion illustrations, and theater performances. Tellingly, at the start of her first scrapbook is a full-page cartoon depicting men trying to play tennis in women's clothes (Figure 2.6). Nor was it unique, especially in the 1890s when, as art historian Melody Davis has noted in her study of narrative stereographs, "the cult of domesticity explode[d] . . . into irony, laughter [and] parody."[61]

An even more prevalent source of satire, much appreciated by Alice and her friends, was blackface and minstrelsy.[62] One of her earliest photographs, taken on Thanksgiving Day 1885, depicts a lineup of fourteen "ragamuffins," neighborhood children in costumes and masks dressed as various American types—the Indian, the frontiersman, the drummer boy. Also shown are boys dressed in girls' clothing and several children in blackface (Figure 4.29). A predecessor of today's Halloween, Thanksgiving was the day that children were relieved of the standards of proper dress and behavior and allowed to roam about begging for treats.[63] Blackface, however, was not limited to

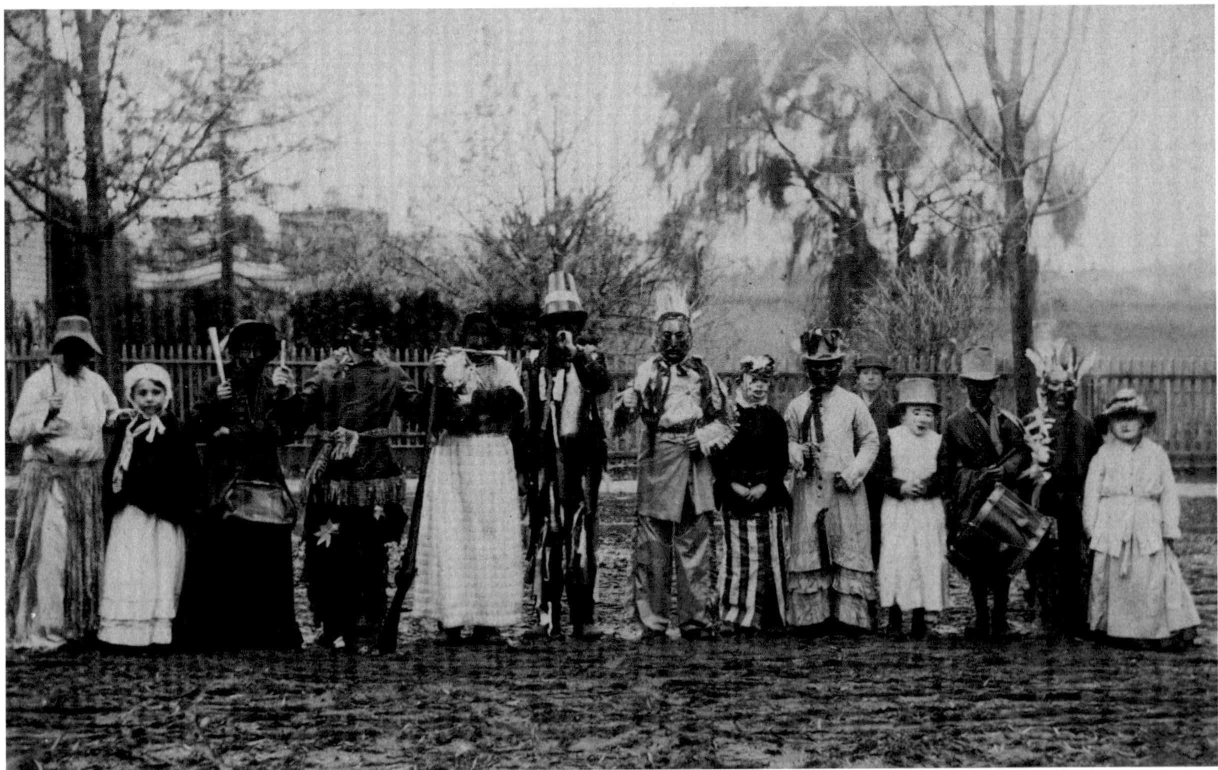

Figure 4.29   Among Alice's first photographs is a tableau of neighborhood children dressed as "raggamuffins" for Thanksgiving.

holidays or children. In Albany in 1893, Jule Martin and a friend went out in public in blackface to entertain their neighbors. As she explained to Alice, "Last night Bertie & I blackened up and went all over the neighborhood. We called on all the staid and dignified people and they seemed to enjoy it all more than a little."[64]

In 1890, Trude attended a minstrel party at Fort Douglas in which women as well as men took part: "The officers are getting up some minstrels before I leave, in which we girls are all to take part, blackening up and dressing in all the colors of the rainbow. I think it will be jolly good fun myself."[65] Afterward, she enclosed a photograph of the party taken by her brother-in-law, which Alice kept in her collection.[66] The racist premise of minstrelsy—that being Black, by its very nature, violated the norms of respectability—emboldened Trude and the other guests to break the rules and have "jolly good fun." Alice's photographs of women acting "badly"—smoking in their undergarments, getting drunk, lifting their skirts to dance, and dressing as men—provided similar opportunities.

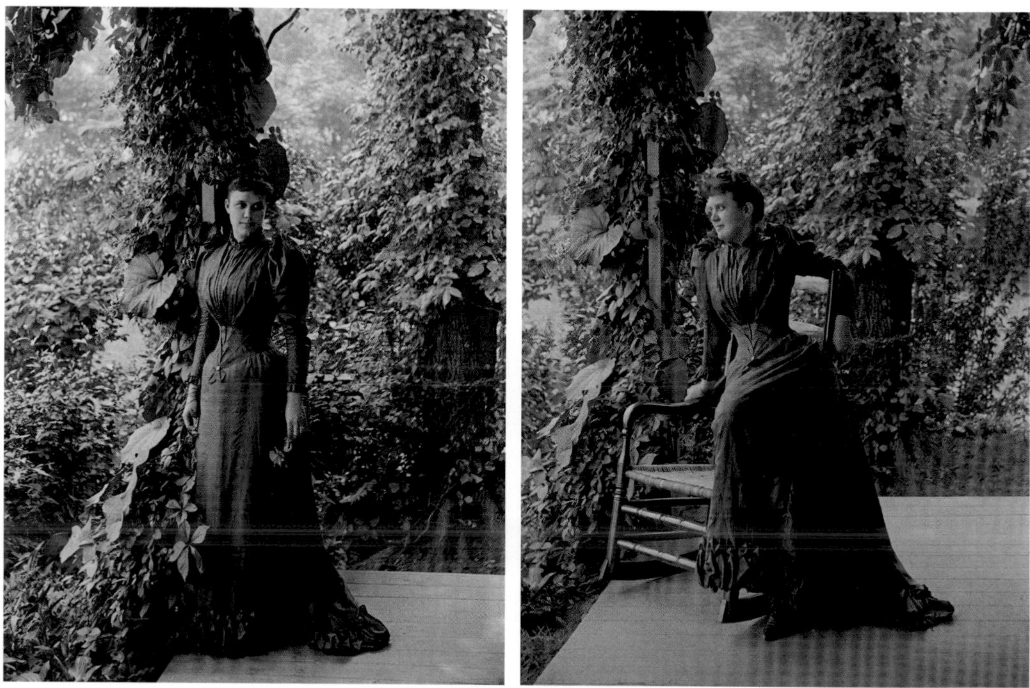

Figures 4.30 and 4.31   In the summer of 1892, Alice set up a portrait niche on the piazza and took formal portraits of Trude in which she posed as a modest maiden and a femme fatale.

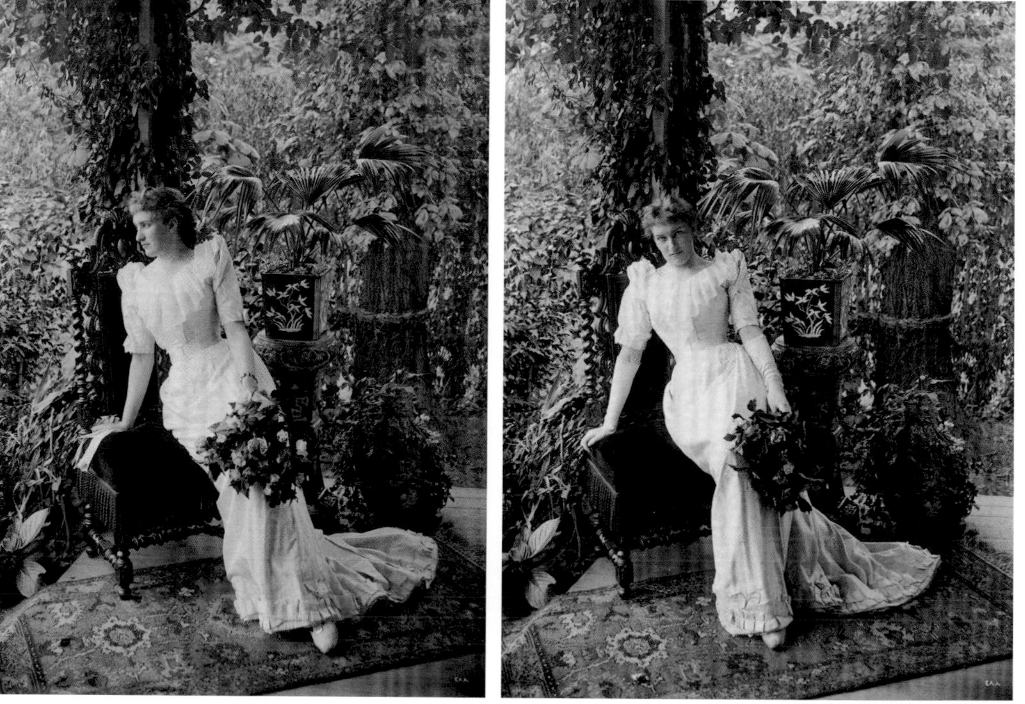

Figures 4.32 and 4.33   When Julia Bredt visited Clear Comfort that September, Alice set up the portrait niche again to capture Julia in the same, contrasting female roles.

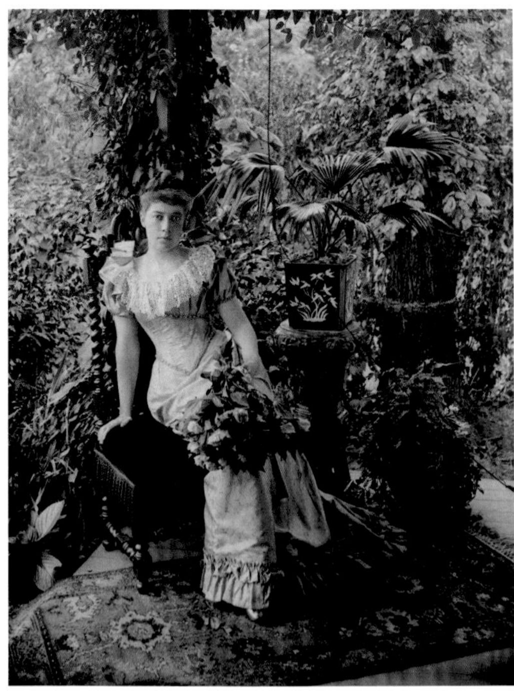

Figure 4.34   Alice participated in this session, dressed like Julia in a formfitting, lacey gown, but she did not role-play for the camera.

Alice was as invested in the performance of idealized respectability as she was in the performance of disrespectability. In July 1892, she made two full-length portraits of Trude in a corner of the piazza at Clear Comfort. In one, Trude stands upright and unsmiling with a flower in her hand, the epitome of the modest minister's daughter (Figure 4.30). In the other, she plays the coquette, perched on the arm of a rocking chair with her arm draped over the back to display her bosom and corseted waist; her hips jut into space; and the tip of her shoe emerges from the flounce of her dress (Figure 4.31). Intended for framing as gifts, these full plate portraits present Trude enacting two stereotypes of Victorian womanhood.

In September 1892, Alice again set up the full plate camera in the corner of the piazza to take two portraits of Julia Bredt and two of herself. She created a studio-like portrait niche by carrying outdoors an upholstered velvet chair, an oriental rug, a Chinese side table and an inlaid planter. Wearing delicate, summer gowns and posing like fashion plates, the women balanced gracefully on the edge of the chair to display the details of their dresses and hourglass shapes. Set against lush, late summer foliage, Alice and Julia embodied the Gilded Age feminine ideal.

In one photograph of Julia, she looks out toward the garden, the afternoon light illuminating her refined profile, and in the other, she stares beguilingly into the camera (Figures 4.32 and 4.33). Alice may have encouraged Julia, as she did Trude, to enact the roles of innocent and seductress, well-worn tropes of popular illustration. In the self-portraits, Alice did not adopt these poses but maintained the direct, serious gaze that she had assumed in earlier photographs (Figure 4.34).[67] Beginning to turn away from "the larky life," Alice was also beginning to turn away from the ideals of Victorian womanhood.

5 THE NEW WOMAN

As top Staten Island tennis players, Alice and Violet Ward had known each other since 1883, but their friendship began to blossom in 1890.[1] Violet was with Alice when Trude Eccleston's ill-fated romance with Lt. Gregg ended, and shortly after he left New York in October 1892, Alice photographed Trude and Violet watching a naval parade while sitting together under the giant honey locust tree at Clear Comfort (Figure 5.1). At the left of the tree stands a camera on a tripod—a surrogate for Alice—and on the right hangs an oversized, well-worn American flag, perhaps the one that was used to signal Grandpa Austen when he passed through the harbor on his European voyages. The scene serves as a coda to Trude's unfortunate affair and signals the end of an era for Alice. Increasingly ambivalent about the romantic game-playing at the heart of the larky life, she used the camera as a visual diary only occasionally.

The years 1893 to 1897 were transitional for Alice and her family. Peter Austen left Rutgers to expand his practice as an industrial consultant, and his family moved from New Brunswick to a sumptuous townhouse in Brooklyn.[2] John Haggerty Austen died in 1894 at the age of eighty-three, and Uncle Oswald became the head of the Austen household.[3] During these years, Alice produced a torrent of photographs of new subjects: a set of twenty-five views of the Chicago World's Fair; a portfolio of "Street Types of New York"; illustrations for Violet's book, *Bicycling for Ladies*; and documentation of the New York State quarantine station, which was supervised by her neighbor, Dr. Alvah H. Doty, the health officer of the Port of New York.

Violet was Alice's collaborator on the last two projects, but her influence as a New Woman pervades them all. The popular press coined the term "New Woman" in 1894 to describe the myriad ways in which young women were challenging the norms of domesticity and dependence that they had inherited from their mothers and grandmothers. Working-class women were seeking employment in offices and department stores, and middle-class women were attending college and training for careers. Women were venturing unchaperoned into public spaces, and fashions were changing to allow them greater freedom of movement. Contrary to conventional medical wisdom, women were asserting that mental and physical exercise were not dangerous to

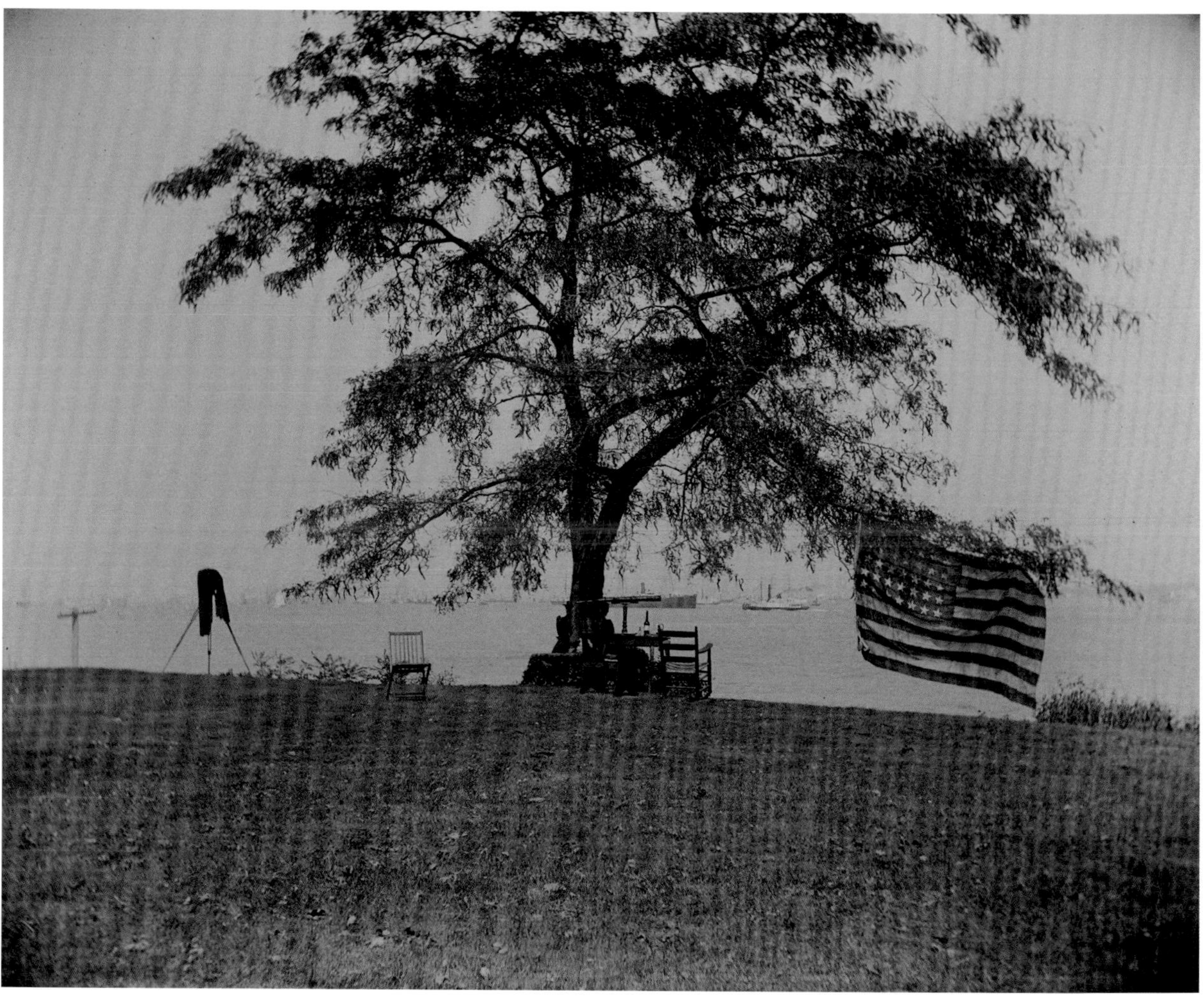

Figure 5.1   Trude and Violet sit on the circular bench surrounding the honey locust tree at Clear Comfort to watch a naval parade. Alice is represented by her full plate camera set up at the edge of the terrace.

their reproductive capacity but beneficial to their health. Many of these controversial trends confirmed Alice's predilections and emboldened her to break Victorian norms. A city shopper since childhood, she took her camera into New York neighborhoods that were well beyond the shopping districts or deemed safe for respectable women, to produce her "street types" portfolio. A seasoned athlete, she became a passionate advocate of women's bicycling, an activity that conservative critics ridiculed. But Alice shunned other aspirations of the New Woman, such as pursuing a career. She copyrighted more than 120 of her new photographs but was ambivalent about asserting authorship of her work and selling it. In an era when many female amateur photographers became successful professionals, Alice opted to remain a woman of her class, sheltered from matters of business.

The Chicago World's Fair

The World's Columbian Exposition in Chicago was a Gilded Age extravaganza, displaying technological wonders, plugging commercial products, and promoting national pride. Situated on 600 acres of parkland designed by Frederick Law Olmsted, the "White City" consisted of temporary, neoclassical pavilions sheathed in white, painted plaster. A spur to urban development, the World's Fair was intended to propel Chicago's recovery from the disastrous 1871 fire. It also marked the 400th anniversary of Christopher Columbus's voyage to America, celebrating the prevailing belief that the United States had delivered European civilization to the New World. A must-see for all Americans who could afford the trip, the Exposition drew 27 million visitors during its six-month run from May through October 1893.[4]

At the start of the year, Alice participated in local preparations for the Fair. A network of women's committees across the country assembled artifacts for the Women's Building, which showcased the art and handicrafts of American women. In early February, an exhibit prepared by the Women's Committee of Richmond County was installed for three days at the Hotel Castleton in Brighton, and Alice's photographs were among the one hundred works of art on display. According to a *New York World* review, the exhibit consisted mostly of "knickknacks, curios and geegaws" that were not headed to Chicago but "right back to the altars and firesides of the old Staten Island families, who dug them up from a cobwebby sleep for this special occasion."[5] Despite the newspaper's criticism, Alice relished the event, keeping several souvenirs, including a committee member's badge and a brochure listing participants.[6]

In the spring, a celebration of the upcoming Fair came to New York, and Alice was there with her camera. On April 27, thirty-five ships from around the world participated in the Columbian Naval Review in New York Harbor, and the next day, crew members marched past cheering crowds down Fifth Avenue and Broadway to the Battery. Alice stood on the balcony of a building at Fifth Avenue near 32nd Street to capture the crowds and formations of armed crewmen (Figure 5.2). Spain's contribution to the Naval Review were replicas of Columbus's three ships, which subsequently headed to Chicago to become a popular display. From the parade, Alice traveled uptown to photograph the largest ship, the *Santa Maria,* which was moored near 95th Street.

On July 1, Alice left for a two-week visit to Chicago. Like her grandfather and Uncle Peter, she had a long-standing fascination with mechanical innovations, so her interest in the exhibits was more than casual. Her grandfather may have regaled her with stories of the 1867 Exposition Universelle in Paris, which he visited numerous times. On occasion, Uncle Peter took her on tours of factories, an unusual pastime

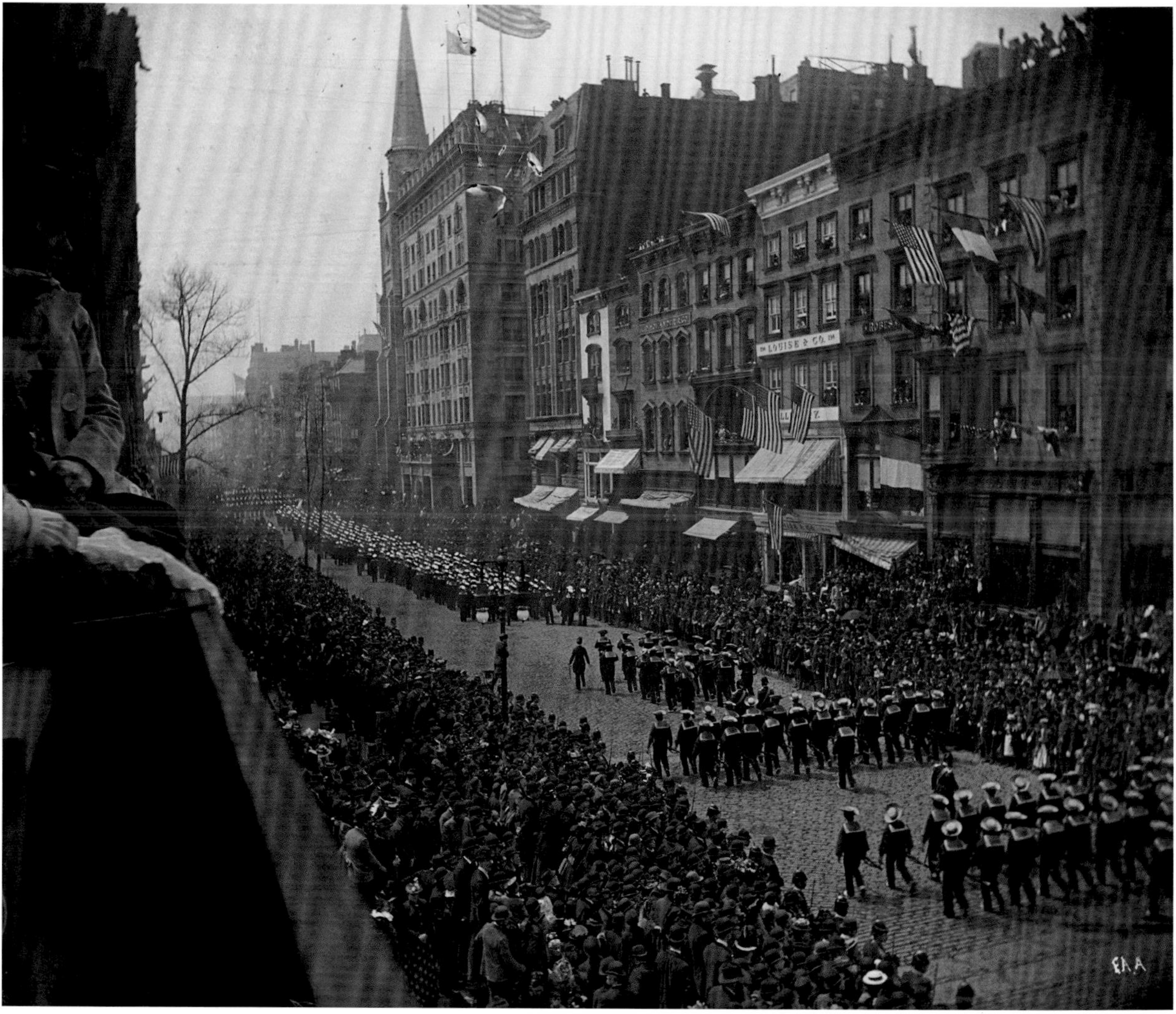

Figure 5.2 Preparations for the 1893 World's Columbian Exposition included a naval review in New York Harbor followed by a Fifth Avenue parade. Alice photographed both events.

for a young woman, as Trude noted in a self-deprecating letter: "If you go through all those factories & digest all you see, I am afraid we will appear very stupid to you on your return, . . . [and you] will have to try & impart some of your knowledge into our dormant brains." She facetiously expressed concern for Alice's safety—"[D]on't get wound up in any of the machinery of the factories"—perhaps a legitimate concern, given the lack of safety regulations at the time.[7]

Alice went to Chicago with Mary Emmons, a Clifton neighbor, and several members of the Emmons family.[8] They stayed in the dormitories of the University of Chicago, whose Hyde Park campus, adjacent to the fairgrounds, had recently opened.[9]

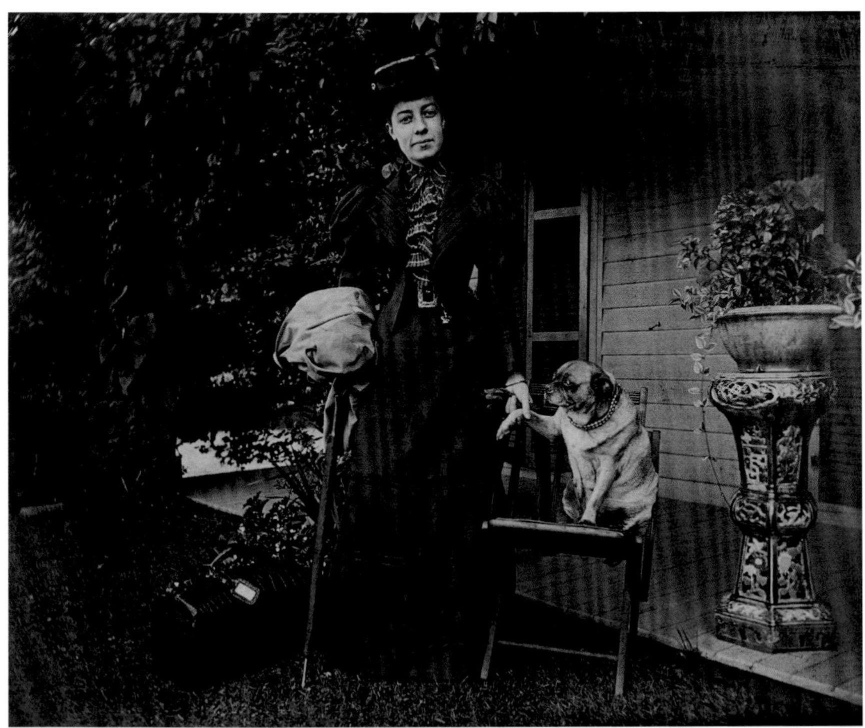

Figure 5.3   When Alice left for the World's Columbian Exposition in Chicago—the farthest she had been from home—she took a self-portrait with Punch.

Chicago was the farthest Alice had traveled from home, and she marked her departure with a self-portrait in which she put down her alligator traveling bag to bid farewell to Punch (Figure 5.3). The purposeful young woman in the smart traveling suit is a far cry from the feminine charmer in lace décolleté and elbow-length gloves of the previous summer.

Alice's photographs of the World's Fair were not personal. Like hundreds of visitors, she set out to create her own souvenirs, despite the plethora of images available for sale.[10] She photographed the major buildings, monumental sculptures, and waterways of the "White City," but unlike many of the official photographs, which were taken before the Fair opened, her liveliest views contrast the crowds of visitors with the grand architecture. One shows pedestrians carrying shade umbrellas along a walkway between the Mines and Electricity Buildings with the distinctive dome of the Administration Building in the distance (Figure 5.4). During her visit, a fire broke out in the chimney of the Cold Storage building, which kept hundreds of pounds of food fresh. Watched by encouraging crowds, firefighters tried unsuccessfully to reach the 191-foot chimney, and thirteen firefighters perished before the flames were extinguished. Alice captured the tragedy from the train that was taking her to the fairgrounds (Figure 5.5).

The Fair's Department of Photography established onerous restrictions for ama-

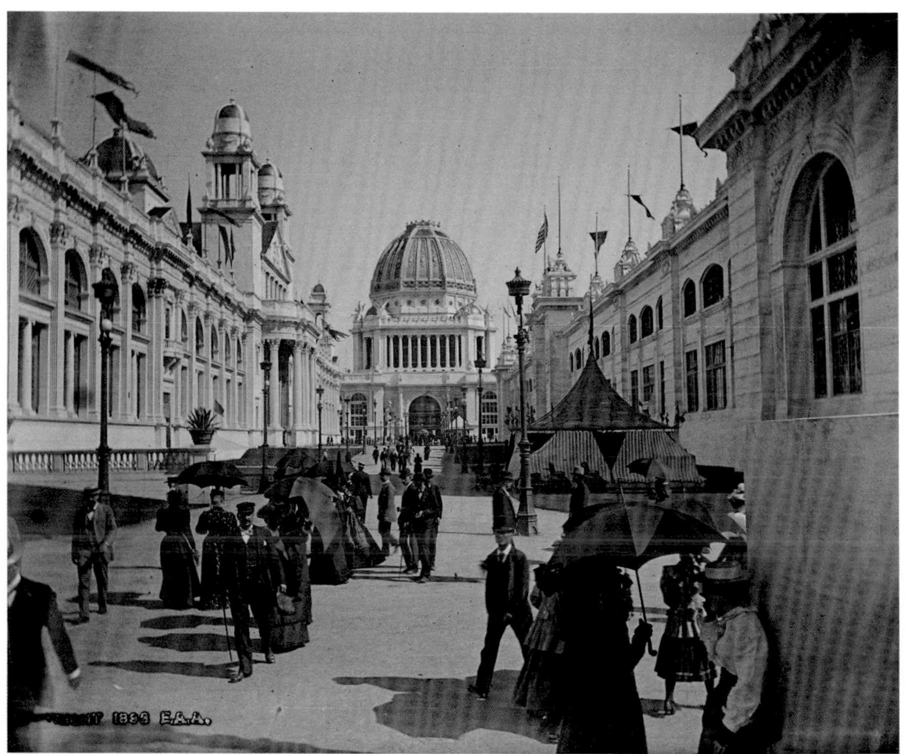

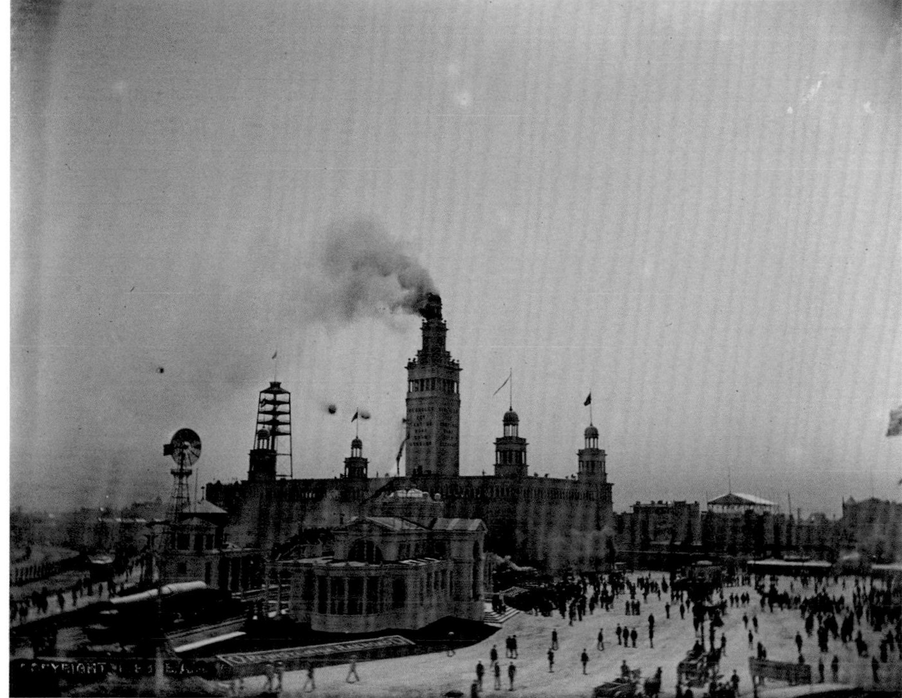

Figures 5.4 and 5.5 The official photographs of the World's Columbian Exposition were void of people and incident. Alice animated her views with strolling visitors and photographed a devastating fire.

teurs: they were not allowed to use cameras larger than 4 by 5; they could not use tripods or photograph the exhibits inside any buildings; and they were required to purchase a two-dollar-a-day permit to bring a camera onto the grounds. The photographic press railed against these restrictions, but they were honored in the breach. A sketch in *Scientific American* demonstrated how a rented folding chair could be used as a tripod.[11] Perhaps following advice in the *American Amateur Photographer*, Alice visited the Fair for several days without her camera before paying for a permit. On July 10, she took twenty-three of her twenty-five views, adhering to a prepared itinerary.[12] She avoided detection long enough to secure an interior view of a fanciful display of a Liberty Bell made of oranges in the California section of the Horticulture Building.[13]

On returning to Staten Island, Alice went on a three-week trip with Trude to visit friends in Lake George, arriving at home in time for the tennis season. In October, she reunited with the Emmons family for the third race of the America's Cup and skillfully captured their party watching the race from the steamship *Columbia* (Figure 5.6). Not until the late fall did she have time to print the Chicago negatives.

Alice's set of twenty-five images, numbered 1 through 25, was unprecedented for her. She mounted them in two ways, one more traditional—silver gelatin prints on brown, gold-edged cardboard—and one more pictorial—platinum prints on 8-by-10 inch sheets of cream-color paper with multiple borders to simulate etchings. In

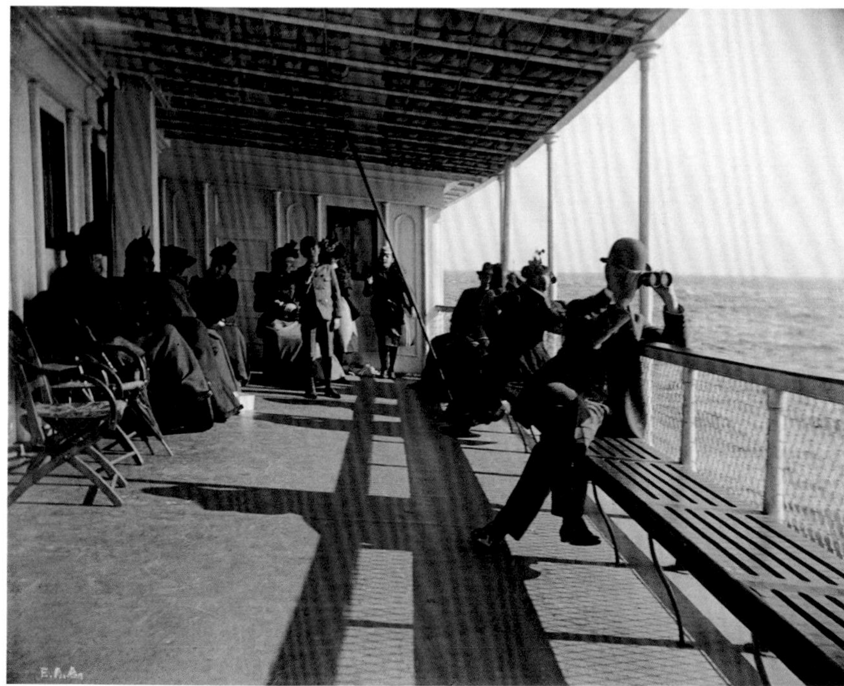

Figure 5.6 Alice joined the Emmons family on the steamboat *Columbia* to watch the third race of the America's Cup.

1892, the Philadelphia photographer John C. Browne had recommended that Alice try platinum paper, and this series was apparently her first opportunity to experiment with it. Printing each negative on both papers provided a textbook comparison of the higher contrast and slicker surface of gelatin silver with the longer tonal range and softer surface of platinum.[14]

Instead of writing her initials in ink on the negatives as she had in the past, Alice used a typeset rubber stamp to mark the negatives: COPYRIGHT 1893 E.A.A., reflecting the copyright she had obtained in December from the Library of Congress.[15] At the time, copyrighting photographs was not universal among professional photographers and extremely rare among amateurs. That Alice applied for copyright suggests she intended to produce an alternative to the readily available commercial souvenirs of the Fair. Violet Ward, who had recently patented a spring-loaded bodkin (a sewing device), may have encouraged her and helped her navigate the application process.[16]

Alice's tentative efforts to sell her work failed. In February 1894, Mrs. Isabella C. King, who lived near Washington Square in Manhattan, ordered prints for four people, each order consisting of a different selection in different "finishes."[17] Alice likely charged Mrs. King for her direct expenses but not for the considerable time it took to fulfill the complicated order. In May 1894, Bessie Strong reported that she had seen the World's Fair photographs that Alice consigned to a New Brunswick bookstore and inquired about them: "They have sold none as yet, but only put them in the window very recently, as they had no awning and the sun was so bright there."[18] Those ineffectual efforts were the extent of Alice's foray into marketing; numerous prints from the Chicago series remained in her possession.

In August, Alice sent a selection of World's Fair photographs to Thomas Quincy Browne Jr., who was a crew member on the 1892 *Wabun* canal trip. He wrote back a newsy, flirty letter which he signed, "'D. Butterball' Ex. 1st mate Yacht": "I did not venture to take photographs at the Fair, so I am doubly glad to have yours. That of the Art Gallery, the Liberty statue, & Columbus, are the best I have seen."[19] Alice felt more comfortable sharing her photographs with friends than selling them.

Street Types of New York

In the spring of 1894, Alice began to photograph "street types of New York."[20] The idea of creating a series of "street types" probably derived from Sigmund Krausz's souvenir book, *Street Types of Chicago, Character Studies,* which was available at the World's Fair. A Hungarian-born writer, Krausz hired a photographer to assist him. He explained his approach in the introduction to his book[21]:

> To collect these studies in such shape and execution as to make a volume desirable to
> every lover of art, it was not sufficient merely to take the kodak and start out to get

a snapshot at a desired subject, but I was compelled for weeks and months to haunt the crowded thoroughfares, the fashionable avenues and the dingy alleys for such characters as seemed to suit my purpose; and when I had found them, persuasion, appeals to their vanity and very frequently pecuniary considerations had to be resorted to in order to induce them to visit a studio in the garb and equipment of their daily vocation.[22]

Krausz created a vaudeville show of street life in his studio. His "characters" played their assigned roles before the camera, and the commentary, written by Krausz and a cadre of local writers (mostly newspapermen), trafficked in ethnic, gender, and racial prejudice.[23] Cartoonist Charles Lederer, for example, lampooned Italian immigrants in his description of "Scissors!," which depicts a knife grinder carrying his whetstone and tools. Humorist Ben King wrote a poem in dialect to accompany "Extry, All about the West-side Murder!," in which a Black child pantomimes selling newspapers.[24]

Alice photographed her New York "street types" *in situ*, an endeavor which Krausz had dismissed as mere snapshooting. Because she recorded the location, date and time of exposure on each negative sleeve, her travels around the city can be tracked. She took preliminary outings in 1894 and 1895, and having refined her technique, completed the project in 1896. She made a dozen excursions that year—three each in March, April, May, and June—which yielded forty-four negatives.

Alice's primary means of transportation were the elevated trains, which converged at South Ferry, where she disembarked from Staten Island. On March 5, 1894, she took the Sixth Avenue elevated to 23rd Street, and in two hours exposed eight negatives. In this initial foray, she made no attempt to gain the cooperation of her subjects. A blind shoelace peddler and a sleeping "crippled newsboy" could not see her, and a knife grinder and a hand organ player were preoccupied with their work. When she photographed a pretzel seller under the elevated tracks and a pair of bootblacks on Fourth Avenue, her subjects were not busy but paid her no attention.

In February and on April 10, 1895, Alice took the elevated to the Fulton Fish Market where she exposed thirteen negatives. A week later, on April 18, she stayed on the train for four more stops to photograph the Jewish pushcart vendors near Grand and Hester Streets, exposing seven more negatives. Because many of these photographs are known only through extant prints (the negatives and their informative sleeves are missing), it is harder to trace Alice's steps. This series, however, shows that she had learned how to approach people and ask them to pose. At the fish market, for example, two men moving empty baskets stopped to look toward the camera, as did an egg vendor and customer on Hester Street (Figures 5.7 and 5.8).

In these busy marketplaces, it was difficult for Alice to isolate individuals. At first, she tried to remedy the problem at home by manipulating her negatives and prints. In an image of a knife grinder, she excluded two boys playing at the right edge of the

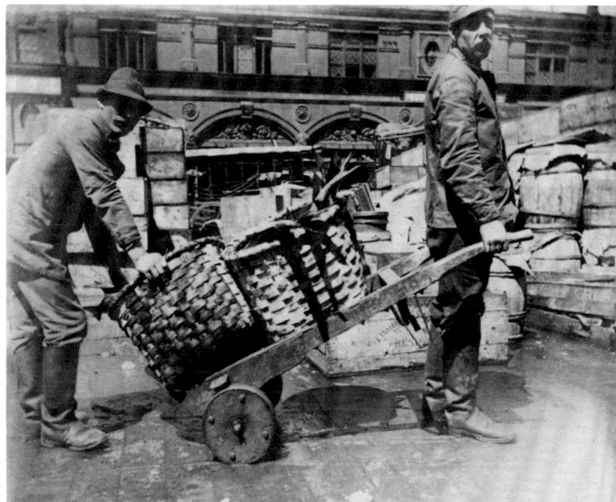
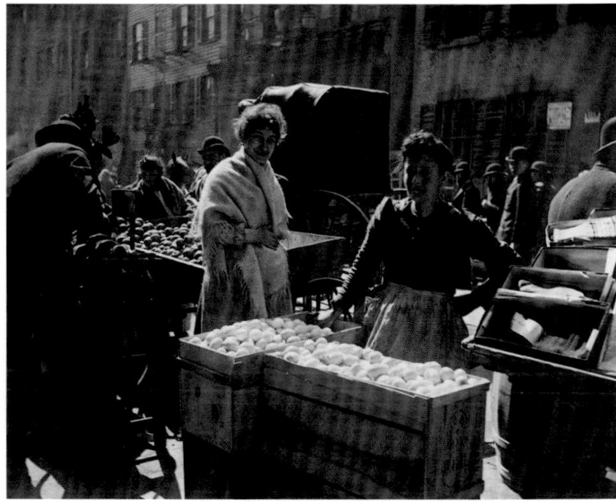

Figures 5.7 and 5.8   Alice photographed the Fulton Fish Market and the Lower East Side, picturesque but tough neighborhoods far from the shopping districts that she knew well.

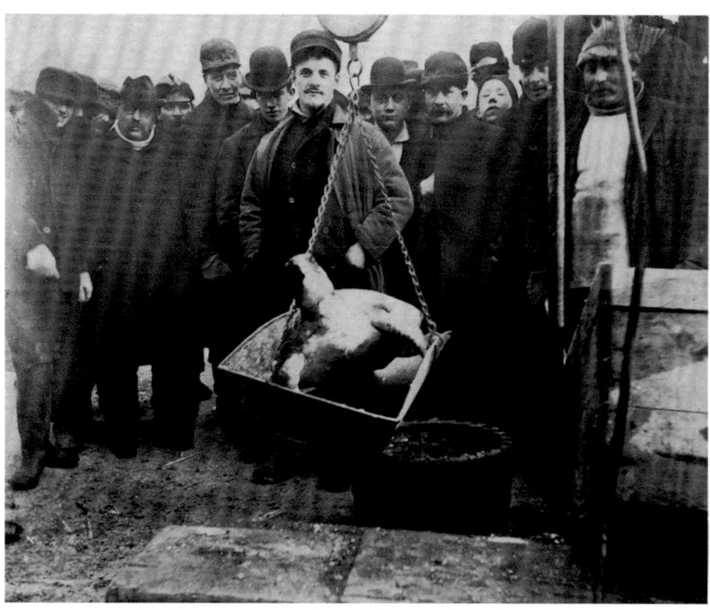
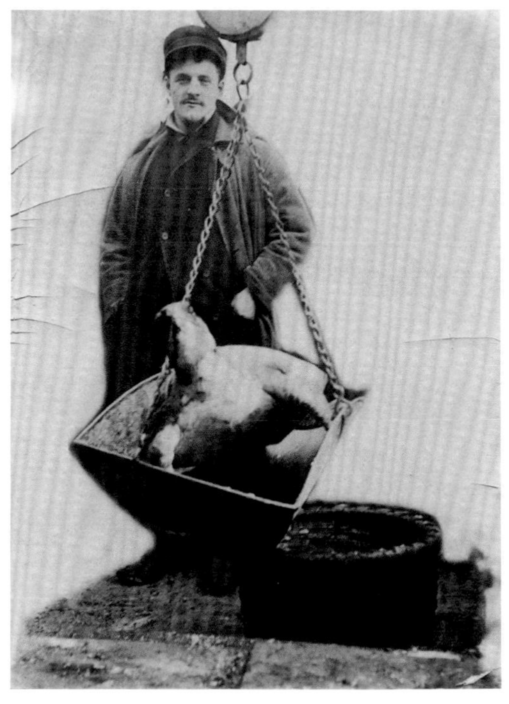

Figures 5.9 and 5.10   Before Alice isolated her subjects from passersby on the street, she resorted to masking her prints.

frame by cutting a print into an oval shape and pasting it onto a gray sheet of paper.[25] In a photograph of a huge turtle being weighed, she masked the negative and cropped the print to eliminate the onlookers (Figures 5.9 and 5.10). By the spring of 1896, when she began the street type series in earnest, she had found a way to keep passersby out of the frame. Walking on the streets with her camera, glass plates, and

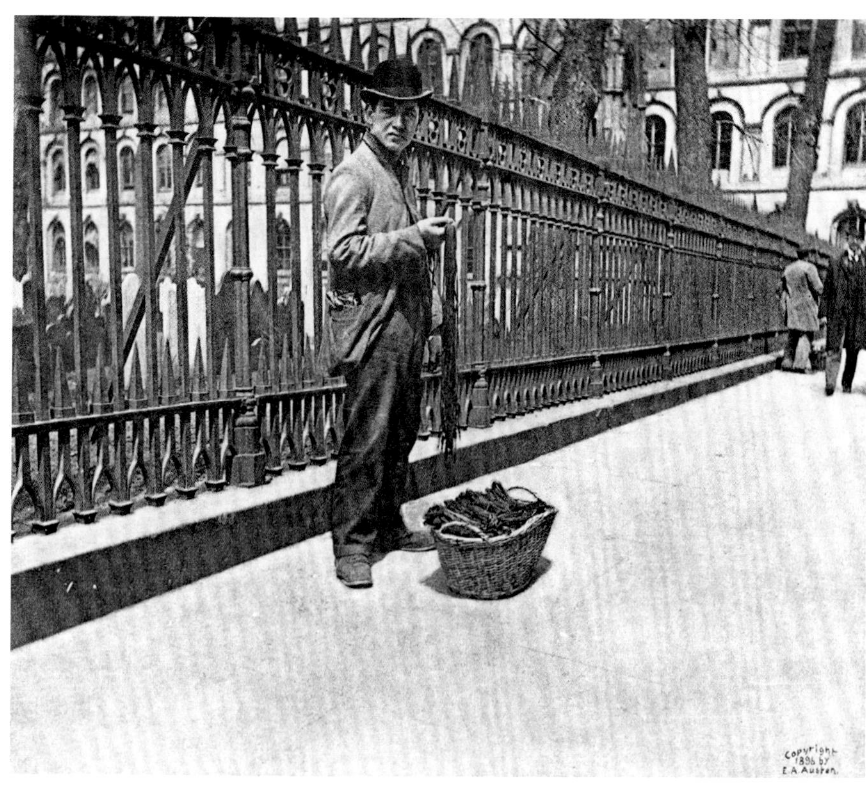

Figure 5.11   This photograph of a shoelace peddler was one of twelve images in the "Street Types of New York" portfolio. These collotypes were printed in ink and were less subtle than Alice's gelatin silver prints.

tripod, she needed someone to help carry equipment and guard her belongings while she photographed. Her helper, perhaps Violet or a family servant, assumed the task of keeping spectators at bay.[26]

Alice worked quickly, interacting with her subjects very little and making several exposures in a few hours. On April 13, for example, she exposed four negatives of emigrants at South Ferry (10:45 a.m. to 11:10 a.m.); hopped onto the Broadway cable car or walked up Broadway to Trinity Church, where she photographed a shoelace peddler (11:20 a.m.) (Figure 5.11);[27] and then walked north to City Hall Park, where she made two exposures of bootblacks (12:35 p.m. and 12:50 p.m.) and a third of a boy and girl selling newspapers (12:55 p.m.). The transgressive nature of her task helps explain her alacrity. "Respectable" women in public were expected to dress and comport themselves unobtrusively and to travel to their destinations without speaking to strangers or taking in the sights. As historian Jessica Ellen Sewell has written, "The ideal invisibility of middle-class women . . . both helped to distinguish them from poorer women and made them less attractive to the gazes of dangerous men."[28] Alice had regularly traveled with her mother to go shopping, a habit which accustomed her to traveling with strangers on public transportation to districts where women congregated. But the "street types" project required her to move beyond these districts, to approach strangers of the lower classes, and to draw attention to herself

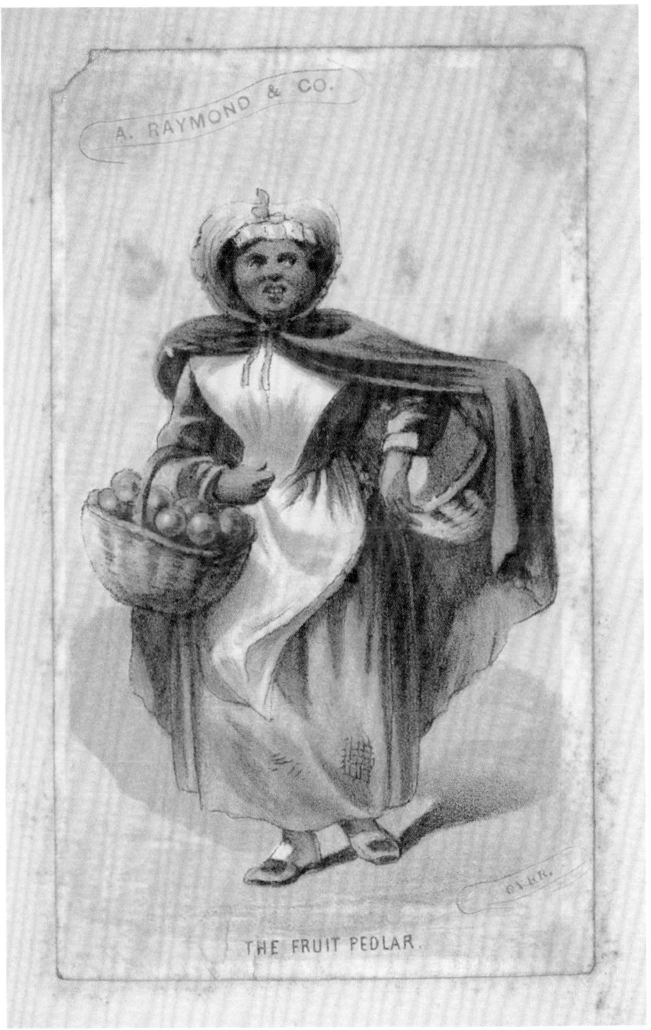

Figure 5.12   This trade card of a fruit peddler which Alice kept in one of her scrapbooks indicates that she was familiar with the European tradition of "street cries."

with her camera and tripod. Once a photograph was taken, Alice and her helper left the site quickly to avoid comments or questions, and after three or four interactions, they were finished for the day.

Although her immediate stimulus for photographing street types may have been Krausz's World's Fair souvenir book, Alice was acquainted with the venerable pictorial tradition of "street cries"—hand-drawn images of tradespeople who walked the streets crying out their wares or services—which dates to seventeenth-century Europe. A lithograph of a fruit peddler in Alice's trade card collection recalls the street cries of the preindustrial era (Figure 5.12).

She was also familiar with the "sunshine and shadow" literature contrasting New York's wealth and poverty, which was well established by the 1890s. Images of tenement life in the city's ethnic enclaves were familiar to readers of national illustrated newspapers, like *Harper's Weekly* and *Frank Leslie's Illustrated*.

On her dozen trips into Manhattan to complete the "street types" project, Alice photographed the same "types" on multiple occasions. She sought out traditional workers—peddlers, bootblacks, newsboys, and street musicians—as well as contemporary workers in uniform, like postmen, bicycle messengers, street cleaners, and municipal policemen. She took several photographs of the "White Wings" (Figure 5.13). Nicknamed for the color of their uniforms, the corps of municipal street cleaners was the brainchild of Col. George E. Waring, who established the Street Cleaning Department in 1895 under the reform Mayor William L. Strong.

Likely working from an itinerary, Alice minimized the time that she spent with each subject. On two occasions she went off script to pursue chance encounters. At South Ferry, she took time to take several photographs of a group of newly arrived immigrants milling around with their baggage. Immigration of Eastern European Jews and southern Italians swelled during the 1890s, and many remained in the city where jobs were plentiful. Their numbers created strains on housing, law enforcement, and charity organizations, and their ethnic and religious differences engendered curiosity and fear. What attracted Alice's attention was a "queer man" (as she described him) who appears in three of the four photographs that she took at South Ferry within thirty minutes.[29] She may have been drawn to his garrulousness or his especially

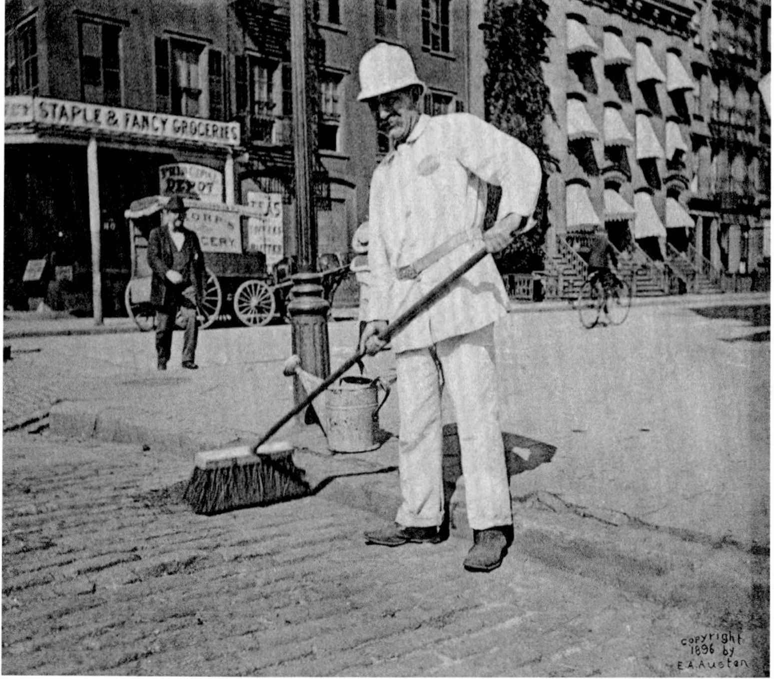

Figure 5.13   A modern "street type" that Alice photographed was a uniformed street sweeper, one of the "White Wings" hired by the newly created Department of Street Cleaning.

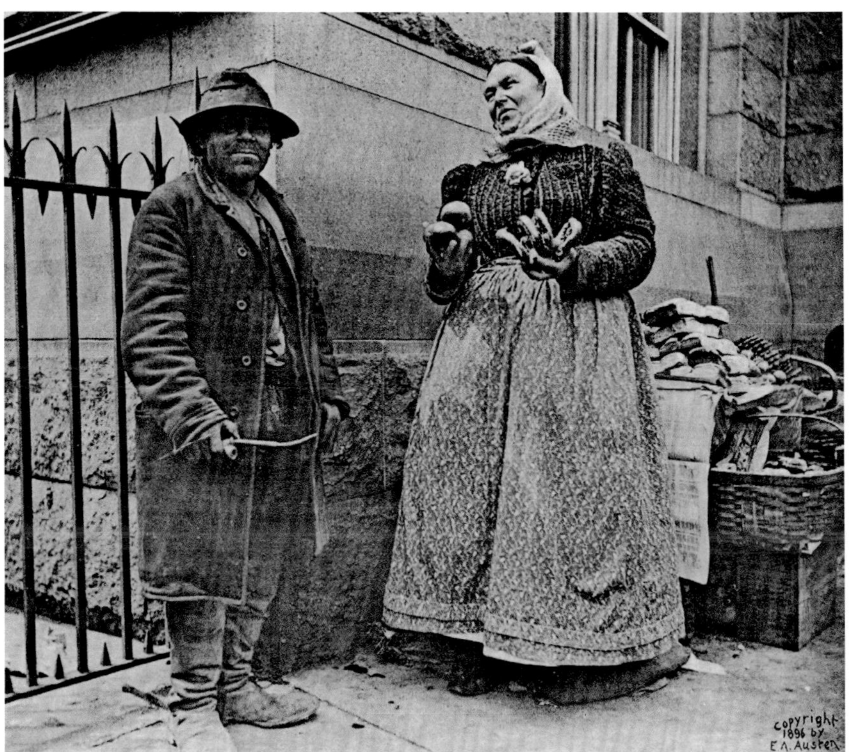

Figure 5.14   Alice took three photographs of this "queer man," a newly arrived immigrant at South Ferry.

shabby appearance which may have affirmed the era's caricature of an Italian immigrant. A photograph of him standing next to a woman selling pretzels became one of the "street types" (Figure 5.14).

On October 30, several months after she stopped photographing "street types," Alice brought her camera to the city to photograph a Fifth Avenue parade for presidential hopeful William McKinley. At Third Avenue and 23rd Street, her attention was drawn to two ragpickers, their handcarts piled high with bundles of rags. Collecting and reselling old rags was a trade practiced primarily by Italian immigrants, who often lived illegally in the city's dumps.[30] Alice took two photographs of the men, one from across the street, which features a spectacular wall of billboards, and the other close-up (Figures 5.15 and 5.16). She worked quickly, as the men's posture and expressions are nearly identical in the two images. The following month when she submitted eighteen images for copyright, Alice included both views of the ragpickers.

Like the World's Fair views, the "street types" presented a printing and distribution challenge. Alice tested a dozen negatives on platinum paper but chose silver gelatin paper to create a set of pictures. She mounted these traditional prints on pictorial mounts: 8-by-10 inch sheets of heavy white paper with an "etching" imprint. The set consisted of forty-two "street types" (all but two taken in 1896), including seventeen of the eighteen copyrighted images (only one of the two ragpickers). Alice used a type-

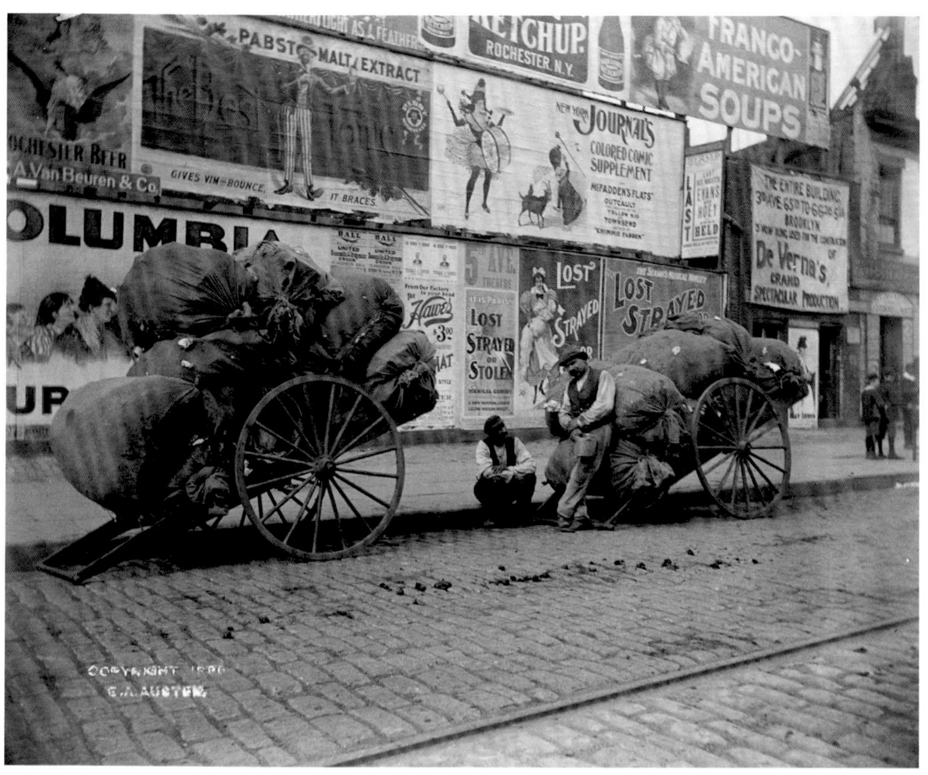
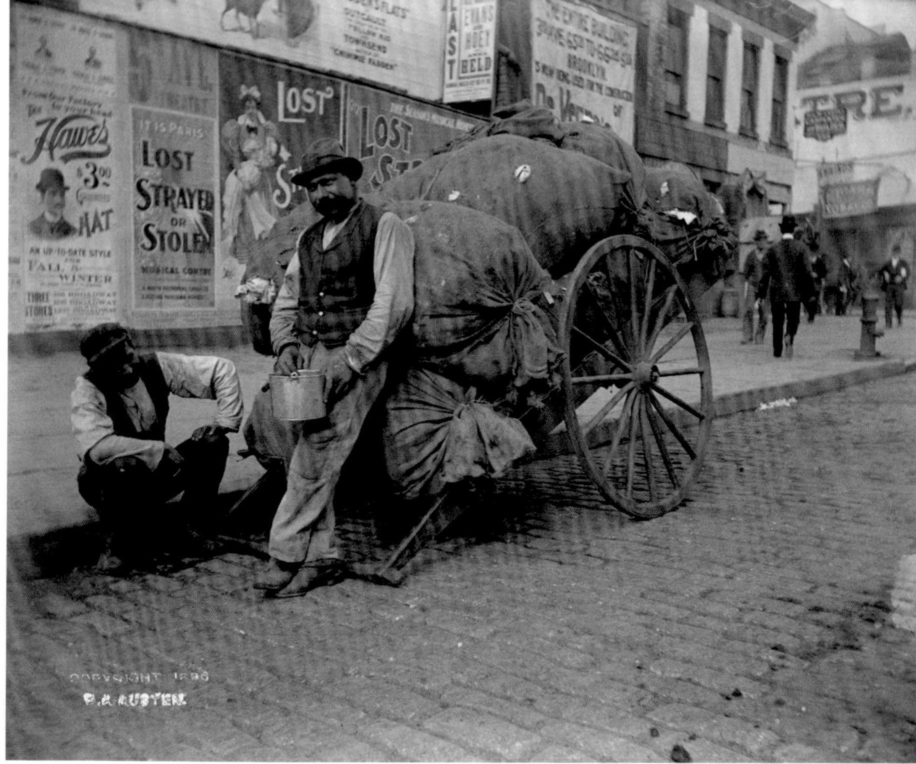

Figures 5.15 and 5.16   At 23rd Street and Third Avenue, Alice photographed a pair of ragpickers with full carts, first from across the street and then at closer range.

set, metal debossing stamp to mark these prints "COPYRIGHTED 1896," and only afterward added her name in ink, "E.A. Austen," perhaps suggesting her reluctance to claim these images as her own.

After completing the set, Alice hired the Albertype Company of Brooklyn to fabricate a portfolio of twelve of the copyrighted images. Founded by Adolph Wittemann, the company specialized in collotype, an ink-based process that did not fade and allowed for printing large quantities cheaply. Wittemann came to the United States from Germany in 1870 and by 1892 was successful enough to buy a five-acre estate on Staten Island.[31] Alice may have known of him locally and may have learned more about his company at the Chicago Fair. A pamphlet prepared for Fair visitors advertised the company's services:

> We offer to prepare, bind, furnish and complete an **Albertype Souvenir** of views of your town, city, establishment, country or section, or a *Catalogue, Pamphlet, Framing Picture, Hanger, Card, Folder, etc* . . . Albertype . . . is the parent process of reproducing photographs on a printing press and renders pictures in full tones and details of the original negative.[32]

A portfolio of loose prints represents a departure from the company's standard format of a bound brochure and may have been done at Alice's request. The 4-by-5 inch collotypes are mounted on 7-by-9 inch sheets of dark brown paper, which complemented the sepia color of the prints. The design of the cardboard covers, which were held together with grosgrain ribbon ties, is oddly rustic: cream-colored paper with a tree-bark texture, and the words, "Street Types of New York," in thin, outlined capital letters in deep red or green ink (Figure 5.17). As instructed by the company, Alice enclosed a list of titles, such as "Street Sweeper, Forty-Eighth Street and Eighth Avenue," or "Pretzel Vender and Emigrant, South Ferry," which comprises the portfolio's only text.[33] Before sending the twelve negatives to the Albertype Company, Alice stamped them, "Copyright 1896, E.A. Austen," having resolved to take credit for them, but her name does not appear on the cover or the contents page of her only self-published work.

The distinct qualities of Alice's "street types" become clearer when compared with photographs taken by her contemporaries Jacob Riis and Alfred Stieglitz. All three photographers used the 4-by-5 camera to photograph New York's lower classes. A Danish immigrant who became a newspaperman, Riis took photographs of New York's slums to arouse the public to action. An inspired writer and orator who claimed he was "no good at all as a photographer," he relied on experienced amateurs to take his first one hundred photographs—including his most famous, "Bandit's Roost"—for a slide lecture that formed the basis of his best-selling book, *How the Other Half*

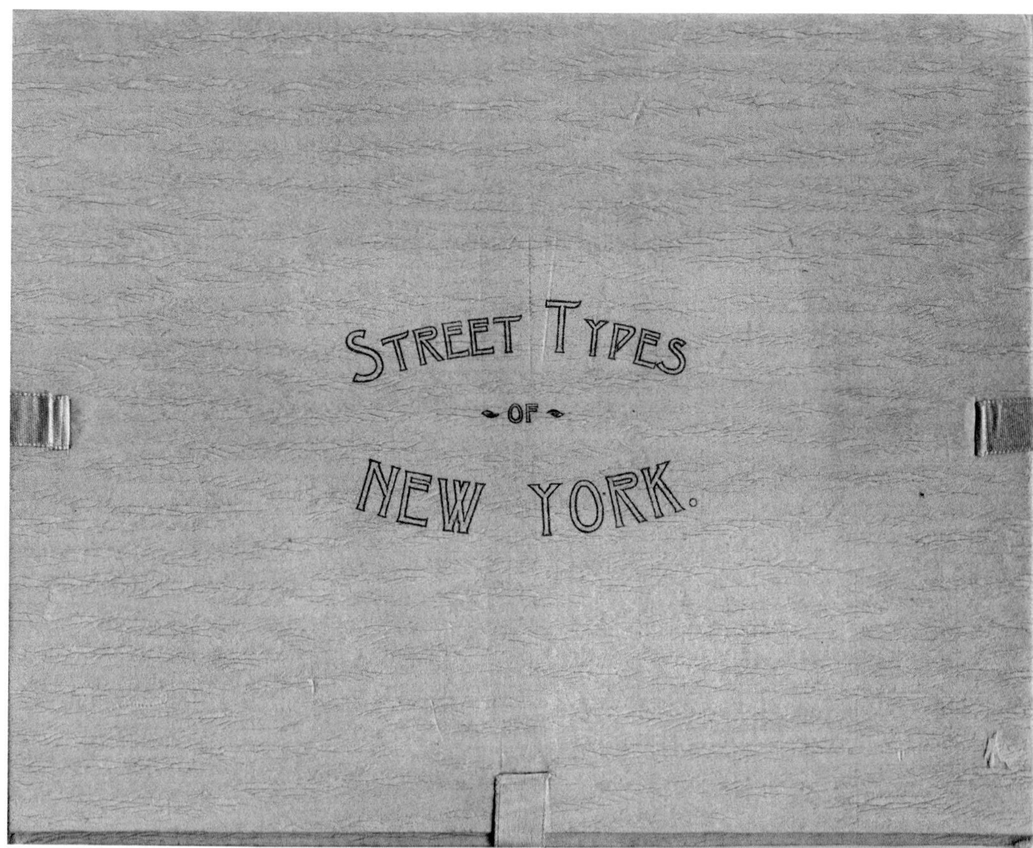

Figure 5.17   The rustic cover of "New York Street Types" was probably designed by the Albertype Company, which routinely created publications from clients' negatives.

Lives (1890).[34] Riis entertained his audience by relying on the literary conventions of the New York slum tour—describing Chinese opium dens, Jewish sweatshops, and Italian rookeries—before appealing to his audience's Christian conscience.

The son of a successful German-Jewish merchant, Stieglitz returned to New York in 1890 after living in Europe for nearly a decade. An ambitious artist and a fierce advocate of pictorial photography, he found his subject in the streets of New York: "I wandered around the Tombs; the old Post Office, Five Points . . . I loved the signs, even the slush, as well as the snow, the rain and the lights as night fell."[35] Stieglitz projected his feelings of isolation onto the streetcar drivers, coachmen, and street sweepers that he photographed, and he identified his quest for perfect negatives with physical hardship: "My picture 'Winter—Fifth Avenue' is the result of a three hours' stand during a fierce snowstorm on February 22, 1893, awaiting the proper moment. My patience was duly rewarded."[36] The negative served as his point of departure in the darkroom, where he enlarged and cropped the image and made carbon prints on rough-textured watercolor paper to soften the atmospheric effect of the snowstorm. Due to his zealous self-promotion, "Winter—Fifth Avenue" was exhibited and published at least twenty-five times before 1900.

Riis, Stieglitz, and Austen all portrayed New York's working poor as types, not as individuals, albeit to different ends. Riis employed ethnic stereotypes to ingratiate himself with his audience; Stieglitz projected his emotions onto laborers; and Austen presented an anthology of tradespeople as a metonymy for a fast-changing city. Their differences were also defined by gender. In photographing on New York's streets, Riis and Stieglitz felt at physical risk. When Riis and his two photographer-colleagues took a camera into Mulberry Bend, they brought along an officer of the sanitary police for protection. Famously hypochondriacal, Stieglitz waited for hours in inclement weather to obtain his most cherished negatives. Austen, by contrast, risked her safety and her respectability in ways unknown to these men by venturing where a woman of her class should not go and speaking with strangers she should not speak to. Gender also shaped the differences in their ambitions. Riis and Stieglitz built their careers on their photographs of New York, while Austen was reluctant to put her name on her portfolio, perhaps seeing authorship as a threat to her respectability.[37]

The question remains: Why did Alice produce the *Street Types of New York*? She was not interested in sales. Although some Albertype publications were advertised and reviewed, there was no public notice of Alice's portfolio. She gave at least two copies to family members—to Aunt Minn and Uncle Oswald and to Ralph Middleton Munroe—and five others are now in public collections.[38] Several empty sets of portfolio covers and numerous unmounted collotypes remained in her collection. As with the World's Fair series, she had no clear idea of her audience beyond family and friends, and she abandoned the idea of distribution, if she had any.

Alice may have been motivated by the sheer audacity of the endeavor. After visiting Chicago under chaperone, she flouted the traditional constraints on women to move around a big city—her city—pushing against boundaries of class, gender, and public space. Wearing her class privilege like armor, she perhaps felt invincible when convincing people to pose as "street types," seeking their cooperation without concern for their reactions to her. As cultural historian Laura Wexler has aptly observed, Alice was "curious about but not comfortable with the 'street type,' and the feeling seems to [have been] reciprocated."[39]

Bicycling for Ladies

In November 1895, Bessie Strong wrote Alice: "What are you doing with yourself I wonder? Probably the bicycle reigns supreme still."[40] That was very much the case.

Alice spent much of 1895 teaming up with Violet Ward to establish the Staten Island Bicycle Club and to help her with *Bicycling for Ladies*, a guide illustrated with drawings after Alice's photographs.

Maria Emily Graham McKnight Ward, called Violet, was the oldest child of William Greene Ward, a Civil War general. Three years older than Alice, she spent winters in her family's Manhattan townhouse and summers at Oneata, an eighteen-acre estate on Grymes Hill, prime Staten Island real estate with panoramic views of the harbor, where the Wards built an eighteen-room Victorian mansion with stables and a tennis court. They touted their ancestors, who helped found the colony of Rhode Island, as well as their wealth, which derived from Ward & Co., the family's banking firm.

Although Violet's family was much wealthier than Alice's, both identified as women of distinguished American ancestry who envisioned futures unencumbered by financial concerns. Violet was an early proponent of the physical culture movement, which proposed organized indoor activity to remedy the myriad physical maladies that plagued city dwellers. The movement arose in men's colleges and spread to women's colleges and wealthy urban women. Violet introduced Alice to Mary Taylor Bissell, a Vassar graduate and medical doctor who promoted physical culture with a steady stream of articles, books, and lectures.[41] In *Physical Development and Exercise for Women* (1891), Bissell argued:

> The obstacles to [a woman's] better physical development are for the most part due to ignorance and to custom; and these, beginning in her early years and continuing to maturity, largely concern her school-life, the restriction of her body by dress, and its limitation from lack of sufficient exercise.[42]

Bissell challenged cultural prejudice with medical authority, enumerating the harms caused by the corset, recommending formal physical education classes in schools, and advocating for gymnasiums during the winter months when outdoor activity was limited.

Violet also introduced Alice to Delia Marie Elliott, called Daisy, who, unlike Alice or Violet, went to school to pursue a career. The daughter of a prominent Brooklyn physician, Daisy graduated from the Brooklyn Normal School for Physical Training, one of the earliest American programs to train physical education teachers.[43] In 1890 at age thirty-three, she began directing classes at the Berkeley Ladies' Athletic Club, an adjunct of the men's Berkeley Athletic Club on West 44th Street, off Fifth Avenue. That year, the Ladies' Club moved into its own clubhouse, with a gymnasium, bowling alleys, swimming pool, dressing rooms, and library. The club was expensive and exclusive with membership restricted to those recommended by existing members.

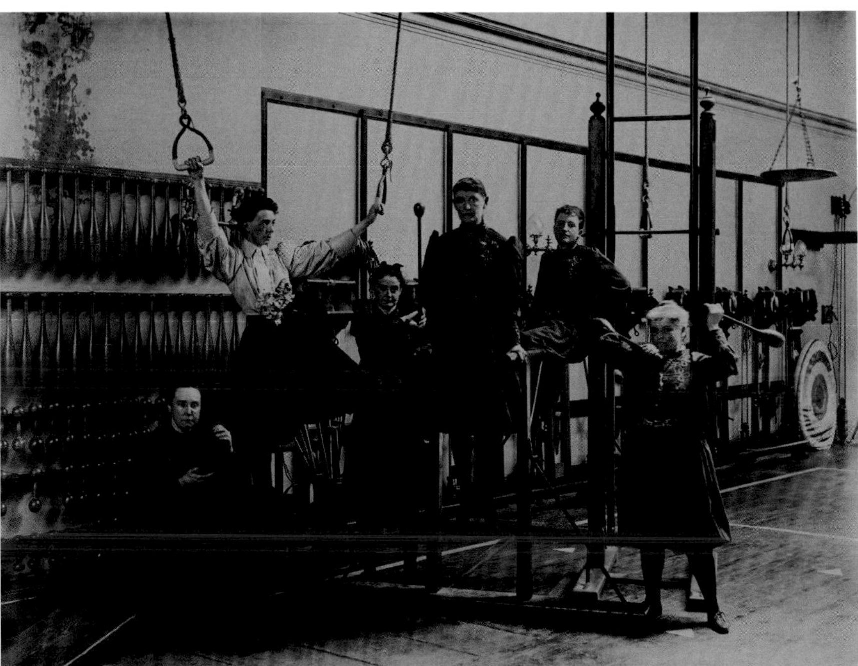

Figure 5.18   Holding the rings, Daisy Elliott poses with her pupils at the Berkeley Ladies' Athletic Club in Midtown Manhattan.

As the club's consulting physician, Dr. Bissell submitted each member to a rigorous physical examination, and Daisy taught a regimen of exercises adapted from men's calisthenics and military drills.[44] Several articles appeared in the popular press that described and illustrated the exercises,[45] and Violet, who was a club member, enlisted Alice to take photographs at the gymnasium. On May 23, 1893, Alice brought her full plate camera to the club and made four exposures. In the photographs, Daisy wears a billowy white blouse and full bloomers, and her four students, including Violet (seated at left), wear military style jackets, which signal the masculine derivation of the women's exercises (Figure 5.18).

Violet's influence on Alice can be seen in their fashion choices in two double portraits. In October 1894, Alice took a second canal trip with Ralph Munroe on the maiden voyage of the *Utilis*, another of his yachts fabricated on Staten Island, and asked Violet to accompany her.[46] Trude, who had retreated to her domestic routines, envied their adventurous spirit, which struck her as exotic: "I wish I could have had some of those lovely sails with you and Violet, what Gipsys [sic] you have become."[47] To commemorate their trip, Alice photographed herself and Violet at Oneata in their "travel costumes" (Figure 5.19). Although they wear matching berets, Alice has on a conventional, tightly fitted traveling suit, which constrained her movements, while Violet has discarded a corset in favor of a skirt and turtleneck sweater, which allow her greater ease of movement and comfort.

In the second portrait taken around the same time, Alice and Violet dress in sim-

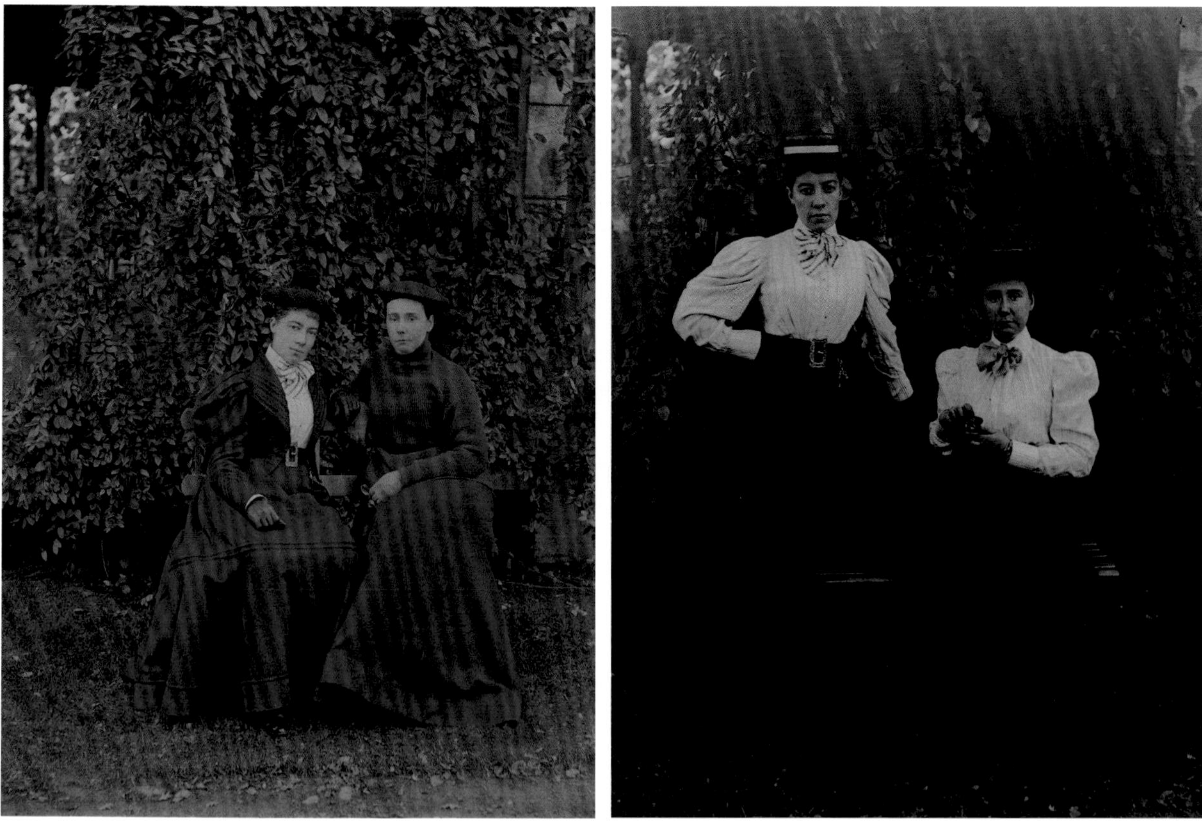

Figures 5.19 and 5.20   Violet encouraged Alice to wear the less confining, more comfortable clothing of the "New Woman."

ilar, loose-fitting shirtwaist blouses, belted skirts, and jaunty straw hats—the New Woman's uniform popularized by commercial illustrator Charles Dana Gibson (Figure 5.20). In Gibson's hands, the radical implications of this unconfining outfit were tempered so that the style became popular. Art historian Holly Pyne Connor captured the Gibson Girl's allure:

> As an ideal Anglo-Saxon woman, the Gibson Girl was a highly reassuring figure . . . [who] had widespread appeal because she simultaneously personified traditional and new aspects of womanhood. Not only was she attractive, chaste and interested in romance and marriage, but she was also independent, self-confident and athletic.[48]

Alice's hand-on-hip pose mimics the Gibson Girl's insouciant glamour. Violet, who was also an amateur photographer, holds a miniature camera, and sits next to a full plate camera.[49] The cameras suggest that these Gibson Girls had skills and work to do.

Past their prime as competitive tennis players, Alice and Violet were perfectly poised

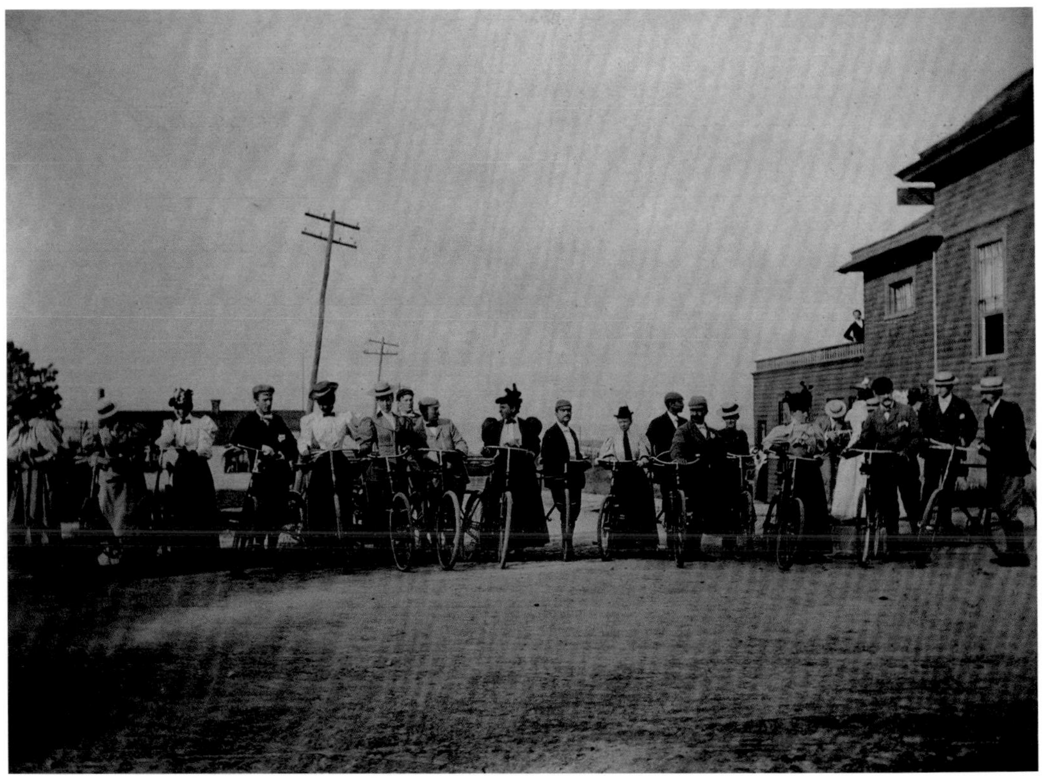

Figure 5.21   Alice photographed the inaugural ride of the Staten Island Bicycle Club.

to take up the two latest sports crazes, golf and bicycling. News coverage of golf, "society's latest pastime," began in 1890, and when the Richmond County Country Club built an eighteen-hole course in 1894, the game was well established on Staten Island.[50] Violet was a more competitive golfer than Alice and even tried to patent an improved golf club.[51] In 1893, the two women took up "wheeling."[52] The passion for bicycles began with the English invention of the safety bicycle, which had two wheels of equal size, a chain drive, pneumatic tires, and, in the women's model, a drop frame with no crossbar between the handlebars and seat. As the weight of the bicycle fell below thirty pounds and the cost below one hundred dollars, bicycling took off. In 1894, 80,000 visitors attended a bicycle trade show in Madison Square Garden, and the following year, 300 American bicycle companies produced half a million safeties.[53]

Bicycle clubs organized long-distance rides, offered lessons, sponsored races, and in exclusive clubs like Manhattan's Michaux Cycle Club where Violet was a member, provided amenities like showers and dressing rooms. In 1895, Violet enlisted Alice to cofound the Staten Island Bicycle Club for what the local press called "the cycling ladies and gentlemen of the island who are prominent in fashionable society." They rented a clubhouse in St. George near the ferry depot, and the club's grand opening consisted of an hour-long ride followed by a tea at the clubhouse.[54] Alice took four photographs of the event, one showing Violet (her dark hat and leg-of-mutton sleeves silhouetted against the sky) at the center of a group of cyclists at the start of the ride (Figure 5.21). By November, they had hired a teacher to provide lessons and opened a rental and repair shop.[55] Despite its auspicious start, a dispute broke out between Violet and the man hired to run the shop, and the club did not see a second season.[56] Violet and Alice had the creativity and energy to launch the bicycle club but lacked the wherewithal to manage it.

Perhaps inspired by Daisy, who was a published advocate for women's physical culture, Violet turned her attention to writing a guidebook for women cyclists. *Bicycling for Ladies* was published in 1896 by Brentano's, a bookstore chain. When her editor asked if Violet wanted her name on the title page to read "Miss M.E. Ward," she responded that she preferred it printed as would a male author's.[57] The title page reads, "The Common Sense of Bicycling; Bicycling for Ladies; With Hints as to the Art of Wheeling—Advice to Beginners—Dress—Care of the Bicycle—Mechanics—Training—Exercise, Etc. Etc. By Maria E. Ward."

While every bit a practical guide, *Bicycling for Ladies* addressed the fierce backlash against women's cycling, which ignited every fear of the New Woman.[58] The bicycle craze challenged fashion norms (the corset constricted breathing, and long skirts interfered with the pedals and gears); it gave women the means to travel alone; and it led to "over-exertion."[59] The popular press regularly published cartoons of an emasculated husband at home with a crying baby while his wife, wearing knickerbockers, went for a ride.[60] The opening of the book's chapter on "Dress" illustrates Violet's approach:

> Clothing should be most carefully selected, with the view to an equal distribution of weight and an even thickness of material; it should have no constricting, no tight bands anywhere, but should permit of absolute freedom of movement, and be warm enough to prevent chilling through too great radiation of heat yet porous enough to allow of free evaporation. . . . The essentials are knickerbockers, shirtwaist, stockings, shoes, gaiters, sweater, coat, no skirt, or skirt with length decided by individual preference, hat and gloves.

At its best, Violet's book edifies and inspires. When she extols the joys of bicycling, she could be writing a New Woman's manifesto:

> Riding the wheel, our own powers are revealed to us, a new sense is seemingly created. The unobserving are gradually awakened, and the keen observer is thrilled with quick and rare delight. The system is invigorated, the spirit is refreshed, the mind, freed from care, swept of dusty cobwebs, is filled with new and beautiful impressions. You have conquered a new world, and exultingly you take possession of it.[61]

The book's illustrations are based on Alice's photographs of Daisy and show the correct (and incorrect) ways to mount, ride, carry, and repair a bicycle. On the lawn at Clear Comfort, the women set up an outdoor studio by placing canvas on the grass as a "floor" and erecting a wooden trellis with tacked up fabric as "walls." In twenty-four photographs taken in four sessions, Daisy wears full-legged bloomers, which provide a clear view of the position of her legs. In four photographs, she wears a full skirt, which shows regard for the sensibilities of the era's more conservative women.[62] To simulate movement, Daisy sometimes balances on the bicycle unassisted (Figure 5.22); in other images, the bicycle is held stationary with a small rock behind the back wheel and a walking stick propped under the seat (Figure 2.23).

Alice's photographs were given to an illustrator who added hats and restyled the clothing to suggest that there was more than one model. The heavily reworked images were then reproduced as halftones (Figure 5.24). Violet did not think to thank Alice or Daisy in her acknowledgments, nor did Alice copyright the photographs. The title page simply noted that the book was "Illustrated."[63]

A month before publication, the *New York Herald* ran, "Fair Ladies and the Wheel, Miss Maria E. Ward Instructs Her Sisters in All the Mysteries of Bicycling," an excerpt that filled a full page and reproduced eleven of the book's illustrations.[64] Appearing at the height of the craze, *Bicycling for Ladies* received favorable reviews from across the country and in England. Some writers recommended the book for men as well as women, and one deemed it "specially suitable for a young man to offer a girl who 'goes a-wheeling' with him."[65] Many reviewers remarked on the "splendid" illustrations that "make very complete the plain text."[66] An influencer before her time, Violet wrote to manufacturers asking them to pay one hundred dollars to be featured in a sequel that would recommend their products to her readers. Her requests fell on deaf ears, and the sequel never appeared.[67]

By the turn of the twentieth century, Violet, Alice, and the rest of the country lost interest in cycling: its novelty wore off and its utility was replaced by the automobile.

Quarantine Station of the Port of New York

A short distance from Clear Comfort along the waterfront stood the headquarters and laboratory of the quarantine station of the Port of New York, as well as the stately home of its health officer. At water's edge was a boarding station, where ships were anchored for inspection to determine if they could proceed to Manhattan or should be diverted to the quarantine facilities on Hoffman and Swinburne Islands. These two islands were built in New York harbor in the early 1870s to isolate contagious immigrants and ships' crews from local populations. In the 1890s, a cholera outbreak in Europe highlighted the inadequacy of the small islands to meet the needs of the vast increase in arriving immigrants. As a result, Hoffman Island was more than doubled

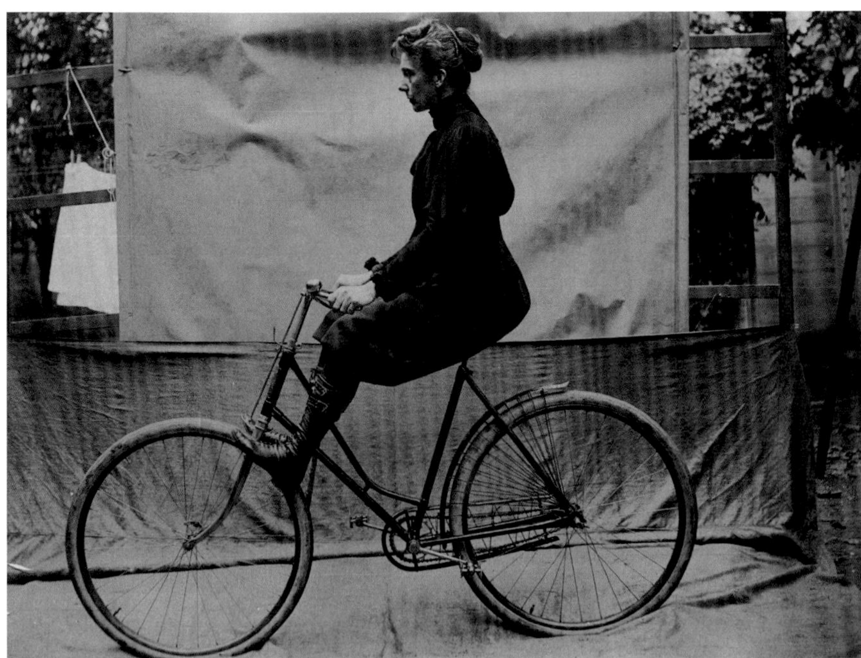

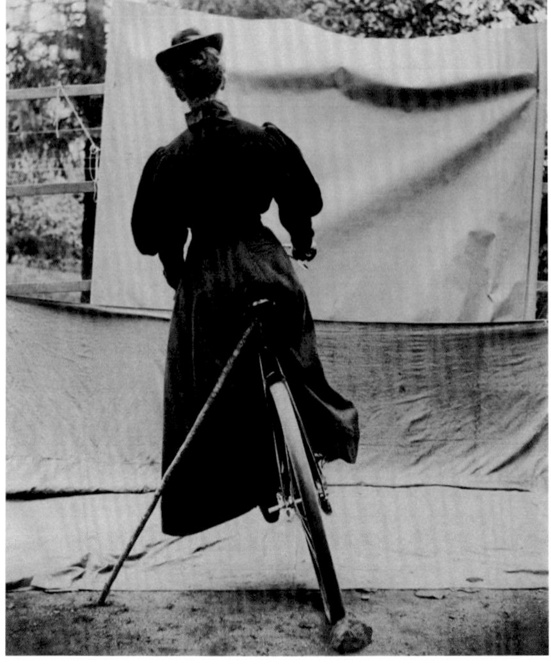

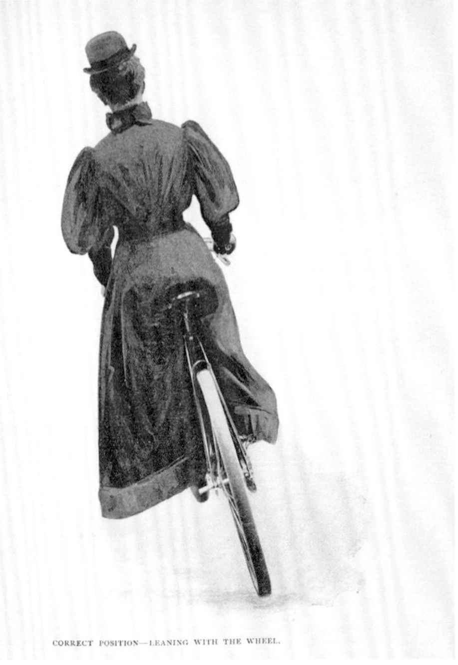

Figures 5.22–5.24   Daisy posed for the illustrations of Violet's guidebook, *Bicycling for Ladies*.

in size to ten acres, and plans were made for dormitories to accommodate 1,200 people. A new hospital and crematorium were designed for Swinburne Island. Those exposed to smallpox, yellow fever, cholera, or bubonic plague but showed no sign of illness were sent to Hoffman Island for observation; those who arrived noticeably ill went to Swinburne Island.

In 1895, Dr. Alvah Hunt Doty, chief of the Bureau of Contagious Diseases for the New York Board of Health, was appointed the health officer of the Port of New York. A good government Republican, Doty was an innovative and ambitious public health official who leaped at the challenge of developing the most up-to-date disinfecting equipment and completing construction on the islands. In his first year on the job, he learned that his neighbor Alice Austen was a skilled photographer and enlisted her to photograph the quarantine facilities. Alice had already photographed ships under quarantine, including the SS *Bourgogne* during the 1892 cholera scare.[68]

Doty's first undertaking was the conversion of an old paddle steamer, renamed the *James W. Wadsworth*, into a disinfection station. Standard quarantine practice required a ship suspected of carrying infection to remain at sea for an incubation period, which could last for weeks. The practice was expensive and inconvenient for passengers and ruinous for shippers if the cargo was perishable. With the *James W. Wadsworth*, Doty aimed to disinfect a ship and its passengers in a few hours. The crew and cabin passengers would disembark onto the steamer so that their ship could be washed with water and fumigated with sulfur gas. On the steamer, the passengers showered, and their belongings were steam-sterilized in vacuum-sealed chambers.[69]

In July 1896, when the *James W. Wadsworth* was ready for use, Doty asked Alice to photograph it for his annual report. Among her early quarantine photographs is a lovely portrait of Doty and his nine-year-old son on deck (Figure 5.25). Her primary task, however, was to depict the disinfection equipment inside the ship's cramped, dark quarters. Assisted by Violet who held the flash, she used the 4-by-5 camera and copyrighted eight of the photographs.[70] Like Alice, Violet was fascinated with machinery, and as the daughter of a military man, was impressed by the role of quarantine in national preparedness. She wrote two articles about the "floating disinfecting plant," one for *Harper's Weekly* and the other for *Appleton's Popular Science Monthly*.[71] Both were illustrated with Alice's photographs, but only *Harper's* gave Alice a byline, "From Photographs by E. A. Austin [sic]," and acknowledged Violet's text only with her initials, "M.E.W."

Alice continued to photograph for Doty, and an 1897 letter clarifies their professional relationship: "Dear Miss Austin [sic]. / Unfortunately the workmen have not finished the new tank & consequently it cannot be photographed to day. . . . The set which you have just sent are very satisfactory & a check will be sent to you."[72] Alice's first and only client, Doty apparently sent payments to Uncle Oswald at his Manhattan office.[73] On one occasion, however, when Alice was out of town, a check was delivered to the Austen house, which took Mamma by surprise:

> A messenger came from the Boarding Station with a handful of papers for you, a check
> from Doctor Doty for 20 dollars, a duplicate unfilled check, and also your bill for the

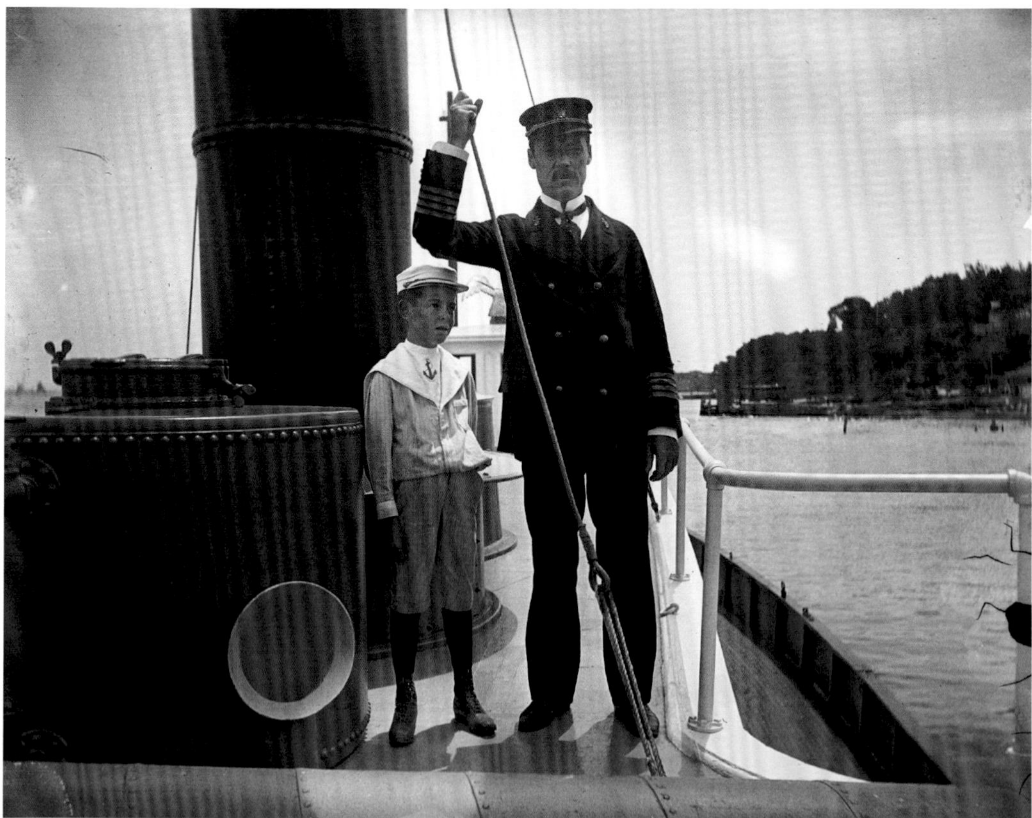

Figure 5.25   Health Officer of New York Dr. Alvah Doty and his son stand on the deck of a steamboat that was converted into a disinfecting station.

> Photographs, they were pinned together with a common pin, no envelope or address, decidedly Doty is a boor in small things. . . . I spoke to the Captain [Uncle Oswald] about it, he said that would be all right, but to let you know about it.[74]

Earning money, it appears, had no place at Clear Comfort, even for work done by Alice.

Alice continued to photograph for Doty on and off until 1910 when he left his position.[75] His most ambitious presentation was an exhibit for the 1901 Pan-American Exposition, a World's Fair in Buffalo. The exhibit was innovative in presentation as well as content, combining photographs, charts, plans, and three-dimensional models.[76] Alice visited Hoffman and Swinburne Islands in February, March, and April 1901 to photograph for the exhibit. She took approximately ninety photographs using her 4-by-5 camera for indoor work and a new 8-by-10 field camera for outdoor architectural work. The presence of a woman carrying a camera in one photograph suggests that Violet accompanied her.[77] Alice copyrighted forty-five of these images,

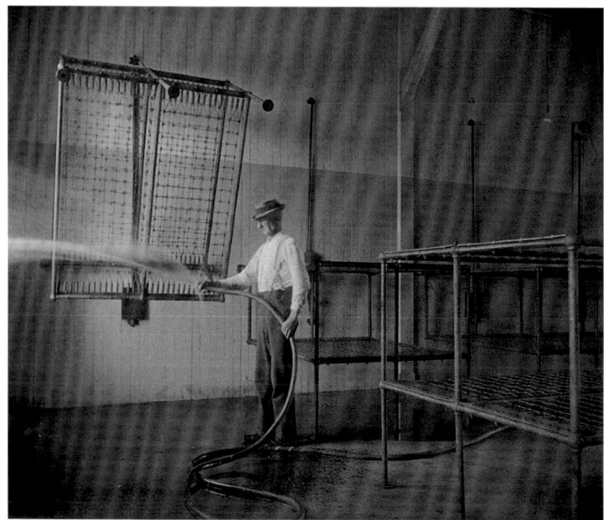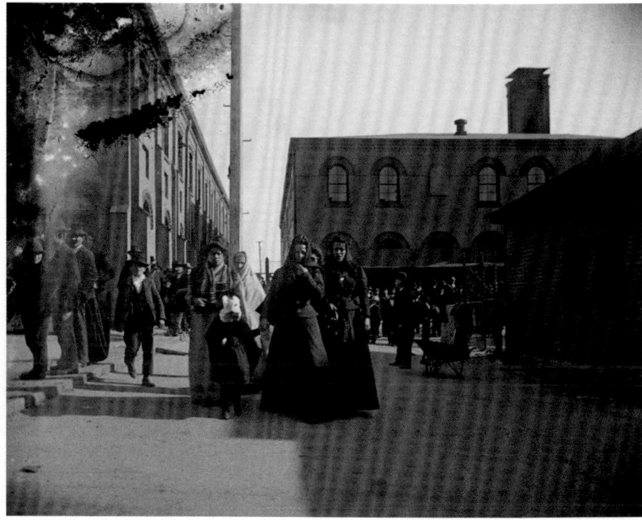

Figures 5.26 and 5.27   For Doty's exhibit at the Pan-American Exposition in Buffalo, Alice documented the new quarantine facilities on Hoffman and Swinburne Islands.

most depicting the dormitories on Hoffman Island (Figure 5.26). Putting herself in harm's way, she photographed immigrants arriving for observation at Hoffman Island from a smallpox ship (Figure 5.27).[78]

Installed in the Manufactures and Liberal Arts Building at the Pan-American Exposition, Doty's exhibit received a gold medal, and the national magazine *Collier's Illustrated Weekly* ran a two-page spread on "How a Quarantine Station is Conducted."[79] Written by Doty, the article included two decorative photomontages with the photographer uncredited. Alice attended the Exposition and photographed the fairgrounds extensively, as she had in Chicago.[80] At night the Fair buildings were lit up with electric light bulbs, a photographer's delight (Figure 5.28). Alice mounted forty masterful prints of the Buffalo World's Fair but did not copyright them. By 1901, her ambition to claim authorship and seek an audience had diminished.

Alice's photographs were missing from another World's Fair, the Paris Exposition Universelle of 1900, which featured an exhibit of "American Women Photographers."[81] Its thirty-one exhibitors were chosen by Frances Benjamin Johnston, who solicited photographs from women she knew or whom editors of photography journals and club leaders had recommended. At the height of her powers, Alice was not part of this network.[82]

Two years older than Alice, Johnston grew up in Washington, D.C., the only child of well-to-do and politically well-connected parents. After studying photography with the first official photographer of the Smithsonian Institution and painting for a year

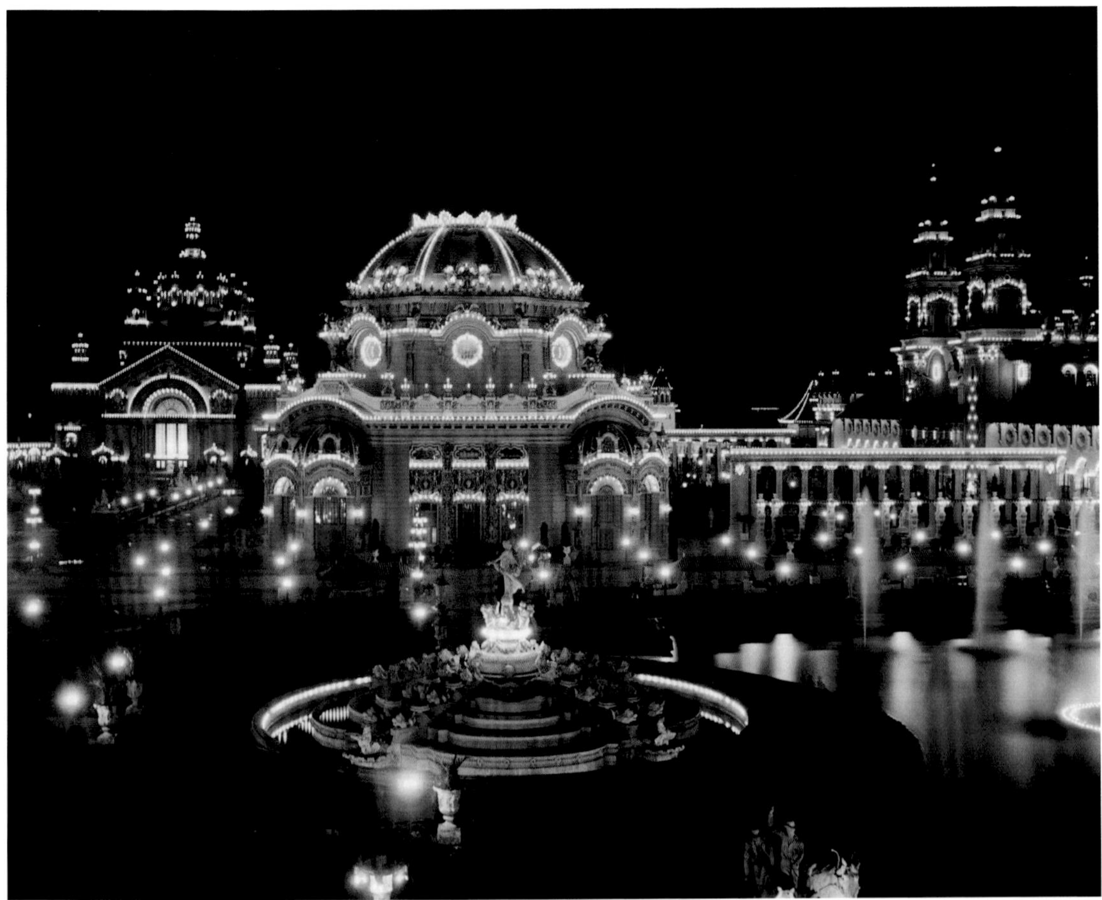

Figure 5.28   Alice photographed the Pan-American Exposition at night when the pavilions were festooned with electric lights.

in Paris, she returned home, where her parents helped her set up a portrait practice by building a spacious studio and handling her business affairs. George Eastman gave her one of his cameras, and she became an agent for the Eastman Kodak Company. She wrote about photography for national magazines and pioneered the field of photojournalism by taking on field assignments. She successfully bridged commercial and artistic circles by exhibiting in prestigious salons worldwide. With articles like "What a Woman Can Do with the Camera," published in *Ladies' Home Journal* in 1897, Johnson received a steady flow of letters from women seeking her counsel. She set a high bar for aspiring photographers:

> The woman who makes photography profitable must have, as to personal qualities, good common sense, unlimited patience to carry her through endless failures, equally

unlimited tact, good taste, a quick eye, a talent for detail, and a genius for hard work. In addition, she needs training, experience, some capital and a field to exploit.[83]

Both skilled and adventuresome photographers, Johnston and Alice had much in common, including a rebellious streak and a love for women.[84] Alice would have enjoyed Johnston's 1896 self-portrait, titled "The New Woman," in which she leans on an upraised knee, holding a cigarette in one hand and a beer stein in the other. In another self-portrait, she wears men's clothes and sports a mustache while holding a high wheel bicycle.[85] But Alice lacked Johnston's support and training, and most important, her drive to forge a career and make an impact on the burgeoning world of photography. Alice kept aloof from the clubs, which in the 1890s were increasingly open to women and where invigorating debates on the means and ends of photography raged, and she retained a Victorian woman's disdain for business.[86] As early as 1888, her Fishkill cousins had urged her to open a studio: "I was telling [photographer John C. Browne] of your small accommodations and he said tell Miss Austen she ought to make her work pay for a studio, that her photographs would pay well and satisfy any customer."[87] The suggestion went unheeded.[88] In 1897, Adolph Wittemann wrote Alice asking her to represent his firm for the winter season in Florida: "Would you possibly consider a trip to St. Augustine, Florida, to handle my Florida books for the winter season on consignment?"[89] She rejected his offer.

Above all, Alice's isolation was geographical. Although Manhattan was only a short ferry ride away and was the center of international ferment in photography, Alice's horizons were defined by Staten Island high society, with its ancestral pride and entrenched prejudices. She infrequently reached beyond family and friends, and standing behind her most enterprising project were Staten Islanders, like Violet Ward, Adolph Wittemann, and Dr. Doty, whom she trusted. She was passionately interested in observing and photographing but not in joining a larger world.

6   LIFE WITH GERTRUDE TATE

"Don't resist my giving to you . . ."

While working on the bicycling book, Daisy Elliott, Violet Ward, and Alice formed a love triangle, fraught with joys and jealousies, as Daisy's letters reveal and the few terse notes from Violet confirm. Daisy was older and more independent than Alice and Violet: she had a career; she traveled to Europe with a companion, not a chaperone; and she had a history of love affairs with women. In 1893 when they began spending time together, Daisy was thirty-six, Violet was thirty, and Alice was twenty-seven. Daisy, it seems, lit the fire that led to several years of drama and heartache for the three of them.

Unlike the intimate but guileless letters that Alice received from her other women friends, Daisy's letters imply amorous emotions in coded prose: "[T]here is a good deal more between the lines than in them," she wrote, "read as much as you care to and you will not be mistaken."[1] Daisy's elliptical language reflects the rise of alarmist views about women's sexuality. In his influential book *Studies in the Psychology of Sex: Sexual Inversion* (1897), for example, English "sexologist" Havelock Ellis explicitly associated sex between women with threats to the social order, including feminism and criminality. Openly acknowledging love for another woman was therefore perilous.[2] But despite their cryptic nature, Daisy's letters yield the basic contours of the three women's tangled affair.

Having attracted the interest of both Violet and Alice, Daisy first chose Violet, which left Alice smarting. In a letter of July 29, 1895, written on Staten Island Bicycle Club stationery, Daisy bid farewell to Alice before leaving for a two-month European sojourn, suggesting a possible future between them:

I am sorry not to see you again before I sail. . . . Sometimes I hope we can again have good times together. As I told Violet the other day I love you and should anything happen to her, you would be the first one I should turn to; I know I have given you no reason to believe this and it is a constant regret and I hate to go away feeling that I have this between us. . . . Goodbye, Alice, Your friend, Daisy M.E.[3]

While abroad, Daisy maintained her relationships with both Violet and Alice: "My thoughts have been away over the water to-day even more than usual; perhaps your letter and one from Violet which came last night together have taken possession of me, for I certainly feel decided longings in that direction."[4]

A year later in August 1896, the three women were still enmeshed. While Daisy was house-sitting at Violet's estate and Alice was vacationing with Trude, Violet pined for Alice, writing to her three times in two weeks. In one letter, she implored, "Don't stay away too long for I shall miss you terribly."[5] By early 1897, Daisy and Violet's relationship had cooled—as perhaps Daisy had anticipated—and on Valentine's Day, Daisy professed her love for Alice:

> You know that I love you darling; there are many things I think of that I would like to do for you, yet there is so little I really can. Whenever there is anything I could do, and don't, please let me know; because there is nothing gives me more true pleasure than doing for one I love as I do you. You have brought me so much happiness at a time when I could see nothing but misery. . . . I would like you to find as much happiness— some time I believe you will darling. / Always faithfully / your / Daisy.[6]

That summer, Daisy went on an eleven-week bicycle trip through the Alps with Caroline Lawrence, a longtime friend and former lover.[7] As Daisy explained to the *New York Times,* she intended to demonstrate that such an arduous journey, previously undertaken only by men, "could be recommended to any woman physically well educated."[8] In numerous letters to Alice, she recounted tales of lost money, flat tires, rain delays, and glorious days of cycling.[9] On August 1, she wrote: "We had the loveliest ride yesterday through the Tyrol. . . we went only 32 miles, but climbed two mountains and the descent of one was so precipitous and winding that we had to walk . . . probably . . . ten miles in all, but I never had a lovelier walk."[10]

Although Daisy wrote Alice weekly, Alice wrote Daisy only twice, and each letter inspired a passionate response. In her first letter, Alice expressed misgivings about Daisy's avowals of love, which prompted protest from Daisy:

> Dear, . . . don't resist my giving to you . . . I don't offer my love and friendship to many as I have to you . . . I want yours—what I have had of it shows me that it is worth having. . . . [P]lease [do] not write any of those slighting things you have insisted upon

plunging at me now and then—they are too suspicious and cynical for utterance by anyone who has any faith in herself.[11]

In her second letter, Alice abandoned discretion and expressed her love for Daisy, albeit on a separate sheet of paper. Daisy promptly responded:

> It is nice too, to feel that the connecting thread stretches across the ocean in both directions from you to me as well as from me to you. . . . I may reassure you, and encourage you to do it again, to know that the separate sheet in your letter is already destroyed; I read it over carefully twice, and destroyed it without even keeping it over night.

When Alice reported that Violet was jealous and hurtful, Daisy comforted her: "I cannot understand it or reconcile myself to [Violet's] way of doing. . . . I have not had a single word, and of course have not written; I can do nothing more—it is the cruelest experience I have had in my life."[12]

Before Daisy returned from Europe, Alice and Violet made peace, and their relationship resumed.[13] In August when Alice was with Trude at Twilight Park in the Catskills, she wrote enthusiastically to Violet and Daisy about her daily mountain hikes. Violet wrote back, "I was delighted to hear from you and regretful that I could not enjoy all the fun of rambling with you."[14] As if in unison, Daisy wrote, "What a good time you seem to be having there. I wish I could take some of those solitary walks with you."[15] Among the guests at Twilight Park that August was Gertrude Tate.

When Alice met Gertrude, the Tate family was in mourning. In February 1897, Gertrude's father, Henry Marshall Tate, had died suddenly at age fifty-two of a heart attack.[16] Educated at Harvard, Tate was a public accountant, well-known for his investigations of political corruption. He settled his family in a townhouse in Clinton Hill, an up-and-coming Brooklyn neighborhood, and Gertrude and her older sister Carrie were regularly mentioned in the Brooklyn society pages as attendees at fashionable gatherings.[17] Tate left enough money to allow his wife and younger daughters, Gertrude and Winifred, to remain in their home and leave the city in summer. (Carrie had married in 1894.) Mrs. Tate leased a cottage at Twilight Park for many years.[18]

Two of Alice's photographs from her 1897 visit to Twilight Park show Gertrude and her family. In a group portrait of guests at the Ledge End Inn, Gertrude (front left), her mother, and eleven-year-old sister Winifred (back right) wear mourning black, and Trude sits next to Gertrude (Figure 6.1).[19] A photograph taken at Haines Falls, which Trude described as "magnif,"[20] shows Trude (fourth from left in white), Gertrude (at center in black with a feathered black hat), and perhaps Winifred (third

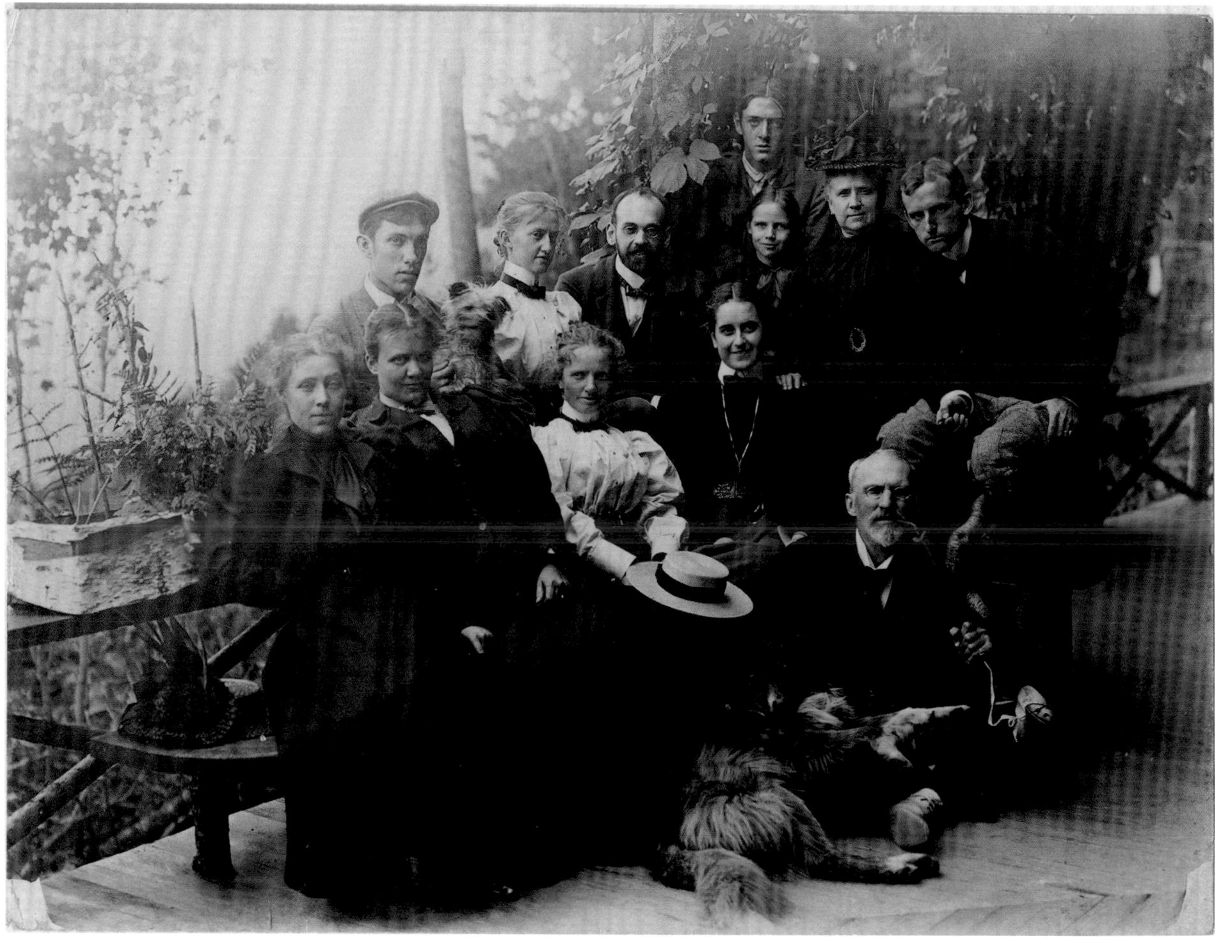

Figure 6.1   Gertrude Tate (front left) and her mother and sister (back right) appear in this group portrait of guests at Twilight Park in the Catskills, where Alice and Gertrude first met in 1897.

from right, her back to the camera) (Figure 6.2).[21] After two weeks at Twilight Park, Alice went home, but the Tates remained until Labor Day. Trude and Gertrude, whom Alice and Trude had nicknamed the "Chipmunk," were inseparable:

> What will you think, [Alice,] when I tell you that the "Chipmunk" & I have taken up Golf. . . . I know this will amuse you very much. I can now challenge you when I come home . . . We (Tatey & myself) got up a Welsh rarebit party . . . We had about twenty and it was a howling success. . . . Mrs Whitney will give a musical Friday evening and . . . I am requested to sing, I am going to take Miss Tate and . . . we expect to have a great lark.

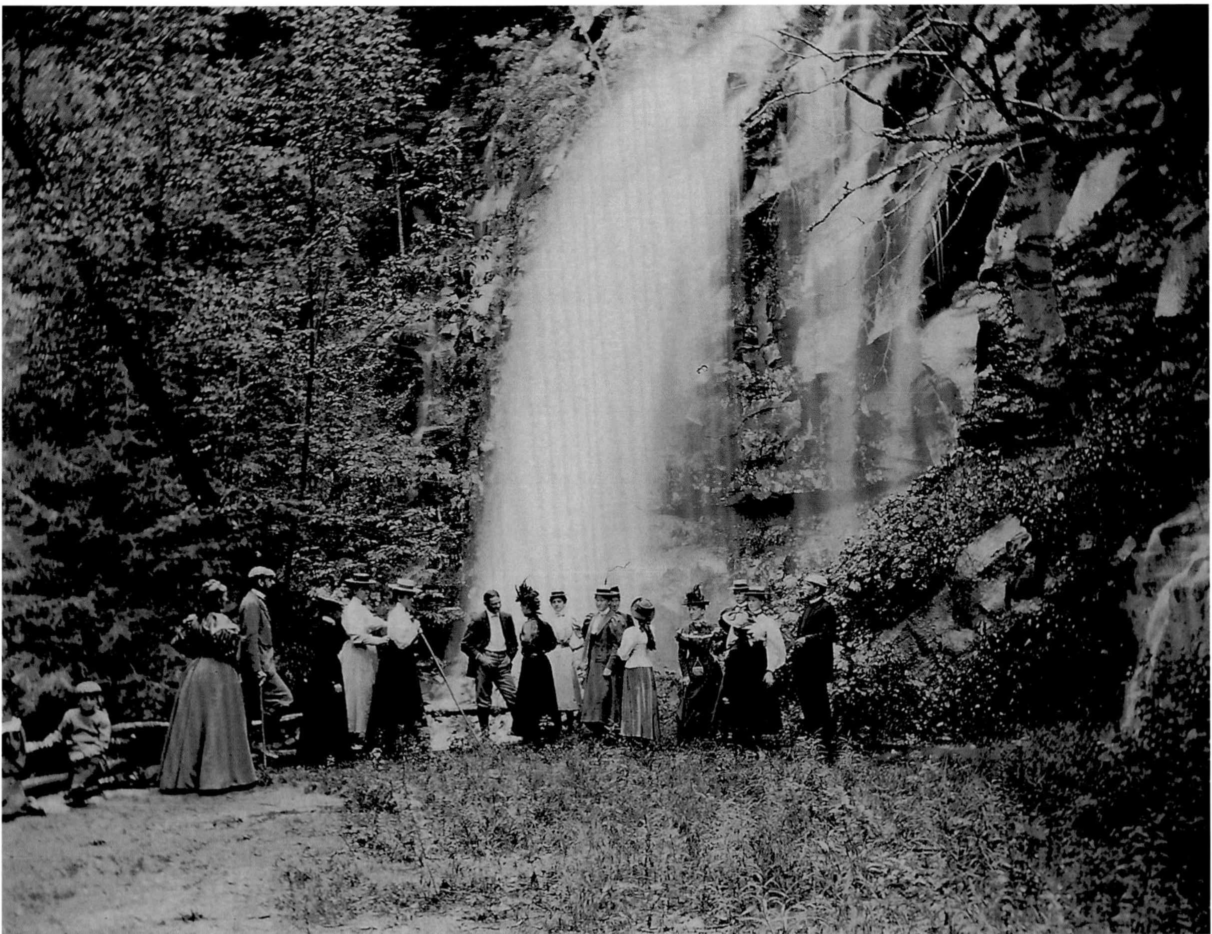

Figure 6.2   Trude (fourth from left in white) and Gertrude (center in black with a black feathered hat) were among the hikers to Haines Falls.

With Gertrude by her side, Trude wrote: "[W]e must keep track of the Chipmunk she is a great girl. She sends lots of love to you & says she misses you more than she can say."[22]

Alice reconnected with Gertrude two years later, and in the meantime, her dalliance with Violet and Daisy continued. In January 1898, Alice's mother suffered injuries in a street accident and was hospitalized in Manhattan. Alice stayed with her great aunt, Sarah Townsend, to attend to Mamma. Alice did not want her Staten Island friends to know about the accident, and the details remain a mystery.[23] But Alice reached out to Violet, who was at her home in Manhattan, and to Daisy, who worked in Manhattan, to report Mamma's injuries and alert them that she would be in the city. Violet, whose home was a block from Aunt Sarah's, sent a note to Alice inviting her to visit: "Dear Alice / Can you come around this evening I am laid up. / With love / V."[24] Daisy, who lived in Brooklyn, arranged to spend the night in Manhattan and offered to help. On January 28, 1898, she wrote: "My own Darling, Your note from the hospital just received and I am concerned indeed for you. . . . If I may call on you, let me know and I will, and if you can get in here please come. . . . Lovingly Your Daisy."[25] Alice accepted Daisy's invitation, and her visit inspired a second letter that same day:

> My darling, you don't know what a brick you are; I triply admire what I saw in you to-day—more still for me to love, and I know how to do that. You have enough now to think of, and I won't <u>allow</u> you to consider me as you showed to-day that you did; you have gotten me on my feet; now I'm the one to look after you. You have made me believe in your love, you never made it more evident than to-day—and now I am willing to be set aside till you again have time for me; I am so confident of your faithfulness that I am not afraid to wait; for I know you won't fail me, ever.[26]

As the letter shows, Daisy could not offer Alice support without seeking to secure her affections. The two letters are the last from Daisy to Alice, and the love triangle appears to have ended sometime that year.

In August 1899, Alice went to Twilight Park where the Eccleston and Tate families were vacationing and fell in love with Gertrude.[27] Alice commemorated the occasion with two small photo albums of 4-by-5 inch photographs, one for herself and one for Gertrude. Gertrude's was inscribed inside the front cover, "G.A.T / Twilight Park / Summer of 1899 / E.A.A" Three photographs taken the same day reveal Alice and Gertrude's nascent attachment.[28] Gertrude and Alice wear the Gibson Girl uniform—white shirtwaists with bowties at the neck, belts cinching the waist, and long, full skirts. In two of the photographs, Gertrude and another guest assume dance poses under an arbor as Alice and a fourth guest pose as their audience, and in a third, Alice and Gertrude lounge together under sun umbrellas on a veranda.

In all but one of the photographs taken that summer, Gertrude wore a short curly wig to cover her bald head, a side effect of typhoid fever.[29] Two remarkable photographs which appear only in Gertrude's copy of the Twilight Park album show her in profile seated in a rocking chair on the veranda with and without her wig (Figures 6.3 and 6.4). In the latter, she reveals her scalp covered with wispy hair, holding up the wig and looking at it with curiosity. The self-deprecating humor that the two women came to share was already on view.

For the next sixteen years, Gertrude and Alice continued to live with their families but reoriented their lives toward each other.

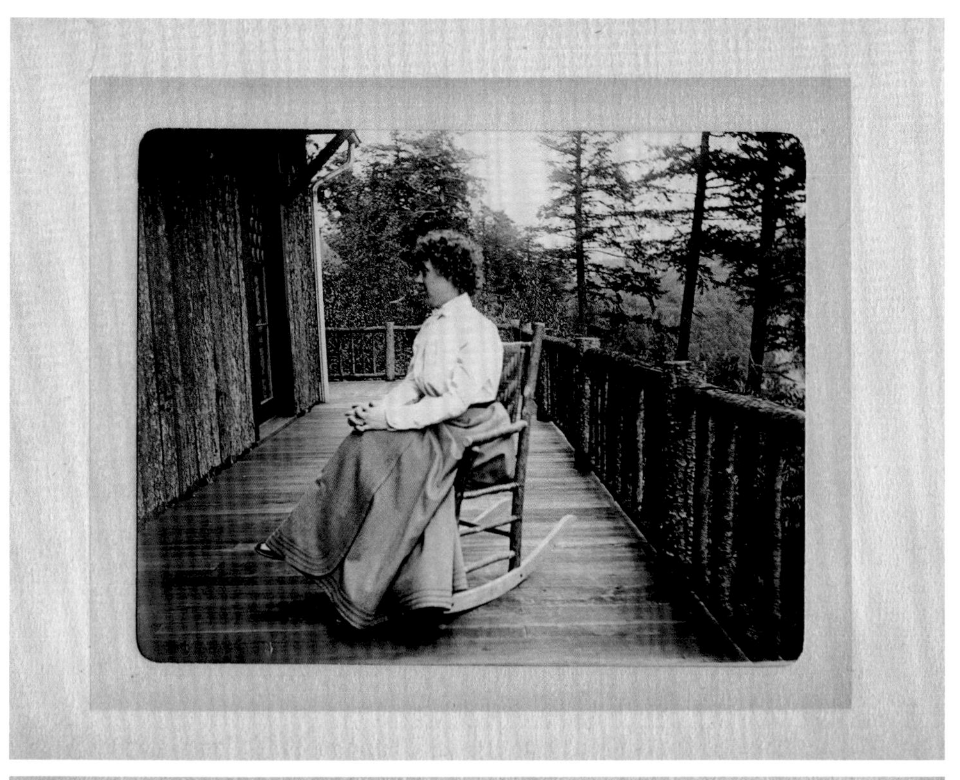

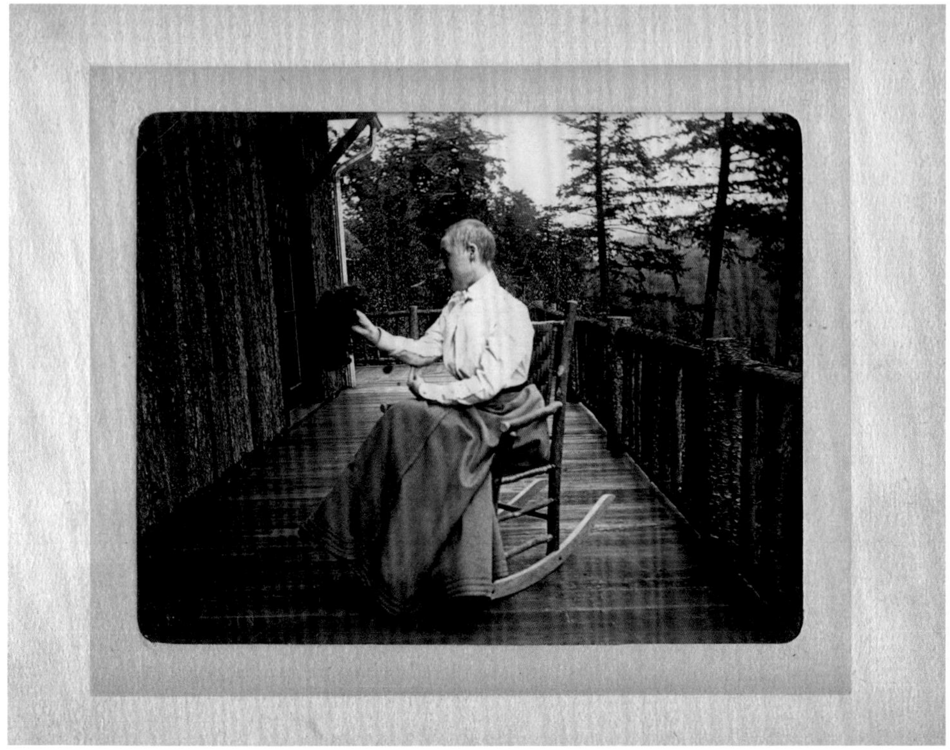

Figures 6.3 and 6.4 When Alice and Gertrude met again at Twilight Park in 1899, Gertrude had lost her hair due to illness and was wearing a short, curly wig. These humorous photographs of Gertrude suggest the trust that had already grown between them.

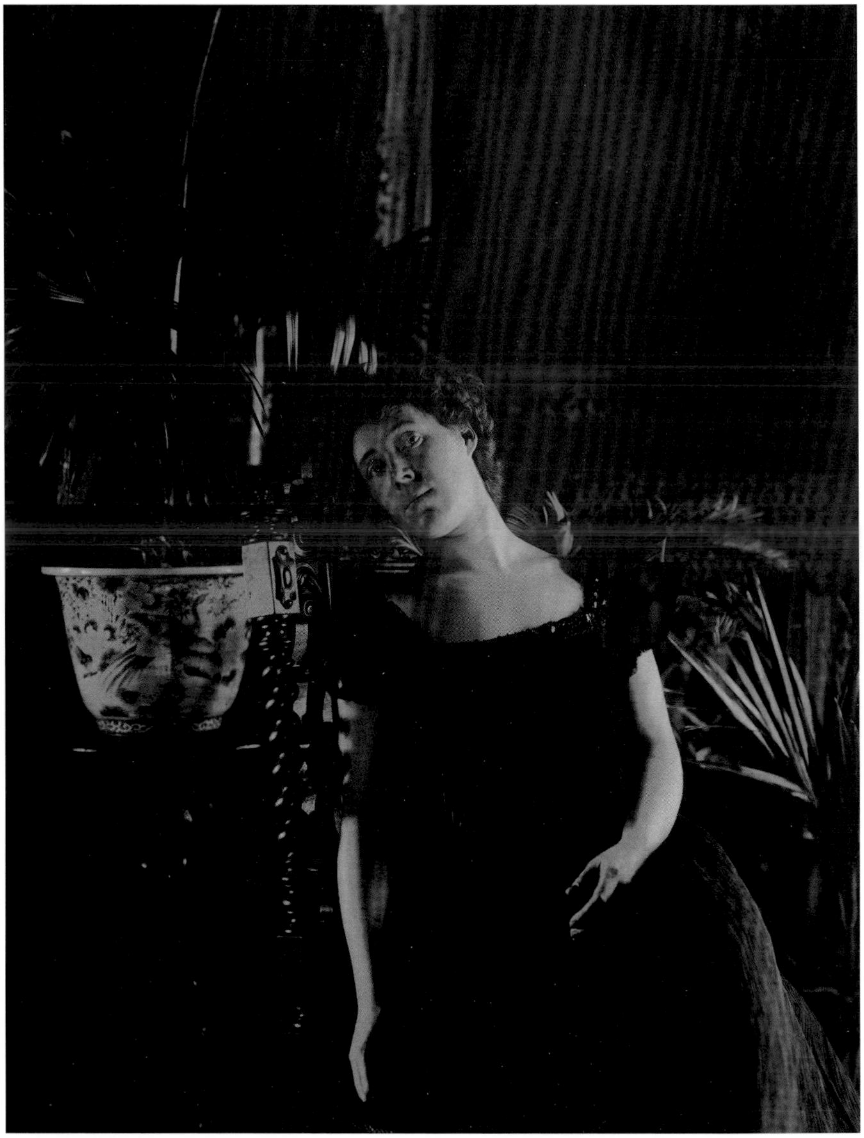

Figure 6.5   In this romantic portrait taken at Clear Comfort, Gertrude still dons a wig, her hair not yet restored.

Alice's Secure World

Alice's photographs of Gertrude at Clear Comfort reveal her pleasure in Gertrude's grace and beauty. Shortly after their 1899 Twilight Park rendezvous, Gertrude posed in the parlor for a formal, 8-by-10 inch portrait taken without flash (Figure 6.5). Still sporting her dark, curly wig, she wears a cap-sleeved, décolleté dress, and as she leans toward a porcelain jardiniere, light pours in from a window illuminating her face, neck, chest, and arms. The emotional vulnerability of photographer and sitter is palpable. In another formal portrait taken after her light brown hair had grown in, Gertrude sits in a parlor chair in the corner of the piazza wearing a ruffled dress

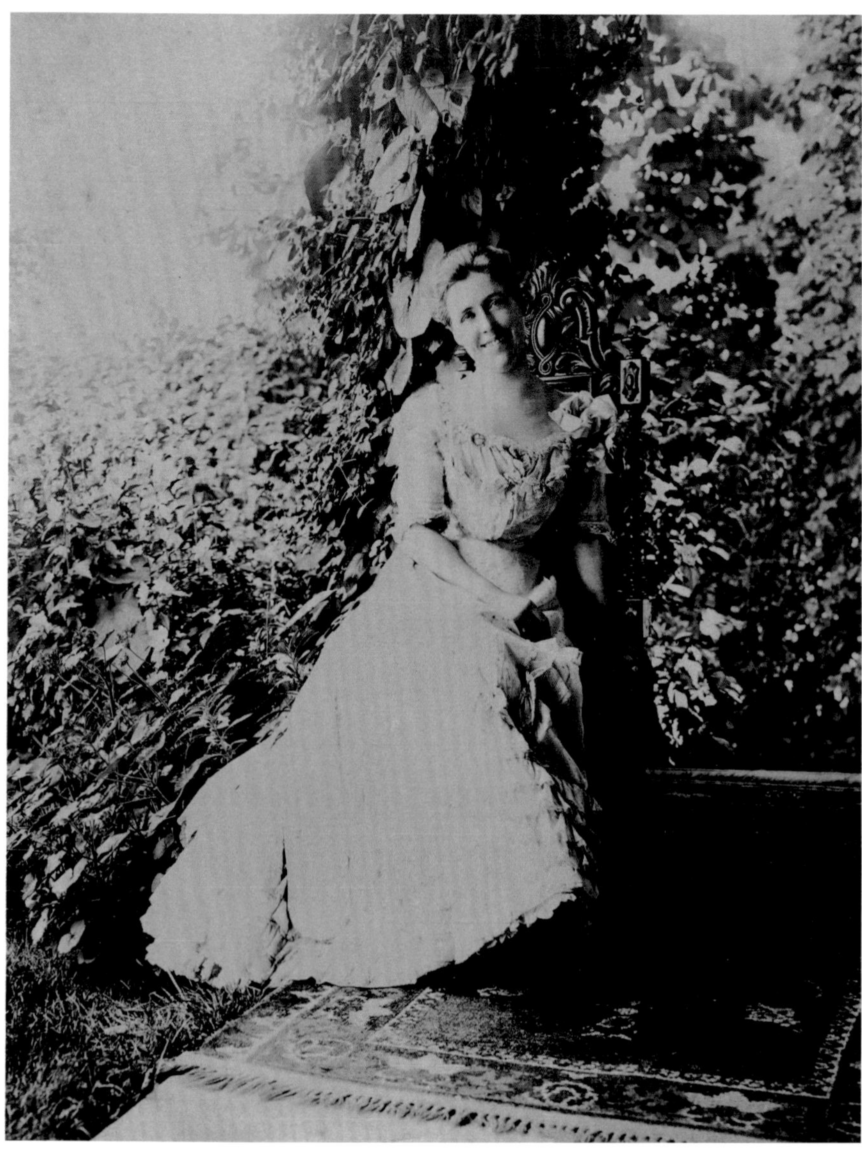

Figure 6.6   After 1900, Alice set up the portrait niche on the piazza once more to photograph Gertrude.

in a reprise of Alice's 1892 portraits of Trude and Julia Bredt (Figure 6.6). Unlike those stylized performances of the virtuous maiden and the femme fatale, Gertrude appears unaffectedly feminine, an ideal personified. Several casual portraits of Gertrude celebrate her presence in Alice's beloved home—sitting on a hammock on the piazza, bathed in sunlight, and watching ships in the harbor at the end of the terrace path (Figure 6.7).[30]

In later years, Gertrude was described by friends as the feminine partner and Alice as the masculine. Pieter Vosburgh, who knew Alice and Gertrude for fifty years, remarked, "Gertrude and Alice were lesbians. Gertrude was the female and Alice was the

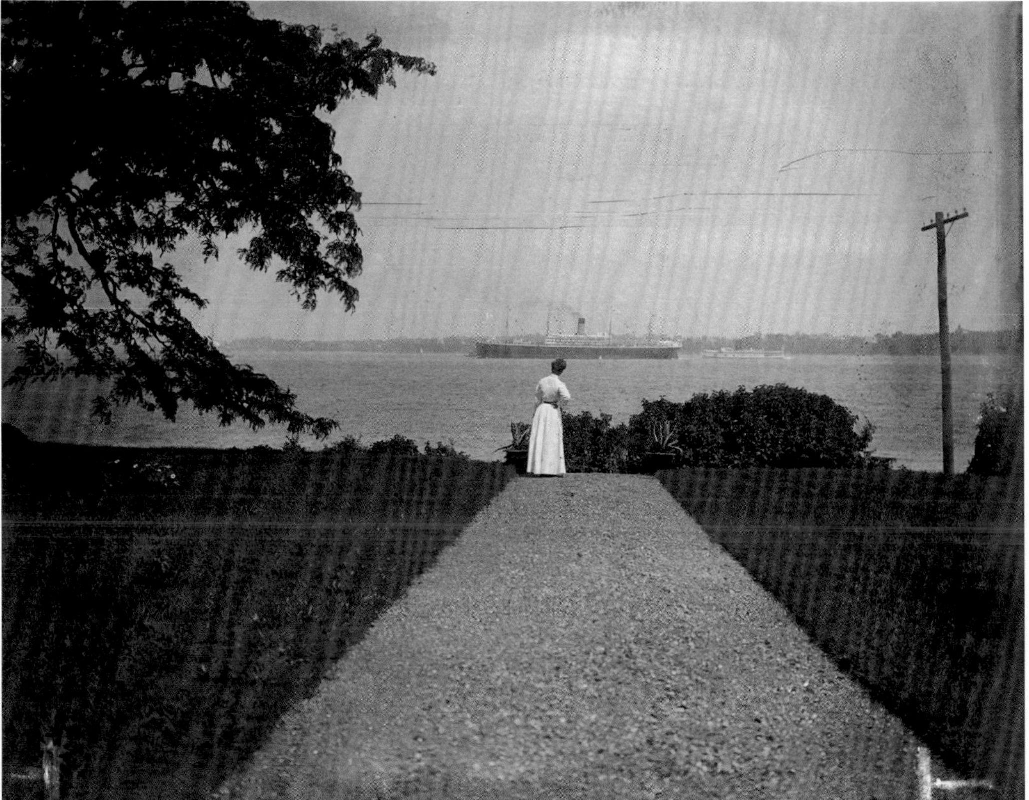

Figure 6.7   Standing at the edge of the terrace, Gertrude watches a steamship pass by Clear Comfort.

male."[31] John Morton, who knew Gertrude and Alice since his childhood, described their personal styles sympathetically without labels: "Miss Tate wore white a good deal; her clothes were often more soft in line, more dainty, than Miss Austen's. Miss Austen, while not at all mannish—far from it—wore clothes that she knew suited her and her temperament; less fussy, with definite line, not trimmed or ornamented beyond a single striking item."[32] Alice rarely photographed herself and Gertrude together, a departure from her earlier work, in which she used a shutter release or put the camera on a timer and entered the frame. A charming portrait of the couple in Gibson Girl garb—in which there is no differentiation of gender roles—was taken at "Pickard's Penny Photo" in Stapleton, a short distance from Clear Comfort (Figure 6.8).

At the start of their relationship, their five-year age difference was significant. In 1900, the year Mamma died, Alice was thirty-four and ready to embrace domestic life with Gertrude after several years of frenetic productivity and emotional turmoil. Gertrude was twenty-nine and at a crossroads. With family finances precarious, she was still expected to parlay her beauty and popularity into marriage.[33] According to Winifred, Gertrude's commitment to Alice flummoxed her friends:

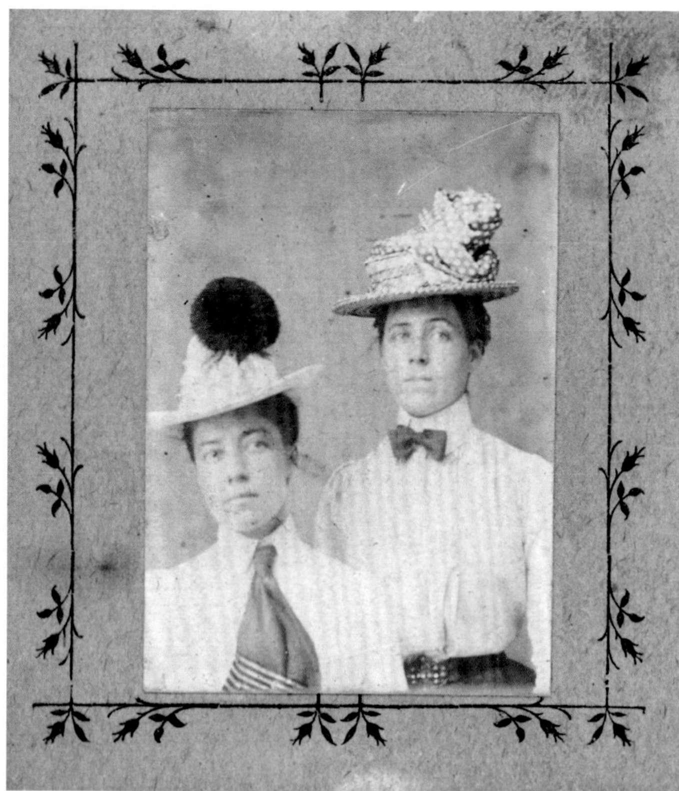

Figure 6.8 Alice rarely photographed herself with Gertrude, but they posed together for this penny photo in nearby Stapleton.

When Gertrude met [Alice] and began to spend all her time on S[taten] I[sland], she dropped her old circle of friends in Brooklyn ... who would phone and ask where Gertrude was, and say, "Is she with That Woman again? I can't understand what she sees in her—she's so homely!"[34]

Gertrude had attended, but did not graduate from Packer Collegiate Institute, a private girls' school in Brooklyn. In the wake of her father's sudden death, she studied for two years to become a kindergarten teacher at Saint Bartholomew's Church in Manhattan. Kindergarten teaching was a new field imported from Germany and dedicated to the then-innovative idea that young children learn through organized play.[35] A naturally gifted dancer, Gertrude also trained in Manhattan at the Chalif Normal School of Dancing. Known as "the dean of dance teachers," Louis H. Chalif, born in Russia, promoted dance as part of the physical culture movement and specialized in training dance instructors to teach diverse styles of dance from folk, to "aesthetic," to ballroom.[36]

Although Alice chose not to pursue a career in photography, she introduced Gertrude to Adeline Robinson, a friend and former tennis champion, to help advance Gertrude's career. Beginning in the 1890s, Adeline taught ballroom dancing to the children of prominent families in many locations on Staten Island and Manhattan, and Gertrude became her assistant for classes held in the ballrooms of Sherry's and Delmonico's, two famous Manhattan restaurants. By 1908, Gertrude was teaching her own classes for adults and children in various hotel ballrooms and private schools in Brooklyn, as well as at the Richmond County Country Club and the Staten Island Academy.[37] She played a leadership role in the New York Society of Teachers of Dancing from its founding in 1914 through the 1930s, and organized "dance tea" fundraisers that garnered press notices like this one in the *Brooklyn Daily Eagle*:

> One of the very best of the *thé dansants* of the hour took place at the Heights Casino yesterday afternoon. It was given by Miss Gertrude Tate, backed by a long array of very representative patronesses, and it proved the most distinctive of successes. Over 250 people subscribed to it, and many of the best known girls and men and older people of society took part.[38]

Like many independent women at the turn of the century, Gertrude built a career by professionalizing the skills that had been traditionally assumed by the women of well-to-do families.

According to Winifred, "Gertrude liked luxury, and Alice could give it to her."[39] While Gertrude was living in Brooklyn with her mother and sister, she and Alice created a sumptuous life together, spending summers in Europe, making excursions by automobile, and cultivating a Manhattan presence. Between 1903 and 1912, they traveled abroad for three-to-four-month vacations, skipping only two summers. Tourist hotels, restaurants, and guided tours were already in place throughout Europe in the 1860s and 1870s, as John Haggerty Austen had described in his letters home. Thirty years later, ocean liner travel was at its peak, and the tourist industry had expanded to meet the needs of the greater numbers of Americans who could afford to travel abroad. Like most tourists, Alice and Gertrude visited the urban centers and picturesque locales in England, Belgium, Holland, France, Switzerland, Germany, Austria, and Italy. In 1909 and 1912, they were more adventurous, traveling to Morocco and Scandinavia.[40]

Alice brought a 4-by-5 camera to Europe and switched from glass to film negatives, which were much lighter and allowed for more exposures. While most of her 1,200 photographs of tourist sites are predictable, the photographs of the travelers themselves offer a glimpse of the growing tourist industry and the deference paid to wealthy Americans.[41] Especially noteworthy is the couple's visit to Morocco in 1909, their only journey to a country whose citizens were neither white nor Christian.[42] Disembarking at Gibraltar, they began their travels with a four-day stay in Tangiers. There they joined a group of intrepid tourists and hired a guide—Mustapha Saidi,

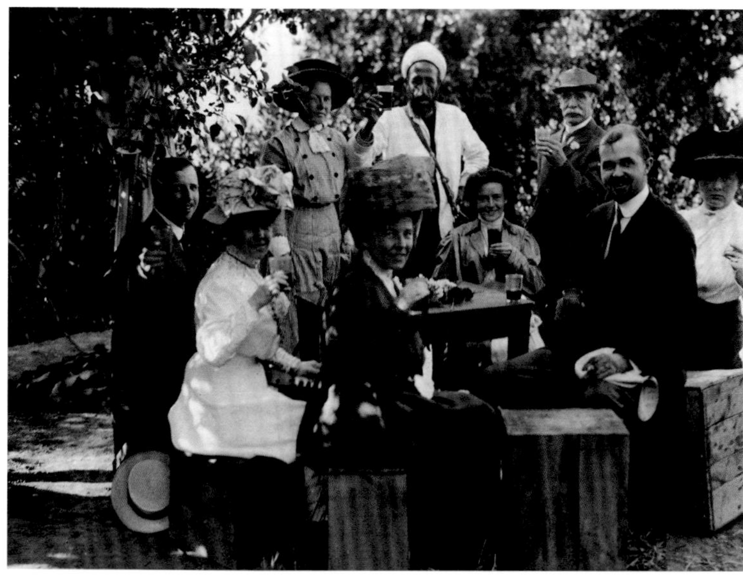

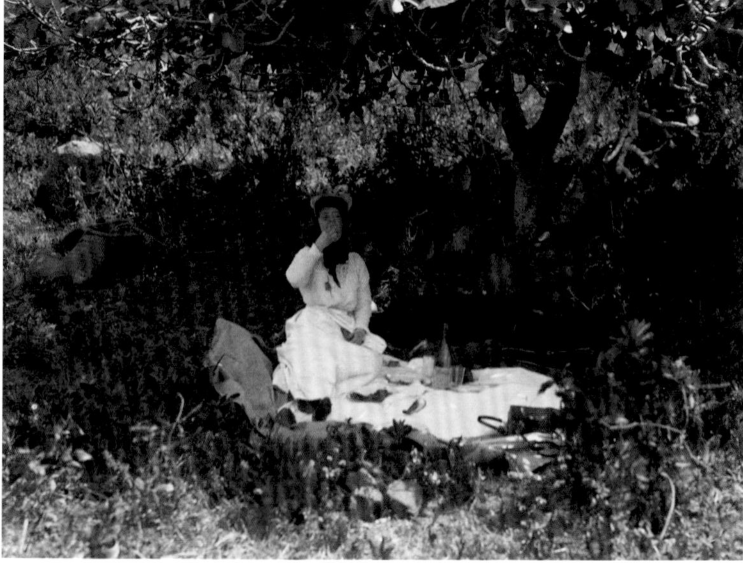

Figures 6.9 and 6.10   During a four-day stay in Tangiers in 1909, Alice and Gertrude traveled nine miles through the desert to Cape Spartel at the Straits of Gibraltar. These photographs show Gertrude (in white) in Tangiers and at Cape Spartel.

whose card Alice saved—to escort them throughout the region. Riding sidesaddle on donkeys, the group ventured nine miles into the desert and visited Bedouin villages on their way to Cape Spartel, a promontory a thousand feet above sea level at the entrance to the Strait of Gibraltar. Alice photographed the group sharing an outdoor meal: Mustapha wears a white turban (standing center rear) and Gertrude a white dress (seated, second from left) (Figure 6.9). Alice took many of the seventy-nine negatives of the Tangiers visit while seated on her donkey with her subjects at some distance. Some of the photographs are wonderfully spontaneous, like one of Gertrude at Cape Spartel gobbling up her lunch (Figure 6.10).

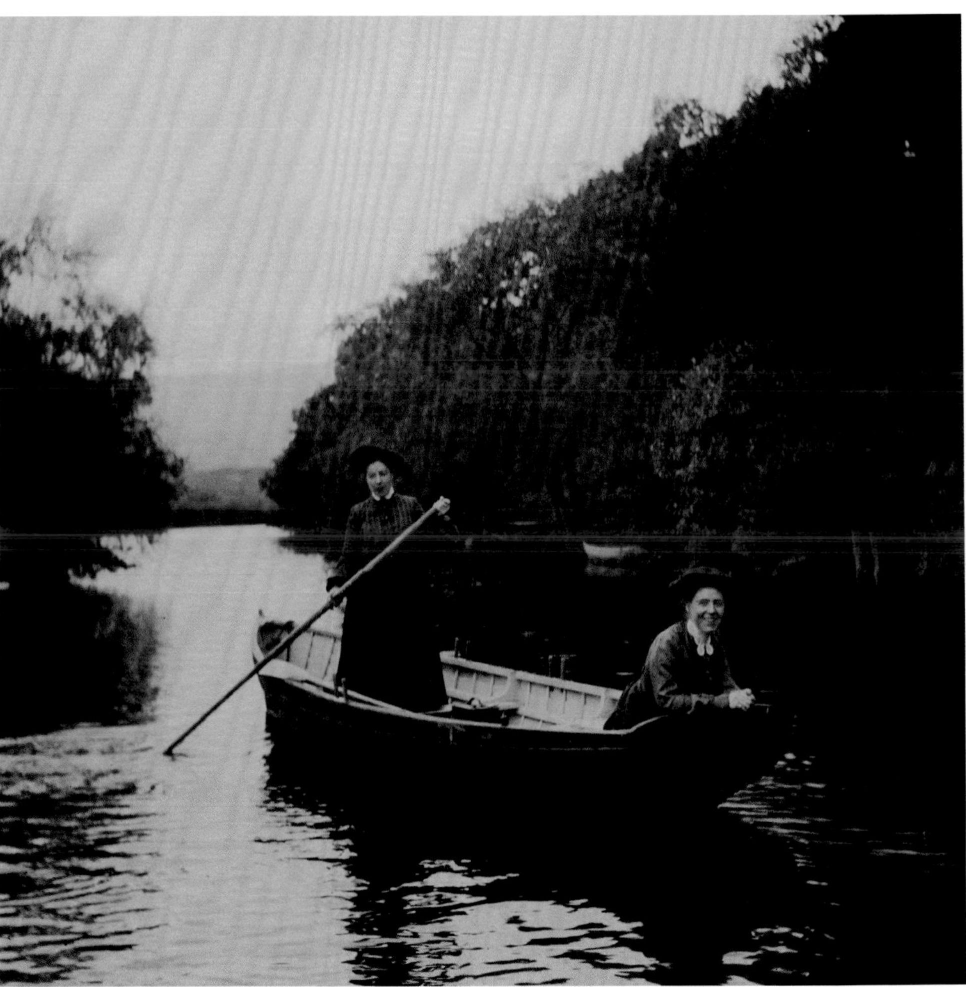

Figure 6.11   Alice's camera remained in the boat when a friend photographed Alice and Gertrude punting in the Scottish Highlands in 1903.

Many of Alice's travel photographs, such as a scene of Alice and Gertrude rowing in the Scottish Highlands, suggest that they experienced greater freedom as a lesbian couple abroad than at home (Figure 6.11). They sometimes traveled with lesbian friends, as shown in a photograph of "Miss Lawrence [Carol Lawrence, Daisy Elliott's former traveling companion], G.A.T. & Effie" on the deck of the SS *Moltke* on route to Naples (Figure 6.12). These glorious vacations were surely the highpoint of their lives together. One of Alice's last travel photographs is a self-portrait, her face reflected in an oval mirror atop a dresser in the tiny cabin that she and Gertrude shared on the SS *Cleveland* on their final transatlantic voyage in October 1912 (Figure 6.13).

At home, Alice and Gertrude walked a tightrope between their private and public lives in order to maintain appearances of respectability. They felt free to reveal their partnership among their friends in Manhattan as they had in Europe. According to

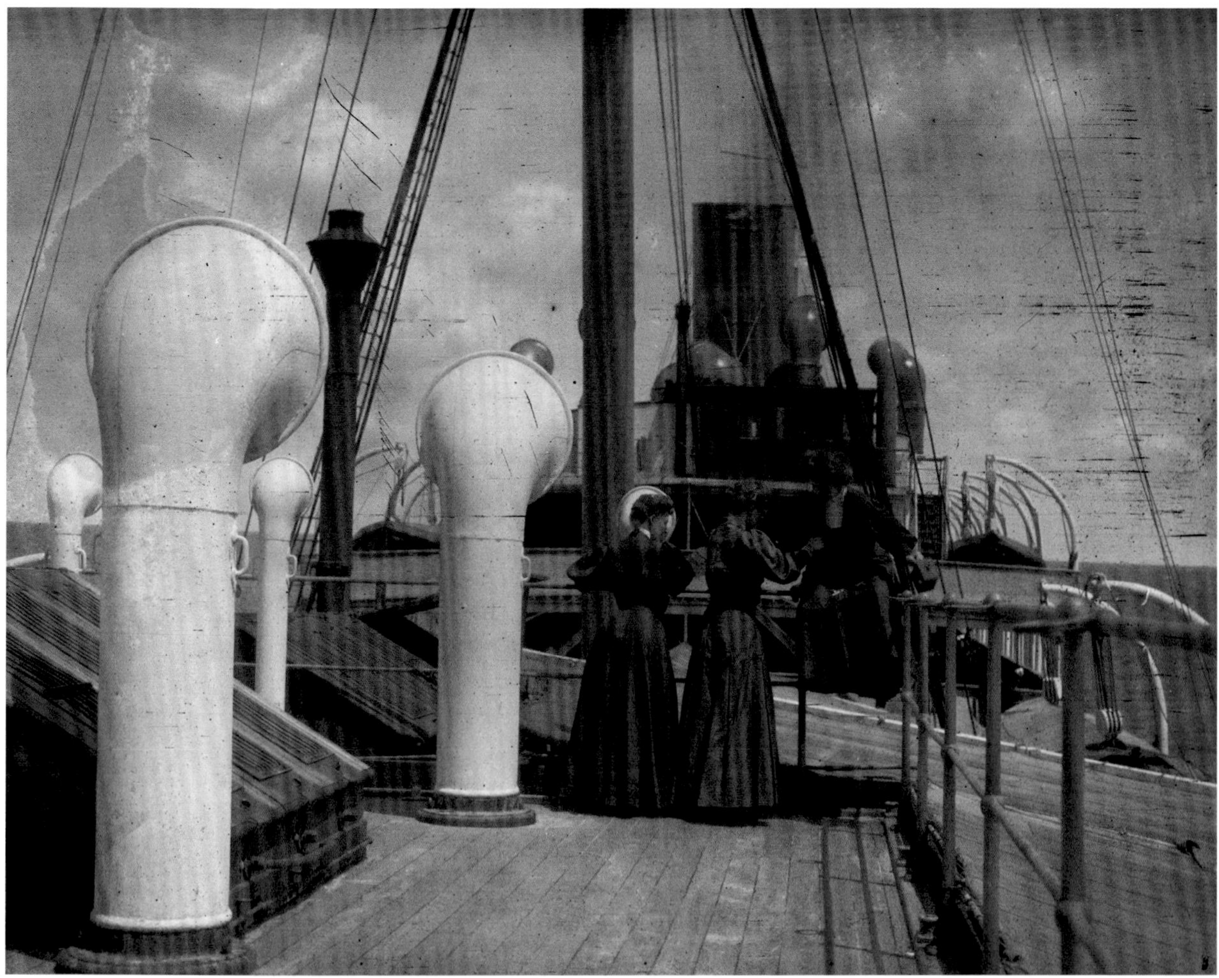

Figure 6.12   Alice and Gertrude traveled to Europe with other unmarried women. Identified aboard this ocean liner headed to Naples in 1906 were Daisy Elliott's former companion Carol Lawrence (left), Gertrude (center), and "Effie."

Winifred, they socialized there with "a small group of homosexual [and] lesbian friends ... never mixing them with the old Staten Island country club families."[43] In Manhattan and Staten Island, however, they lived within communities defined by class privilege. In 1909, Alice joined the New York *Social Register*, a publication inaugurated in the Gilded Age to distinguish people with old wealth and colonial ancestry from parvenus; she paid for the listing, which granted her entrée into New York high society.

Alice also joined the Colony Club, another marker of class status. Modeled on New York's many prestigious men's clubs, it was founded in 1903 by a coterie of wealthy women, including Anne Morgan, whose father J. P. Morgan raised the funds for its

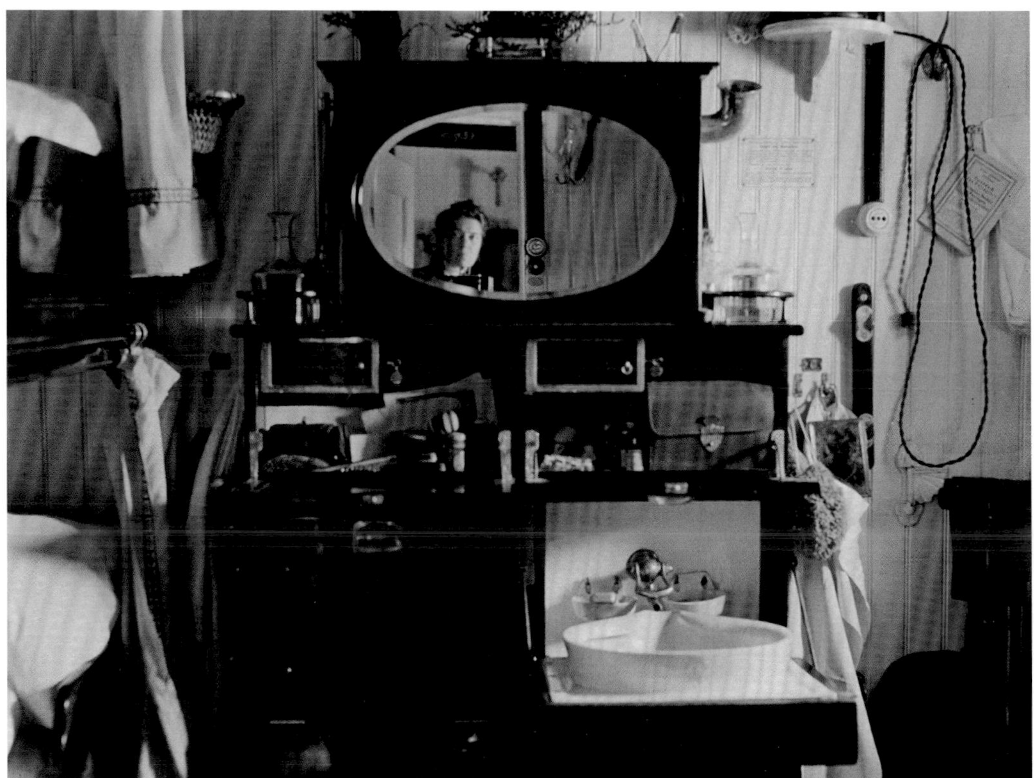

Figure 6.13 Although she did not know it was their last European journey, Alice memorialized their travels by photographing the cabin she and Gertrude shared aboard the SS *Cleveland* in 1912.

first headquarters. The building was designed by society architect Stanford White, and the interior was decorated by Elsie de Wolfe, who went on to develop a thriving career as a decorator. Anne, Elsie, and Elsie's partner Elisabeth Marbury set the tone for the club, which attracted many New Women who, like them, were accomplished and partnered with women.[44] By 1914, when Alice joined the club, it had outgrown its original building and moved to a seven-story headquarters on Park Avenue—still in use today—with two dining rooms, two ballrooms, a swimming pool, and gymnasium, as well as twenty-five guest bedrooms. Alice had a subscription to the Metropolitan Opera, and she and Gertrude likely took advantage of the guest rooms on opera days.

Alice was enamored of automobiles, which in the early 1900s were handcrafted, luxury machines that required technical know-how and promised unprecedented mobility at unprecedented speeds.[45] Alice's fascination was captured by a friend in a photograph, ca. 1908, which shows her hoisted up onto a fence rail to better take her own photograph of an automobile race (Figure 6.14). Alice purchased her first car sometime after 1910; it was manufactured by the Overland Company, which produced 5,000 cars a year, making it one of the three major American manufacturers. An expensive plaything used primarily for recreational "touring," the Overland cost more than $1,000 ($32,000 today).

Accompanying Alice and Gertrude at the race was Guy Loomis, who was their frequent traveling companion. Loomis was a millionaire and a friend of Gertrude's from their youth. He and his brother ran their father's Brooklyn lumber company until they sold it in 1916 and retired early. Known as a "society man," Loomis belonged to numerous men's clubs and owned three yachts and many luxurious automobiles. In 1904, he was severely injured and an employee was killed when he drove his car through a railroad crossing and was hit by a train.[46] This tragedy did not dampen his love of automobiles, and he drove Alice and Gertrude on numerous holidays, even

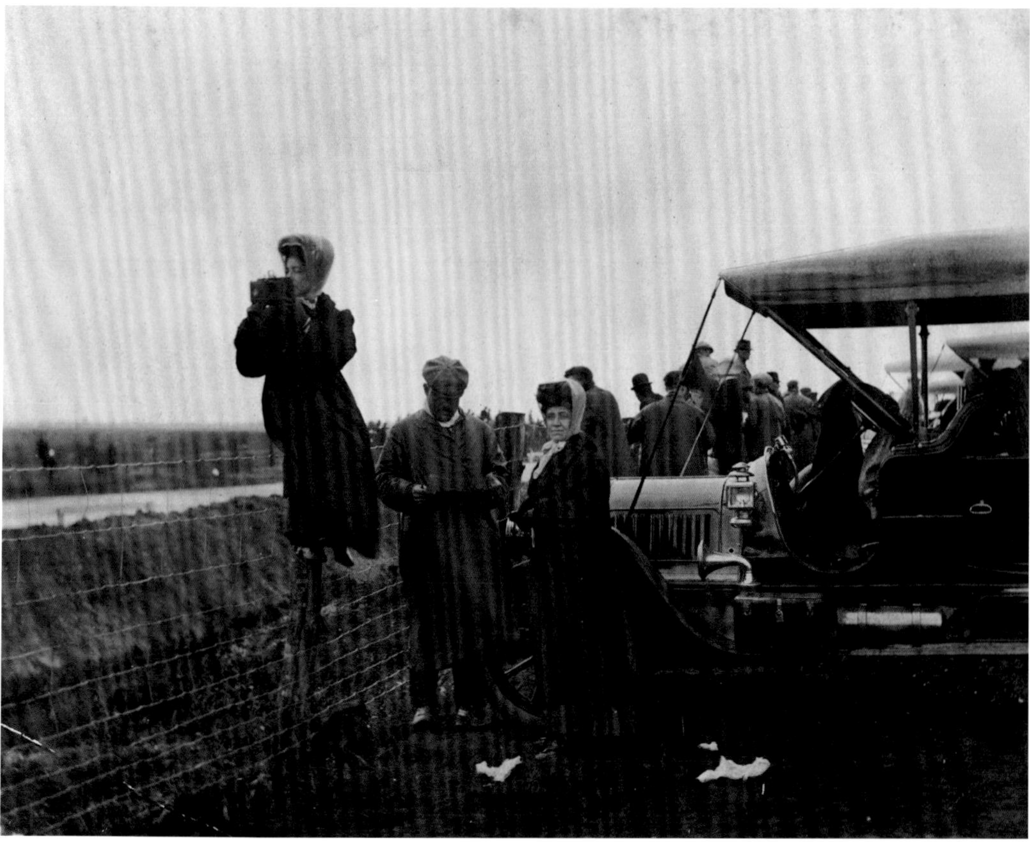

Figure 6.14   Gertrude's close friend Guy Loomis was a wealthy collector of automobiles and yachts. In this picture taken by a friend, Alice sits astride a fencepost to photograph an auto race, Guy studies what may be the racing schedule, and Gertrude faces the camera. Bundled up on a cold day, they stand beside one of Guy's European-made automobiles.

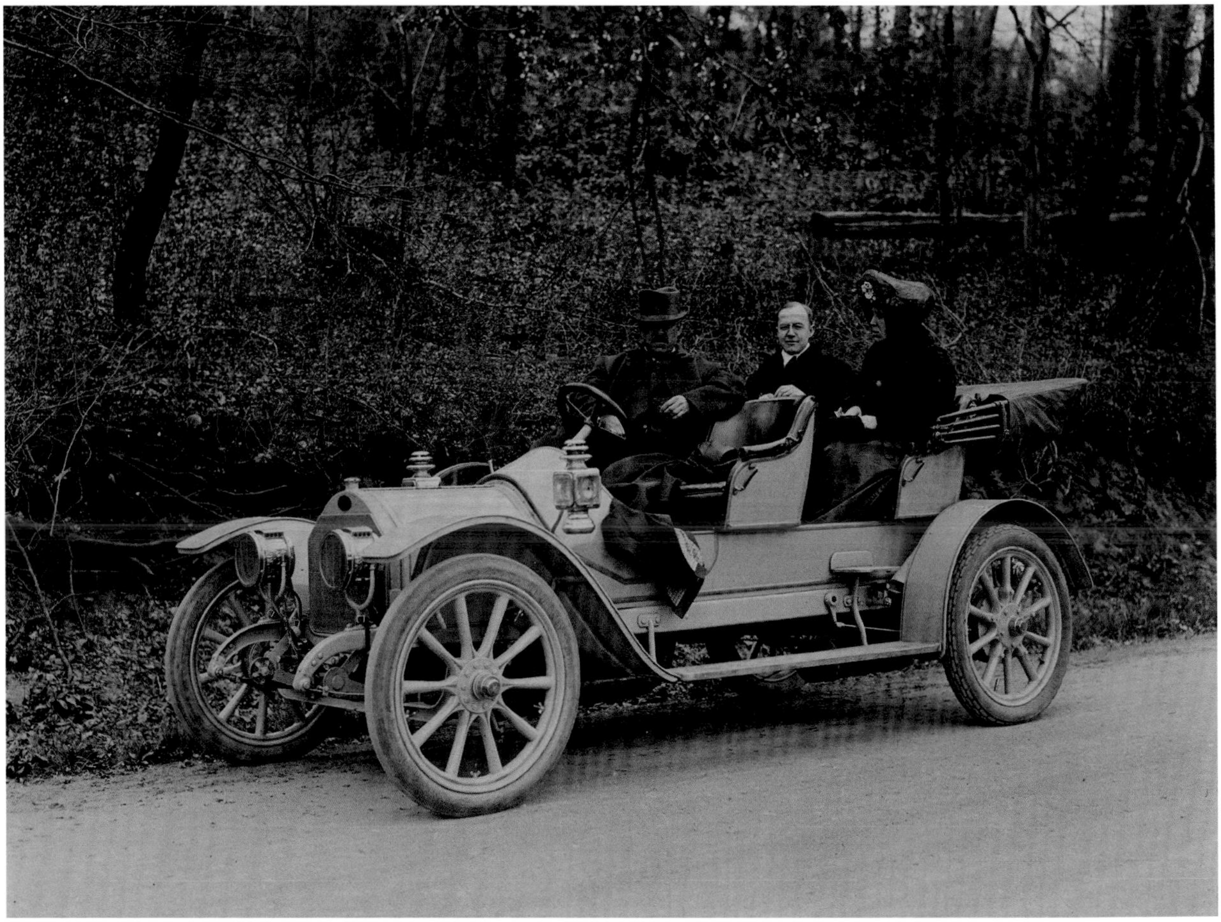

Figure 6.15   Gertrude took this photograph of Guy, Alice's cousin Henry Rogers Winthrop, and Alice in Guy's touring car on route to Long Island.

shipping a touring car to Europe to accompany them.[47] On their excursions, Alice often took more photographs on route than at their destinations. In April 1910, on the way to Centerport, Long Island, they stopped to record Loomis's elegant vehicle. Alice, Gertrude, and Alice's cousin, Henry Rogers Winthrop, took turns with the camera, while Loomis remained seated behind the wheel (Figure 6.15).

Alice brought Gertrude into the circle of Staten Island's "country club families," whom she had known all her life. In a 1904 photograph of the "lunch club" at Clear Comfort, Alice (standing at left), Gertrude (seated left), Trude (standing at center), and Julie (standing at right) gather around her grandfather's desk in the parlor (Figure 6.16). Alice also maintained her membership in the Richmond County Country Club and grew especially close to Jessie McNamee Simons, whose Tudor-style mansion overlooked the club grounds.[48] Jessie's mother was a niece of Cornelius

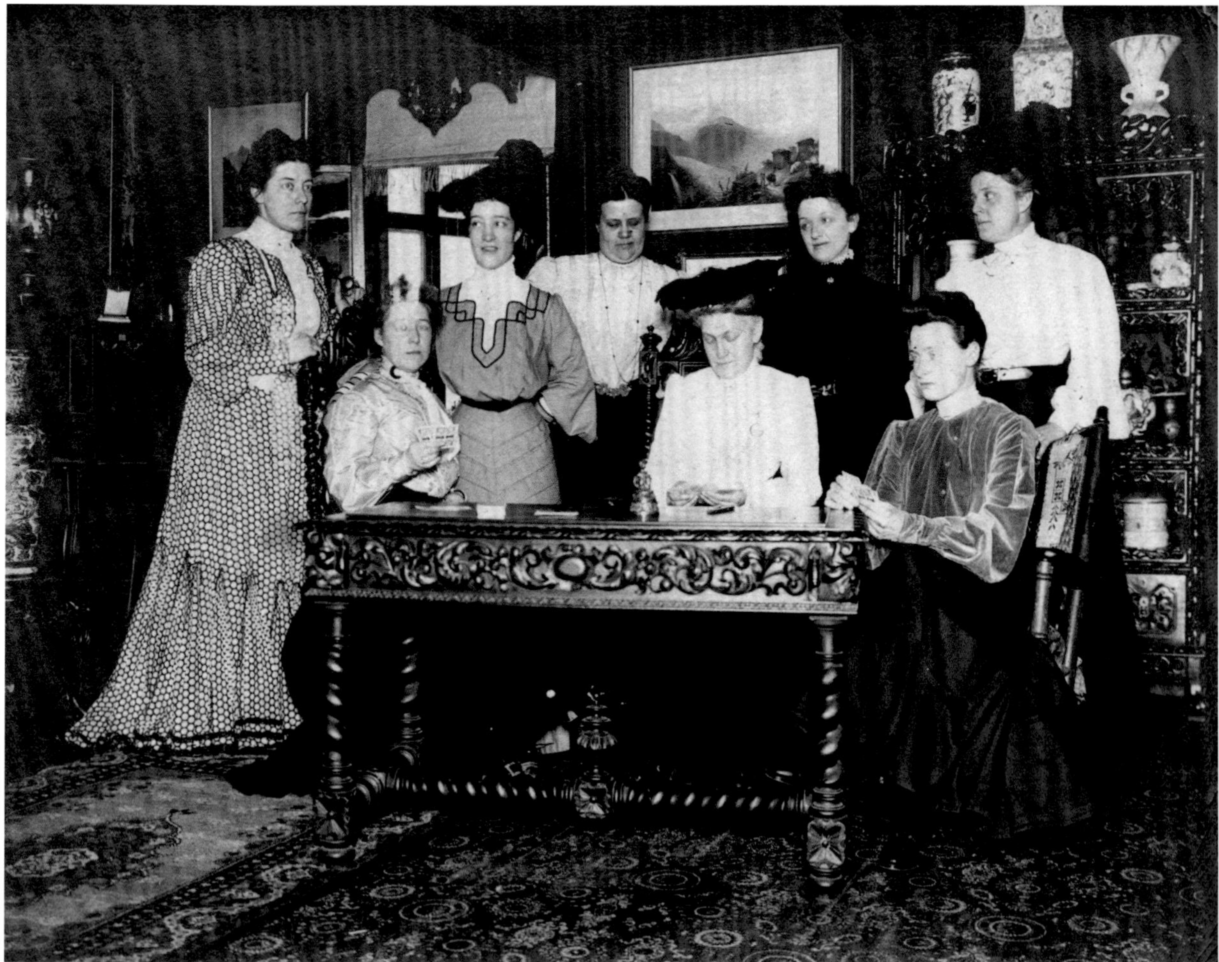

Figure 6.16   In 1904, Alice hosted a meeting of the "lunch club." Alice photographed her guests gathered around the Victorian card table in the parlor: Alice stands at left; Julie Lord stands at right; Trude Barton stands at center; and Gertrude, holding cards, sits in front of Alice.

Vanderbilt, and her father managed Vanderbilt properties on Staten Island. Although she wished to be known for her own accomplishments as a published songwriter and athlete, Jessie lived like a Vanderbilt and relished the connection.[49] In 1901, Jessie married a stockbroker, Charles Dewar Simons. In 1910, Alice photographed a lavish picnic on the Simons's farm, in which a four-horse carriage and three automobiles squired the guests to a wooded clearing where servants served lunch on white linen tablecloths spread on the ground. After the picnic, the entourage visited the Vanderbilt mausoleum at Moravian Cemetery.[50]

Gardening at Clear Comfort became increasingly important to Alice as it had been to her grandfather. According to John Morton, Jessie's nephew, Alice was "an energetic gardener who thought nothing of spading over a large flower bed in a morning in old clothes."[51] She treasured the gigantic wisteria vines, perhaps brought home by Oswald and Minn from their travels, which in spring covered much of the back of the house with their aromatic, purple blossoms. She also prized a night-blooming cereus, an exotic cactus loved by Victorian gardeners whose annual flowering often occasioned a party.[52] In April 1914, Alice hosted the first meeting of the Staten Island Garden Club at Clear Comfort and was elected its president. Once again, she was ahead of a trend, which by the 1920s was nationwide. Although garden clubs were sometimes dismissed as mere gatherings for women to exchange plant cuttings, each meeting of the Staten Island club featured a lecture by a professional writer, editor, or horticulturalist.[53]

By the end of its first year, the Garden Club had one hundred members, too large a crowd to meet in private homes. At the same time, the Staten Island Antiquarian Society was incorporated to preserve historic landmarks and promote proper appreciation of the island's history. The Garden Club and the Antiquarian Society joined ranks and with support from the local chapter of the Daughters of the American Revolution purchased the Perine House as headquarters for both organizations. The *New York Tribune* captured the spirit of the enterprise:

> It is a fitting thing that at a moment when the landmarks of Europe are being transformed into unsightly ruins, if not totally removed from view, a new society should be formed on Staten Island for the preservation of an old house around which cluster stories of those brave and noble days before our birth as a nation.[54]

Alice worked hard to save the Perine House, which was even older than the Austen House and in serious disrepair. The Garden Club raised a third of the $2,500 down payment and began meeting at the house in January 1915, immediately after its purchase. Alice organized twice-a-week teas to contribute to the house maintenance fund,[55] and rallied club members to plant an "old fashioned" garden and a vegetable garden on the grounds.[56] Gertrude was a member of the club, as were Julie Lord, Trude Barton, and Jessie Simons. In appreciation of her efforts, the Antiquarian Society voted Alice to its board of directors.

In 1917, Winifred Tate and her mother moved to an apartment building, and Gertrude, at age forty-six, moved to Clear Comfort. As Winifred explained, Gertrude and Aunt Minn, then seventy-seven, got along well:

> Alice was not much company for Minn, she was always dashing off in her car, or going sailing, or cycling. So Minn was glad to have Gertrude around for company. Gertrude liked staying at home, was not at all athletic, never learned to ride a bicycle.[57]

Indeed, Gertrude may have felt more at home on Staten Island than in Brooklyn, where she faced the opprobrium of her mother and older sister. As Winifred reported, neither her mother nor her "puritanical sister Carrie" admitted openly that Gertrude was a lesbian, "but that was undoubtedly what upset them so much."[58] Minn died in 1918, and Alice inherited Clear Comfort in accordance with her grandmother's wishes that the house not be sold if a family member wished to live there.[59]

While continuing to teach dance in Brooklyn and on Staten Island, Gertrude took responsibility for serving tea at the Perine House. Eventually she became the manager of the Box Tree Inn, the Perine House tearoom that began to serve luncheon and supper as well as afternoon tea. Tearooms, like garden clubs, were run by women of taste and means for women of taste and means. Eschewing the large meals, alcohol, and heavily decorated Victorian interiors of male-owned restaurants, tearooms provided women the opportunity to convert home cooking and decorating into small businesses.[60] With the Colonial Revival in full force, the Perine House décor—with its Windsor chairs, wide-board floors, and family heirlooms—appealed to fashionable women of leisure and attracted motorists looking for a scenic destination. An advertisement in a 1922 automobile travel guide read: "The Box Tree Inn / One of the few Revolutionary Houses Intact—Built 1668. / Now building our reputation by serving Motoring Tourists delightful things in a delightful way."[61] The Box Tree Inn was short-lived. In 1922, the Staten Island Antiquarian Society merged with the Staten Island Historical Society, putting the Perine House under different leadership who abandoned it.

When the United States entered World War I, Alice and Gertrude responded with fervent patriotism. Alice photographed warships as they passed through the harbor—with Gertrude on the lawn waving a large American flag—as well as several military parades in Manhattan. She volunteered to teach numerous classes in motor vehicle driving and drove an ambulance for the Red Cross Motor Corps. In 1918, the Army hastily built a receiving hospital with 2,500 beds in Fox Hills, not far from Clear Comfort, and Alice transported wounded soldiers arriving from Europe to the hospital. She also served in the hostess house and the canteen at Fox Hills.[62] Meanwhile. Gertrude taught classes on surgical dressings for the Red Cross on Staten Island and at the Colony Club in Manhattan.[63]

When the war ended, the two women embraced the spirit of the Roaring Twenties with investments and business enterprises, but with limited success. In 1920, Alice and two of her cousins sold a tenement building in Hell's Kitchen, which Uncle Peter had acquired as an investment.[64] Two years later, she bought a luxury apartment in a new building within walking distance of the Colony Club.[65] The purchase suggests that Alice and Gertrude were spending more time in Manhattan than before the war.

In November 1922, Alice and Gertrude partnered with Florence Richards, a fellow Garden Club member, to open the Agency Shop in St. George.[66] The *New York Herald* announced the opening:

> Society women on Staten Island, like many in Manhattan, have entered the field of business. The first venture is a novelty shop, opened Monday by Mrs. Eugene Lamb Richards, in partnership with Miss E. Alice Auten [sic] and Miss Gertrude A. Tate. . . . The shop will have for sale such novelties as radio heaters, scissors sharpeners, Christmas cards and articles suitable for gifts. The organization will also act as an agency in some lines of goods and also display models of new inventions.[67]

The gadgets and inventions reflected Alice's tastes, but the shop did not catch on; it opened for the Christmas season and soon closed.

In August 1923, when Alice and Gertrude were traveling from Saratoga to Glens Falls, they were involved in a car accident with a man who was allegedly driving drunk on the wrong side of the road. In 1925, they filed a lawsuit against the man in which Alice sought $2,000 for personal damages and $1,200 for her car, and Gertrude $10,000 for her injuries, an amount large enough to suggest substantial lost income and medical expenses.[68] The accident apparently halted Gertrude's dance classes, which were not mentioned in the newspapers again until 1928.

Through their affiliations with the country club, the garden club, and the Perine House, Alice and Gertrude were comfortably integrated into Staten Island society. They did not feel the need to hide their spouse-like behavior from friends, as an anecdote told by John Morton shows:

> [Miss Austen's] speech was to the point and brief . . . never rambled on. Miss Tate, on the other hand, did sometimes get carried away by words when she was interested in something. Miss Austen would catch a neighbor's eye and . . . with a quick grin would mutter, "She talks so much!" at the same time giving Gertrude an affectionate pat on the head as a delicate touch of understanding. Miss Tate would just laugh and carry on.[69]

In the right circumstances, Alice was comfortable addressing head-on any undercurrent of opinion that she was "mannish." In January 1917, she attended a "hen dinner" at Jessie's house.[70] "Hen dinners" were typically held by women when their husbands were occupied at all-male events. Abandoning the decorum usually expected of them, attendees dressed in costumes that allowed for raucous role-play. Among the twelve women at Jessie's were a knight in armor, a bullfighter, a Scotsman, a harem girl, and a "mammy" in blackface. In her photograph of the party (sadly out of focus), Alice

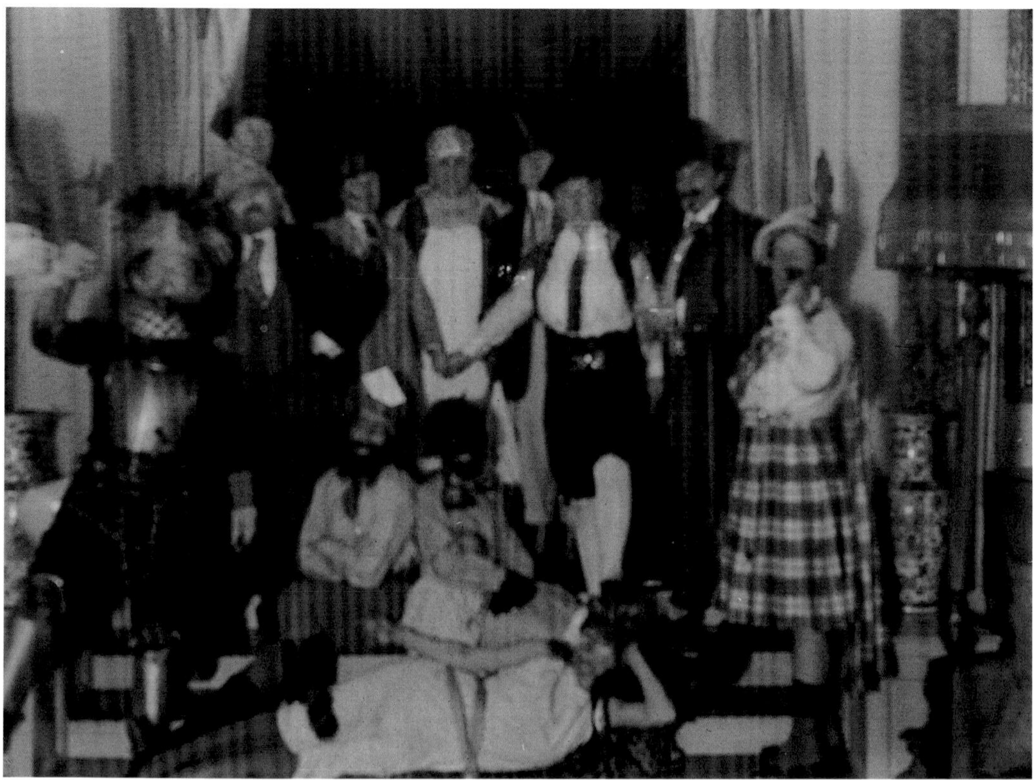

Figure 6.17   At this 1917 "hen dinner" held at Jessie Simons's house, Alice dons a fake mustache and wears men's clothes (back row, right). Like many of Alice's later negatives, it is of poor quality and was probably never printed.

stands in the back (right), sporting a mustache and goatee, a wide-brimmed hat, and a man's suit with vest and tie (Figure 6.17). Other than Alice and Gertrude, the guests were married women associated with the garden club or country club.[71]

By the 1920s, Alice and Gertrude formally presented themselves as a couple in the listings of the Social Register, the Richmond County Country Club (where Gertrude became a member in 1922), and the Colony Club (where Gertrude became a member in 1932).[72] Their age and the discretion of their peers protected them from the overt discrimination that younger and less privileged lesbians experienced.

Photography

Today Alice is remembered for her photographs and for her relationship with Gertrude, but Alice's photographs were mostly unmemorable after she met Gertrude. In 1903 when she first went to Europe, Alice switched from glass plate to 4-by-5 film negatives, a practical decision based on the exigencies of travel abroad. The film negatives came in packs of twelve—each with a paper tab at the top edge—which fit into the back of the camera. To expose a negative, Alice had only to pull the paper tab, and the negative moved into place behind the lens, allowing her to quickly take several exposures. The ease in handling encouraged experimentation. While shipboard, Alice photographed the organic forms of the churning ocean and the geometric patterns of masts, rigging, and funnels on deck.

On her way to Europe in 1909, Alice stood on the upper deck and photographed the passengers in steerage eating their supper (Figure 6.18). Unlike Alfred Stieglitz, who famously looked down on the crowd in steerage on their voyage to Europe, Alice called out to the passengers who looked up toward her camera.[73] In the 1910s and 1920s, the organic forms of nature, the geometric forms of industry, and studies of the working classes became hallmarks of modern art. For Alice, these same subjects were rooted in her earlier studies of the grounds of Clear Comfort, her love of machinery, and her "street types" project. She shared with modernists less an interest in modern art than an interest in modern life.

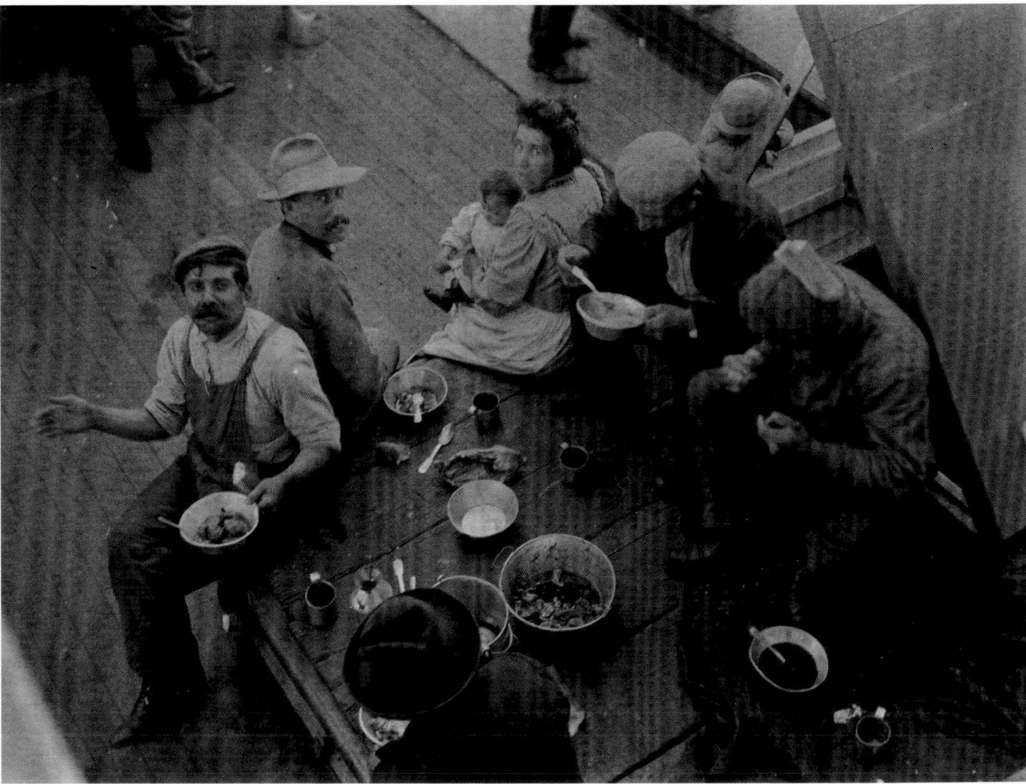

Figure 6.18   Alice used the camera freely while traveling, as in this view of steerage from the upper deck of an ocean liner, but she rarely printed her negatives.

Although film packs encouraged Alice to be more experimental, they all but put an end to her printing. Film pack negatives were difficult to process, and the packs were meant to be developed and printed commercially. When Oliver Jensen asked about her film negatives, Alice replied that "the films were too expensive," and she had "better results with the glass plates."[74] The expense was the cost of commercial printing, and the results were disappointing compared to the products of her own darkroom. The shift in Alice's practice is apparent in the way she handled the two types of negatives. When she printed her glass plates, she discarded poor ones and placed the good ones in individual sleeves, which she meticulously annotated. The film negatives remained in their packs, unedited, cursorily identified as groups, usually undated, and mostly unprinted. Of the nearly 3,000 film negatives, relatively few vintage prints exist.

Alice's reliance on film packs accompanied a change in her ambitions. In the 1880s, photographs were Alice's social currency, garnering gratitude and praise from her family and friends. In the early 1890s, photography helped her assess and reject Victorian norms of femininity and marriage. In the mid-1890s, she expanded her horizons—most notably with the "Street Types of New York" portfolio—but failed to find an audience and was left with scores of unsold prints. Once she settled into domestic life with Gertrude, the importance of photography to her social self weakened. Exposing a negative is only the first step in creating a photograph for a serious amateur, and Alice no longer wished to pursue the process of developing negatives and prints, and mounting prints on boards or in albums. Her film negatives provide valuable biographical information and insight into Alice's visual thinking, but they are not finished works.[75]

On occasion, Alice returned to glass plates and her darkroom, using the 8-by-10 inch camera that she had acquired in 1897.[76] She rephotographed the interior and grounds of Clear Comfort, a project perhaps inspired by two newspaper articles published in 1911, which were illustrated with "photographs by Alice Austen." Most likely, Alice was acquainted with the author of the syndicated column, "A Page for Misses," which offered instruction to young girls. The two articles—"Makeshift Photography" and "The Winter Garden for Girls"—present Alice's idiosyncratic views on photography and gardening in the guise of instruction. The illustrations are wonderfully eccentric. The opening photograph of "Makeshift Photography," captioned "Utilizing Furniture as a Tripod," shows one chair perched upon two others in front of an étagère filled with Asian ceramics; a 4-by-5 camera rests on the seat of the top chair. The arrangement serves as a symbolic portrait of Alice, a "figure" made up of Austen family furniture bearing a camera with an issue of *Popular Mechanics* slipped under a chair leg (Figure 6.19). In "The Winter Garden for Girls," a photograph captioned "Transforming an Old Country Estate" shows the grounds of Clear

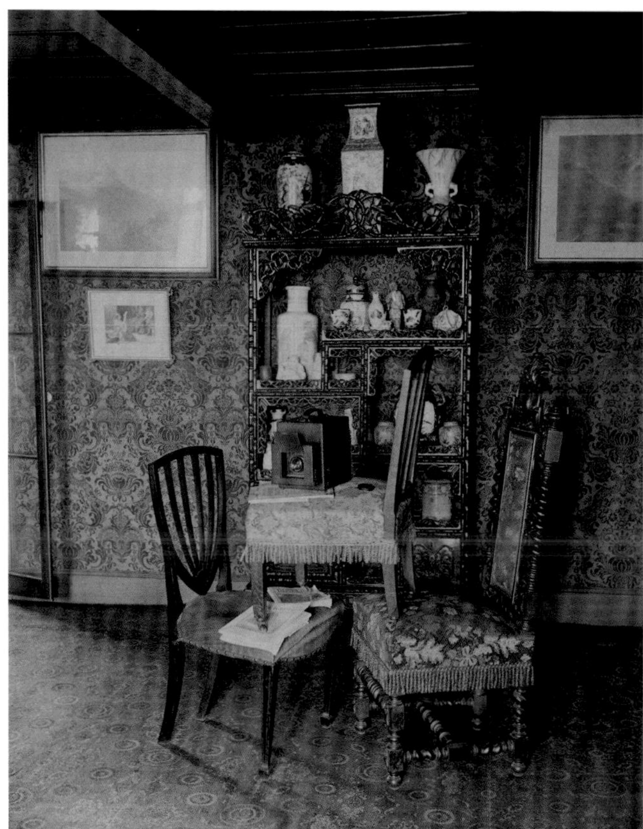

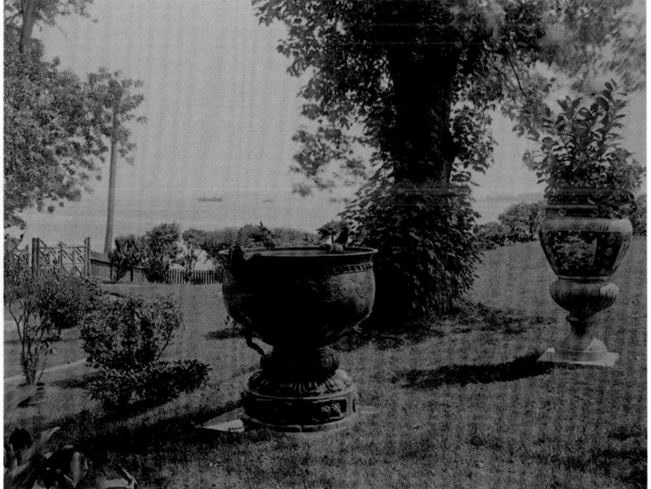

Figures 6.19 and 6.20   In 1911, these photographs of Clear Comfort were published in the syndicated advice column, "A Page for Young Misses."

Comfort dotted with vases and urns that Oswald and Minn had brought home from Asia (Figure 6.20). Alice also used 8-by-10 glass plates to pay homage to Gertrude's endeavors and perhaps for advertising purposes. She made a series of formal photographs of a dance class (Figure 6.21) and deftly documented the interior of the Box Tree Inn (Figure 6.22).

An aficionado of gadgets, Alice experimented briefly with a variety of cameras that were aimed at capturing motion and required minimal skill. In 1905 she took a roll-film camera with 1.5-by-2 inch negatives to Europe. Of the thirteen negatives on the roll, the best depicts Gertrude walking by a Parisian newsstand (Figure 6.23).

Alice placed the tiny contact prints from the roll in a photo album, but they were poorly processed and have faded.[77] Between 1929 and 1935, she used a movie camera to shoot eleven reels of 16mm film, three in color. The footage depicts the same Clear Comfort subjects that she was photographing with the still camera: ships passing in the harbor, cats playing in the yard, friends visiting the house, and blooming flowers, most notably the wisteria. Alice did not edit the film, nor is it known if she projected it.[78] Photography became a private matter for her, a treasured habit of mind and eye.

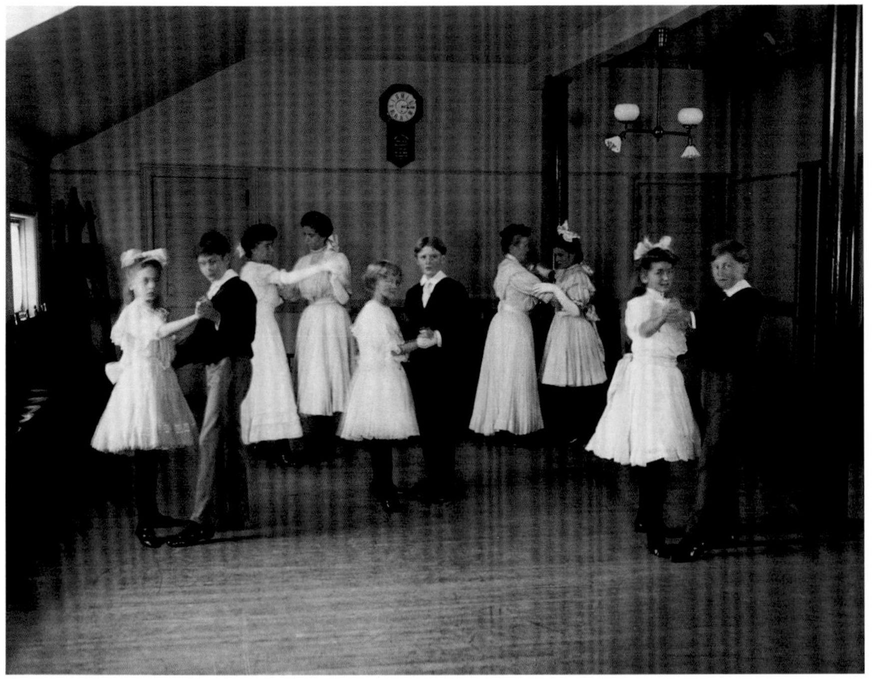

Figure 6.21   Alice often attended Gertrude's dance classes. The nine children range in age from approximately nine through fifteen. Gertrude (back right) joins in to complete the fifth couple.

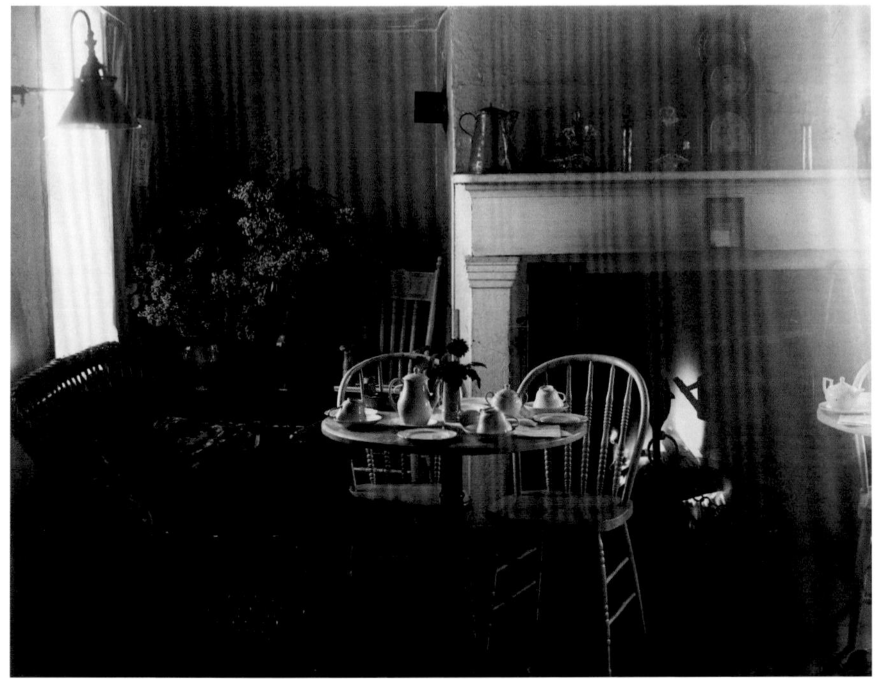

Figure 6.22   The Box Tree Inn exhibits the Americana décor popular in 1920s tearooms: antique chairs freshened up with white paint; modern white china; odd pieces of pewter and brass on the mantelpiece; and dried flowers cascading out of old ceramic jugs.

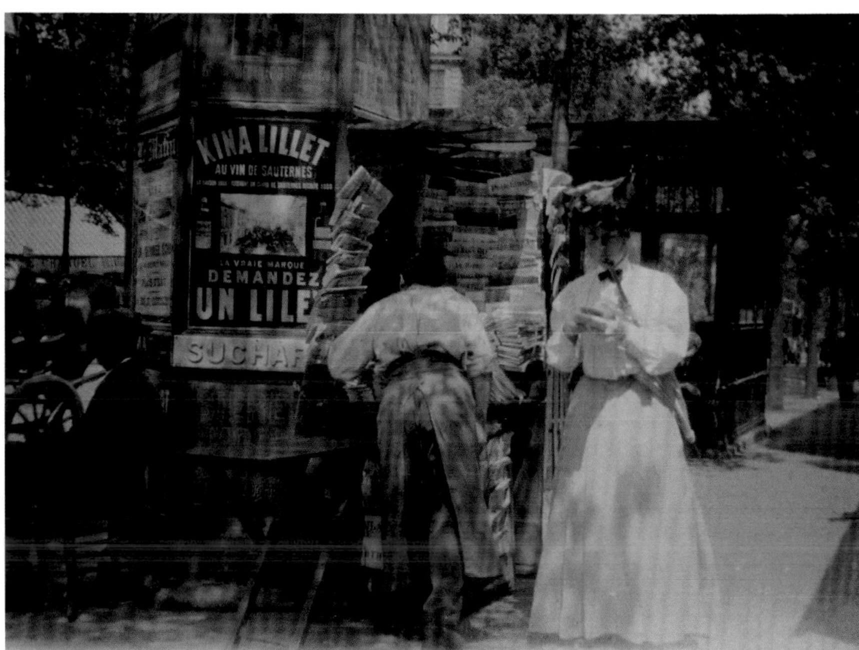

Figure 6.23   Alice captured Gertrude walking down a Parisian street with a camera that produced 1.5-by-2 inch negatives.

After the Crash

Although Gertrude contributed her small earnings to their household, the two women lived primarily on Alice's investment income. During the bullish stock market of the 1920s, Alice made the fatal mistake of entrusting her savings to a financial advisor who bought assets on margin, leaving her vulnerable in 1929 when the market crashed.[79] Like many Americans, she assumed the economy would recover quickly, took out a $10,000 mortgage on Clear Comfort, and in 1930, vacationed in Nova Scotia and Cuba.[80] In 1931, she borrowed another $10,000, and the two mortgages were combined and transferred to Banker's Trust, which extended the repayment date for three years.[81] Seeking out the counsel of realtors and lawyers, Alice failed to follow their advice. One realtor wrote, "I know just what it will mean to you to sell, pull up stakes and live somewhere else from where you have spent so many happy years, but . . . I think you should not let sentiment hold you back now."[82]

For years, Alice ignored the encroaching changes that put her and Gertrude at risk and turned down opportunities to sell Clear Comfort for large sums. In the 1920s, she was offered $100,000 from an oil company and $150,000 from a dry dock company but refused both offers.[83] By the late 1920s, the waterfront directly north of Clear Comfort was heavily industrialized. The Pouch Terminal docked as many as ten freighters at a time; the Wrigley's gum factory employed 150 workers; and a marine and salvage company, another 200. The dirt, smells, and noise were two short blocks away, and the Wrigley's factory sign was easily seen from Clear Comfort's rustic gate (Figure 6.24). During these years, Alice photographed a reunion of her oldest friends at the house, including Julie Lord (seated left) and Trude Barton (standing right). Alice is seated at right (Figure 6.25). By then, Julie and George Lord had moved from their waterfront property to New Jersey.

To make ends meet, Alice sold many of her beloved family heirlooms. The Colonial Revival of the 1920s created a collecting frenzy for Early American furnishings, and among Alice and Gertrude's close friends was J. A. Lloyd Hyde, a leading Americana dealer.[84] Hyde and his partner Arvid Knudsen were visitors to Clear Comfort—they appear in one of Alice's motion picture reels—and likely met Alice and Gertrude through queer friends in Manhattan.[85] Hyde helped Alice sell her most valued pieces, including a Duncan Phyfe sofa and a "Chippendale" chair, the latter to the Metropolitan Museum of Art.[86] In preparation for sale, Alice photographed many items, including the giant Revolutionary War chain link, which had sat atop the parlor fireplace for almost a century (Figures 1.6 and 6.26).

In 1934, when Alice could not repay her mortgage, Banker's Trust foreclosed on

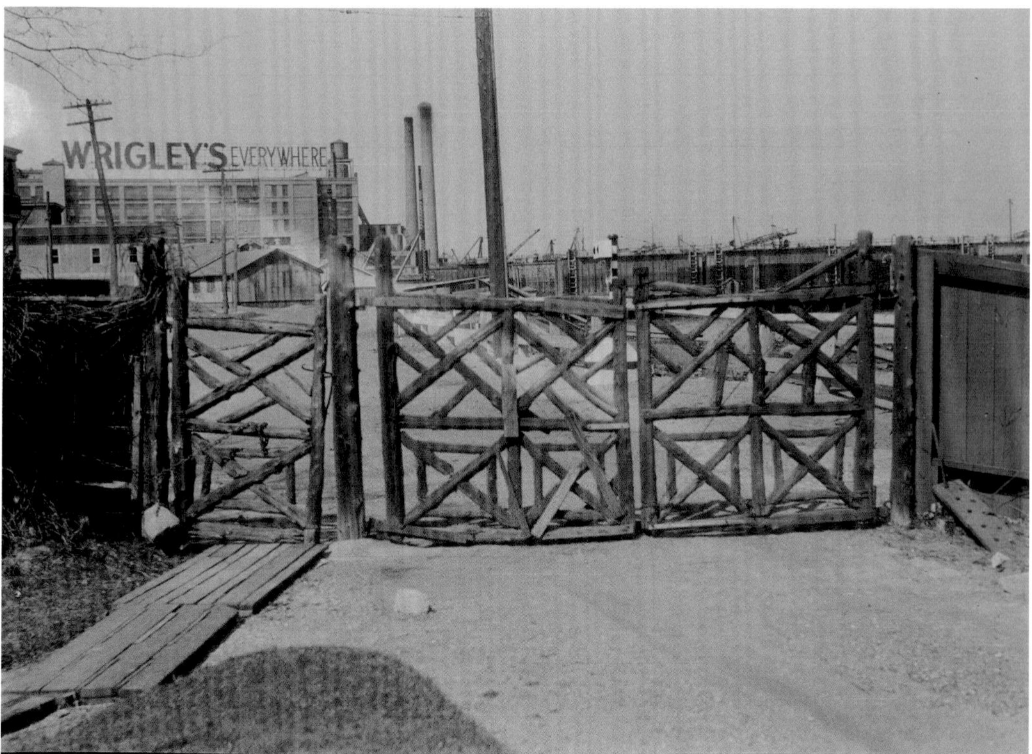

Figure 6.24   **A 1930 photograph of Clear Comfort's rustic entrance gate shows the encroachment of shipping and manufacturing that was surrounding the property.**

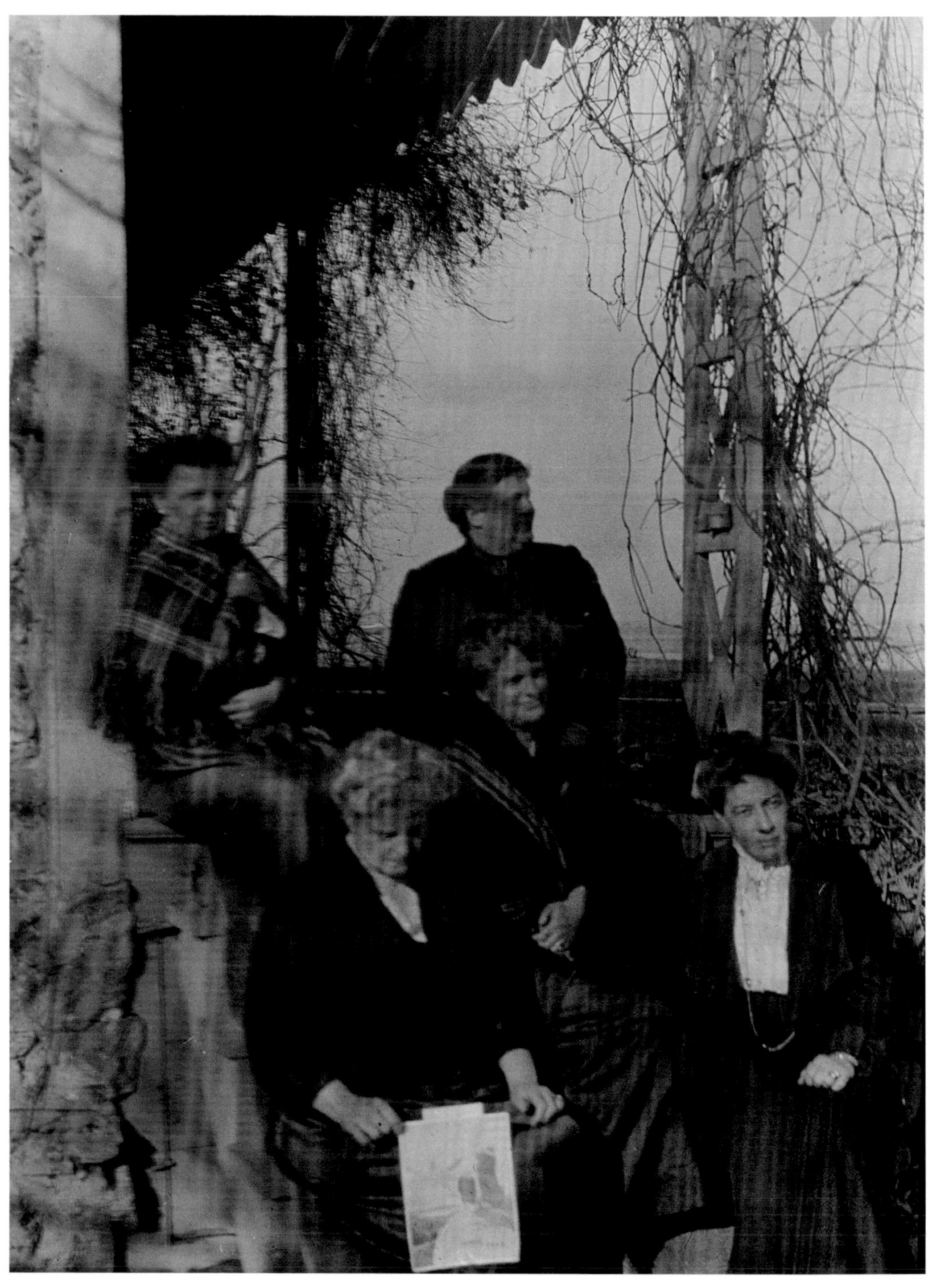

Figure 6.25   Alice and her oldest friends remained close. Probably taken by Gertrude, this photograph includes Trude Barton (back right), Alice (front right), and Julie Lord (front left).

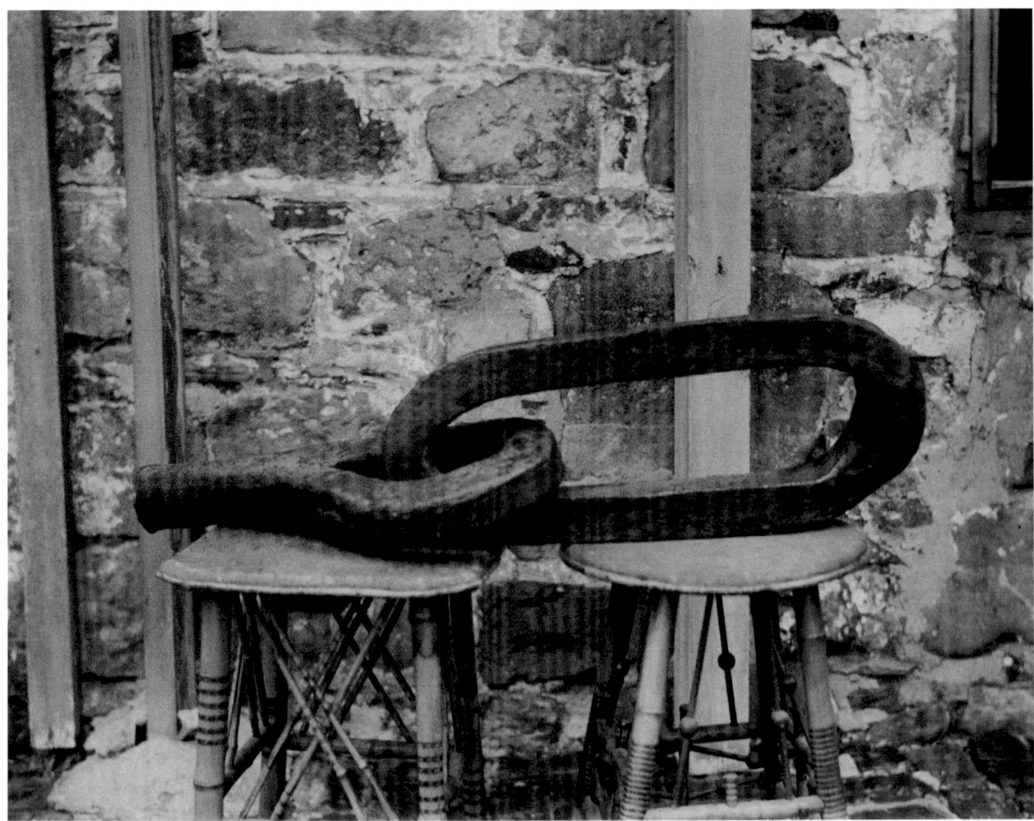

Figure 6.26   In preparation for sale, Alice placed the giant chain link on stools on the piazza to photograph it. Its current whereabouts is unknown.

the property. Several women's organizations, including the Daughters of the American Revolution, beseeched the court for an extension of time, to no avail.[87] A sympathetic bank officer, however, permitted Alice and Gertrude to remain as caretakers, provided they maintain the house and pay a token rent of ten dollars a month.[88]

Shortly after the foreclosure, in an effort to capitalize on Clear Comfort's old world charm and spectacular harbor view, Alice and Gertrude opened a tearoom, setting out tables and chairs in the garden. A postcard advertisement beckoned guests:

Watch the Ships Sail by at "Clear Comfort" [The Old Austen House]. No. 2 Hylan Blvd., Rosebank, Staten Island. Hostesses Miss E. Alice Austen and Miss Gertrude A. Tate. Tea will be served from 3 until 6 o'clock every day [including Sundays]. Luncheons . . . suppers . . . and bridge parties may be arranged for by telephone St. George 7-1229. Take any Bus at St. George to Hylan Boulevard, then walk one block toward the water.[89]

The tearoom was occasionally noted in the *New Yorker* and *Vogue*, and for several summers drew Manhattanites on a lark.[90] Gertrude did the cooking; Alice managed the house; and local teenagers waited tables and cleaned up at day's end. In time, the tearoom became increasingly difficult for the elderly proprietors to maintain, and it closed after the 1941 season. Alice claimed that the commanding general of nearby Fort Wadsworth requested the closure for fear that German spies would use the garden to monitor troop movements in the harbor.[91] That same year, the Kende Galleries in Midtown Manhattan auctioned off a large portion of Alice's remaining valuables.[92]

Another attempt to earn income was renting out the Mullers' "quarterdeck" as an apartment. Richard Cannon, a medical intern who worked at the nearby US Public Health Service hospital, lived there with his wife Mary in 1944. Cannon photographed Alice—seated, with a camera by her side—and Gertrude, her feet in a dancer's position and her hand placed protectively on Alice's chair (Figure 6.27).

In May 1944, Bankers Trust reneged on its informal agreement and sold the Austen property for $7,500 to Grace Mandia, whose father owned a local tavern. Once again Alice and Gertrude avoided eviction, this time because the Mandia family violated the terms of purchase, which required the owners to live there. The press sensationalized the story: "78 Years In House. Eviction Revoked. Spinster Is Said To Have Once Refused $125,000 For Staten Island Home."[93]

The reprieve led to nightmare. In one of her few extant letters, Alice described what happened next to Henry Rogers Winthrop, a wealthy cousin who occasionally sent her modest sums:

> The hurricane last September 14th [1944] wrecked the kitchen end of the house, a huge tree fell across it, had to send for the firemen, & they cut all the wires, & for over two months we had neither light, water or heat, and the owner refused to correct the pipes, so they froze tight, froze & burst the radiators. No fire since January the cold has been frightful, it made my knees so stiff that the doctor made me go to the Hospital for six weeks to get out of the cold damp house. Now I am back but very lame & have to walk with two canes, there is so much to do to move, it is a frightful prospect.[94]

Although impoverished, Alice and Gertrude retained their Social Register listing until 1942 and their Colony Club membership until 1944. In notes for a memoir, John Morton summarized Alice's perilous conservatism:

> Alice's secure world—with defined social order, and a benevolently and generally Episcopalian God in charge of matters—began to crumble. It was a world that was comfortable, as sound as J.P. Morgan's bank on Wall Street, as assured as Mr. Taft in the

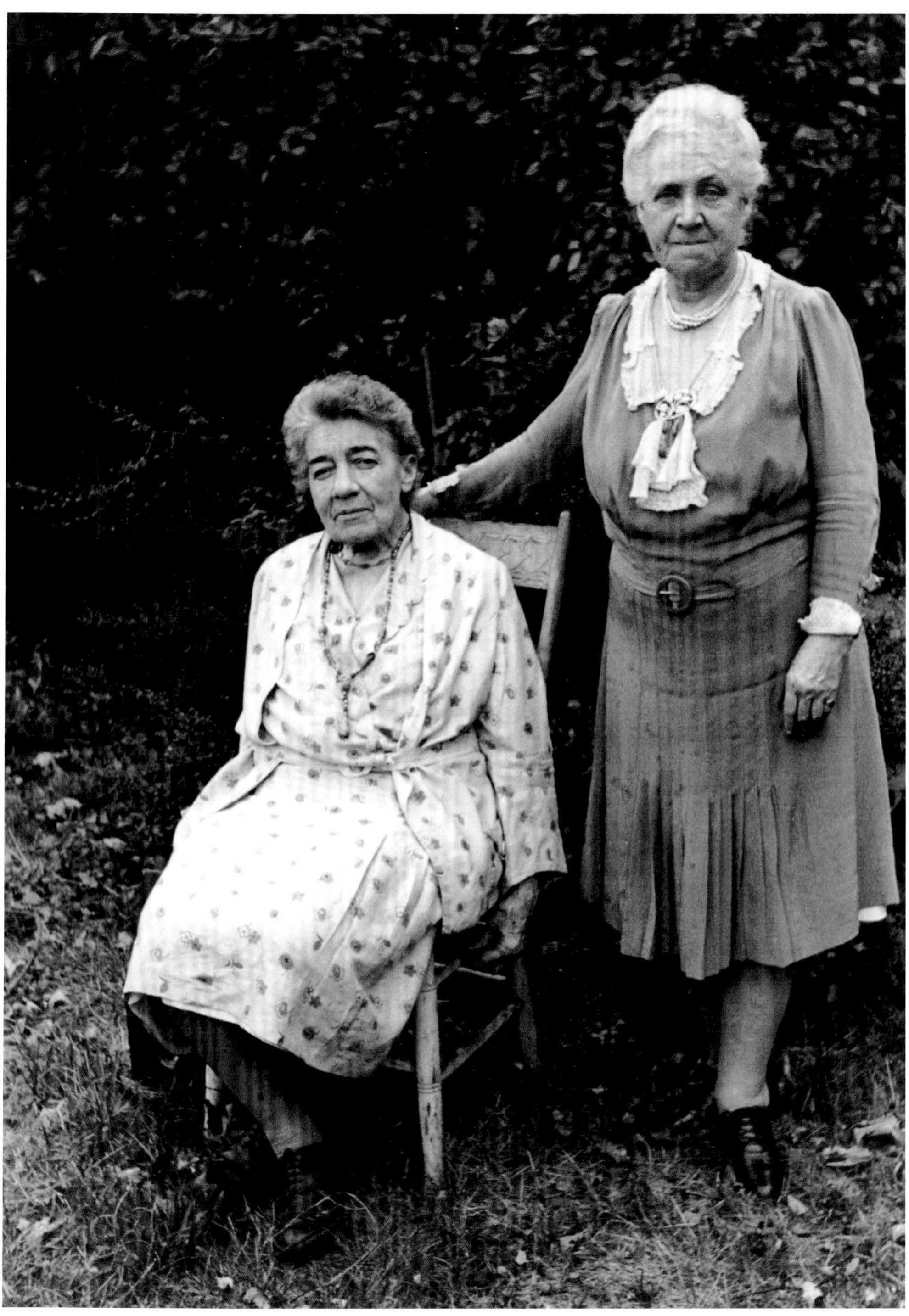

Figure 6.27 Richard O. Cannon and his wife, who lived with Alice and Gertrude in 1944, fell under the spell of the decrepit house and its occupants.

White House, as predictable as rib roast for Sunday dinner at one o'clock, or reading Charles Dickens aloud on Christmas Day.[95]

Alice and Gertrude skillfully negotiated the defined social order of Staten Island society without the legal protections of marriage and despite the growing prejudice against lesbians, but their success depended upon Austen family money. In 1945, after fifteen years of valiant struggle, they were finally evicted from Clear Comfort and moved into a three-room apartment in St. George, Staten Island's civic center. Four years later, when Alice's arthritis worsened, Gertrude could no longer manage her care, and Alice moved to the Mariners' Family Home near Clear Comfort. Gertrude stayed in the apartment so they could remain in close contact. She phoned Alice every day; Alice came to dinner once a week; and Gertrude visited Alice once a week. The arrangement worked well enough for a year, but in late 1949, Gertrude yielded to Winifred's urgings and moved to her home in Jackson Heights, Queens, which left Alice alone. Regular phone calls were now expensive, and as Gertrude recounted, Alice "[wa]s desolate at having me go."[96] An obstinate resident, Alice was shunted from one nursing home to another until June 1950, when she was admitted to a public facility, the Staten Island Farm Colony.[97] To qualify, Alice, age eighty-four, transferred her remaining assets to Gertrude and declared herself a pauper.

7 LEGACY

If she had not been evicted from Clear Comfort, Alice Austen and her photographs would have slipped through the pages of history. The intricate story of how her photographs were saved, how she was introduced to the public, and how her reputation evolved touches on many topics: historic preservation, the institutional acquisition of photographs, the periodical press, urban planning, early public television, the history of photography, and feminist and lesbian activism.

The Austen Archive

On July 17, 1945, Alice frantically telephoned Loring McMillen, the director of the Staten Island Historical Society, seeking his assistance. When he arrived at Clear Comfort, he found her quarreling with Benjamin Jaffe, a secondhand furniture dealer from New Jersey, who had purchased the house's contents.[1] In a memo to the file, McMillen described the scene:

> Miss Austen and her engaging companion Miss Tate have moved from the old house. Not quite broken in spirit but broken in health and finance Miss Austen has at last been forced to leave the only home she has ever known. . . . Pride beset her to the end and in spite of countless friends such as . . . myself, she made a disgusting bargin [sic] with a Newark "junk dealer" a Jaffe by name to sell the contents of the house after she had removed what she wanted. The amount involved was $600 which was too low even considering that for years she had been selling her better pieces. The trouble arose when neither she nor Jaffe having clearly defined the articles she was to take became involved in arguments and recriminations.

McMillen resolved the controversy by having the Society's lawyer draw up an agreement between buyer and seller and removing many items for safekeeping. "Miss Austen," he wrote, "seemed too dazed to make up her own mind." He added, "The finest material we secured as a loan is the remarkable photographs and negatives made by Miss Austen and her uncle I believe, [which] . . . we are now examining."[2]

Years earlier in 1931, when McMillen first visited Clear Comfort, he encountered an intact house and a lively Miss Austen. He was then a twenty-five-year-old engineer for the New York Telephone Company, who devoted his spare time to studying Staten Island's oldest buildings.[3] His summary of the 1931 visit reflects a sophisticated knowledge of Colonial construction techniques and a distaste for the Gothic Revival renovations of Alice's grandfather: "The trim of poor design scream[ed] of the early Victorian era." Alice's financial difficulties were not yet apparent, nor was she yet afflicted with arthritis. He described her as "a woman of about 55 [she was 65 at the time] active and alert," who "has a remarkable old house filled with equally remarkable and interesting relics of the past. . . . [A] Duncan Phife [sic] sofa, a Chipendale [sic] wing back chair are but a few of a household of many."[4]

As Alice's fortunes fell, McMillen's star rose. He converted the abandoned Richmond County Clerk's Office into the Society's Historical Museum, and in 1936, he was appointed director of the Historical Society and named Staten Island's official borough historian. In his new roles, McMillen routinely kept in touch with longtime Staten Island residents, including Alice,[5] who was a lifetime Society member.[6]

In 1945, as Alice and Gertrude left the house, McMillen removed thousands of photographic prints and negatives and a variety of other items, which the Society subsequently acquired. The chaos of moving day is reflected in the acquisition, which ran the gamut from the treasured to the trivial: a seventeenth-century family Bible; scrapbooks of trade cards that Alice assembled in her teens; albums of mounted photographic prints of the kind she gave to friends and family; and a cache of letters, postcards, greeting cards, calling cards, tickets, and programs. In his notes, McMillen chastised Alice for entrusting the contents of her home to a New Jersey "junk dealer" ("pride beset her in the end").[7] If she had only called him, she and her belongings would have been treated respectfully; the Society could have chosen selectively; and he could have helped her dispose of the remainder for a fair price. The ill-fated choice of the "junk dealer," however, was a symptom of the larger challenge facing Alice. Depleted by illness and trauma, she could not imagine, much less plan for, leaving her home. Rita Beschner Newell, a waitress at the Clear Comfort Tearoom, who helped Alice and Gertrude move out of the house, reflected on the experience:

> Well, Miss Austen, I think, always lived in a world of her own . . . I think in later years I knew her the most because their friends sort of deserted them . . . Miss Austen had her bedroom on the first floor . . . You couldn't get in that room! She saved everything. You had to have a path to go through it . . . There were closets and closets that had never been opened in years and years, I guess. I remember we did open one closet, and they found a big chest of silver, and they sent that to the bank to the vault.[8]

After Alice and Gertrude were gone, the house was left unlocked. Alice's friend and neighbor, Rudolph Cender, described seeing papers and furniture on the lawn, the work of vandals and curious children, including his own:

> I went through there, you know . . . I just was looking to see if <u>she</u> was in there, I thought maybe she was dead or something. Because the front door and the back door was open and you could walk right through the house. . . . And then I figured, well, let me get out of here before somebody, you know, accuses me of stealing something. . . . There was a lot of stuff in there, some nice stuff there. . . . And then my son said, "Why can't we take some of the stuff? . . . There's nobody here?" I said no.[9]

At the time, McMillen was formulating his great vision, Richmondtown Restoration. Inspired by John D. Rockefeller's Colonial Williamsburg and Henry Ford's Greenfield Village, McMillen wished to restore the buildings of Richmond, the former county seat, and bring to the site additional historical buildings to create a village where visitors could experience everyday life in preindustrial America.[10] In light of his mission, he valued Alice's photographs of Staten Island subjects and hoped to find a suitable home elsewhere for the rest of her collection.

In 1948, Clarence Coapes Brinley, a sixty-year-old engineer nearing retirement, began volunteering at the Society.[11] McMillen assigned him the photographic files, and he began to unpack Alice's glass plates from their dusty boxes in the museum's basement. Holding the plates up to the light, he was captivated. Later describing his discovery, he offered the first critical assessment of Alice's achievement:

> There was a touch of the professional. The exposures were properly timed, the developing had been done with great care. Each plate was encased in a separate jacket, on the face of which was recorded the subject, the date, the time of day, the weather condition, the lense [*sic*] used; the exposure time and the shutter speed. There was a touch of the historian. Many of the negatives recorded contemporary events of importance and of lasting interest. But above all there was a touch of the artist. Most of the pictures were carefully posed. They had balance, that rare thing among early photographers, that balance which indicated that the person behind the lense [*sic*] was not merely someone who happened to own a camera.[12]

To pursue McMillen's goal of dividing Alice's collection, the Society needed to own it outright. On the understanding that the Society, which had little resources, would invest time and effort in the photographs, Gertrude sold the collection for fifty dollars: "It is understood that all those objects and collections which have Staten Island associations are to be retained by the Society in its collections permanently."[13] Gertrude's letter of receipt indicates that she was pleased with the arrangement: "I'm quite happy to have you in possession of so many things that were dear to the heart of Miss E. Alice Austen & to me. To feel they have a permanent home with the Society I know will gladden her heart.[14]

The same month that Alice entered the Farm Colony, the Society gained title to the collection, and Brinley immediately set to work writing museums to interest them in the non-Staten Island photographs.[15] By fall, curators from the Museum of the City of New York, the New-York Historical Society, and the Library of Congress had found their way to Staten Island to examine the collection. No deal was made, but Brinley began to understand the strengths of the collection and that it would be unwise to break it up.[16] In November, he reached out to national magazines and local newspapers offering "exclusive rights" for fifty "New York character studies" of street workers and enclosing a vintage print in each letter.[17] Brinley received one positive response, from the *Daily News*, which was beginning a series in its Sunday magazine on "New York's Changing Scene." The *Daily News* paid $150 for the rights to fifteen "character studies," which it did not publish until 1965, but it did publish two of Alice's Manhattan street views. For the latter, Brinley charged the *Daily News* twenty dollars and sent two original negatives, which were never returned.[18] Despite his mixed results, Brinley's crash course in museum work earned him the title of the Society's Associate Curator of Photography.[19]

Saving Miss Austen

As Brinley was accumulating rejection letters, he received an inquiry on behalf of Oliver O. Jensen, a veteran of New York publishing, who was searching for little-known photographs of nineteenth-century American life. Jensen hit the jackpot with Alice's photographs.

After years of writing and editing for *LIFE* magazine, Jensen, at age thirty-six, was looking for a new challenge. He wished to adapt the format of the magazine photo-essay, in which a narrative unfolds through captioned photographs, to a less hurried, less commercial form than *LIFE*. In 1950, he cofounded a publishing company, Picture Press, and began to prepare a picture book documenting the radical changes in the lives of American women since 1880. Jensen brought his mastery of mass media to a thesis that was ahead of its time:

> No country disputes so passionately about its women—about their careers, their clothes, their education, their housekeeping, their behavior in marriage, their morals, their sex practices and almost their every move in our complicated civilization. . . .

[O]ur women are renowned all over the world not only for their good looks, their health, their wealth and their longevity, but also for their widely publicized spiritual difficulties.[20]

The letter from Constance Foulk, Jensen's assistant who had worked for him at *LIFE*, landed on Brinley's desk on December 27, 1950.[21] Soon Jensen and Foulk were spending days in the Society's basement looking at Alice's glass plates and jotting down the inscriptions from the negative sleeves. Having chosen thirty-four negatives and seeking more information about the photographer, Jensen was thrilled to learn that Alice was still alive but shaken to learn of her ignominious fate. When he went to visit her at the Farm Colony, Alice was resting in her bed. She ignored him until, as he explained, "I passed a few of my prints [from her negatives], which were fortunately big 11 by 14 enlargements, rather rudely in front of her nose. Then she stared at them, sat up, fished some glasses off her table and studied the pictures intently."[22] Fully alert, Alice offered lively commentary on the people and places depicted in the modern prints, which looked strangely unlike her gold-toned contact prints of the 1890s.

Initially drawn to the photographs, Jensen was even more intrigued by Alice. He immediately saw in her fascinating life and tragic circumstances the potential for a gripping magazine story and a way to assist her. Jensen and Foulk selected several hundred negatives to sell to magazines for stories about her life and times. In an era when photographs were the magazine industry's most valuable commodity, Jensen charged as much as $2,000 for a story in exchange for which Picture Press supplied work prints from Alice's negatives. Brinley signed a five-year contract allowing Picture Press to market the collection with a 50/50 split of net profit, with the proviso that while she was alive, Alice would receive 60 percent of the Society's share.[23] Jensen succeeded in placing feature stories in *LIFE*, *Holiday*, and *Pageant*,[24] which engendered additional requests for Alice's images. On August 19, 1951, with proceeds from *LIFE*,[25] Alice left the Farm Colony for the home of Mrs. Carrie Park, who cared attentively for twenty-five elderly people; Alice paid Mrs. Park one hundred dollars a month.[26] As Alice settled in, Gertrude wrote gratefully to Jensen: "I am writing on behalf of Miss Austen, to thank you for all you have done to keep the change in her surroundings. Certainly for her it is heaven sent. To me it reads like a fairy-tale with you the Prince Charming who started it all."[27]

On September 24, 1951, a month after Alice left the Farm Colony, "The Newly Discovered Picture World of Alice Austen, Great Woman Photographer Steps Out of the Past," appeared in *LIFE*. Although there is no byline (often the case in *LIFE*), Jensen penned the text, and the captions were based on Alice's commentary.[28] The introduction even pitched Jensen's new company:

Only Alice's friends ever saw this marvelous record of her life and times. Eventually the huge collection went to the Staten Island Historical Society where this year it was rediscovered by the editors of Picture Press, in the course of preparing a photographic history of American women which will be published by Harcourt, Brace.

The eight-page photo-essay featured twenty images and established the template for future presentations of Alice's work and life: family and home ("The Family at Clear Comfort" / "Alice Grew Up in a Big Mansion Devoted to Culture and Curios"); leisure and travel ("A 'Larky' Life" / "Alice Loved Every Bit of It"); and Alice's visual satire ("Work and Wit" / "She Had a Light Touch and a Heavy Camera"). Florid lettering and photographs with rounded corners evoked the Victorian era. The last two pages melodramatically contrasted a full-length self-portrait of Alice in her prime ("What happened to Alice? Turn the page") with a photograph of her in a wheelchair at the Farm Colony taken by staff photographer Alfred Eisenstadt ("Alice Austen, crippled and a pauper, is still alive.").[29] Like many *LIFE* photo-essays, it ended with a thinly veiled solicitation: thanks to print sales, Alice had moved to a private nursing home, where "there is enough money to keep her in relative comfort for another 14 months." The essay garnered much needed donations, and a letter to the editor praised its "sheer drama" as worthy of a Pulitzer award.[30]

Despite *LIFE*'s manipulative handling of Alice's story, Jensen's correspondence with Gertrude displayed mutual affection,[31] and he brought out the best in Alice. After a visit, Jensen reported to Brinley: "[I] took Miss Austen out to a lobster dinner. There is nothing wrong with her appetite. We had a very pleasant day identifying pictures and Miss Austen's memory covers about 75 to 80% of the pictures more than adequately."[32] After the *LIFE* essay appeared, Jensen arranged for a television interview on "Vanity Fair," a popular CBS program, for which Alice was paid one hundred dollars.[33] Years later, host Dorothy Doan recalled the episode: "Of course they showed those fabulous photographs she had taken. . . . She was a very poised well-bred person, advanced in years but not overwhelmed in the least by all this sudden fame."[34]

On October 7, 1951, two days after the television interview, the Society sponsored "Alice Austen Day" (Figure 7.1). With one hundred modern prints on display, the celebration was the first public showing of Alice's works. With 300 guests in attendance, including a group of Alice's childhood friends,[35] Brinley made a gracious speech recounting the efforts of the Picture Press and the Society on Alice's behalf.[36] Alice was in fine form, announcing to the photographers, "I'd be taking these pictures myself if I were 100 years younger."[37] The *New York Times* ran stories the day before and after the event.[38]

Although the Society made the arrangements for Alice Austen Day, the idea was

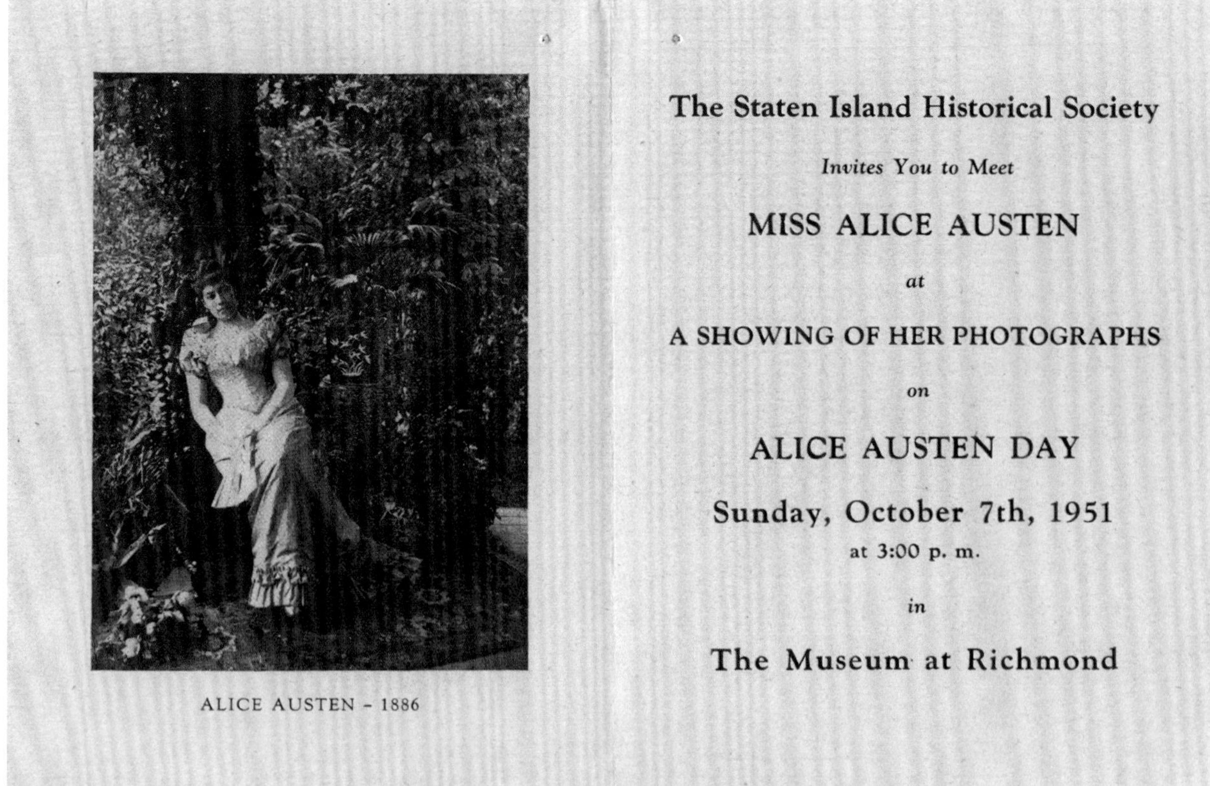

Figure 7.1   The invitation to Alice Austen Day was illustrated with her 1892 self-portrait (incorrectly dated 1886).

Jensen's. *LIFE* ran a two-page "Sequel" about the celebration and featured photographs of Alice greeting old friends.[39] Gertrude wrote Jensen "to thank [him] and congratulate [him] for making Sunday 'Alice Austen Day' such a tremendous success." About Alice, she reported, "I saw her Monday, yesterday, & apparently she was not the worse for all the excitement. She certainly thrives on it."[40]

Meanwhile behind the scenes, the Society delayed dispensing money earmarked for Alice's care. In early September 1951, its board of directors held a special meeting to discuss the unexpected windfall from selling the rights to Alice's photographs. The board agreed to give its share of $1,425 from the *LIFE* article to Alice—in four quarterly payments—but disagreed about its obligation to give additional funds.[41] Paul Maddaus, who was representing Gertrude and serving as board treasurer, resigned from the board in protest:

I represented the Society [in purchasing the Austen collection of photographs from Miss Tate] and accepted [Miss Tate's] belief that the Society would be above dealing with her in the greatest of good faith. Now the honorable thing I can do is represent her, if necessary in the courts of law, in order to insure that she does not sustain severe loss because of her good faith in the good faith of such Society.[42]

In the wake of Alice Austen Day, Gertrude wrote Jensen to express her disappointment in the Society's inaction: "I don't want to seem grasping but I feel that you & I are interested in guarding her future, so that I'm bringing to your attention the fact that the Museum has not taken care of this for Miss Austen."[43] Having no alternative, Gertrude accepted the inconvenient quarterly payments but complained to Mc-Millen when the second payment was late: "Could you jog the memory of whoever is in charge of this & ask him to forward the second quarter's check in the amount of $365.25 one month of which you will note I have already paid [to Mrs. Park]."[44]

In December, Alice suffered a mild stroke and needed extra care, but the Society continued to drag its feet. Gertrude managed to pay the bills until June when the New York City Department of Hospitals determined that Alice, who could not walk unassisted, could no longer stay at Mrs. Park's. To avoid sending her to the city's hospital for the poor on Welfare Island ("It means just murder for she wouldn't survive it"), Gertrude hired a nurse to take in and care for Alice. On June 4, 1952, Gertrude wrote Jensen: "The whole situation is certainly tragically sad. . . . I doubt if anyone could credit such callousness."[45]

Alice died five days later, but even her death did not loosen the Society's coffers. A year later, the Surrogate's Court opened an inquiry into "the assets and funds belonging to Elizabeth Alice Austen," and subpoenaed the Society's lawyer and treasurer to testify about "transactions between [the Society] and the decedent." The matter was not settled until October 5, 1954, when the Society paid Alice's funeral expenses of $397.85. Concerned that the payment might bind it to Gertrude and her heirs, it specified to the funeral home that the payment was a donation, not an obligation to the estate.[46]

Alice did not live to see "Alice Austen's America," a six-page photo-essay that appeared in *Holiday*, a large-format travel magazine, in August 1952.[47] *Holiday* staffer Roger Angell wrote a sensitive appreciation of her work to accompany a potpourri of city and country scenes. Describing Alice as "a magnificent artist," Angell continued:

Her pictures of workers, the faces and scenes of New York are an imaginative and revealing documentary, the kind of honest reportage which no mere snapshooter ever attempts. She could photograph the simple look of a hot New England day—a rowboat, shade trees and an old man with an umbrella—and give it the composition, the sharp feeling of time and place, the soft magic of a Renoir painting.[48]

Alice also missed the publication of Jensen's book, *The Revolt of American Women: A Pictorial History of the Century of Change from Bloomers to Bikinis—from Feminism to Freud,* which appeared in November 1952. The book began with a fourteen-page photo-essay on Alice, reproducing twenty-two photographs. The essay fit awkwardly into the book's first chapter, which aimed to establish the Victorian backdrop to subsequent change. Alice hardly represented Jensen's thesis that the American woman of the 1880s "led a short, sheltered life in a man's world."[49] Jensen sent the book to Gertrude, who loved it: "Your article & the photographs concerning Alice, I found delightful & I most sincerely congratulate you in giving this delightful, informative work to the present day world with its varied contrasts both mental & physical."[50]

The Revolt of American Women was less well-received at the Society. Indeed, it widened the breach between Jensen and Brinley, which had been barely concealed from the beginning. Jensen's claim that his assistant, Constance Foulk, had "discovered" Alice's photographs rankled Brinley,[51] and Jensen and Brinley perceived Alice's legacy differently. Brinley valued her photographic achievement, while Jensen valued her life story, in which he had played a pivotal role.

In April 1956, Brinley notified Jensen that their five-year contract had ended and requested the return of all Austen negatives and prints.[52] Jensen responded that he had just negotiated a contract to publish an Austen biography, which would include 200 to 250 of her photographs.[53] Brinley rejected this proposal, insisting on editorial control: "To us, the Holiday article [written by Roger Angell] . . . presented Alice Austen the Artist. This we think should be the approach in all further publications." He also demanded that the publisher pay for permissions in advance: "It may be that we could be persuaded to scale down the price [from $10 per picture] to make your publication possible, but we would want a fixed fee to be paid at the time of publication."[54] He hoped to use the money to finance a darkroom for the Society to print Alice's negatives.

Alarmed, Jensen arranged an emergency lunch with his editor, Cass Canfield, and Brinley, but it proved unsuccessful. Afterward, Canfield wrote Brinley reiterating that a beautifully produced and nationally distributed book would redound to the Society's benefit,[55] but Brinley could not bear the condescension:

> In our meeting you threatened to walk out. . . . I have had a long business career. Many years ago I adopted the canon that when a person threatens to walk out of a conference, ipso facto he has walked out. I do not propose to renew the negotiation.[56]

Brinley's response put an end to Jensen's project; it would be twenty years before an Austen biography appeared.[57]

The Alice Austen House Museum

Today the Austen House affords a view of the elegant sweep of the Verrazzano-Narrows Bridge, a lynchpin in Robert Moses's master plan to connect New York's five boroughs. Opened in 1964, the bridge almost spelled doom for the Austen House. Its salvation coincided with an ideological shift that signaled the end of Moses's power.

In 1960, when bridge construction was underway and the value of Staten Island waterfront property began to rise, the Mandia family sold the Austen property for $10,000 to the Bevex Realty Corporation of Manhattan, which planned to demolish the house and build a cluster of high-rise apartments with harbor views. Meanwhile, McMillen's vision of creating Richmondtown was materializing. The Historical Society entered a contract with New York City to create an ambitious $3 million open-air museum with thirty-eight building projects, to represent local architecture, history, and culture from the seventeenth through the nineteenth centuries. McMillen's primary patron was none other than Moses who, as parks commissioner and city construction coordinator, included Richmondtown in his 1951 plan to acquire Fresh Kills to build a citywide garbage "sanitary landfill."[58] Soliciting major donations, Moses served as honorary chairman of Richmondtown Restoration, Inc., the project's private, non-profit fundraising organization.[59]

On April 23, 1964, the *Staten Island Advance* noted that the Austen House "now belongs to the Staten Island Historical Society, which plans to move it to Richmondtown."[60] The story was wrong: the Historical Society did not own the house, but McMillen apparently considered the idea seriously. That year, the Society acquired four portrait paintings of Alice's ancestors, which her cousin Henry Rogers Winthrop had purchased from her in 1945.[61] When Winthrop died in 1958, responsibility for disposing of the portraits had fallen to his secretary. In a letter to McMillen, she wrote, "It has given me great pleasure to learn that you are willing and pleased to accept [the portraits] to be placed back in the old Austen home when it comes to 'Richmondtown.'"[62]

Oliver Jensen also responded to the threat to the Austen House. The August 1966 issue of *American Heritage*—which Jensen cofounded in 1954 and edited until 1976—included an article on the history of Staten Island, which featured Alice and her photographs. Written by Archie Robertson, the article celebrated the early history and natural beauty of the island and decried the loss of its distinct character, especially since the opening of the Verrazzano Bridge, which "will probably ruin what is left of any rural charm." Robertson invoked the image of a deteriorated Clear Comfort to warn against unbridled development: "Alice Austen's ancient home still stands, as of now, overlooking the Narrows, but it is empty and decaying. . . . Miss Austen's pictures remain to ask us quietly, what we are doing to our country."[63]

Robertson's despair reflected a citywide—indeed national—shift in public opinion regarding historic preservation and environmentalism. In 1962, the city established an advisory Landmarks Preservation Commission,[64] and, fueled by public outrage over the demolition of Pennsylvania Station, Manhattan's majestic, Beaux-Arts rail terminal, a city landmarks bill was signed into law in 1965.[65] At the same time, historic preservation was gaining national attention: in 1966, the National Historic Preservation Act was passed, which established the National Register of Historic Places and the National Historic Landmarks Program. As a result, many of Moses's long-planned expressways were denied funding, including significant parts of a Staten Island expressway system, which would have transected a large verdant area that his opponents dubbed the "Greenbelt."[66]

The Austen House presented the Landmarks Preservation Commission with a novel problem: Should the house, which met the commission's historical and architectural criteria, be landmarked as a building or *in situ*? The *Staten Island Advance* weighed in decisively: "Divorcing the Austen House from its site would be like moving the Statue of Liberty to City Island."[67] In January 1967, advocates for saving the site met to form the Friends of the Alice Austen House.[68] Jensen, the Friends' first president, enlisted Margot Gayle, a cofounder of the Victorian Society of America and a press officer for the City Planning Commission, to spearhead their efforts. The Friends moved fast. In February, they launched a $100,000 fundraising drive, and in March, they secured the support of the Mayor's office to add the Austen House property and the adjacent old New York Yacht Club to a nascent plan for the Rosebank Esplanade, a recreational pathway along the Staten Island waterfront.[69]

In September, the Friends sponsored a picnic buffet at sunset on the lawn of the Austen House to bring together potential supporters. All guests received the July issue of *Infinity Magazine*, published by the American Society of Magazine Photographers (ASMP), which featured Alice's self-portrait on the cover and a photo-essay entitled, "The Friends of Alice Austen." The essay ended with this lament: "How long her house will last and whether her unique historic photographs will be preserved is anyone's guess."[70] In the *New Yorker*, architectural critic and preservationist Brendan Gill reflected on his visit: "Was it possible that this dark, snug house, this jungle of a garden, this green lawn running down to the beach were about to disappear forever?"[71]

The Friends' early initiative culminated in its 1968 publication of an illustrated brochure, *Gateway to America: The Alice Austen House and Esplanade*, which outlined an integrated house, garden, park, and esplanade design. With forewords by

New York City's Parks commissioner and the Staten Island borough president, the brochure lambasted the city for its history of permitting "a barricade of steel and concrete to be erected along its shoreline until the waterfront is inaccessible to the pedestrian in all but a few places." It proposed instead "a unique combination of recreational potential and historical value to be set aside now for the benefit of the public that needs it so badly."[72] The Austen House would be a museum devoted to photography; the yacht club, a restaurant, and shop for visitors; and an esplanade would extend from the Austen House all the way to Fort Wadsworth.[73]

McMillen's role in the effort to save the Austen House evolved from the old preservation model to the new. He quickly embraced the Friends' cause to save the house on site.[74] In February 1967, Richmondtown opened an exhibition of 280 Austen photographs, which was billed as "the first effort in a concerted drive by 'Friends of E. Alice Austen' to save her former home, the lovely Austen Cottage overlooking the Narrows."[75] The Friends' brochure proposed that Richmondtown "should be designated to administer the museum, and with the aid of Miss Austen's pictures, to restore the interior and exterior of the house as it was when Clear Comfort was in its heyday."[76]

Over the course of the 1970s, the Friends succeeded in saving Clear Comfort. The wheels of bureaucracy turned slowly but surely. In September 1970, the Austen House was placed on the National Register of Historic Places; in November 1971, the Landmarks Preservation Commission designated it a New York City landmark; in 1975, the Department of Parks purchased the house and six surrounding acres from the Bevex Realty Corporation; and in June 1979, a contract between the Friends and the Parks Department authorized the commission of a Historic Structures Report that provided a blueprint for the restoration of the house and gardens.[77] New York's 1970s fiscal crisis, however, gutted the esplanade plan, and it was not until 1984 that city funding for the restoration was approved.

Alice's World

On Christmas Day 1975, a half-hour documentary called "Alice's World" aired on Channel 13, New York's PBS station. The film was the work of Gordon Hyatt, the executive producer of "The 51st State," an innovative news program about New York City, and Stuart Hersh, a young freelancer, who wrote and directed it. McMillen, Jensen, and Ann Novotny, who was hard at work on an Austen biography, were interviewed on camera. Novotny borrowed Hersh's title, *Alice's World*, for her book, which appeared the following fall.

The film grew out of a phone call from Margot Gayle to Hyatt, a fellow preservationist. Gayle hoped that Hyatt would produce a piece for "The 51st State" on the plight of the Austen House, which was landmarked but still privately owned. As Hersh later recalled, "To mollify [Gayle], Gordon sent me out to do a story, and to mollify Gordon, I went." Hersh assumed he would produce "at best a five-minute segment," but after visiting the house, he realized "the story is not the house, the story is Alice Austen."[78] The feature story took two to three months to complete. Hersh reviewed hundreds of copy prints, and the Historical Society sent out more than 200 original negatives to make 8-by-10 enlargements for the film. "Alice's World" was narrated by Helen Hayes, the grande dame of the New York stage, who was then fighting to save Broadway's turn-of-the-century theaters. It ended with Hayes describing the plans for a photography museum, park, and esplanade as the camera revealed the rundown house, overgrown gardens, and littered shoreline of 1975.

With "Alice's World," Alice's name reached a large general audience for the first time since the 1950s.[79] Hyatt amplified the film's message by interviewing Gayle and Jensen on WNYC, New York's public radio station.[80] Shortly after the film aired, a new Staten Island elementary school, P.S. 60, was named the Alice Austen School. The naming was a victory for the principal, who "wanted her school to commemorate someone whose life would be of interest (and serve in some sense as a role model) for the children—not . . . some unhappy martyr, whose significance lay largely in the moment and manner of death."[81]

A freelance picture researcher, Novotny learned about Alice while working on her first book, *Strangers at the Door: Ellis Island, Castle Garden, and the Great Migration to America* (1971).[82] Investigating Alice's photographs of Staten Island's quarantine station, she was captivated by the entire archive. Even before her Ellis Island book was completed, Novotny brought together her publisher and the Staten Island Historical Society to discuss an illustrated Austen biography.[83] She then reached out to Jensen, who shared his notes for his unpublished biography, allowed Novotny to interview him, visited Staten Island with her, and wrote the introduction for her book.[84] Novotny painstakingly studied Alice's negatives and consulted the Photographic Historical Society of New York about her equipment, while Novotny's coworker, Rosemary Eakins, transcribed Alice's negative sleeves, Alice's only written legacy.[85] The two researchers located many surviving friends and relatives, including Gertrude's sister, Winifred Tate Baker, and Alice's first cousin, Elizabeth Patty Austen Miller (called Patty).[86]

Novotny wrote for a mainstream American audience accustomed to magazine picture stories and saw Jensen as a mentor and valuable contact. Sending him the outline of her book, Novotny wrote: "[T]he story of Alice's life and the charm of her photographs have a simple, human appeal that reaches and touches people who are not normally at all interested in photographic history."[87] Admiring Novotny's efforts, Jensen expressed regret that he had not spent more time with Alice. "I confess that after Alice was installed in her new life [after leaving the Farm Colony], I did not go [see her] as much as I should have."[88]

At times, Novotny's eagerness to capture the reader's imagination got the best of her. Alice had told Jensen that she began photographing at the age of ten. That would have been in 1876, several years before commercial dry plate negatives spurred the growth of amateur photography among the American leisured class. Novotny knew that Alice's earliest known photographs were dated 1884, when she was eighteen, but accepted Alice's account and compared her to Jacques-Henri Lartigue, a recently discovered child prodigy of early twentieth-century photography.[89]

Novotny's zeal for detective work led her on several wild-goose chases, most notably the search for thousands of supposedly lost glass plate negatives, the loss of which remains part of Austen lore today. The idea derived from a story to Novotny told by Rita Beschner Newell, who recalled smuggling boxes of large, glass plate negatives out of the house to a neighbor's basement shortly before the eviction.[90] Novotny excitedly reported to Jensen that she had located the neighbor, who confirmed the story "in most general terms" but "did not remember, specifically, any photographs." The neighbor reported that she had turned over the items when "the nasty auctioneer from Newark" demanded them. On this basis, Novotny speculated that "perhaps 2,000 8 by 10 glass plates" were missing and might "turn up yet if we are persistent enough."[91] Alice, however, did not acquire her 8-by-10 camera until 1897, after her active years. It is therefore implausible that she produced 2,000 now-missing 8-by-10 glass negatives.

After *Alice's World* appeared in December 1976, Novotny immediately threw her energies into book promotion, which merged with her role as president of The Friends of the Alice Austen House (Figure 7.2).[92] Novotny reported to Gayle, "I am speaking to any group interested in Alice and always mentioning the urgent need for funds." Every time she sold a book, Novotny told the purchaser that one dollar was reserved for the house restoration.[93]

Despite her scattershot methods, Novotny was an effective leader of the Friends. On March 17, 1977—Alice's birthday—a group of Austen devotees, including children from P.S. 60, celebrated the placement of a headstone on her grave in the Austen family plot in Moravian Cemetery. In January 1978, the Neikrug Gallery exhibited thirty photographs from Alice's negatives, the first Manhattan exhibition of her work.[94] In 1979, Novotny teamed up with Historic Richmond Town Curator Charles L. Sachs to organize an exhibition of sixty-eight prints at the fledgling South Street Seaport Museum in Lower Manhattan, and in May 1980, she penned an article on Alice for

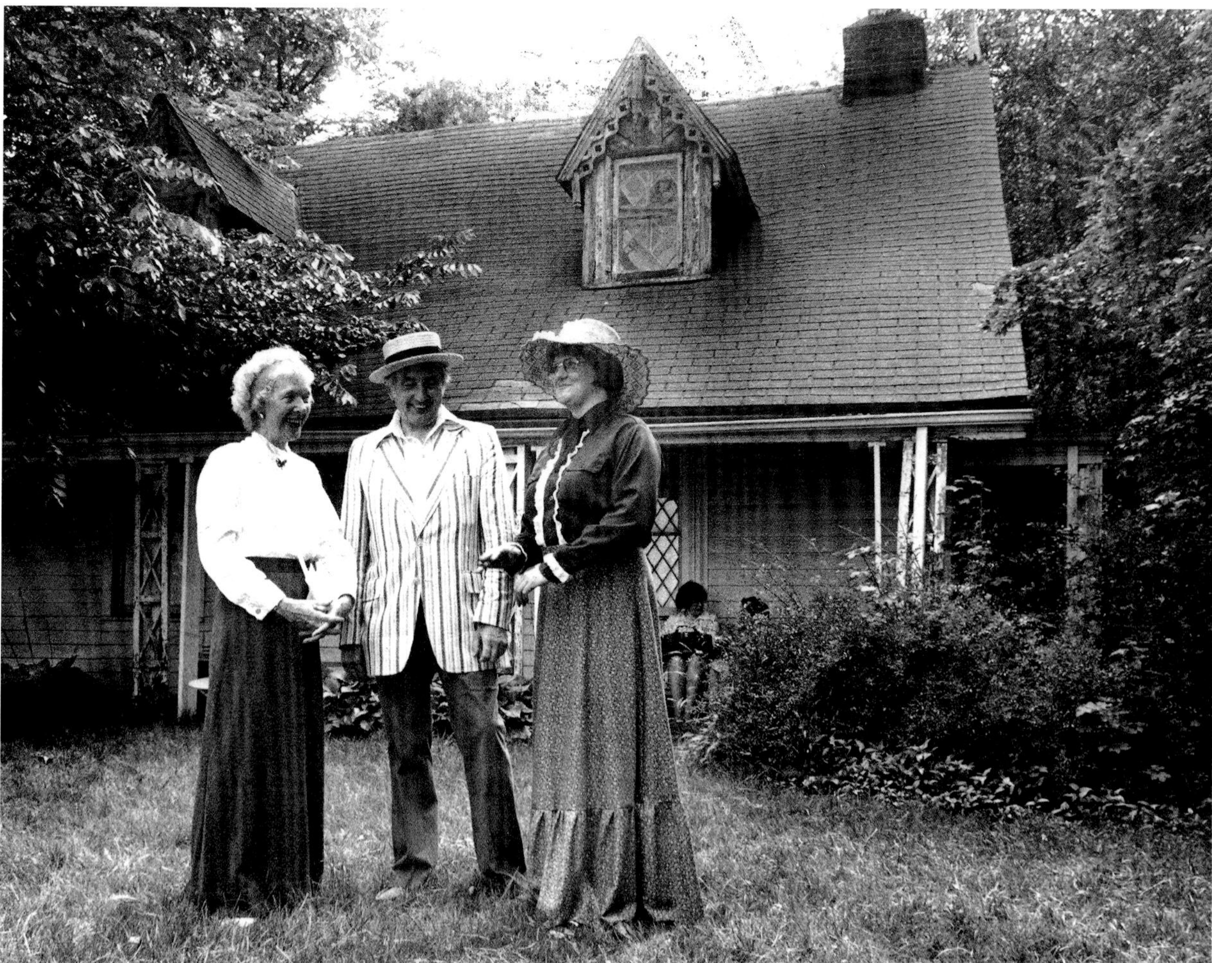

Figure 7.2   In this press photograph for the *Staten Island Advance*, Ann Novotny (right) wears "Victorian dress" to a fundraiser for the Friends of the Alice Austen House.

Camera, a venerable magazine for photographers.[95] Most important, she raised the funds and oversaw the production of the Historic Structures Report, the prerequisite for restoration of the Austen House.[96]

Novotny also became proficient at sparring with bureaucrats, as her letter to the head of Capital Projects for the Department of Parks reveals:

> To have an appropriation for design funds . . . is the happy culmination of 15 years' work by your department and our volunteers. However . . . the thought of further de-lays distresses us deeply. . . . The Austen House remains habitable (or rather, inhabited) only through the tenacity of [our tenants] the Stephensons. . . . If [they] should move out

before restoration work begins, we really do not believe that an empty Austen House would long survive vandalism or arson, or the brush fires accidentally but regularly set by fisherman on the shore. You share our concern, I know.[97]

Tragically, in December 1982, Novotny died of a stroke at age forty-six, before city funding for the restoration was approved. Margaret (Peggy) Buckwalter, who had worked for Oliver Jensen at *American Heritage*, took over as president of the Friends, and in 1984, the restoration was efficiently completed with the plans and personnel that Novotny had assembled.

Alice's Closet

In *Alice's World*, Novotny discreetly described Gertrude Tate as "the friend who shared Alice Austen's older years" and characterized their relationship as a "fifty-year companionship . . . [that] was for both of them a satisfactory alternative to marriage."[98] At the same time, she contributed articles to small lesbian and feminist journals, in which she announced that Alice and Gertrude were lesbians.

Novotny's description of Alice and Gertrude's "fifty-year companionship" was a remnant of the Victorian notion of a "Boston marriage," a socially acceptable partnering of two women in which the likelihood of a sexual relationship was beyond mention, if not beyond the imagination.[99] Following the wishes of those she interviewed for *Alice's World*, Novotny employed the delicate language of an earlier era to protect the couple from a homophobic culture. One interviewee was Gertrude's sister Winifred, who told Novotny that "Alice and Gertrude's relationship was probably lesbian," which upset her mother and older sister greatly. Although Winifred regularly visited Clear Comfort and was supportive of her sister, she too was disapproving of their relationship, describing it as "wrong devotion on both sides."[100] In 1949, Gertrude moved to Winifred's house in Queens, but after several years and without warning, she left to spend her final years in New Jersey with Pieter Vosburgh, an old friend who had accepted Alice and Gertrude.[101] Winifred, however, had the last word. When Gertrude died in 1962 at age ninety-one, Winifred buried her in the Tate family plot in Brooklyn, not with Alice on Staten Island as Gertrude had wished.[102]

Vosburgh was among those who expected Novotny to maintain secrecy about the nature of the two women's relationship. "I will say confidentially," he wrote, "and not to be repeated, Gertrude and Alice were lesbians. . . . My personal conviction is that if you prefer to be a homosexual, that's your business, not mine."[103] Novotny replied, "Yes of course I did realise [sic] that they were lesbians—happy ones—and I agree with you that that choice is no one else's business. In a few days I'll send you a xerox copy of the manuscript so you can see for yourself how I handled that question (gently and with courtesy to the two ladies, I hope)."[104] Discretion also mattered to Stuart Hersh, who wrote and directed the 1975 PBS television show. He recognized that Alice and Gertrude were lesbians but believed it was their wish not to mention it.[105] Jensen, who wrote the introduction to Novotny's book, followed the same course.

In the acknowledgments of *Alice's World*, Novotny reserved her last and most heartfelt thanks for Eakins, "my friend and business partner," who "spent countless days and long evenings . . . helping me through all the exacting and exciting stages of making this book."[106] By the time the book was published, Novotny and Eakins had left their husbands and were living together in a one-bedroom apartment.[107]

A few months before *Alice's World* appeared, Novotny proposed an article to the editors of *Dyke, A Quarterly*, written "by and for lesbians," which produced six issues between 1975 and 1979. Novotny did not write the article, but the editors thanked her for her "help, information and photographs." The article did not mince words and began, "Alice Austen was a Lesbian born on Staten Island, New York, in 1866."[108] The cover design placed the journal's logo against a red background above "The Darned Club," vividly capturing *Dyke's* brash tone (Figure 7.3).

Shortly after the publication of *Alice's World*, Novotny wrote an article for *Heresies*, the eponymously named journal of a recently founded women's collective dedicated to feminism, politics, and art. The journal's third issue was devoted to "lesbian art and artists" and arose out of the "need to challenge the heritage of secrecy, silence, and isolation which has been a necessity for lesbians who make art." It was "designed, edited and put together by lesbians [and] all contributors to the issue are lesbians."[109] With her article, Novotny announced her solidarity with the lesbian community. She began with a description of a photograph of Alice and Gertrude at an auto race (Figure 6.14) and invited the reader to celebrate their love:[110]

> [We] can see Elizabeth Alice Austen up there still, athletically balanced on a precarious perch, concentrating single-mindedly on the pictures she was taking, oblivious to her observer and to the other spectators around her and not giving a tinker's damn that her ankles are exposed below her long skirt in a most unladylike manner. The lover who was to share Alice's life and enthusiasms for over fifty years, Gertrude Amelia Tate, is smiling quizzically at the second photographer: she and he may be sharing amusement at how very characteristic this unconventional pose is for Alice.[111]

Novotny mentioned that Alice was forty when the photograph was taken, the same age as Novotny.

When she died in 1982, Novotny was memorialized as a married woman with no acknowledgment of her partnership with Eakins. The *New York Times* obituary

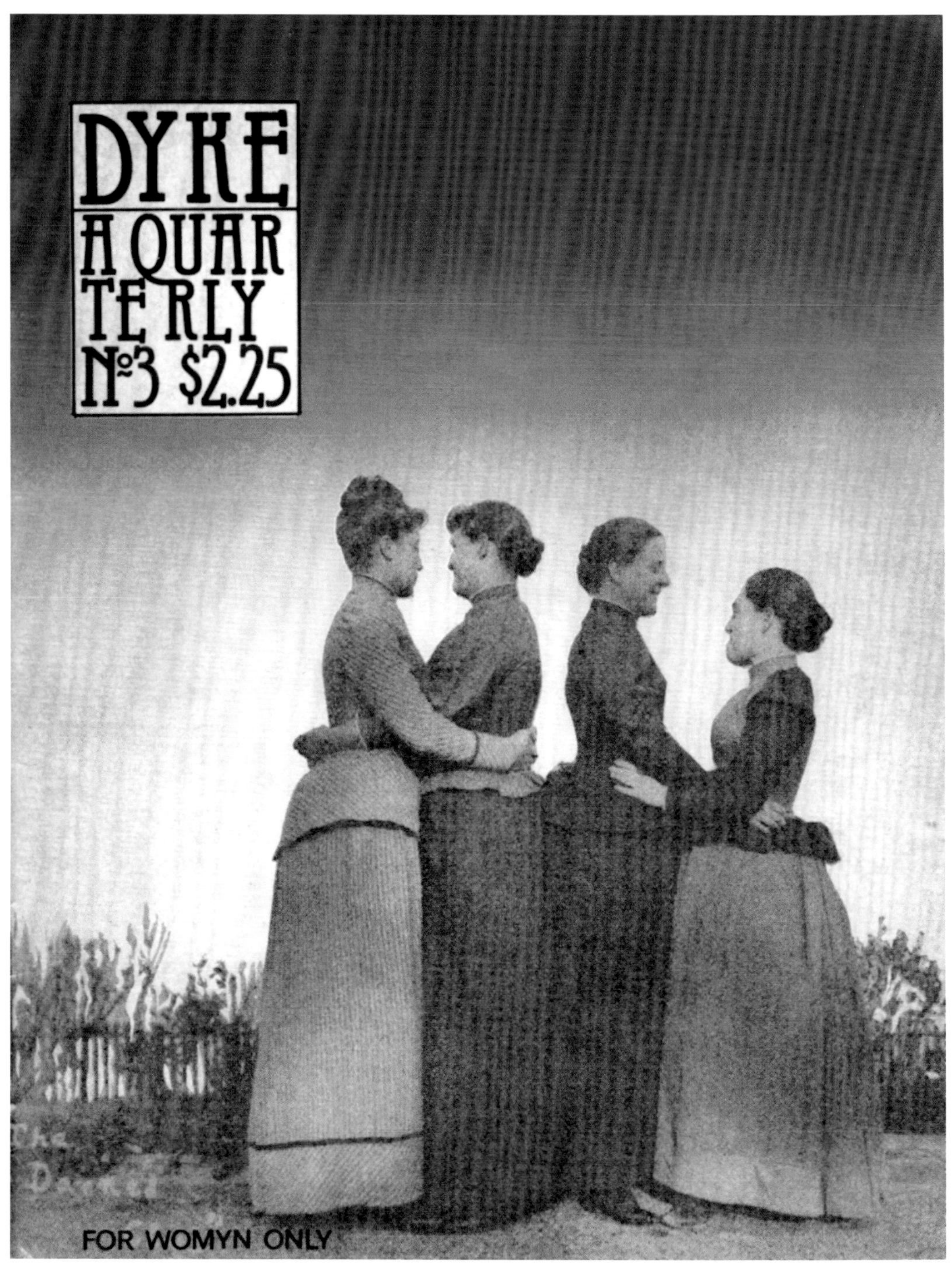

Figure 7.3 "Alice Austen–Photographs" appeared in the third issue of *Dyke*, a journal "for womyn only."

listed her husband and parents as her survivors.[112] In 1986, the Friends of the Alice Austen House published a full-color journal about the house with a dedication page to Novotny written by her parents and featuring a twenty-year-old photograph taken by her husband George Novotny.[113] Eakins was not mentioned in the journal, but the Friends' newsletter published a three-part tribute to "Alice and Ann" by "Dr. Rosemary L. Eakins." Eakins called Novotny "Alice's ideal biographer who shared [with Alice] a love of photography, a love of excellence, and a love of life."[114]

Alice's World introduced Alice to the photography community. By the 1970s, an elite group of photographers, collectors, and curators dedicated to photography as a fine art was burgeoning. Although they admired the pioneer efforts of pictorialists to champion photography as "an art of personal expression," they dismissed pictorial aesthetics as artificial. For Novotny, Alice's lack of interest in pictorialism was an asset:

> Alice Austen lived in the real world and photographed people and places as they actually appeared. . . . She approached her subject straightforwardly, without any attempt at the "refinement, grace and decorative sense" encouraged in the photographic journals of her most productive years.[115]

As a picture researcher immersed in the world of the periodical press, Novotny imagined that "if Alice Austen had been born a few years later . . . she might have made a name for herself as one of the country's first newspaper photographers or photojournalists."[116] Thanks to Novotny's book, Alice's work appeared in numerous surveys of photography and art of the modern city. Scholars favored the New York "street types," which they related to the photographs of Jacob Riis and Lewis Hine and the paintings of the Ashcan School.[117] In 1984, cultural historian Peter Bacon Hales, who "dismissed" most of Alice's work "as the family photography of a devoted and talented amateur," heralded the "street types" as precursors to contemporary street photographers "Diane Arbus, Lee Friedlander, Tod Papageorge and Garry Winogrand."[118]

Meanwhile, Novotny's *Heresies* article introduced Alice into feminist and lesbian discourse. In *Eye to Eye*, photographer JEB's 1979 collection of portraits of lesbians, Alice was mentioned as a predecessor.[119] Alice appeared in Emmanuel Cooper's 1986 survey, *The Sexual Perspective: Homosexuality and Art in the Last 100 Years in the West*.[120] In the 1986 exhibition *Staging the Self* at the National Portrait Gallery (London), Alice's photographs were said to illustrate "what happens when a women takes over the predominantly male prerogative of the look to create a place for herself as a subject who looks."[121] And in 1991, the conceptual artist Nina Levitt created four enlargements of "The Darned Club," masking parts of each image to comprise a work entitled, "Submerged (Alice Austen)." By multiplying, fracturing, and obscuring Alice's

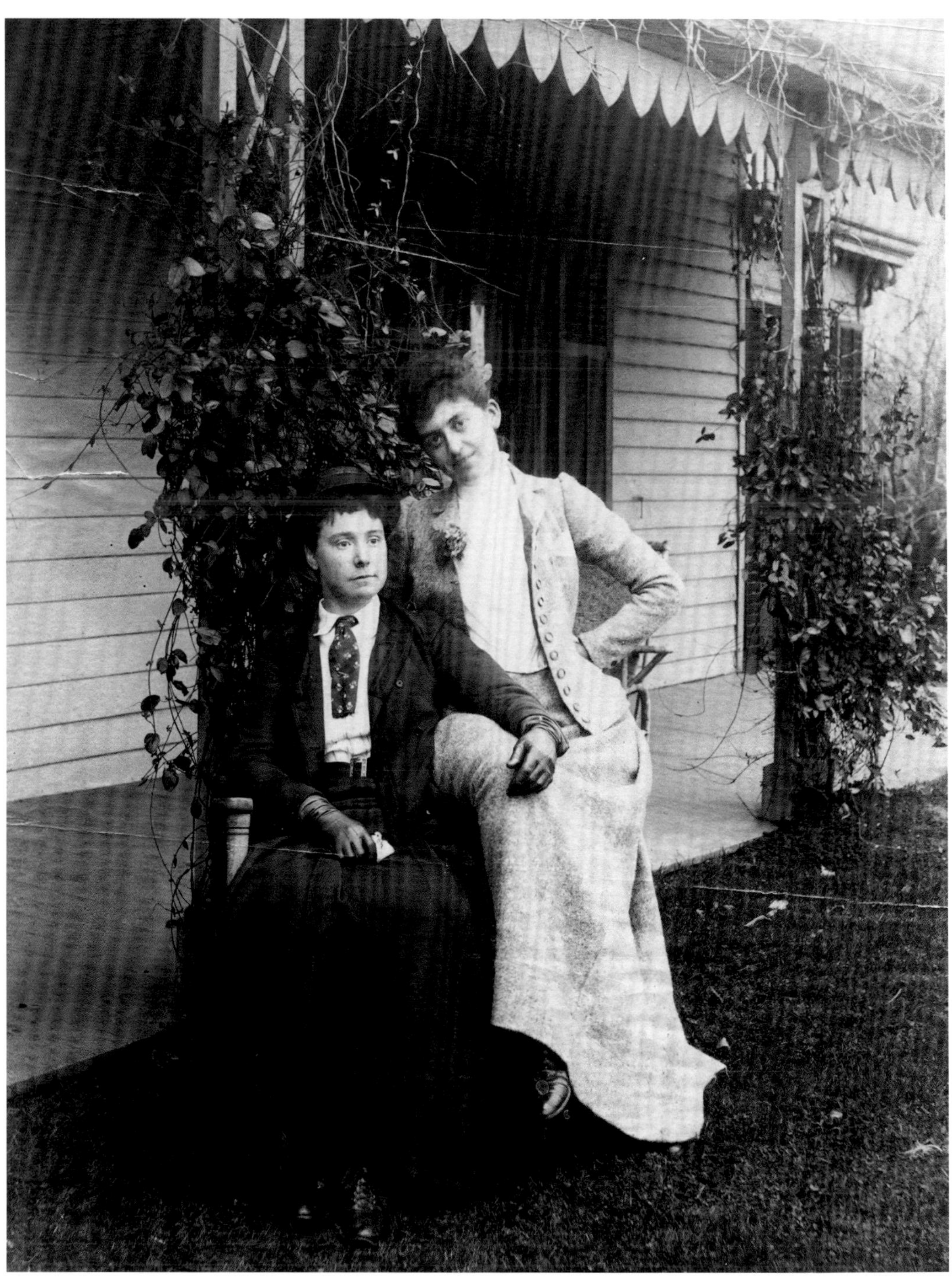

Figure 7.4 The woman sitting on the arm of Violet's chair has not been identified, but the caption in *Dyke* reads, "Violet Ward and her lover."

image, Levitt paid homage to "a Victorian lesbian existence and [sought to] refute attempts by historians to neglect, negate and erase this existence."[122]

A telling example of the disconnect between Alice's divergent publics occurred in 1990, when the publisher of Lillian Faderman's *Odd Girls and Twilight Lovers*, a now-classic history of lesbian life in twentieth-century America, wrote to the Staten Island Historical Society requesting permission to reproduce one of Alice's photographs for the book's cover.[123] The photograph showed Violet Ward seated, draping her arm over the thigh of an unidentified woman perched on the side of the chair (Figure 7.4). It had been published in *Dyke* and in *Heresies* without the Society's knowledge or permission, and a staff member responded to the request incredulously:

> We are not credited on the xeroxed page of the book that you sent. Can you let me know the title and author. . .? [B]efore giving permission to use this photograph . . . the Staten Island Historical Society must be satisfied with the context in which our photograph is used. Has your book or research have [sic] any documented proof that Violet Ward was lesbian? We would need that information to grant permission.[124]

The collision between Alice's mainstream and lesbian readers emerged into public view in the summer of 1994 with The New York Public Library's landmark exhibition, "Becoming Visible: The Legacy of Stonewall," which commemorated the 25th anniversary of the uprising.[125] With a disco ball and a sound system dominating the space, the show celebrated lesbian and gay culture and attracted more than 100,000 visitors. Michael J. Fressola, the arts editor of the *Staten Island Advance*, highlighted Alice's presence in his review of the exhibition, which the newspaper headlined with the Gay Pride slogan, "We are here, we are queer, get used to it."[126] An irate James Thompson, the chair of the Alice Austen House board, wrote a rebuttal entitled, "Contrary to rumor, Alice Austen was not gay."[127]

The Austen House's attempt to keep Alice in the closet backfired. Amy S. Khoudari, a volunteer who wrote a much-needed visitors' guide to the house and gardens, was barred from the collection when she gave a public lecture in St. George describing Alice and Gertrude's relationship as lesbian.[128] She reported the board's homophobia to the Lesbian Avengers, a newly formed group dedicated to "fighting for lesbian visibility and survival," who sprang into action.[129] On July 31, they arrived at the Austen House annual nautical festival wearing makeshift Victorian bathing costumes and donning "Dyke preservers" to "save Alice" from the board (Figure 7.5). True to their practice of "having fun doing serious things," the Avengers sang customized sea shanties, like this one, to the tune of "My Bonnie Lies Over the Ocean":

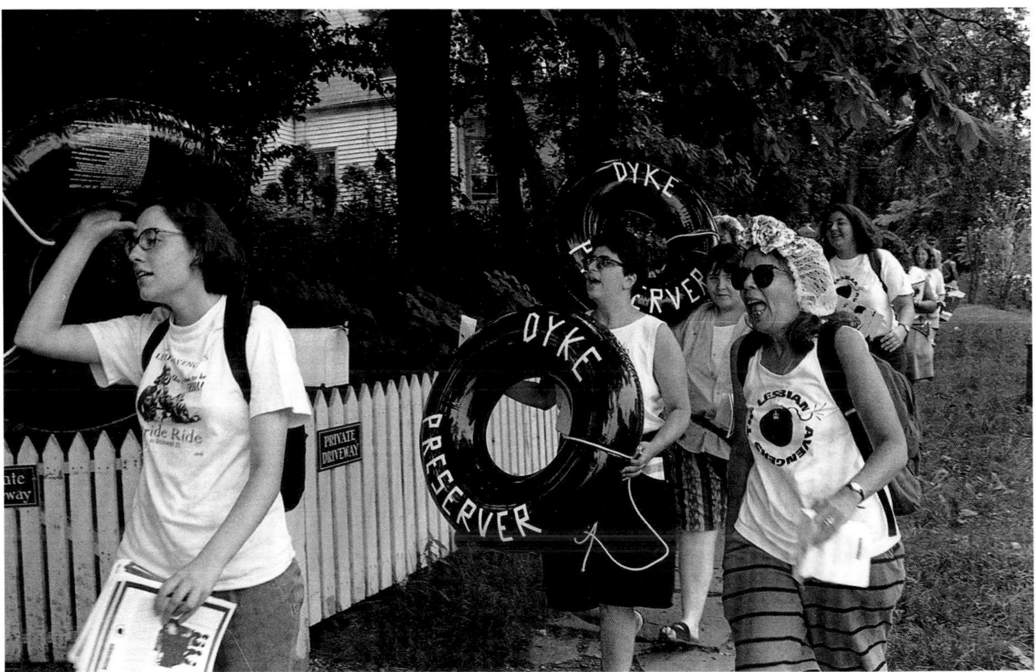

Figure 7.5 In 1994, Saskia Scheffer photographed the Lesbian Avengers protest at the Alice Austen House.

> Gertrude and Alice were lovers
> It was plain for the whole world to see
> But the Board of Directors deny this
> So they should go jump in the sea.[130]

The controversy surrounding Alice was brilliantly captured by Barbara Hammer, in her 1998 documentary, "The Female Closet," which featured three lesbian artists of different generations: Alice Austen, Hannah Hoch, and Nicole Eisenman.[131] Hammer interspersed interview clips of Austen experts and protest participants with close-ups of Alice's photographs. Hammer's video camera caressed the images to suggest Alice's affection for the women before Alice's lens.

The board, however, remained intransigent. It fired Mitchell Grubler, a capable executive director and experienced preservationist, for his refusal to back its position. In 2001, a new executive director, Amy Hufnagel, quit her job when the board rejected her strategic planning report, which recommended recognizing Gertrude's role in Alice's life.[132] Hufnagel's successor, Carl Rutberg, sought to steer a middle ground. In 2010, he wrote, "Today, we do not claim that Austen was a lesbian, and we do not hide Gertrude Tate. Instead we present what we know and let the visitors make up their own minds."[133] It was not until 2015, the year the US Supreme Court legalized gay marriage, that the tide finally turned. That year, Rutberg's successor Janice Monger worked with the NYC LGBT Historic Sites Project to achieve designation of the Alice Austen House as a national site of LGBTQ history. Alice and Gertrude's story is now central to the visitor experience.

EPILOGUE   ALICE'S FRIENDS

Alice's decision to forego marriage and partner with Gertrude Tate was radical, but once together, they kept within the confines of elite society and hid the nature of their relationship. Having fallen in love in 1899, they did not live together until 1917. During their years of caution, the presumption that women should be devoted to hearth and home was challenged on many fronts. Greater numbers of women sought higher education, developed careers, and became professional advocates for progressive causes. In the early 1910s, the word "feminism" entered common parlance, and the cause of women's suffrage, which had gained momentum at the beginning of the century, succeeded in 1920 with the passage of the Nineteenth Amendment. While Alice and Gertrude patronized the Colony Club, an Upper East Side women's club in which admission depended upon pedigree, more freethinking women, many of them queer, belonged to Heterodoxy, a feminist club in Greenwich Village, which required its members "not to be orthodox in her or his opinions."[1]

Alice's generation of women represented the greatest number of unmarried, childless women in American history.[2] Of her closest friends, most did not marry and only one had children. But like many women of wealthy families, who did not attend college and did not pursue ambitious careers, they were among the more conservative members of their generation. Their stories provide context for Alice's and illustrate how a group of privileged women navigated changing times, some more contentedly than others.

Julia Marsh Lord, called Julie (1862–1950)

Julie Lord's mother and Alice's grandmother were Townsends, and Julie and Alice, who grew up together as neighbors, may have been distant cousins. Like Alice, Julie was high-spirited and an avid athlete, but unlike Alice, she modeled her life on her mother's by marrying young, having children young, and assuming the role of society matron. Julie and her husband George O. Lord, also a member of their Clifton set, built a house near Clear Comfort. She was five months pregnant with the first of two daughters in October 1891 when Alice took the photograph of "The Darned Club."[3]

After the birth of her first child, Julie's letters to Alice stopped, but their friendship continued, as seen in Alice's photographs.[4] Julie's extracurricular activities conformed to the expectations of a socially responsible community leader. From the early 1900s through the 1930s, she was an officer of the Society for the Relief of Destitute Children of Seamen and a founding member, with Alice, of the Staten Island Garden Club. After World War I, the Lords moved to New Jersey where, according to Novotny, Julie opened a restaurant, and Alice and Gertrude drove there to visit for lunch.[5] Julie and her husband were buried in the Marsh family plot in Moravian Cemetery, the same cemetery as the Austens.

Gertrude Eccleston Barton, called Trude (ca. 1865–1952)

Alice's closest friend growing up was Trude Eccleston, whose family played a major role in Alice's youth. Reverend and Mrs. Eccleston were respected leaders of the Clifton community, and their four children were like siblings to Alice, an only child. The Ecclestons included Alice in the social events they attended—her name was always mentioned next to Trude's in press reports—and most summers, Alice joined them on vacation.

A natural performer who loved attracting attention, Trude—at least on vacation—was preoccupied with being courted by young men, which resulted in her engagement to Lt. John C. Gregg. Alice staged "Trude & I Masked, Short Skirts" and "Trude & I in Bed," as well as the series of photographs with Willie Hopper mocking courtship, in response to Trude's romance with Gregg. Humiliated by her broken engagement, Trude lost her bravado. She attended to domestic duties and accepted the attention of Charles Barton, a family friend whom she had rebuffed as a romantic partner for years. From a venerable family, Barton was a stockbroker and an athlete and was active in Staten Island civic affairs. In 1900, when Trude was thirty-five and Barton was forty-two, they married but did not have children.

As the daughter of a prominent minister, Trude bowed to family expectations and chose an appropriate mate within the tight-knit community of wealthy Staten Island. In 1951, she had the opportunity to revisit her "larky life" when she attended "Alice Austen Day" at the Staten Island Historical Society and saw Alice, Gertrude, and the prints from Alice's old negatives. She died in July 1952, a month after Alice, and was buried in the Barton family plot in Moravian Cemetery.

Elisabeth Briard Strong, called Bessie (1865–1952)

The youngest child of a New Jersey common pleas court judge, Bessie Strong lived her entire life in New Brunswick. She knew Alice through the Peter Austen family, and in their teens, they attended Rutgers College graduation festivities together. Bessie and Alice shared interests in sports, music, and photography, and they remained friends at least through 1898 (when Alice's letter collection ends). In the 1880s, Bessie was excited but insecure about socializing with young men and urged the more self-confident Alice, who had attracted the attention of two men in Bessie's circle, to visit often. As more of her friends married, Bessie's letters became more anxious. In 1894, she complained, "You can scarcely turn a corner without running up against an engaged person these days."[6] Perhaps in response, Alice arranged a date for Bessie with a Clifton friend, but it fell through.[7]

Bessie's brothers had first-rate educations, illustrious careers, and married into wealthy, prestigious families. As the Strongs' only daughter, Bessie was expected to do little more than serve her parents. When a servant left (which happened often), Bessie filled in, and she canceled social engagements when needed at home. Bessie lived with her parents until their deaths when she was in her forties. Her brother Theodore, a New Jersey state senator, and his large family moved into the Strongs' imposing mansion (which Alice had photographed for Bessie's mother in 1892), and Bessie moved to a boarding house.

Bessie fulfilled the stereotype of a "spinster"—a woman of low status within her family who failed to find a husband and to whom fell the task of caring for aged parents. Once on her own, however, she built a meaningful life of public service. The Republican fervor of her youth—she had railed against a Democratic victory parade in downtown New Brunswick—gave way to support of innovative social service agencies spearheaded by Progressives.[8] She was a board member of a residential nursing home and a longtime president of the New Brunswick Visitor's Nursing Association. By 1913, she was a suffragist, and in 1921, she was among the first women to serve as a juror in a New Jersey courtroom. She died in 1952—a month before Alice—at age eighty-eight.

Julia Bredt (1869–1949)

Three years younger than Alice, Julia Bredt was her Clifton neighbor until 1882, when Julia's parents separated and her mother and four siblings moved to Bethlehem, Pennsylvania. Alice and Julia's friendship intensified between 1890 and 1892, when they visited each other regularly. The Bredt family lived near the campus of Lehigh University, and Julia's home became the setting for social gatherings. As with Bessie Strong in New Brunswick, Alice was a social asset who added excitement and gossip to Julia's circle of friends. On a visit to Clear Comfort, Julia posed with Alice and Jule Martin dressed in men's clothes.

The Bredt family's move to West Orange, New Jersey in 1893 may have been precipitated by a scandal involving Julia's younger sister Ernestine. According to the

Chicago Daily Tribune, Ernestine and seven other girls at the Moravian Seminary for Young Ladies were denied diplomas due to their "improper behavior," although the girls claimed that professors had inappropriately touched them.[9] Perhaps in response to the scandal, Julia's mother tried to rein in Julia's social life, but to no avail. Not long after she arrived in New Jersey, Julia wrote Alice: "Thank goodness I can go to matinees alone with men this winter, some girls can and some can't, but I am wild on this subject of chaperones, lately, and especially all this summer I have had so much of it, it has really made me much worse than I was before."[10]

Julia's letters to Alice end in 1895 when she was twenty-six and give little indication of the adult she was to become. Neither she nor Ernestine married, and they lived together in a house near their brother Arthur and his family in West Orange. Arthur was an engineer for the American Telephone and Telegraph Company, where Julia served as librarian for many years. She was a championship golfer, still playing tournaments in her sixties. There is no indication that she and Alice remained friends in later years.

Julia Taber Martin, called Jule (1866–1937)

On October 15, 1891, when Jule Martin posed with Alice and Julia Bredt dressed in men's clothes, she was momentarily relieved of the crisis that began that May, when her father was accused of stealing company funds and fled to Canada. Five days later, Jule left Staten Island for Albany, where, stripped of family and wealth, she found herself working for Mrs. Angelica Cooper, her stepmother's cousin. In 1894, she followed Mrs. Cooper to Santa Barbara, where she established "The Palms," a boarding house for a wealthy clientele. While struggling to create a business from scratch—renovating and decorating a house, cleaning rooms, waiting on customers, paying bills, hiring staff, and advertising—she regularly sent funny, buoyant letters to Alice. About the "swell, fast, rich set of San Francisco," she wrote:

> They think the earth not quite good enough to hold them . . . & I am so amused by their selfishness and egotism, never having come across such like before. . . . They all like me & I hate the lot, but they do not know it.[11]

In 1898, The Palms was doing well enough that Jule bought a nearby house with plans to expand. She told Alice, "This is my home now and I like it—only it is just 3,000 miles too far away."[12]

Jule had become a New Woman in the 1890s, not by choice but by necessity. In building a career for herself, she discovered capabilities that she did not know she had. The tragic story of her later life is therefore especially shocking. In 1904, her brother Walton, a successful New York physician, committed her to a mental hospital in Westchester County, New York, and after sixteen years, she was transferred to a hospital on Long Island, where she died in 1937 at the age of seventy-one.

Jule's medical records reveal that her mental breakdown in 1904 was ascribed to a sexual pathology. When she entered the hospital in New York, she had already been in two hospitals and had twice tried to commit suicide. A case abstract summarized her personal history:

> Patient's initial symptoms began one year and a half ago. These were inability to fix her attention, and slight exhilaration. Delusions of a sexual character began six months ago when patient was at Santa Barbara, and she was then placed in a sanitarium, escaped from there and walked three miles to drown herself. Was brought East and placed in Dr. Bowman's [hospital in] Greenwich, Conn. While there said people were making remarks about her, also went to a friend's house and turns on the gas. Told Dr. Bailey she had practiced onanism [masturbation] and had abnormal sexual relations with other women, also that she was pregnant. Later told her friend she became so at Dr. Bowman's.[13]

What precipitated Jule's suicide attempts? Had she been sexually assaulted or were her reports of sexual assault and impregnation "delusions of a sexual character"? Because she suffered other delusions—that she was married, that she had killed someone—her experiences in the Santa Barbara sanatorium and Dr. Bowman's hospital remain a mystery.

The routine case notes in Jule's file suggest that she was kept physically safe, but her mood swings were intense—she was often violent—and she became increasingly disabled over time. Shortly before she left Westchester for the Long Island hospital, a doctor noted in her file that "she frequently misidentifies the physician, is evidently very deteriorated and there is not even a shell of her normal personality remaining."[14]

Jule's heroic struggle to thrive outside the protection of her family, so beautifully documented in her letters to Alice, was fragile. Her success in business, which buoyed her self-confidence, may have been perceived by friends and family as a fall in class status. When Walton committed Jule to the Westchester hospital, he reported that she was a music teacher, an acceptable profession for a wellborn unmarried woman, but untrue.

Maria Emily Graham McKnight Ward, called Violet (1863–1941)

Three years older than Alice, Violet Ward spent winters in Manhattan and summers at Oneata, her parents' Staten Island estate. Alice and Violet played tennis together in the 1880s but did not become close friends until the 1890s. With Violet's encouragement, Alice devoted less time to Staten Island society and took on new challenges in photography, including for Violet's trailblazing book, *Bicycling for Ladies*. Violet and Alice were both romantically involved with Daisy Elliott until Alice began seeing Gertrude Tate in 1899, and Alice's friendship with Violet seems to have ended soon thereafter.

Violet was named for her mother, Emily Graham McKnight Ward, who died in 1877 when she was fourteen and her younger sister Carrie was only eight. Their father, General William G. Ward, did not remarry, and it became his daughters' responsibility to care for him. For Violet, her father's needs always came first. In 1896 when Alice and Violet were constant companions, Violet reported: "My Father is now on a milk diet, which of course will make him weak and I must watch him all the closer as he still goes down town every day."[15] A larger-than-life character, General Ward filled Violet's head with stories of illustrious ancestors, Civil War valor, and postwar business deals. In 1922, she recorded a number of his stories, including one in which her father rushed to Washington to see President Lincoln when war was declared: "[He] offered his services to the President . . . [and] returned to New York with a marshal's warrant and a general's commission, and he and his regiment . . . were ordered to Washington for the defense of the capital, and that regiment became Mr. Lincoln's body guard."[16]

When General Ward died in 1901, Violet and her sister retreated from Manhattan life, renting out the family's city house and living year-round on Staten Island. Violet continued to play competitive golf, and although Alice and Violet both belonged to the Richmond County Country Club, they seem not to have remained close friends. As she retreated from society, Violet became increasingly preoccupied with her family's history, and in 1915 when she was fifty-two, she told a scandalous story about her youth that landed her in court. She claimed that when she was twelve years old, her father married her to an army officer, and that after the ceremony, she and the officer stayed together in an army tent for two days. When they emerged, the officer was sent away, and the marriage was kept secret, but Violet allegedly became pregnant, giving birth to stillborn twins. When the Lincoln Trust Company, the executor of her father's $200,000 estate, heard Violet's story, they petitioned the court to declare her incompetent, and the case went to trial, at which a doctor testified that Violet suffered from "chronic delusional insanity."[17] Not surprisingly, the sensational story was picked up by newspapers nationwide.

After only a fifteen-minute deliberation, the jury denied the bank's petition and determined that Violet could manage her financial affairs. One can only imagine her courtroom performance that led to this outcome, but why had she put herself at such risk? And was her account true? Violet's story reflects the fantastic nature of her father's tales, one in which the protagonist is not a commanding patriarch but a disempowered daughter bursting with rage.

Violet died in 1941 and her sister the following year, and the auction of the contents of their home drew antique dealers from up and down the Eastern Seaboard. In its report on the auction, the *Staten Island Historian* described the Ward sisters as "recluses," a term that throws a veil over their lives.[18]

Delia Marie Elliott Fosdick, called Daisy (1857–1951)

Violet Ward introduced Alice to Daisy Elliott, who lived in Brooklyn, was nine years older than Alice, and managed the athletic program of the Berkeley Ladies' Athletic Club in Manhattan. In 1897, the club moved to Carnegie Hall, and Daisy remained its athletic director until 1905. A professional advocate for women's athletics with a history of romantic relationships with women, Daisy was a more radical New Woman than any of Alice's Staten Island friends.

In middle age, however, Daisy changed course. In 1911 when she was fifty-four, she met Frederick Fosdick of Fitchburg, Massachusetts while on vacation in England, where they married on the spot.[19] Despite their hasty decision to wed, the marriage was long-lasting. A widower with four children, Fosdick was president of the Fitchburg Steam Engine Company and served as the city's mayor. In Fitchburg, Daisy was an ardent suffragist and active member of clubs advocating for women and girls. After Fosdick's death in 1924, she traveled extensively in Europe with her old friend, Caroline Lawrence. In her final years, she moved to New Jersey to live with a sister, but when she died in 1951 at the age of ninety-four, she was buried in Fitchburg next to her husband.

ACKNOWLEDGMENTS

This book would not have been possible without the unflagging support of Historic Richmond Town, which has cared for Alice Austen's photographs since 1945. I am especially grateful to Executive Director Jessica B. Phillips, who inherited my project when she took the helm in 2018 and adeptly brought the book to fruition. I also wish to thank Peter Aigner, Director of The Gotham Center for New York City History at The Graduate Center, City University of New York, which awarded me a Robert D. L. Gardiner Writing Fellowship in 2020. Both organizations provided intellectual guidance as well as financial support. Victoria Munro, Executive Director of the Alice Austen House, and Kristine Allegretti, Director of Collections and Operations, offered invaluable assistance by allowing me unlimited access to their collections. Alice Austen's descendants—Martha Cole, Mary Miller, and James Miller—shared their extensive collection of family memorabilia and offered encouragement at every turn.

After leaving my position as Curator of Prints and Photographs at the Museum of the City of New York in 1991, I have worked as an independent scholar and curator, organizing exhibitions and writing books on New York photographers, including Berenice Abbott, Alfred Stieglitz, and Jacob Riis. I knew little about Alice Austen until 2001, when I was asked to serve on a planning committee for a new visitor interpretation of the Austen House. Alice's photographs, I learned, belonged to Historic Richmond Town, where researchers could peruse a set of three-ring binders filled with modern prints from her glass plate negatives. I also learned that the only book on Alice was Ann Novotny's *Alice's World*, published in 1976.

Several years later, Maxine Friedman, then Historic Richmond Town's Chief Curator, asked my advice on updating the access and preservation of the Alice Austen Photograph Collection. In addition to the 3,500 glass plate negatives that had been printed for researchers, there were several thousand prints and film negatives unknown to the public. Maxine directed the digital scanning and cataloging of the collection's over 7,800 items, and in the years following, and largely as a labor of love, she researched Alice's photographs, identifying the people and events depicted. My approach to research and writing evolved from my curatorial practice: by studying photographic archives, I developed fresh narratives about photographers already known to the general public but in need of up-to-date scholarly attention. Alice Austen, who had not been carefully researched for nearly fifty years, fit this model perfectly. I contracted with Historic Richmond Town to write a book and was given a laptop that allowed me to study in detail the photographs and their documentation.

In 2017, when I began my research in earnest, I quickly assembled a mountain of primary sources that took several years to digest. In addition to Alice's photographs, Historic Richmond Town owns the Austen Family Papers, which includes business documents and correspondence as well as scrapbooks, photo albums, oil portraits, and a hodgepodge of exuberant Victorian ephemera. Although there are only a handful of extant letters written by Alice, the Alice Austen House owns a collection of 700 letters written to her by friends and family, which illuminate her relationships with the cast of characters that she photographed. Carli DeFillo, now Collections Manager at Historic Richmond Town, transcribed them—an epic task, given the eccentricities of Victorian letter writing. Under Carli's supervision, Nicole Giacomino-Azzarelli transcribed a book of letters in the Austen Family Papers by John Haggerty Austen, Alice's grandfather. The Alice Austen House also holds Ann Novotny's research papers—especially valuable because her book is without footnotes.

The staff of four other collections generously helped me complete my primary research. The Schlesinger Library at the Radcliffe Institute for Advanced Study, Harvard University, owns a scrapbook assembled by Alice. This scrapbook and a second one in the collection of the Alice Austen House offer invaluable documentation of Alice's busy social calendar from 1881 through 1889. The University of Miami Libraries holds the Papers of Ralph Middleton Munroe, Alice's uncle by marriage and an amateur photographer. The Concord Free Public Library owns negatives and photo albums by Alfred Munroe, Alice's cousin by marriage and an amateur photographer. The University of Connecticut Library holds the Papers of Oliver O. Jensen, who introduced Alice to the American public in *LIFE* magazine in 1951 and planned a book about her that was never published.

My deepest thanks go to Maxine Friedman and Charles L. Sachs, who preceded Maxine as Curator at Historic Richmond Town, for their generous contribution to my research. As I formulated questions, they found answers by scouring numerous online resources: genealogies, newspaper archives, real estate records, census records, ship passenger lists, and more. As a research team, we solved many mysteries presented by the photographs and were able to amend and correct Novotny's research. Along with Curator Sarah Clark, Maxine and Charlie carefully read chapter drafts from this book.

My Gardiner fellowship took place during COVID, and in lieu of public programs,

I organized an online exhibit, "Miss Alice Austen and Staten Island's Gilded Age." Beautifully designed by Anke Stohlmann, the exhibit was my first attempt to publicize the previously unknown chronology of Alice's life and photographs. The fellowship supported two readers of the manuscript, who helped me step back from the minutiae of Alice's story to consider the larger questions that needed to be addressed. Lillian Faderman, whose seminal books guided my research in gender studies, pushed me to develop connections between Alice's photographs, correspondence, and her evolving sexual identity. Equally valuable were the comments of Britt Salvesen, Curator and Head of the Photography Department at the Los Angeles County Museum of Art, who encouraged me to articulate Alice's conservative but original photographic practice in the context of pictorialism, the dominant genre of the era.

Albert LaFarge, my literary agent, brought the book to Fordham University Press. Working with Fordham has been a pleasure, thanks especially to the leadership of Director Fredric Nachbaur. Production and design manager Mark Lerner, copy editor Lis Pearson, and assistant managing editor Kem Crimmins brought their years of experience to guiding the project from manuscript to book. In providing scans from their collections, I am deeply indebted to Carli DeFillo and Kristine Allegretti. I also wish to thank Xuemeng Zhang, who generously contributed original photography and prepared the scans for printing.

Finally, I thank my family, who offered much more than moral support. My husband Paul Shechtman read the manuscript several times for clarity and brevity. My daughters, Anna and Emily Shechtman, sharpened my political thinking when considering Alice's social conservatism and the rise of first-wave feminism. Their tutelage was essential to writing this book.

Too Good to Get Married took more time and was more challenging to write than I expected, but I believe I have met my goal of reintroducing Alice Austen to the public. Working with both Historic Richmond Town and the Alice Austen House, I was able to bring together the two halves of Alice's legacy. My hope is that the book will provide a sound foundation for Alice Austen enthusiasts and scholars of photography and gender to better appreciate her intriguing photographs and compelling life story.

ABBREVIATIONS

HRT	Historic Richmond Town
SIHS	Staten Island Historical Society
AAH	Alice Austen House Museum
Novotny Papers	Ann Novotny Papers, AAH
AAH Scrapbook	Alice Austen Scrapbook, AAH
AAH Letters	Alice Austen Letter Collection, AAH
Schlesinger Scrapbook	Alice Austen Scrapbook, Schlesinger Library, Radcliffe Institute, Harvard University
Jensen Papers	Oliver O. Jensen Papers, Thomas A. Dodd Research Center, University of Connecticut, Storrs

ILLUSTRATIONS

Unless otherwise noted, the items illustrated belong to Historic Richmond Town. Photographs from the Alice Austen Photograph Collection begin with the accession number 50.015. Titles from this collection without brackets are based on Alice Austen's negative sleeves; bracketed titles are descriptive only.

NOTES

Introduction

1. Oliver Jensen, Research memo, July 12, 1951, Box 5, Jensen Papers (hereafter cited as Research memo, July 12, 1951, Jensen Papers).

2. Oliver Jensen, *The Revolt of American Women: A Pictorial History of the Century of Change from Bloomers to Bikinis—from Feminism to Freud* (New York: Harcourt, Brace and Company, 1952), 15.

3. Vavelda von Steinberg, Research memo, September 10, 1951, Box 5, Jensen Papers (hereafter cited as Research memo, September 10, 1951, Jensen Papers).

4. Jensen, *The Revolt of American Women*, 15; "Members of [Alice's] family died, and since she never married, she was finally left alone at Clear Comfort with her old friend, Gertrude Tate, who had come to live with her." "The Newly Discovered Picture World of Alice Austen, Great Woman Photographer Steps Out of the Past," *LIFE* (September 24, 1951), 144.

5. Ann Novotny, *Alice's World: The Life and Photography of an American Original: Alice Austen, 1866–1952* (Old Greenwich, CT: The Chatham Press, 1976), 60.

6. Anne Maguire, *Alice Austen and Gertrude Tate House: A National Historic Lesbian Landmark, Museum and Biographical Guide*, Lesbian Avengers file, Lesbian Herstory Archives, Brooklyn, NY.

7. Laura Peimer vividly describes the Lesbian Avengers' protest in "Alice's Identity Crisis, A Critical Look at the Alice Austen Museum," *History of Photography* 24, no. 2 (2000): 175–79.

8. See Lillian Faderman, "Lesbian Exoticism," in *Surpassing the Love of Men: Romantic Friendship and Love Between Women from the Renaissance to the Present* (New York: Quill, William Morrow, 1981), 254–75.

9. Richard Meyer, "Inverted Histories: 1885–1979," in Catherine Lord and Richard Meyer, eds., *Art and Queer Culture, 1885 to Present* (London: Phaidon Press 2013), 20.

10. Letter of Gertrude Eccleston to Alice Austen, August 28, 1895, AAH Letters.

11. Letter of John A. Morton Jr. to Ann Novotny, December 27, 1975, Novotny Papers.

12. The term "larky life" first appeared in *LIFE* (September 24, 1951), 140. A three-page spread was titled, "A 'Larky' Life, Alice Loved Every Bit of It." The text begins, "For Alice Austen life on Staten Island in the 1880s and 1890s was, as she put it, 'larky.'"

13. Jensen, *The Revolt of American Women*, 25.

Chapter 1: Clear Comfort

1. This is the only letter written by Alice in the AAH letter collection. In the Novotny Papers, there are four letters that Alice wrote to her cousin Henry Rogers Winthrop in the 1940s seeking financial assistance. The Metropolitan Museum of Art has a 1933 letter by Alice (see note 17).

2. Letter of Alice Austen to John H. Austen, August 25, 1892, AAH Letters.

3. See Ira Cohen, "The Auction System in the Port of New York, 1817–1837," *The Business History Review* 45, no. 4 (Winter 1971): 488–510. Cohen writes this about Haggerty & Austen: "The older auction houses continued to dominate the auction business, especially the firms growing out of the separation of the 1820s partnership of Haggerty & Austen," 507.

4. "In 1827, Haggerty, Austen & Co. sold at auction, $6,000,000. Amount of duty on this amount was $72,000," *Documents of the Assembly of the State of New York*, Seventy-Second Session, No. 218, "Report of the Committee on Trade and Manufactures on Auction Duties" (April 9, 1849), 8.

5. Moses Yale Beach, *Wealth and Biography of the Wealthy Citizens of New York City: Comprising an Alphabetical Arrangement of Persons Estimated to be Worth $100,000, and Upwards, With the Sums Appended to Each Name* (New York, 1845), 5. Beach's figures may be exaggerated. See Edward Pessen, "Moses Beach Revisited: A Critical Examination of His Wealthy Citizens Pamphlets," *The Journal of American History* 58, no. 2 (September 1971): 415–26.

6. William Rhinelander Stewart, *Grace Church and Old New York* (New York: E. P. Dutton & Co., 1924), 125–28.

7. *Daily National Pilot* (Buffalo, NY), February 7, 1846; The *New York Daily Herald* (February 11, 1846) listed the auction purchasers and the prices, from $40 to $950. David Austen purchased two $950 pews (the equivalent of $64,000 today).

8. Remarks published in *"The Commercial"* (most likely the *New York Commercial Advertiser*) were cited in the *New York Tribune*, March 6, 1851.

9. Thompson testified in court: "I am a dry goods merchant, and have been engaged in that trade for about 30 years," *Morning Herald*, May 24, 1839.

10. For the history of the American Art Union, see https://ahpcs.org/publisher/the-american-art-union.

11. John H. Austen Scrapbook, HRT, Austen Family Papers, MS001, Box 17.

12. For a discussion of John and George Austen's role in the early kerosene trade, see Abraham Gesner and George Weltden Gesner, *A Practical Treatise on Coal, Petroleum, and Other Distilled Oils* (New York: Bailliere Brothers, 1865), 10–11.

13. A keyword search for John H. Austen in nyshistoricsnewspapers.org from 1857 through 1883 yields 405 auction advertisements, which list the companies he worked for.

14. When John Austen traveled to Europe from 1867 to 1872, he asked Elizabeth to save his letters, which are pasted in a book, along with his sister Sarah Ann Austen's letters to him (1832–1834) and his 1874 letters from the American West. John H. Austen Letter book, HRT Austen Family Papers, MS002, Box 1 (hereafter cited as JHA Letter book).

15. John H. Austen's bankruptcy notice was published in the *New York Times* on May 5, 1868; he was listed as auctioneer in thirty-one auctions that year.

16. See Lincoln Diamont, *Chaining the Hudson: The Fight for the River in the American Revolution* (New York: Fordham University Press, 2004).

17. John Haggerty Austen married Elizabeth Alice Townsend; Sarah Ann Austen married William Hawxhurst Townsend; and Mary Austen married Isaac Townsend. In a 1933 letter, Alice noted, "Three Townsends married three Austens." Letter of Alice Austen to Joseph Downs, January 19, 1933, curatorial object file "Easy Chair 33.26," Department of the American Wing, Metropolitan Museum of Art, New York (hereafter cited as Metropolitan Museum of Art Letter).

18. "My grandparents (John) Austen lived in Vesey Street, No. 2 Bowling Green, Union Square, & had a country place at Throgg's Neck," Metropolitan Museum of Art Letter.

19. The original house was probably built by Lambert Dorland, a weaver, and his son Jan, a farmer and cordwainer, between 1700 and 1725. Shirley A. Zavin et al., *Alice Austen House: Historic Structures Report*, 1979, 44 (hereafter cited as Historic Structures Report). On a post-card advertising the Clear Comfort Tea Room in the 1930s, Alice, following family tradition, dated the house "prior to 1669," HRT Austen Files.

20. For an excellent discussion of the early development of Staten Island, see Adam Zalma, "Staten Island in the Harbor Metropolis: The Making of the Region and the Disappearance of the Island, 1790–1858," PhD diss. (Rutgers University: New Brunswick, NJ, 2014).

21. Both sons were buried in the David Austen family vault, Trinity Cemetery. Elizabeth's mourning ring currently belongs to a great-granddaughter of Peter Austen.

22. One of Elizabeth's brothers, William Hawxhurst Townsend, who was married to John Austen's sister Sarah Ann, purchased a twenty-acre hillside property about a mile from the Austen House. It may be that the two families intended to raise their families together, but the William Townsends moved back to Manhattan in the 1860s. For the Townsend compound, see Charles W. Leng and William T. Davis, *Staten Island and Its People: A History, 1609–1933*, Vol. 5 (New York, 1933), 134; and James G. Ferreri, "Miss Errington Could Teach Us Something About Respect," *Staten Island Advance*, January 29, 2004, D2.

23. Samuel Akerly, "Agriculture of Richmond County," *Transactions of the New York State Agricultural Society . . . for the Year 1842*, 199–200.

24. For a detailed history of the Austen House, see Historic Structures Report.

25. Herman Hoyer, a German-born, New York photographer, produced a set of stereographs, "Illustrations of Staten Island," that were advertised in the *Richmond County Gazette* between August and November 1859; See Charles L. Sachs, "Alice Austen's Predecessors and Contemporaries: Photography on Staten Island in the 19th and Early 20th Centuries," *Staten Island Historian*, 11 n.s., no. 1 (Summer–Fall 1993): 3–4.

26. On December 5, 1851, Renwick purchased the first four lots (numbered 2, 3, 4, and 5 on the 1848 survey map of property of W. W. Van Wagenen) for $2,000 and three days later, transferred them to the Austen's attorney who put the lots in a trust for Elizabeth, subject to a mortgage from Renwick. See Richmond County Deeds 24, 548–49, 604–06.

27. Elizabeth acquired the remaining lots in two separate purchases: on February 1, 1859, she bought lots 6, 7, 8, and 9, from Charles Edgar Appleby for $1,600; and on March 1, 1859, lot 10 from Henry E. Dibble. See Richmond County Deeds 43, 437–38, 537–38.

28. In his letters to Elizabeth from Europe, John Austen described visits to churches and cathedrals, some of which he recalled from his extensive collection of stereographs.

29. The neo-Gothic modernization of the old farm dwelling was suggested by Downing in his journal, *The Horticulturist*, and was undertaken elsewhere on Staten Island. Historic Structures Report, 16.

30. Alice sold the wing chair to the Metropolitan Museum in 1933; it is currently on view at the Alice Austen House.

31. Alice photographed the bust and pedestal in the dining room twice (50.015.5246 and 50.015.7372).

32. The quarantine station, which stood near the Austen House on the Staten Island waterfront, was home to the health officer of the Port of New York. Alice's quarantine photographs are discussed in Chapter 5.

33. W. H. Rideing, "A Spring Jaunt on Staten Island," *Harper's New Monthly Magazine* 57, no. 3 (September 1878): 548.

34. Rideing, "A Spring Jaunt on Staten Island," 548.

35. Examples of other feature stories about the Austen House include, "Rosebank's Old House," *New York Sun*, December 1, 1895, 7; and "Old House Once Guided Packets," *New York Sun*, January 11, 1930. In the 1890s, the Austen House began to appear in Staten Island guidebooks.

36. Alice pasted this article in her scrapbook, and wrote the date in pencil, "May 22, 1889," AAH Scrapbook. A similar article, "Commodore Vanderbilt's Courting," with engraved illustrations, appeared in the *New York World*, March 27, 1887, 26.

37. Letter of John H. Austen to Elizabeth A.T. Austen, June 22,1867, JHA Letter book.

38. Letter of John H. Austen to Elizabeth A.T. Austen, July 25, 1867, JHA Letter book.

39. While John Austen was in Europe, Elizabeth managed a dispute with their neighbors regarding water rights and the construction of curbs on Pennsylvania Avenue. John wrote, "The answer you gave about the curb & gutters business was just right. When Christie does his I will do mine & not one minute before." Letter of John H. Austen to Elizabeth A. T. Austen, July 24, 1872, JHA Letter book.

40. Letter of John H. Austen to Elizabeth A.T. Austen, July 25, 1867, JHA Letter book.

41. Catharine E. Beecher and Harriet Beecher Stowe, *American Woman's Home: or Principles of Domestic Science,* 1st ed. 1869 (Watkins Glen, NY: American Life Foundation, 1979), 13.

42. Elizabeth Alice [T.] Austen Last Will and Testament, May 1, 1884. Richmond County, NY, Surrogate's Office, Wills, vol. U, 473–78. (hereafter cited as Elizabeth A.T. Austen Will). She died January 8, 1887, at the age of seventy-four. John H. Austen died intestate at the age of eighty-three in 1894, leaving an estate valued at $15,000, approximately $500,000 today. For the Letter of Administration of John Haggerty Austen, June 7, 1894, see Richmond County, NY, Surrogate's Office, Decrees of Administration, vol. 4, 80.

43. Letter of John H. Austen to Elizabeth A.T. Austen, June 15, 1867, JHA Letter book.

44. Edward Stopford Munn, b. June 21, 1828, Day Book of Baptisms, 1827–1839, Parish Registers of St. Mary's Church, Islington, England. The manifest for the ship *Caroline and Mary Clark*, leaving from the port of Le Havre, France, and arriving in the port of New York on April 14, 1851, listed the entire Munn family—Benjamin, 49, Merchant; Sarah, 49; Edward, 23; Eleanor, 21; Frederick, [age illegible]; Sarah, [age illegible]; Benjamin, 16; and Thomas, 14.

45. From 1860 to 1862, Munn was in a "note and exchange brokerage" partnership—Munn & Marsh, brokers—with Steward C. Marsh Jr., in Manhattan. Trow's New York Directories, 1861 through 1866, list Edward S. Munn, broker, in Manhattan.

46. A 3-by-5 inch notecard recording the marriages performed at St. John's Episcopal Church in Clifton reads: "Munn, Edward S / 6–1-1863 / to Alice C Austen / by Rev Thomas K Conrad / Witnesses: Mr. and Mrs. Mann [sic] and Mrs. Austen." Novotny Papers.

47. Elizabeth and John Austen purchased Woodbine Cottage on Sylvaton Terrace on February 16, 1864, for $3,500. Richmond County, NY, Clerk's Office, Deeds 53, 552–55. After Ally moved back to Clear Comfort, the Austens kept Woodbine Cottage as a rental property. Austen Family Property Ledger, Box 2, Austen Family Collection, HRT. They sold the cottage, which has since been torn down, for $1,800 in March 1885. Richmond County Deeds 157, 240–42.

48. The 1865 New York State census lists Edward Munn as head of household. New York, Richmond County, Town of Southfield, 2nd Election District, p. 29, Dwelling 153.

49. By the time John embarked on his first trip to Europe in June 1867, mother and daughter were living at Clear Comfort. "And now dear Elizabeth I must say send love to Ally, Minn, & Peter & kiss the baby your devoted JHA." Letter of John H. Austen to Elizabeth A. T. Austen, June 14, 1867, JHA Letter book.

50. The 1870 US census lists Benjamin Munn as head of household. Edward's mother Sarah

died in 1870, shortly before the census. New York, Kings County, Brooklyn Ward 2, p. 25, Dwelling 176.

51. In the 1870 US census, mother and daughter are still listed with the surname "Munn": household headed by "Eustin [sic], John H," including "Munn, Alice" (33) and "Munn, Elizabeth" (4) (New York State, Richmond County, Town of Southfield, p. 100, Dwelling No. 680). In her will, Elizabeth Austen lists her daughter as "Alice Cornell Austen" and her granddaughter as "Elizabeth Alice Austen Mann [sic]" (Elizabeth A.T. Austen Will). The 1900 US census lists "Alice Cornell Austen" as "widow" and her daughter as "Elizabeth A Austen." (New York, Richmond County, Ward 4, Enumeration District 10, Sheet 8). The *New York Times* obituary, September 22, 1900, reads: "Alice Cornell Austen of Clifton, S.I., daughter of the late Elizabeth Townsend and John. H. Austen." The 1915 New York State census (Election District 36, Ward 4, New York City, Richmond County, Town of Southfield, Assembly District 1, 15) lists "Minnie Miller" as head of household and includes "Munn, Alice, Niece" (45). In her will, prepared in 1915, Minn refers to her niece as "Elizabeth Alice Austen, also sometimes known as Elizabeth Alice Austen Munn."

52. "Alice's father is still an unmentionable subject and very little is known about him. Apparently, he sailed for England, promising to send for his wife as soon as he was settled, and never did. The impression is that he never saw his daughter. Alice's mother probably heard something about him after he left because her vehement attitude suggests she knew she had been deserted rather than that he was lost at sea or had died before he could send for her." Research memo, September 10, 1951, Jensen Papers.

53. "Munn.—In Brooklyn, on the 15th inst., of pneumonia, Edward S. Munn, aged 52 years," *New York Daily Herald*, November 19, 1879.

54. Letter of Ellen Munn Whittaker to Mrs. Edward Munn, May 25, 1881, Box 2, Austen Family Collection.

55. Alice photographed the room that she shared with her mother in 1887, 1894, and 1898. Photographs taken after her mother's death in 1900 indicate that Alice hardly changed the arrangement of the room.

56. Letters of Alice C. Austen to Alice Austen, June 18, 1892 and August 17, 1893.

57. Ally's scrapbook, a gift from her maternal grandmother when she was ten, featured articles on European history and natural history but nothing on American topics. Alice C. Austen Scrapbook, Box 3, Austen Family Collection. Unlike her mother, Ally wished to go to Europe with her father, but the timing of Alice's birth and her collapsing marriage presented roadblocks. In his last letter from Europe, John wrote: "As far as Ally [is concerned,] when could she have gone. . . . Certainly there is no chance whatever." Letter of John H. Austen to Elizabeth A.T. Austen, July 24, 1872, JHA Letter book.

58. The 1865 New York State census for Richmond County, Town of Southfield, Second Election District lists Dwelling No. 78 (p. 14) household headed by Frances Hicks, including son "Sam Hicks" ([age] 26, Broker); and Dwelling No. 166 (p. 31) household headed by "Jno. H Austen," including daughter "Minnie Hicks" ([age] 25). Richmond County, Town of Southfield, Second Election District.

59. Letter of John H. Austen to Elizabeth A.T. Austen, June 19, 1869, JHA Letter book.

60. Richard E. Morris, "The Victorian 'Change of Air' as Medical and Social Construction," *Journal of Tourism History*, 2018, https://doi.org/10.1080/1755182X.2018.1425485.

61. "Died. Hicks. On board of ship Agra, off Batavia, on Tuesday, July 5, of consumption, Samuel Hicks, eldest son of the late John H. and Frances Hicks, of this city," *New York Daily Herald*, November 26, 1870.

62. "A Piano Voyage Twice Around the World," *New York Times*, May 14, 1875, 7.

63. Letter of John H. Austen to Elizabeth A.T. Austen, August 5, 1874, JHA Letter book.

64. On May 2, 1872, the *Brooklyn Daily Eagle*, 2, reported: "The ship *Agra*, from Hong Kong for New York, Capt. Miller, was lost on the Parsels reef in the China Sea." On May 7, the *New York Herald* printed a correction, noting that the ship lost was not the *Agra* but a German vessel.

65. The Austen House, filled with artifacts from Europe and Asia, illustrates the "cosmopolitan domesticity" described by Kristin L. Hoganson, in *Consumers Imperium: The Global Production of American Domesticity, 1865–1920* (Chapel Hill: University of North Carolina Press, 2007), but the Austen consumers were uncharacteristic. John H. Austen was a European traveler and a purveyor of European luxury goods, and Captain Oswald and Minn Muller brought home souvenirs from their world travels.

66. Mrs. Maurice I. [Eleanor] Pitou, November 4, 1975, Interview notes, Novotny Papers.

67. The grandchildren of Elizabeth Patty Austen Miller, Alice's first cousin (hereafter cited as Patty Miller) own a photograph of the Potter Family installed in the Austen house bathroom. Ann Novotny, *Alice's World: The Life and Photography of an American Original: Alice Austen, 1866–1952* (Old Greenwich, CT: The Chatham Press, 1976), 25. One grandchild donated a Potter Family figurine to the Alice Austen House (1990.1.1).

68. "The fact that Uncle Oswald secreted 'naughty' literature in their rooms is recalled to this day by Alice's Cousin Patty, Uncle Peter's only daughter," Novotny, *Alice's World*, 23. Novotny visited Patty Miller in Upstate New York for two days in 1975, and they corresponded afterward, but Novotny's papers do not include interview notes with her.

69. Letter of Alice C. Austen to Alice Austen, February 14, 1892.

70. "Boarding School for Young Ladies. Mad. Petibeau and Miss Errington have recently established their Boarding School on Staten Island, at one of the most beautiful, healthy and commanding spots that can be found on the bay. . . . The ladies are . . . eminently qualified by their acquirements, moral worth and experiences, to take charge of and educate young ladies. . . . Parents may with entire confidence place children under their management," *The Evening Post*, October 23, 1843.

71. In 1864, Harriet Errington traveled to California to tutor the children of Frederick Law Olmsted, who lived on Staten Island. There she met geologist Clarence King and photographer Carleton Watkins of the US Geological Survey. In a letter to her brother, Harriet reported on her collection of fossils: "My collection of specimens, all I believe new species, are in the care of the paleontologist of the Geo. Survey. . . . One is named Lima Erringtoni in honor of my discovery," PBA Galleries, *Americana, Travel and Exploration*, March 22, 2006, lot 112.

72. On the first page of her first scrapbook, Alice pasted the obituary of Georgiana Errington. At the top edge of the clipping, she wrote in pencil: "Died January 24th age 64 years." Schlesinger Scrapbook.

73. Miss Errington's note suggests that Alice regularly sent her a Christmas card: "Many thanks for your pretty card and the kind thought of me that never fails," Letter of H. N. Errington to Alice Austen, December 26, 1891.

74. Autograph album of Grace Simonson, HRT (69.002.0005).

75. For seminal discussions of romantic friendship, see Carroll Smith-Rosenberg, *Disorderly Conduct: Visions of Gender in Victorian America* (New York: Oxford University Press, 1986), 53–76; and Lillian Faderman, *Surpassing the Love of Men: Romantic Friendship and Love Between Woman from the Renaissance to the Present* (New York: Quill, William Morrow, 1981), 157–77.

76. Letter of Grace Simonson to Alice Austen, August 28, 1885.

77. Elizabeth A.T. Austen Will.

78. Metropolitan Museum of Art Letter.

Chapter 2: The Sporting Society Set

1. AAH owns Alice's children's magazines.

2. R. Gordon Kelly, *Children's Periodicals of the United States* (Westport, CT: Greenwood Press, 1984), 455.

3. For an overview of the trade card fad, see Robert Jay, *The Trade Card in Nineteenth-Century America* (Columbia: University of Missouri Press, 1987). Jennifer N. Black, in "Exchange Cards: Advertising, Album Making, and Commodification of Sentiment in the Gilded Age," *Winterthur Portfolio* 51, no. 1 (Spring 2017), offers an extensive review of the scholarly literature on trade cards collected in scrapbooks.

4. The oldest Austen scrapbook belonged to Alice's grandmother, Elizabeth A.T. Austen. Compiled before she married in 1835, it features exquisitely hand-colored magazine engravings. John H. Austen's scrapbook, given to him by his daughter Alice C. Austen in 1852, includes programs and news clippings related to his role in the sale of the Art Union collection and the early years of the New York Yacht Club. Alice C. Austen's scrapbook was given to her in 1847 by her grandmother, Alice Townsend, and includes articles on European natural history and the arts. Peter T. Austen's incomplete scrapbook begins in 1869 when he was seventeen and includes articles that increasingly specialized in the sciences. HRT, Austen Family Papers, M001, Boxes 3, 11, 12, 17.

5. Alice's three trade card scrapbooks, HRT Austen Family Papers, MS001, Box 4.

6. See Ellen Gruber Garvey, "Scrapbook, Wishbook, Prayerbook: Trade-Card Scrapbooks and the Missionary Work of Advertising," in Susan Tucker et al., eds., *The Scrapbook in American Life* (Philadelphia: Temple University Press, 2005), 97–115.

7. Letter of Alice C. Austen to Alice Austen, undated, AAH Letters. The meaning of the expression "within effect" is uncertain.

8. Letter of Alice C. Austen to Alice Austen, June 17 [no year], AAH Letters.

9. Letter of Alice C. Austen to Alice Austen, May 5, 1892, AAH Letters.

10. Alice's photographs offer excellent source material for a study of New York Gilded Age fashion.

11. The three children of Peter and Nellie Austen were William Munroe, called Munroe (b. 1883); Elizabeth Patty, called Patty (b. 1884); and Oswald Townsend (b. 1885).

12. In the 1882 program for the Rutgers College commencement exercises, Alice wrote in pencil a dollar amount (e.g., $30, $20) next to each prize. In the 1885 program for the graduating exercises of the Rutgers College Grammar School, she starred the history and valedictory orations and added other comments, in pencil. Schlesinger Scrapbook.

13. "Broadway Theater HMS Pinafore, Gorman's Original Philadelphia Church Choir Company, An augmented orchestra under the direction of Mr. J.P. Sousa," April 25, 1879, Schlesinger Scrapbook.

14. Comparing Alice's scrapbooks to her photographs of women "cross-dressing and mocking courtship customs," Ellen Gruber Garvey incorrectly concludes that Alice's scrapbooks were self-censored. *Writing with Scissors: American Scrapbooks from the Civil War to the Harlem Renaissance* (New York: Oxford University Press, 2011), 18.

15. To save space, Alice cut off the names and dates of newspapers but penciled in the date at the end of almost every article.

16. The first two scrapbooks were not removed from the Austen House in 1945 by Loring McMillen and eventually showed up at auction. The first album was purchased in 2004 by the Schlesinger Library, Radcliffe Institute, Harvard University. On the front inside cover is the date, August 27, 1883, and on the back inside cover is the date, January 20, 1887. The second belonged to a tennis ephemera collector who lent it to Ann Novotny in 1981 and is now at AAH. The title page of the second scrapbook reads, "1887 / 1888 / 1889." The scrapbooks are unpaginated, but items are arranged chronologically. A third, unfinished scrapbook and loose clippings dated 1889 to 1893 intended for it can be found in the HRT Austen Family Papers, MS001, Boxes 5 and 8. In 1902, Alice started a scrapbook with fabric pages to secure pins and buttons. A remarkable collection of commercial objects, the scrapbook includes Republican political buttons, bicycling ephemera, and pins celebrating St. Patrick's Day, which was Alice's birthday. HRT Austen Family Papers, MS001, Box 17.

17. Research memo, July 12, 1951, Jensen Papers.

18. See Brigid M. Boyle, "Athleticism and the New Woman, Lawn Tennis at the Staten Island Ladies' Club," *Winterthur Portfolio* 54, no. 3 (Winter 2019): 231–68.

19. The Staten Island Ladies' Club for Outdoor-Sport was often called the Staten Island Ladies' Club and, after its move in 1886, the New-Brighton Ladies' Club.

20. Charles E. Clay, "The Staten Island Cricket and Baseball Club," *Outing Magazine* 40, no. 2 (November 1887): 107. AAH Scrapbook.

21. *New York Herald*, June 9, 1880.

22. Editor of the *Amateur Athlete* (M.A.H.), "Ladies' Club for Outdoor Sports," July 13, 1884, Schlesinger Scrapbook.

23. The second location for the Staten Island Cricket and Baseball Club was often identified as Livingston, the name of the station on the Staten Island Railroad.

24. The Kirmess took place in late May 1886 in the German Club Rooms in Stapleton. The renowned "Professor Carl Marwig" choreographed a suite of dances in the "Dutch, Spanish, Dresden China, and Gipsy" styles. Most exciting for the spectators was the finale, a "Lawn Tennis Dance," in which young men wielded tennis racquets. The Schlesinger Scrapbook includes the Kirmess program and several press accounts.

25. "August 31, 1887, The Ladies Club," *Richmond County Gazette*, AAH Scrapbook.

26. Undated article, AAH Scrapbook.

27. Staten Island hosted the national tournament only in 1888.

28. Edward H. Clarke, MD, *Sex in Education: Or, a Fair Chance for Girls* (Boston: James R. Osgood and Company, 1875), 117.

29. "Beauty on the Green," *New York Herald*, September 8, 1888.

30. Patricia Campbell Warner, *When the Girls Came Out to Play: The Birth of American Sportswear* (Amherst: University of Massachusetts Press, 2006), 46.

31. "How A Girl Plays Tennis," *The [Philadelphia] Times*, October 10, 1886.

32. Adeline K. Robinson, "Lawn Tennis Hints for Girls," *Harper's Young People* (October 30, 1888), 920, AAH Scrapbook.

33. Alice won the women's singles on October 2, 1888, and took this photograph (see Figure 2.7) on the Fort Wadsworth grounds a month later, on November 6, 1888.

34. *The Racquet of the Clifton Tennis Club*, a program for a fundraising fair held in May 1889, noted: "Last year, when the Club had become firmly established, the ladies' purpose being achieved, they magnanimously dropped their title from the name of the club, and adopted the present title," HRT, Austen Family Papers, MS001, Box 2. In "Sporting Notes," May 18, 1890, the *New York Herald* reported: "The Clifton Tennis Club has been organized on the east shore

of Staten Island with fine grounds at Arrochar." The officers listed were all men. On October 18, 1890, Alice photographed the new clubhouse (50.015.6011).

35. The match was for the championship in ladies' and gentlemen's doubles; Alice and her regular partner Harry Wright successfully defended their title against Julie Marsh and Theodore Townsend. "The Clifton Ladies Club," October 11, 1883, Schlesinger Scrapbook.

36. "The Clifton Tennis Club," *New York Times*, May 22, 1893.

37. "Ladies at the Sculls. A Pretty Sight on the Narrows at the Clifton Boat Club," *New York Times*, September 6, 1885.

38. "The minstrel entertainment held by the Clifton Boat Club last Friday evening at the boathouse was in every way a success. The members of the club were most excellent in their impersonations of plantation darkeys," November 20, 1885, Schlesinger Scrapbook.

39. Warner, *When the Girls Came Out to Play*, 61.

40. The Richmond County Country Club was established on the twelve-acre former Ellingwood estate near Grymes Hill for hunting and lawn tennis. In 1897, the club moved to a thirty-acre site on Todt Hill, one of Staten Island's highest and most scenic locales. The country club took over the childhood home of Alice's close friend, Louisa Alexander, as its clubhouse, which remains the clubhouse today.

41. A fourth member may have been Julie Marsh's cousin Sue Ripley. See the discussion of "The Darned Club" in Chapter 4.

42. "They Took a Great Risk," May 12, 1886, Schlesinger Scrapbook.

43. "The Famous Bean Soup Club of Clifton," *Richmond Gazette*, July 26, 1889, AAH Scrapbook.

44. Five hundred guests from Staten Island and New York attended this party at the home of Erasmus Wiman, a leading patron of Staten Island society events. "The reception . . . assembled the best of Staten Island's very good society [which] . . . could easily form another 'four hundred.'" "Reception at Tantalon, Mrs. and the Misses Wiman Receive Their Friends," December 12, 1888, AAH Scrapbook.

45. The slight that started the "war" was the failure to invite Mrs. Nathaniel Marsh, Julie Marsh's mother and Clifton's premier hostess, to attend a planning committee meeting for the annual charity ball. Alice and her close friends boycotted the charity ball and organized a ball for Clifton residents only. "Social War in the Suburbs, Staten Island Society Divided into Two Camps," *New York Sun*, February 18, 1888.

46. March 18, 1889, AAH Scrapbook.

47. The poem was written by Mary Wortley Montagu (1689–1762), an English writer and diplomat. March 3, 1886, Schlesinger Scrapbook.

48. Letter of Elisabeth Strong to Alice Austen, July 19, 1885, AAH Letters. In 1892, another friend of Bessie's, Charles Ludlow, took interest in Alice, who sent him her photograph; he then traveled to Staten Island to visit her.

49. Letter of Gertrude Eccleston to Alice Austen, June 21, 1893, AAH Letters.

50. Letter of Grace Simonson to Alice Austen, September 25, 1887, AAH Letters.

51. Thorstein Veblen, *The Theory of the Leisure Class* (Oxford: Oxford University Press, 2007 ed.), 28–29.

Chapter 3: Makeshift Photography

1. Research memo, July 12, 1951, Jensen Papers.

2. The Austens' stereoscope, which sat on a table in the middle parlor, can be seen in the background of Alice's photograph of a fake poker game (see Figure 4.26).

3. Letter of John H. Austen to Elizabeth A.T. Austen, June 26, 1869, JHA Letter book.

4. Letter of John H. Austen to Elizabeth A.T. Austen, July 21, 1869, JHA Letter book.

5. On a visit to the new Victoria and Albert Museum in London, John told a copyist who sat in front of an Edwin Landseer painting that "a print of it hung in my house nearly 2,000 miles away." (June 19, 1867). From Lake Lucerne in the Swiss Alps, John referred to "that high bluff that you see in the picture that hangs over the sofa with snow on the summit." (July 4, 1870). Letters of John H. Austen to Elizabeth A. T. Austen, JHA Letter book.

6. Letter of John H. Austen to Elizabeth A.T. Austen, July 17, 1869, JHA Letter book.

7. Letter of John H. Austen to Elizabeth A.T. Austen, July 13, 1867, JHA Letter book.

8. John mentioned the demonstration on June 29, 1867, and reported on July 6 that he was not going to purchase the camera. He first mentioned the Dubroni camera on July 13, and on July 25, reported that he had rejected buying it. Letters of John H. Austen to Elizabeth A. T. Austen, JHA Letter book.

9. Letter of John H. Austen to Elizabeth A.T. Austen, July 25, 1867, JHA Letter book.

10. Peter Townsend Austen Scrapbook, HRT, Austen Family Papers, MS001, Box 12.

11. In 1984, fifty-two glass negatives and forty-one lantern slides by Peter Austen were donated to HRT by the widow of photographer Raymond Borea. Novotny had given the collection to Borea in the 1970s. Most of the photographs depict Peter's family.

12. "The New Photographic Course at Rutgers," *The Photographic Times and American Photographer* 18, no. 375 (November 23, 1888): 589; Gary D. Saretzky, "Nineteenth Century New Jersey Photographers," *New Jersey History* (Fall/Winter, 2004), http://www.gary.saretzky.com /photohistory/resources/photo_in_nj_July_2021.pdf.

13. Letter of Nellie Munroe Austen to Alice Austen, March 27, 1892, AAH Letters.

14. The Munroe family moved to Staten Island from Concord, Massachusetts in 1854, when Ralph Munroe's father Thomas became the New York sales representative for his family's pencil manufacturing firm. In 1869 when Ralph was eighteen, the Munroe family moved to Townsend Avenue near Clear Comfort.

15. Ralph Middleton Munroe and Vincent Gilpin, *The Commodore's Story: The Early Days on Biscayne Bay* (Miami: Historical Association of Southern Florida, 1990), 44.

16. Munroe and Gilpin, *The Commodore's Story*, 26.

17. Munroe and Gilpin, *The Commodore's Story*, 44.

18. Munroe and Gilpin, *The Commodore's Story*, 44.

19. When he married, Ralph Munroe built Breezy Knoll, an octagon-shaped house facing the water at Great Kills. There are twenty-five mounted photographs of Breezy Knoll in the Ralph M. Munroe Family Papers, University of Miami Libraries.

20. "Captain Muller showed her how to operate the camera and Alice began taking pictures. She staunchly maintains that except for showing her how to first work the camera, Captain Muller taught her nothing about photography. . . . Another uncle of Alice's, Peter Townsend Austen, was a prominent chemist at Rutgers and he taught her a little about developing, but Alice again claims that she learned all but the first things by doing it herself." Research memo, July 12, 1951, Jensen Papers.

21. Novotny assumed that Peter Austen built the Clear Comfort darkroom for Alice, but he may have installed it earlier for his own use.

22. Letters of Alice C. Austen to Alice Austen, June 17, 1885 and June 16, 1891, AAH Letters. An early negative in Alice's collection was by Ralph Munroe (50.015.6732). The negative sleeve reads: No. 42, Steamer 'Ethiopia' / clear sunny day / May 2nd 1886. 4.30 P.M. / Taken by Mr. R. Munroe.

23. Alice credited Oswald Muller on four negative sleeves: three full-length portraits of Alice taken in 1887 and 1888 (50.015.6687, 50.015.6688, and 50.015.6692) and an 1891 view of Ralph Munroe's yacht *Micco* in the harbor (50.015.6715). Five family portraits of Oswald, Minn, and Alice show Oswald holding the shutter release in his hand.

24. The group consists of twenty-four negatives and one print. The original negative sleeves have been lost, and the photographs, attributed until recently to Alice, are far more likely the work of Oswald Muller, based on their date, the location next to Oswald's South Street business office, and the subject matter: many of the ships were owned or operated by Roderick W. Cameron, a friend of Oswald and Minn.

25. Two oil sketches of Clifton scenery by Elizabeth A.T. Austen belong to HRT (P01.0030 and P01.0031).

26. Research memo, July 12, 1951, Jensen papers.

27. In *Camera Mosaics: A Portfolio of National Photography*, 1894, Alice's ten prints were credited to "Miss E.A. Austin [sic], Jersey City (N. J.) Camera Club." Gary Saretzky, an expert on the subject, told the author that Alice was not listed as a member of any New Jersey camera clubs.

28. For a defense of women's membership, see Catherine Weed Barnes, "Why Ladies Should be Admitted to Membership in Photographic Societies," *The American Amateur Photographer* 1, no. 6 (December 1889): 223–24.

29. There are four full plate portraits of Minn, Oswald, and Alice consisting of three prints and one negative, none matching (50.015.1920, 50.015.2341, 50.015.2342, and 50.015.6640). Copies (a 3.5-by-4 inch glass positive at HRT and a 3.5-by-4.5 print at the AAH) are variants of 50.015.6640.

30. This print is mounted on an 8-by-10 inch board, indicating that it was especially valued; the negative is lost.

31. See John Rohrbach, ed., *Acting Out: Cabinet Cards and the Making of Modern Photography* (Fort Worth: Amon Carter Museum, Fort Worth; and Oakland: University of California Press, 2020).

32. During the summer of 1885, Alice attempted to make a "stereograph" by mounting two prints of a photograph of Aunt Minn on a single 5-by-8 inch board (50.015. 2334). Apparently, she did not understand the mechanical principle underlying stereoscopy: the three-dimensional illusion of the stereograph requires the use of a camera with two lenses mounted side by side that mimic binocular vision.

33. Despite the limitations of her equipment, Alice persisted in trying to capture motion. In this early group are a cricket match and a boat race, both photographed from a great distance.

34. The full plate camera was fitted with a Dallmeyer lens, which Alice referred to on the negative sleeves as "Dalh lense." In June 1888, she replaced the Dallmeyer lens with a Perken lens. Alice used Carbutt, Cramer, Cramer Light, and Seed dry plates.

35. Alice's photography and her gardening were the subject of two 1911 articles for the syndicated column, "Pages for Misses," which are discussed in Chapter 6.

36. "Makeshift Photography," *New York Herald, Magazine Supplement*, May 28, 1911, 14.

37. This album could have been assembled later, but all the negatives date from 1886, 1887, and 1888.

38. For Christmas 1897, Alice gave an album of Clear Comfort photographs to her Uncle Peter, whose great-grandchildren now own it. HRT owns thirteen photo albums, two of full plate size. The Austen House owns five albums, one of full plate size. In 2021, a privately owned full plate album was disassembled, and the boards sold individually on eBay.

39. "Makeshift Photography," 14.

40. According to Jensen, "Alice claims her first camera was a Waterbury 4 x 5 given to her by a cousin." Research memo, July 12, 1951, Jensen Papers. Alice's camera (A45.0075) was donated to HRT in 1964 by Einar Thulin Jr., who lived in the same apartment building in St. George as Alice and Gertrude, ca. 1948.

41. Research memo, July 12, 1951, Jensen Papers.

42. Arva Moore Parks, *The Forgotten Frontier: Florida Through the Lens of Ralph Middleton Munroe* (Miami, FL: Banyan Books, 1977). For photographs by Ralph Munroe, see the Ralph M. Munroe Family Papers, University of Miami Libraries, Digital Collections.

43. Letter of Thomas Quincy Browne Jr., to Alice Austen, April 22, 1893, AAH Letters.

44. Letter of Ralph Middleton Munroe to Alice Austen, April 18, 1893, AAH Letters.

45. Alfred Munroe (1817–1904) was recorded in the Staten Island censuses of 1870 and 1875. When his nephew Ralph Munroe moved to Florida in 1886, Alfred spent winters in Coconut Grove. Munroe and Gilpin, *The Commodore's Story*, 164, 179. The Concord Library owns a collection of 183 of Alfred Munroe's negatives and two beautiful albums of his Concord prints. Alfred published *Concord: Out of Door Sketches* (Concord, MA: The Erudite Press, 1903), which included reproductions of some of his photographs, including "Under the Hemlocks."

46. Letter of Mary Munroe to Alice Austen, July 22, 1892, AAH Letters.

47. Letter of Alice C. Austen to Alice Austen, June 18, 1892, AAH Letters.

48. Alice's Fishkill cousins were Emily Denning Van Rensselaer; Emily's sister Jane Denning; and Emily's daughter, also named Emily. They lived on an estate named Presqu'ile, that jutted out into the Hudson River. Alice photographed at Presqu'ile on summer visits in 1886, 1888, 1890, and 1892.

49. Alice sent Browne one of her views of the waterfall at Watkins Glen. In his reply, Brown described his "exact formula for oxalate developer . . . for time pictures." A few weeks later, Alice sent two portraits of Browne, one taken at Presqu'ile (50.015.6902) and the other at Milsingah Falls (50.015.6404). Letters of John C. Browne to Alice Austen, September 6, 1892 and October 18, 1892, AAH Letters.

50. HRT has an extensive collection of Isaac Almstaedt photographs, and in 2004 held an exhibition, "Staten Island Gems: Photographs by Isaac Almstaedt." Also see John B. Woodall, "Isaac Almstaedt, Staten Island's Famous Artistic Photographer," *Staten Island Historian* 5, nos. 3 and 4 (Winter–Spring, 1988): 26–27.

51. Charles E. Clay, "The Staten Island Cricket and Baseball Club," *Outing* 11, no. 2 (November 1887): 98–112. Alice pasted the entire fourteen-page article into her scrapbook. AAH Scrapbook.

52. Alice's print of the Isaac Almstaedt L.I.S.C. tennis portrait of L.I.S.C. (PH01.0048) can be seen in the photograph "Middle room from hall piano," January 2, 1895 (50.015.5252).

53. Isaac Almstaedt, [Alice Austen, Trude Eccleston, and Julia Bredt], n.d. (49.002.0004).

54. Compare Isaac Almstaedt, St. John's Church, Chapel & Rectory, n.d. (96.019.0029B) and [St. John's Church, Rectory and Sunday school], n.d. (50.015.7531.001). The two children standing at the entrance gate of the church appear in both photographs, and the clock on the church steeple reads 3:30 in Alice's photograph and 3:35 in Almstaedt's. There are no extant negatives of these photographs, but Alice's photograph is in an album of photographs of St. John's Episcopal Church, dated 1892.

55. Letter of Edith Blunt to Alice Austen, September 18, 1892, AAH Letters.

56. Alice's photograph, "Bessie & Dr. Van Dyke with camera," of March 17, 1892, is known only from a badly damaged negative (50.015.5502).

57. Letters of Elisabeth Strong to Alice Austen, December 7 and December 27, 1890, AAH Letters.

58. Alice sent prints to *Camera Mosaics: A Portfolio of National Photography, Being a Collection of Many Hundred Pictures Made by Leading Members of American Photographic Societies in the Course of Their Travels.* The large-format, two-volume set was not selective (it included works by eighty-eight photographers of all stripes) and was poorly printed in halftone. Ten prints by "Miss E.A. Austin" [sic] appeared on pp. 225, 233, and 273. The text was marred by misspellings of proper names, including Alice's.

59. The extant exhibition prints were made from full plate negatives and mounted on 10-by-12 inch boards. Written in black ink in Alice's hand on the back of each mount is a title in quotation marks and in the lower right: Miss E.A. Austen, Rosebank P.O., Staten Island, New York. Four of the prints are at HRT: The bridge behind Rip Van Winkle's house (50.015.2470); A Colonial Interior (40.015.2490); Team of oxen (50.015.2494); and Brook (50.015.2468). Two prints are at AAH: A Cartful, Staten Island (1995.9.142); and Ready to Start, Staten Island (1995.9.145).

60. "E.A. Austen, Rosebank, N.Y." was among the entrants for the second amateur photography contest in *Frank Leslie's Illustrated Newspaper* (November 15, 1890), 260. A selection of winning photographs and the list of prizes appeared on February 7, 1891, 8–11.

61. Letter of Elisabeth Strong to Alice Austen, December 28, 1892, AAH Letters. Alice's three issues of *Sun and Shade* (September 1890, November 1890, and February 1893) are at AAH.

62. Letter from Elisabeth Strong to Alice Austen, June 23, 1888, AAH Letters.

63. For Christmas 1890, Alice sent a self-portrait to her Fishkill cousins and to Bessie Strong. Letter of Emily Denning Van Rensselaer to Alice Austen, December 29, 1890; and letter of Elisabeth Strong to Alice Austen, December 27, 1890. In 1892, Percival Drayton, who Alice met when visiting Julia Bredt in Bethlehem, Pennsylvania, thanked Alice for her photograph and promised to send his to her in a few weeks. Letter of Percival Drayton to Alice Austen, March 30, 1892, AAH Letters.

64. Alice's initials inked in reverse on the emulsion side of the negative first appear in July 1886. They indicate that at least on some occasions, she wanted her authorship to be known.

65. Letter of Hetty Furniss to Alice Austen, November 21, 1889, AAH Letters. Alice took the portrait of Hetty and her children on September 19, 1889 (50.015.6646).

66. Letter of Maud Wright to Alice Austen, September 19, 1889, AAH Letters.

67. Letter of Clifford R. Chapman to Alice Austen, July 2, 1891, AAH Letters.

68. Letter of Gertrude Eccleston to Alice Austen, August 27, 1888, AAH Letters.

Chapter 4: The Passing of the Larky Life

1. The church, based on Shakespeare's church in Stratford-on-Avon, was completed in 1871 and the rectory in 1881.

2. Reverend Eccleston was absent for this portrait taken in the parlor but was present for an outdoor portrait made on the rectory porch the same day (50.015.5558 and 50.015.5559).

3. Alice kept an album of twenty-three photographs of St. John's Church, the rectory, and the Sunday school (50.015.7531).

4. The three children from Nathaniel Marsh's first marriage were grown by the time Julie and her siblings came of age.

5. Letter of Julia Marsh to Alice Austen, August 1885, AAH Letters.

6. Letter of Gertrude Eccleston to Alice Austen, July 20, 1888, AAH Letters.

7. Letter of Gertrude Eccleston to Alice Austen, July 27, 1888, AAH Letters.

8. "For St. John's Library, A Performance of 'The Doctor of Alcantara,' on Wednesday night," 1888 newspaper clipping, AAH Scrapbook.

9. Letter of Gertrude Eccleston to Alice Austen, July 20, 1888, AAH Letters.

10. Letter of Gertrude Eccleston to Alice Austen, May 12, 1890, AAH Letters.

11. *New-York Tribune*, December 19, 1888, AAH Scrapbook.

12. Letter of Alice C. Austen to Alice Austen, July 17, 1897, AAH Letters.

13. In November 1888, a month before Julie Marsh's wedding, Alice photographed her bedroom (50.015.6809) and the exterior of the Marsh house (50.015.6808). In October 1889, she photographed the Lords' house (50.015.6806 and 40.014.6807). In March 1893, Alice visited Mary Butler Alburger and her husband in Germantown, Pennsylvania, and photographed their home (50.015.6371 and 50.015.6370). In May 1893, she visited Lou Alexander Richards in Cambridge, Massachusetts, and photographed their home (50.015.6125 and 50.015.6124).

14. Letter of Julia T. Martin to Alice Austen, March 8, 1892, AAH Letters.

15. Letter of Julia Marsh to Alice Austen, August [n.d.] 1885, AAH Letters.

16. Letter of Gertrude Eccleston to Alice Austen, March 15, 1892, AAH Letters.

17. According to Alice's notations on the negative sleeve, the photograph was taken by Louise Scofield, Julie Lord's cousin. Louise, age fifteen, was an aspiring photographer.

18. Ellen R. Wheeler of Fairfield, Connecticut, "Letters to the Editors," *LIFE*, October 15, 1951, 19.

19. Letter of Alice C. Austen to Alice Austen, June 21, 1891, AAH Letters.

20. The caption for "The Darned Club" in *LIFE*, September 24, 1951, 141, which was based on Alice's recollections to Oliver Jensen, reads: "'The Darned Club,' named by disrespectful Staten Island men, strikes a pose of girlish friendship on the Austens' lawn overlooking the Narrows. Alice (left) and her three friends Trude Eccleston, Julia Marsh and Sue Ripley went to school together for years, later spent most of their time at each other's homes." Borrowing Jensen's language, Novotny elaborated a bit: "Trude Eccleston, Julia Marsh and Sue Ripley strike a pose of girlish friendship on the Austen lawn overlooking the Narrows. They spent much of their youth in each other's homes, forming a club that was nicknamed by the excluded young men of the neighborhood." Ann Novotny, *Alice's World: The Life and Photography of an American Original: Alice Austen, 1866–1952* (Old Greenwich, CT: The Chatham Press, 1976), 54.

21. The Cooking Club met at a vacant house owned by Mrs. Marsh where the girls prepared family recipes. "They Took a Great Risk" is a press account of a tea that the Cooking Club held for young men. May 12, 1886, Schlesinger Scrapbook. See Figure 2.10 for Alice's photograph of the Cooking Club taken on May 4, 1886. In the photograph, Alice, Julie, and Trude are easily identified; the fourth girl may be Sue Ripley. The club was still active in 1888. Letter of Julia Marsh to Alice Austen, March 1, 1888, AAH Letters.

22. Letter of Gertrude Eccleston to Alice Austen, May 12, 1890, AAH Letters.

23. In June 1891, Gregg took a six-month furlough to visit friends and family and pursue Trude. He returned to Fort Douglas in October 1892 and was killed in 1899 while serving in the Spanish-American War.

24. Letter of Gertrude Eccleston to Alice Austen, March 5, 1892, AAH Letters.

25. Trude reported to Alice what had occurred between her and Lt. Gregg in a letter that Alice did not receive because it was sent to the wrong address. In a follow-up letter, Trude wrote,

"I simply cannot write all that stuff again so will wait & tell you all about what has happened since your departure." Letter of Gertrude Eccleston to Alice Austen, June 23, 1892, AAH Letters.

26. Letter of Gertrude Eccleston to Alice Austen, June 23, 1892, AAH Letters.

27. After Alice left Watkins Glen, Hopper convinced his parents to let him stay to spend more time with Trude. While under her spell, he wrote to Alice that Trude had tried on a bathing suit that "fit like a dream" and that they had strolled together at 11 p.m. Letter of Augustine Minshall Hopper to Alice Austen, August 11, 1892, AAH Letters.

28. Hopper also photographed the cemetery scenes, but only Alice's photographs came out well. Letter of Augustine Minshall Hopper to Alice Austen, August 11, 1892, AAH Letters.

29. The five-part series was called, "Symphony in Two Flats." In "Opening Movements," (1), the wooing couple prepares to kiss; in "Introduction of Relative Minor," (2), a young boy interrupts them; in "Resumption of Theme with Variations," (3), the couple opens a parasol for privacy; in "Reappearance of Dominant Minor Third," (4), the boy appears right in front of them; and in "Closing Measures," (5), the couple opens a second parasol, creating a cocoon in which they can kiss unobserved. *LIFE*, July 23, 1891, 38–39.

30. "Bon Voyage," July 14, 1887, AAH Scrapbook. On the return of Trude, Jule, and Dr. Eccleston from Europe, they went hiking in the Alps and lost their way. After several hours, they found a hamlet, hired a cart and mule, and returned to their hotel at 10 p.m. "Dr. Eccleston's Brave Girls," August 17, 1887, Schlesinger Scrapbook.

31. Obituary of Mrs. I. K. Martin, *Richmond County Sentinel*, Wednesday, June 27, 1877.

32. One of Alice's photo albums includes twelve full plate prints from the Bennington visit (49.002.0006).

33. Like "Trude and I in bed," this photograph required the use of a flash timer. Alice took off the lens cap in a darkened room, set the timer, and returned to bed to await the flash going off.

34. Letter of Mrs. Eliza Snively to Alice Austen, September 14, 1890, AAH Letters.

35. Letter of Julia T. Martin to Alice Austen, September 17, 1890, AAH Letters.

36. Julia Bredt did not know Alice's other friends before her Staten Island visits, 1889–1892. Letter of Julia Bredt to Alice Austen, November 10, 1890, AAH Letters.

37. Letter of Julia T. Martin to Alice Austen, November 29, 1891, AAH Letters.

38. Letter of Julia T. Martin to Alice Austen, December 16, 1891, AAH Letters.

39. Letter of Julia T. Martin to Alice Austen, August 1, 1893, AAH Letters.

40. In January 1891, Jule met Hattie and Bertie Pruyn, sisters of a leading society family in Albany. They remained loyal to her, giving her their discarded French couture even after she moved to California.

41. Letter of Julia T. Martin to Alice Austen, March 8, 1892, AAH Letters.

42. The Pruyn sisters recommended Jule for a teaching position at St. Agnes School for Girls in Albany. Poorly educated, Jule was not qualified for the job and was not hired.

43. Letter of Julia T. Martin to Alice Austen, May 7, 1894, AAH Letters.

44. Letter of Julia T. Martin to Alice Austen, July 8, 1894, AAH Letters.

45. In 1868, the New York Yacht Club built a clubhouse on the eastern edge of the Austen property and remained there until 1871, when it moved its headquarters to Manhattan. Frederick Bredt purchased the clubhouse and owned it until 1874, when he bought Beach Lawn for his family. The clubhouse still stands and is called the McFarlane-Bredt House.

46. In her letters, Julia mentioned an uncle and children, but Bredt relatives in Bethlehem remain unidentified. The Bredt family lived at two different houses on Centre Street, which suggests that they rented. Alice photographed the façade of the second home in June 1891, and in

February 1892, she also photographed Julia's bedroom, with one wall covered in photographs (50.015.6349).

47. Letter of Julia Bredt to Alice Austen, September 17, 1889, AAH Letters.

48. Rigged poker games were a staple of Victorian comic photography. Bessie Strong described such a scene to Alice. Letter of Elisabeth Strong to Alice Austen, March 13, 1889, AAH Letters.

49. Letter of Julia Bredt to Alice Austen, January 1, 1892, AAH Letters.

50. Letter of Julia Bredt to Alice Austen, March 9, 1892, AAH Letters. Alice mailed her negatives to George Booth who had them printed and returned them. Letter of George Booth to Alice Austen, March 15, 1892.

51. Two photographs of a costumed couple of ambiguous gender illustrate Alice's interest in cross-dressing (50.015.5526 and 50.015.5527). Four of Julia's February guests belonged to Lehigh's Mustard and Cheese Drama Society, which featured men in female roles in its productions. These photographs may depict two of Julia's guests in theatrical costume at her home during one of her February 1892 soirees.

52. "Many thanks for the picture & poetry which you so kindly sent me. . . . I will be delighted to keep to my promise & will send you a chromo as soon as I have them taken, which will [be] in a few weeks." Letter of Percival Drayton to Alice Austen, March 30, 1892, AAH Letters.

53. Letter of Julia Bredt to Alice Austen, November 28, 1890, AAH Letters.

54. Letter of Julia Bredt to Alice Austen, March 9, 1892, AAH Letters.

55. "Stole from his Partners, Arthur Coit Gilman, who Died Last December," *New York Times,* April 30, 1891.

56. Letter of Henry K. Gilman to Alice Austen, February 18, 1892, AAH Letters.

57. Letter of Alice C. Austen to Alice Austen, February 10, 1892, AAH Letters.

58. Letter of Elisabeth Strong to Alice Austen, September 16, 1893, AAH Letters.

59. Letter of Henry K. Gilman to Alice Austen, November 12, 1893, AAH Letters.

60. "Henry K. Gilman's Peculiar Death," *New York Times,* December 28, 1893. Gilman was found near death in his room, was revived, and died three days later of pneumonia.

61. Melody Davis, *Women's Views: The Narrative Stereograph in Nineteenth-Century America* (Durham: University of New Hampshire Press, 2015), 53.

62. Alice kept a printed announcement for "Callender's Consolidated Spectacular Colored Minstrels, The Only Colored Organization in the World," who performed at a Broadway theater in May 1883 (45.002.0077). For mention of minstrel shows by Alice's friends, see Letter of Julia Bredt to Alice Austen, March 9, 1892; Letter of Gertrude Eccleston to Alice Austen, April 2, 1893; and Letter of Elisabeth Strong to Alice Austen, March 5, 1894, AAH Letters.

63. On Thanksgiving and ragamuffin parades, see Carmen Nigro, The New York Public Library blog, https://www.nypl.org/blog/2010/11/23/thanksgiving-ragamuffin-parade. In 1910, Alice again photographed ragamuffins at Clear Comfort (50.015.2843).

64. Letter of Julia T. Martin to Alice Austen, April 14, 1893, AAH Letters.

65. Letter of Gertrude Eccleston to Alice Austen, June 17, 1890, AAH Letters.

66. Attributed to Albert Blunt, [Minstrel show], May 1890 (50.015.0417).

67. In the second self-portrait, Alice holds a fan instead of a bouquet (50.015.6693).

Chapter 5: The New Woman

1. In 1889, Alice and Violet began to reconnect. On March 24, 1889, Alice took two formal portraits of the Ward family at home (50.015.6633 and 50.015.6634), and on June 11, 1890,

she took a series of informal photographs of Violet and Violet's sister Carrie on the grounds of Oneata (e.g., 50.015.6697).

2. In 1893, Peter took a position as chair of chemistry at Brooklyn Polytechnic Institute and expanded his practice as an industrial consultant. His family moved into a grand, newly built townhouse in Park Slope, Brooklyn.

3. In her will, Elizabeth A.T. Austen bequeathed Clear Comfort to her family. In 1894, John H. Austen died intestate, and Minn and Oswald Muller inherited the property.

4. The cost of the trip was beyond the means of many women. The Women's Committee of Richmond County offered twenty-five dollars to any woman who was a "serious worker" and "self-supporting." "For the World's Fair," *Staten Island Advance*, April 1, 1893, 1.

5. "Staten Island Relics, Richmond County Women Have a World's Fair of Their Own," *The World*, February 3, 1893, 9.

6. The badge has been accessioned (45.002.0051). The brochure, *Reports of the Women's Committee of Richmond Co. N.Y. for the World's Columbian Exposition*, is at HRT, Austen Family Papers, MS001, Box 2.

7. Letter of Gertrude Eccleston to Alice Austen, March 5, 1892, AAH Letters.

8. The Emmons family lived in a huge, neo-Gothic villa that Alice photographed in October 1888 and again in May–June 1890. Alice was friends with the two oldest Emmons children, Effie and Kintzing.

9. Mrs. Emmons was a director of the Women's Committee of Richmond County, which gave her access to the dormitories at the University of Chicago.

10. Alice bought the *Chicago Tribune*'s souvenir book at the World's Fair. *Glimpses of the World Fair, A Selection of Gems of the White City and the Midway Plaisance*, AAH.

11. See *American Amateur Photographer* 5, no. 7 (July 1893): 319; and *American Amateur Photographer* 5, no. 9 (August 1893): 369–70.

12. Alice took two photographs on the University of Chicago campus: the fair's famous Ferris wheel (50.015.5259) and the new buildings of the university (50.015.6079).

13. "Liberty bell made of oranges," July 10, 1893 (50.015.5282).

14. See Chapter 3 for John C. Browne's advice to use platinum paper.

15. *Catalogue of Title Entries for Book and Other Articles*, No. 130, entered in the office of Library of Congress under the Copyright Law, week of Dec. 25–Dec. 30, 1893.

16. Violet patented her bodkin on December 19, 1893, the same month that Alice filed for copyright. Patent number 510,943. HRT, Ward Family Papers, MS004, Box 5.

17. In March, Alice sent Mrs. King her prints and an invoice. Mrs. King sent Alice a check but requested that Alice send four receipts so that she could more easily collect from her friends. Letters of Isabella C. King to Alice Austen, February 14 and March 3, 1894, AAH Letters.

18. Letter of Elisabeth Strong to Alice Austen, May 23, 1894, AAH Letters.

19. Thomas Quincy Browne Jr. to Alice Austen, August 28, 1894, AAH Letters.

20. In 1891, Alice photographed her grandfather and Julia Bredt in Central Park (50.015.5597 through 50.015.5604), and in 1893, she photographed the Naval Review Parade on Fifth Avenue and the docked Spanish ships at the West 95th Street pier (50.015.5621 through 50.015.5628 and 50.015.5778).

21. Sigmund Krausz wrote several books. His only known photographs are the "Chicago Street Types," copyrighted in 1891. They were also printed as cabinet cards, some of which were exhibited in 1951 in *Forgotten Photographers* at the Museum of Modern Art.

22. Sigmund Krausz, *Street Types of Great American Cities* (Chicago and New York: The Werner Company, 1896), 3. Krausz revised his 1892 book, *Street Types of Chicago: Character*

Studies, changing the title and adding an introduction and ten new images with his accompanying text.

23. Krausz's "street types" include several New Women, including one walking in public unaccompanied ("Out for a Stroll") and "Tennis-Girl." The second edition of his book opens with "Bicycle Girl."

24. Sigmund Krausz, *Street Types of Chicago: Character Studies* (Chicago: Max Stern & Co., 1892), 3–4, 17–18.

25. Compare 50.015.0955 and 50.015.0956.

26. When she was working on the "street types," Alice enlisted Violet's assistance to photograph the quarantine station for Doty.

27. There is an error on Alice's negative sleeve for the shoelace peddler at Trinity Church (11:20 a.m.): it would take longer than ten minutes to get from South Ferry (11:10 a.m.) to the church. The time for the whole series from South Ferry to City Hall—between 10:45 a.m. and 12:55 p.m.—is plausible.

28. Jessica Ellen Sewell, *Women and the Everyday City: Public Space in San Francisco, 1890–1915* (Minneapolis: University of Minnesota Press, 2011), 3.

29. The sleeve of the negative 50.015.5940 reads: "Emigrants, queer man & baggage."

30. Jacob Riis photographed and interviewed Italian ragpickers living in several of the city's dumps for a series of newspaper articles in 1892.

31. On Adolph Wittemann and the Albertype Company history, see https://www .collectableivy.com/collectible-ivy-blog/the-albertype-company-view-books-and-postcards-/.

32. [Albertype sales brochure] (New York: Albertype Co., 1893) in David A. Hanson *Collection of the History of Photomechanical Reproduction*, Sterling and Frances Clark Art Institute Library, Williamstown, Massachusetts, https://library.clarkart.edu/view/UniversalViewer/01 CLARKART_INST/1223654080008431?c=&m=&s=&cv=&xywh=-558,256,3580,1679&r=0.

33. The content list includes, "Ragman and Cart, Twenty-Ninth Street, between Third and Lexington Avenues," which does not appear in the portfolio. Instead, the portfolio includes another copyrighted image, "Ash Cart," which Alice identified on the negative sleeve as, "Street Cleaning Cart & Men, 50th Street."

34. See Bonnie Yochelson, "Jacob A. Riis, Photographer 'After a Fashion,'" in Bonnie Yochelson and Daniel Czitrom, *Rediscovering Jacob Riis: Exposure Journalism and Photography in Turn of the Century New York* (Chicago: University of Chicago Press, 2014), 121–227.

35. Dorothy Norman, *Alfred Stieglitz: An American Seer* (New York: Random House, 1960), 39, in Bonnie Yochelson, *Alfred Stieglitz New York* (New York: Seaport Museum New York and Rizzoli, 2010), 13, note. 6.

36. "The Hand Camera—Its Present Importance," *American Annual of Photography and Photography Times Almanac*, 1897, in Yochelson, *Alfred Stieglitz New York*, 15, note 10.

37. Alice always used her initials when signing her work, but since her recipients were usually people who knew her, it is unlikely she was masking her gender.

38. The Alice Austen House owns two portfolios, one inscribed, "For Auntie and Uncle." Ralph Munroe's portfolio can be found in the Ralph M. Munroe Family Papers, University of Miami Libraries. Other portfolios belong to the Nelson-Atkins Museum, Kansas City, Missouri; the George Eastman Museum, Rochester, NY; the Museum of the City of New York; and the National Gallery of Art, Washington, D.C.

39. Laura Wexler, *Tender Violence: Domestic Visions in an Age of U.S. Imperialism* (Chapel Hill: University of North Carolina Press, 2000), 212.

40. Letter of Elisabeth Strong to Alice Austen, November 7, 1895, AAH Letters.

41. Alice photographed Dr. Bissell at Oneata, ca. 1891 (50.015.5443).

42. Mary Taylor Bissell, MD, *Physical Development and Exercise for Women* (New York: Dodd, Mead and Company, 1891), v.

43. The school was founded by William Gilbert Anderson, who also founded the American Physical Education Association, of which Daisy was a member.

44. See Eleanor Waddle, "The Berkeley Ladies' Athletic Club," *Outing Magazine* 15, no. 1 (October 1889): 57–63.

45. See "Gymnastics for Girls," *Scientific American Supplement*, no. 753 (June 7, 1890): 12036–38.

46. Alice gave Violet thirteen mounted photographs to commemorate their 1894 canal trip. The photographs were donated to the New-York Historical Society by Henry Marion Ward in 1942.

47. Letter of Gertrude Eccleston to Alice Austen, October 2, 1894, AAH Letters.

48. Holly Pyne Connor, "Not at Home: The Nineteenth Century New Woman," in *Off the Pedestal: New Women in the Art of Homer, Chase, and Sargent* (Newark, NJ: Newark Museum; and New Brunswick, NJ: Rutgers University Press, 2006). Fig. 1 (page 5) shows Charles Dana Gibson's cover of *Scribner's Magazine*, June 1896, a classic example of the Gibson Girl, here riding a bicycle.

49. When visiting Washington, D.C., Violet wrote to Alice: "I only wish you were along, what fun we would have together. My camera is here and I hope to take back some work with me." Letter of Violet Ward to Alice Austen, January 18, 1891, AAH Letters.

50. "Golf is fast becoming popular. Among society people it has got to be quite a thing." "Society's Latest Pastime," *New York Times*, June 10, 1894. The Richmond County Country Club's move in 1897 to Todt Hill (its current location) was inspired by the need for a golf course.

51. The Ward Family Papers contain drawings of a golf club with a whalebone neck, which Violet invented, dated June 13, 1908. HRT, Ward Family Papers, MS004, Box 4.

52. A series of five photographs of Alice, Violet, and Daisy riding bicycles at Port Richmond are dated November 22, 1893 (50.015.5202 through 50.015.5206).

53. "National Bicycle Show," *New York Times*, January 13, 1895; Margaret Guroff, *The Mechanical Horse: How the Bicycle Reshaped American Life* (Austin: University of Texas Press, 2016), 39.

54. "A Bicycle Tea was given yesterday at St. George, S.I., under the auspices of the Staten Island Bicycle Club." "The Social World," *New York Times*, June 26, 1895.

55. "Two Enterprising Women. Miss Violet Ward and Miss Alice Austin [sic] . . . seeing the necessity of a cycle club, have organized one, and called it the Staten Island Bicycle Club," *Richmond County Advance*, November 9, 1895. The article mentions the hiring of a teacher and repair shop attendant.

56. "There is a small war in progress at this place over the possession of the headquarters of the Staten Island Bicycle Club, which . . . has a membership of about fifty, fully half of whom are ladies." *The Journal* (New York), April 3, 1896. The article describes the dispute in detail. For follow-up, see *New York Tribune*, April 26, 1896; and *New York Herald*, May 31, 1896.

57. Letter of Frank Allen to Violet Ward, January 13, 1896, HRT, Ward Family Papers, MS004, Box 4.

58. In 1895, Frances E. Willard published, *A Wheel Within a Wheel: How I Learned to Ride a Bicycle, With Some Reflections by the Way*. The founder of the Women's Christian Temperance Union and a well-known suffragist, Willard recounts how at age fifty-three, she took up cycling.

59. For a concise summary of the arguments against women's bicycling, see Guroff, *The Mechanical Horse,* 39–47.

60. For versions of this cartoon, see Evan Friss, *On Bicycles: A 200 Year History of Cycling in New York City* (New York: Columbia University Press, 2019), 69, Fig. 2.15; and Newark Museum, *Off the Pedestal,* 34, Fig, 19.

61. Maria E. Ward, *Bicycling For Ladies: With Hints as to the Art of Wheeling—Advice to Beginners—Dress—Care of the Bicycle—Mechanics—Training—Exercise, Etc., Etc.* (New York: Brentanos, 1896), 93, 12.

62. Daisy's costume changes suggest that the photographs were taken in four sessions. There are thirty-four illustrations in the book: twenty-four depict Daisy on a bicycle and correspond to photographs at HRT. There are five views of feet on bicycle pedals, and five of hands with tools. Daisy or Violet may have posed for these; there are no extant prints or negatives.

63. In the Preface, Violet thanks the author and publisher for permission to quote from "Physiology of Bodily Exercise."

64. *New York Herald,* May 2, 1896, Fifth Section, 6.

65. *The Publishers' Weekly, American Book-Trade Journal* 50 (July–December 1896): 59–60.

66. *The Inter Ocean* [Chicago], May 30, 1896.

67. In the HRT Ward Family Papers (MS004) are letters to Violet from bicycle manufacturers rejecting her solicitation of support for her sequel. The New-York Historical Society owns a scrapbook of Violet's clippings and correspondence about bicycles. Newspaper clippings related to cycling and cycling clubs, New-York Historical Society.

68. "La Bourgoine [sic] & steamers quarantined for cholera," September 5, 1892 (50.015.5830).

69. Those who traveled in steerage disembarked at Hoffman Island before their ship was disinfected. The *James W. Wadsworth* was only the first stage of Doty's master plan, in which the needs of steerage passengers were addressed.

70. On the negative sleeves of two photographs of the fumigation chamber, Alice wrote, "Vi flashed light." (50.015.5697 and 50.015.5698). In 1896 and 1897, Alice copyrighted a total of fifteen photographs of the disinfecting equipment on the *James W. Wadsworth.*

71. "A Floating Disinfectant Plant," *Harper's Weekly,* August 8, 1896, 788; "Disinfection at Quarantine, A Floating Disinfecting Plant," *Appleton's Popular Science Monthly* 50 (January 1897): 344–53. The latter article included eight Austen photographs, which were not credited to her. See also Alvah H. Doty, "Quarantine Methods," *The North American Review* 165, no. 489 (August 1897): 201–12 (unillustrated); and *Annual Report of A.H. Doty, Health Officer, Port of New York, For Year 1897,* Transmitted to the Legislature, March 30, 1898. Doty's report relied heavily on charts and included only five photographs, none attributed.

72. Letter of Alvah H. Doty to Alice Austen, March 1, 1897, AAH Letters.

73. Among a group of quarantine negative sleeves at AAH, one is inscribed: "Miss. E.A. Austen / c/o Capt. Miller / 26 So Williams St / City," Muller's business address.

74. Letter of Alice Cornell Austen to Alice Austen, May 19, 1897, AAH Letters.

75. Alice returned to photograph the quarantine facilities in 1906 and 1910. In 1911, a newly elected Democratic governor accused Doty of incompetence. Fiercely defended by the medical establishment, Doty nevertheless lost his job. See Doty's obituary, *New York Times,* May 28, 1934.

76. Doty's exhibition was modeled on the landmark New York Tenement House Exhibition

of 1901, which attracted 10,000 visitors during its two-week run and led to the establishment of the New York Tenement House Department, https://exhibitions.library.columbia.edu/exhibits/show/css/housing/tenementexhibit.

77. See "Hoffman Island, Engine House and Chimney," April 8, 1901 (50.015.5666).

78. Six of the thirty quarantine photographs copyrighted in 1901 depict "Hoffman Island, immigrants from smallpox ship held for observation."

79. *Collier's Illustrated Weekly* 27, no. 12 (June 22, 1901): 18–19.

80. Alice exposed 130, 4-by-5 inch negatives at the Pan-American Buffalo Exposition. The negative sleeves identify the subject but do not include the date or technical data. She made some platinum prints and mounted forty silver gelatin prints on 7-by-9 inch paper.

81. See Verna Posever Curtis, "Frances Benjamin Johnston in 1900," in *American Women Photographers in Paris, 1900–1901* (Giverny: Musée d'Art Americain; and Washington, D.C.: Library of Congress, 2001), 24–37.

82. Alice Austin (1862–1933), a professional, pictorial photographer from Boston, was one of the Americans included in the Paris exhibition.

83. *Ladies' Home Journal* 14, no. 10 (September 1897): 6–7. The full article is reproduced in Katherine Manthorne, *Women in the Dark: Female Photographers in the US, 1850–1900* (Atglen, PA: Schiffer Publishing, 2020), Appendix 2, 129–34.

84. In 1901, Johnston met photographer Mattie Edwards Hewitt, and in 1909 they set up a business and a home together in New York City, an arrangement which lasted until 1917. See Bettina Burch, *The Woman Behind the Lens: The Life and Work of Frances Benjamin Johnston 1864–1952* (Charlottesville: University of Virginia Press, 2000).

85. The self-portrait of Johnston in men's clothes and mustache holding a high wheel bicycle belongs to the Frances Benjamin Johnston Collection, Library of Congress, and is reproduced in Susan Turner-Lowe, "The Pride and Practice of Frances B. Johnston," Verso, Huntington Library, Art Museum and Botanical Gardens. https://huntington.org/verso/pride-and-practice-frances-b-johnston.

86. The Paris Exposition commissioners asked Stieglitz to organize an exhibit of American photography, but he insisted that his exhibit be hung in the Fine Arts section, not the Photography section, and they refused. Johnston's exhibit was hung in the Photography section in its stead.

87. Letter of Jane L. Denning to Alice Austen, September 19, 1888, AAH Letters.

88. The cousins in Fishkill regularly ordered multiple prints of Alice's photographs and regularly offered to pay for them. In 1894, Cousin Emmie wrote, "[N]ow you must charge a sufficient sum to pay you for the trouble & expense." Letter of Emily Denning Van Rensselaer to Alice Austen, December 25, 1894, AAH Letters. On at least one occasion, Bessie Strong sent Alice money without asking: "The pictures came safely and are fine. I will enclose the money for them." Letter of Elisabeth Strong to Alice Austen, December 7, 1890, AAH Letters.

89. Letter of Adolph Wittemann to Alice Austen, January 2, 1897, HRT, Austen Family Papers, MS001, Box 2.

Chapter 6: Life with Gertrude Tate

1. Letter of Daisy Elliott to Alice Austen, June 19, 1897, AAH Letters.

2. See Lillian Faderman, *Surpassing the Love of Men: Romantic Friendship and Love Between Woman from the Renaissance to the Present* (New York: Quill, William Morrow, 1981), 239–53.

3. Letter of Daisy Elliott to Alice Austen, July 29, [1895], AAH Letters.

4. Letter of Daisy Elliott to Alice Austen, undated, AAH Letters.

5. Letter of Violet Ward to Alice Austen, August 29, 1896, AAH Letters.

6. Letter of Daisy Elliott to Alice Austen, February [no day], 1897, AAH Letters.

7. Caroline T. Lawrence (1852–1937) was photographed by Alice at the Ladies' Berkeley Athletic Club in 1893 (50.015.6591 and 50.015.6632). Alice identified her as "Miss Lawrence" on the negative sleeves; Daisy referred to her as "Miss L" in letters to Alice. Never married, she lived her entire life at 45 East 29th Street in Manhattan.

8. "An Alpine Cycle Tour," *New York Times*, November 13, 1898. The article describes the itinerary of an 1897 trip of the two women cyclists: "Miss S. [sic] M. Elliott is a Director of the Berkeley Gymnasium and her companion is a regular exerciser there." Caroline Lawrence was not mentioned by name.

9. Alice saved eleven letters and one postcard that Daisy sent from Europe in the summer of 1897.

10. Letter of Daisy Elliott to Alice Austen, July 30, 1897, AAH Letters.

11. Letter of Daisy Elliott to Alice Austen, June 19, [1897], AAH Letters.

12. Letter of Daisy Elliott to Alice Austen, July 25, 1897, AAH Letters.

13. On September 14, 1897, Alice took a series of photographs of the Ward estate. Prints can be found in HRT, Ward Family Papers, HRT, and a small photo album (50.015.7529).

14. Letter of Violet Ward to Alice Austen, August 12, 1897, AAH Letters.

15. Letter of Daisy Elliott to Alice Austen, August 21, 1897, AAH Letters.

16. Obituaries for Henry Marshall Tate appeared in the *Brooklyn Daily Eagle* (February 8, 1897) and the *New York Times* (February 9, 1897).

17. A report on fashionable summer residences noted that "the Taylor Cottage [in Great Barrington, Massachusetts] is occupied by Mr. and Mrs. H.M. Tate, of the Hill [i.e., Clinton Hill], and their three attractive daughters, of whom Miss Gertrude and Miss Carrie Tate are well known in Society," *Brooklyn Life*, August 5, 1893.

18. "Miss Winifred Tate, who is one of the most popular girls at Twilight Park every summer (for she has been there with her mother some ten or twelve seasons), is the third in this little family of quite exceptionally pretty, attractive girls," *Brooklyn Life*, August 29, 1913.

19. Pamela Bannos recognized that this photograph was taken at Twilight Park in 1897, and that the photographs in the commemorative albums were taken on a second visit in 1899. https://mydearalice.org/chapter-9/. Alice exposed two negatives of this group, which are missing. An uncropped print belongs to AAH (see Figure 6.1), and two cropped prints are at HRT (50.015.0418 and 50.015.0419).

20. Letter of Gertrude Eccleston to Alice Austen, August 25, 1897, AAH Letters.

21. A letter from a guest at Twilight Park thanking Alice for a print verifies that the photograph was taken in 1897. Letter of Alice Southworth Waterman to Alice Austen, September 19, 1897, AAH Letters.

22. Letter of Gertrude Eccleston to Alice Austen, August 25, 1897, AAH Letters.

23. A woman who came to the aid of Alice's mother on the street wrote Alice a week after the accident: "I am glad I happened to be near your Mother at the time she was in need of help." Letter of Caroline M. Sweet to Alice Austen, February 5, 1898, AAH Letters. A letter from Trude Eccleston was addressed to "Miss Alice Austen / 77 Park Avenue, New York City / NY / Cof Mrs. Townsend." Trude explained that she learned of Alice's mother's accident from the Austens' servant and, apologizing to Alice, gave her a list of Staten Island people who knew about it. Letter of Gertrude Eccleston to Alice Austen, January 27, 1898, AAH Letters.

24. Letter of Violet Ward to Alice Austen, January [26–27,] 1898, AAH Letters. Violet lived at 315 Lexington Avenue, around the corner from Aunt Sarah's house.

25. Daisy explained her whereabouts, noting: "Shall be in town tonight at Miss Lawrence's." Caroline Lawrence lived ten blocks from Aunt Sarah's house. Letter of Daisy Elliott to Alice Austen, January 26, 1898, AAH Letters.

26. Letter of Daisy Elliott to Alice Austen, January 28, 1898, AAH Letters.

27. In August 1899, Alice and her mother visited the Catskill Mountain House, a famous Hudson Valley resort not far from Twilight Park. Among the photographs Alice took there is one showing her mother seated on the columned piazza (50.015.6405).

28. Gertrude's copy belongs to the Alice Austen House and Alice's to HRT. The two albums are nearly identical: Gertrude's copy holds twenty-four photographs and Alice's twenty-three, and the ordering of prints is slightly different. AAH owns a second album with many of the same photographs. The negatives for all these photographs are missing.

29. Winifred Tate Baker interview notes, Novotny Papers.

30. Novotny speculated that this photograph depicted Alice, not Gertrude.

31. Letter of Pieter Vosburgh to Ann Novotny, April 18, 1976, Novotny Papers.

32. John A. Morton Jr. interview notes, February 1976, Novotny Papers.

33. Ann Novotny believed that "Gertrude, in effect [was] the main support of the Tate family since the early death of her father," *Alice's World: The Life and Photography of an American Original: Alice Austen, 1866–1952* (Old Greenwich, CT: The Chatham Press, 1976), 46. It is unlikely that Gertrude's teaching income could support three women, a Brooklyn townhouse, and a summer cottage rental.

34. Winifred Tate Baker interview notes, Novotny Papers.

35. The kindergarten movement was heavily influenced by John Dewey's progressive educational philosophy. In the early 1900s, kindergartens proliferated in settlement houses and urban public schools.

36. "Louis H. Chalif, 71, Master of Dancing," *New York Times*, November 25, 1948.

37. Winifred described how Adeline Robinson helped Gertrude start teaching dance. Winifred Tate Baker interview notes, Novotny Papers. *The Richmond County Advance*, April 14, 1894, announced Adeline's classes at the Hotel Castleton on Staten Island; and the *New York Times*, April 20, 1900, announced her classes for "many of New York's most prominent families" at a small ballroom at Sherry's restaurant in Manhattan.

38. *Brooklyn Daily Eagle*, April 12, 1914.

39. Winifred Tate Baker interview notes, Novotny Papers.

40. Based on dated photographs and travel records, the European trip itineraries can be reconstructed as follows: 1903 England, France, Scotland, Holland, and Germany; 1905 France, Switzerland, Italy, and Austria; 1906 Gibraltar, Italy, Switzerland, and France; 1907 no extant photos but ship manifest of return from France in September; 1908 no extant photos but ship manifest of return from France in October; 1909 Azores, Gibraltar, Morocco, Spain, France, Belgium, and Holland; 1910 few extant photos and ship manifest of return from France in October; and 1912 Denmark and Sweden.

41. There are 174 film negatives from the 1903 trip; sixty-seven from the 1905 trip; 226 from the 1906 trip; more than 500 from the 1909 trip; and 289 from the 1912 trip.

42. The 1909 trip is the best documented. Alice kept a pocket-sized *Photographic and Exposure Record and Diary* in which she recorded the subject, date, time of day, and exposure data for her photographs. There are no other extant record books like this one.

43. Winifred Tate Baker interview notes, Novotny Papers.

44. For the role of Anne Morgan and Elsie de Wolfe in the founding of the Colony Club, see Alfred Allan Lewis, *Ladies and Not-so-Gentle Women: Elisabeth Marbury, Anne Morgan, Elsie de Wolfe, Anne Vanderbilt, and their Times* (New York: Viking, 2000), 207–10, 220–27.

45. See Margaret Walsh, "Gender and the Automobile in the United States," in *Automobile in American Life and Society*, Science and Technologies Studies Program, University of Michigan, Dearborn, 2004–2010, http://www.autolife.umd.umich.edu/Gender/Walsh/G_Overview1.htm.

46. "Killed in Auto Crash, Brighton Train Hits Car—Morris Ward Dead, Guy Loomis Hurt," *New York Times*, November 24, 1904.

47. Winifred reported that Loomis "was in Europe many times with Alice and Gertrude and car." Winifred Tate Baker interview notes, Novotny Papers. He, Alice, and Gertrude were listed on the ship manifest of the SS *Friedrich der Grosse* from Cherbourg, France on October 14, 1908.

48. On October 26, 1912, Alice photographed the country club clubhouse from Jessie's bathroom (50.015.7278).

49. Jessie's musical compositions were featured in a concert at the Waldorf-Astoria when she was twenty-three. Jessie jokingly remarked to a reporter, "Please don't say anything about the family . . . I'm so tired of hearing it recited that I belong to the Vanderbilt family, just as if that must constitute my only claim to recognition," *Boston Globe*, November 11, 1897.

50. On May 31, 1910, Alice photographed the horse-drawn carriage and picnic guests in front of the Vanderbilt mausoleum (50.015.5042).

51. John A. Morton Jr. interview notes, Novotny Papers.

52. Alice photographed a group gathered to witness the annual night-blooming of the cereus at her Fishkill cousins' home in July 1890 (50.015.6246). Alice's cereus, which she photographed many times, was planted in the garden next to the piazza (50.015.2869).

53. Among the first garden club lecturers were Leonard Barron, editor of *Garden Magazine* (*New York Press,* April 10, 1914) and Richardson Wright, editor of *House and Garden Magazine* (*New-York Tribune*, December 20, 1914).

54. "Society Buys House of the 'Missing Silver Buckles,'" *New York Tribune*, December 14, 1914.

55. The Staten Island Garden Club contributed $800 of the first payment of $2,200 on February 15, 1915. See Charles Gilbert Hine, *The Story and Documentary History of the Perine House* (Staten Island Antiquarian Society, 1915), 8.

56. Alice photographed the planting of a vegetable garden at the Perine House in May 1917 (50.015.2927 through 50.015.2930).

57. Winifred Tate Baker interview notes, Novotny Papers.

58. Winifred Tate Baker interview notes, Novotny Papers.

59. On July 26, 1919, Peter Austen's children—William, Patty, and Oswald—signed an indenture that ceded their rights to the Austen House to Alice. HRT Austen Family Papers, MS001, Box 3. In 1915 when Patty married, their widowed mother Nellie moved with Patty to Upstate New York. Both sons eventually moved to Miami, where their uncle Ralph Middleton Munroe resided.

60. See Jan Whitaker, *Tea at the Blue Lantern Inn: A Social History of the Tea Room Craze in America* (New York: St. Martin's Press, 2002).

61. *Automobile Blue Book* 1, 1922, 108.

62. "Miss E. Alice Austen . . . with the authority from the New York Red Cross and the Staten Island Branch, organized four classes of 100 or more women to study to become ambulance drivers and mechanics to be ready to form a motor corps when we entered the war. . . .

Miss Austen was a Lieutenant in the Canteen and a Hostess at Hostess House at the Fox Hills Hospital through the entire war." Mabel Keep, ed., *Directory of Women Members of Clubs, Welfare Bodies, Political Organizations and Associations in Staten Island* (New York, 1927–1928), 19 (hereafter cited as Directory of Women). Alice appears in nurse's uniform in two group photographs of the Fox Hill Hospital staff in "Women Workers in the War," *New York Herald*, April 20, 1919.

63. Directory of Women, 17.

64. "James H. Cruikshank bought from Elizabeth Alice Austen, William Munroe Austen and Elizabeth P. Miller a five-story tenement flat (25 by 100 feet) at 527 West Fifty-Second Street, through Brown, Wheelock and Company," *New York Herald*, June 29, 1920, 19. William Wheelock was Alice's cousin.

65. The list of buyers of co-op apartments on the east side of Lexington Avenue between East 69th and 70th Streets included "Miss E. Alice Austen, Colony Club."; "Buy Fine Suites from Plans," *New York Herald*, August 27, 1922.

66. The early accounts of the Agency Shop include this list that belongs to the Alice Austen House: "Disbursements by Mrs. F.W.E. Richards" totaled $247.42; and "Money received" totaled $82.85, with a balance of $164.89 owed to Mrs. Richards. On November 6, 1922, Alice photographed the building in St. George before the Agency Shop opened there (50.015.2985).

67. "Shop is Started by Society Women of Staten Island, Trio in Venture to Sell Novelties," *New York Herald*, November 12, 1922.

68. "Start Negligence Action," Schenectady *New York Gazette*, March 4, 1925, 3; and "Sues Cohoesier," *Troy Times*, March 3, 1925, 8; *Albany Times Union*, March 5, 1925, 4. The Schenectady newspapers list the date of the accident as August 6, 1922, and the Troy newspaper lists it as August 6, 1923. The driver, Henry M. Shaver of Cohoes, countersued. In the Austen-Shaver suit, the jury decided both drivers had been careless and were at fault, and the case was dismissed. In the Tate-Shaver suit, a mistrial was declared, but the case does not seem to have been retried. See Albany County Hall of Records, E. Alice Austen v. Henry M. Shaver and Gertrude Tate v. Henry M. Shaver. Supreme Court (Albany County) Minutes, March 18, 1925 Trial Term—Civil (1925), 289, 296.

69. John A. Morton Jr. interview notes, Novotny Papers.

70. Alice made two exposures of another hen dinner at Jessie's house in which she is dressed in men's clothes and donning a mustache. These undated photographs are also out of focus (50.015.2832 and 50.015.4302).

71. For a report on the benefit and the names of the hen dinner guests, see *Brooklyn Life*, May 13, 1916.

72. The Social Register notes that Alice and Gertrude were members of the Richmond County Country Club and the Colony Club.

73. Stieglitz took his photograph of passengers in steerage in 1907; he first printed it in 1911 and continued to print it in various ways throughout his life. In old age, he declared *The Steerage* a turning point in his evolution from pictorial to modern artist. Alice took a similar photograph under similar circumstances, but there are no extant prints from her negative.

74. Research memo, September 10, 1951, Jensen Papers.

75. Notable exceptions are six prints of pastoral scenes of sheep and windmills in Belgium and Normandy photographed on the 1909 trip. To make prints, Alice ordered 8-by-10 inch enlarged copy negatives from film negatives, and some of the prints are hand-colored. These retardataire attempts at artistic photography, which Alice copyrighted, underscore her isolation from the pictorial movement.

76. Alice's 8-by-10 Folmer & Schwing camera came to HRT in 1945 and was accessioned in 1949 (49.002.0008).

77. There are two small albums with 1.5-by-2 inch photographs: one is incomplete with thirteen photographs (50.015.7528), and the other, which belongs to AAH, is a complete album with twelve pages, four prints per page (2017.005). A highlight of the album is a series of images of Gertrude dancing outdoors.

78. Charles L. Sachs, SIHS chief curator, procured funding for the conservation of Alice's eleven reels of 16mm film, which date from August 1929 to summer 1935. He organized a public program, "Alice Austen's Home Movies," held in March 1983. A VHS tape of the program selection has been digitized.

79. Paul Maddaus phone interview notes, July 29, 1951, Jensen Papers.

80. Alice went to Cuba with Jessie Simons in January 1930, and in June to Nova Scotia with Gertrude. There are a handful of negatives and two prints of Nova Scotia at HRT.

81. Richmond County Clerk, Mortgage Libers, vol. 631, 1; vol. 656, 26 and 28; vol. 664, 431 and 578; vol. 665, 137 and 144.

82. Letter of Philip L. Watkins to E. Alice Austen, November 16, 1931, Alice Austen Folder, Jessie Vanderbilt Simons Papers, Archives and Manuscripts, Duke University Libraries.

83. Research memo, July 12, 1951, Jensen Papers. Fenton Brown, a wealthy lawyer and Austen family friend, confirmed the oil company offer and mentioned another offer of $125,000 from a dry dock company. Fenton Brown interview notes, March 1975, Novotny Papers. Clear Comfort was briefly threatened when the city contemplated a subway or rail tunnel from Bay Ridge, Brooklyn to Clifton. For a history of subway plans to Staten Island, see Kenneth M. Gold, *The Forgotten Borough: Staten Island and the Subway* (New York: Columbia University Press, 2023).

84. See Jennifer Carlquist, "The antiquarian career of J.A. Lloyd Hyde: Americana as business and pleasure," MA thesis (Cooper-Hewitt National Design Museum, Smithsonian Institution and Parsons, The New School for Design, 2010).

85. Pamela Bannos identified Hyde and Knudsen in a film clip. https://mydearalice.org /chapter-10.

86. A photograph of the sofa appeared in *American Country Life* (April 1933), 72. HRT Austen Files. The acquisition of Alice's wingback chair in 1933 (acc. no. 33.26) is described in the Museum's *Bulletin* 19 (June 1934). Later determined to be English-made and not made in New York, the chair is currently on view at AAH.

87. "Mansion Built in 1669 Overlooking Narrows is Sold in Foreclosure," HRT Austen Files.

88. Letter of Pieter Vosburgh to Ann Novotny, April 18, 1976, Novotny Papers; and Paul Maddaus phone interview notes, July 29, 1951, Jensen Papers.

89. HRT Austen Files.

90. See *New Yorker*, July 24, 1937, 61, and August 9, 1941, 53; and *Vogue*, August 15, 1941, 36. Rita Beschner Newell, who worked at the tearoom as a teenager, recalled: "Most of the people came from New York to the tearoom. It wasn't a local thing, you know, people from the neighborhood didn't come, because it was very fancy." Rita Beschner Newell interview notes, October 28, 1975, Novotny Papers.

91. Research memo, September 10, 1951, Jensen Papers; and Novotny, *Alice's World*, 189–90. Although Jensen and Novotny expressed skepticism about Alice's spy story, two German spies were arrested on Staten Island in 1943. "FBI Traps Engineer Who Gave Nazi Spy Data on U.S. Arms," *New York Times*, June 30, 1943.

92. Kende Galleries, Inc., *Bibelots, Jewelry, Painting and Prints, Furniture, Oriental Rugs,*

Fine Laces, Property of Miss E. Alice Austen, "Clear Comfort," S.I., N.Y. (February 12 and 13, 1941), HRT Austen Files. Kende Galleries was at 730 Fifth Avenue at 57th Street in Manhattan, the center of the art gallery district.

93. The headlines read, "OPA [Office of Price Administration] Calls Off Eviction of Austen House Resident," (August 19 '44, in pencil); "Court Voids Sale of Old Residence"; and "78 Years in House, Eviction Revoked, Spinster Is Said To Have Once Refused $125,000 for Staten Island Home Saved by OPA."

94. Letter of Alice Austen to Henry Rogers Winthrop, May 20, 1945, Novotny Papers. Winthrop's secretary, who knew Alice well, gave a group of letters between Alice and Winthrop to Novotny.

95. John A. Morton Jr. interview notes, Novotny Papers.

96. Letter of Gertrude Tate to Loring McMillen, December 5, 1949, HRT Austen Files.

97. Research memo, September 10, 1951, Jensen Papers. The memo traces Alice's movements from late 1949 to June 1950, from the Mariners Family Asylum, to Pleasant Haven Nursing Home, to a brief stay at the Dresden House in Manhattan, to the Staten Island Farm Colony.

Chapter 7: Legacy

1. In the 1940s and 1950s, Benjamin Jaffe (1907–1967), a Russian immigrant, owned the East Orange Art Antiques and Furniture Galleries, Inc., in the heart of Newark's Jewish shopping district.

2. "Austen House, Notes by L. McMillen," July 17, 1945, HRT Austen Files.

3. Alfonso A. Narvaez, "Loring McMillen, 85, An Engineer and a Founder of S.I. Restoration," *New York Times*, March 21, 1991; Harlow McMillen, "Loring McMillen and the Staten Island Historical Society: A Tribute"; and Charles L. Sachs, "Loring McMillen, Preservationist and Public Historian," *Staten Island Historian* 9, no. 1, n.s., (Summer–Fall 1991): 1–11.

4. "Austen House, Notes, by L. McMillen," September 17, 1931, HRT Austen Files.

5. "Loring had been interested in acquiring Alice Austen's photographs for years. He would visit her often . . . During these visits he would ask her to donate the photographs to the Society. She would say, 'I'll think about it.' Loring believed she would eventually give them to the Society." Margaret Robinson, SIHS Treasurer under Loring McMillen, interview notes, Ed Weisman, July 17, 2009, HRT Austen Files.

6. Alice was a member of the Staten Island Antiquarian Society, founded in 1915. The Antiquarian Society merged with the Staten Island Historical Society in 1922, and members of the former became lifetime members of the latter.

7. "Austen House, Notes by L. McMillen," July 17, 1945, HRT Austen Files.

8. Rita Beschner Newell interview notes, October 28, 1975, Novotny Papers.

9. Rudolph Cender, interview notes, October 27, 1975, Novotny Papers.

10. Interview with Loring McMillen on "Museum Week," WNET TV, July 2, 1968, https://www.wnyc.org/story/staten-island-historical-society/.

11. "A Hobby That Paid Off," *Tudor City Views*, May 1952, HRT Austen Files.

12. "Remarks for Alice Austen Day," (handwritten notes), HRT Austen Files; "Alice Austen Day," *Staten Island Historian* 12, no. 4 (October–December 1951): 27.

13. Bill of Sale, May 10, 1950, HRT Austen Files.

14. Letter of Gertrude Tate to Loring McMillen, May 15, 1950, HRT Austen Files.

15. In June 1950, Brinley sent similar letters to the New-York Historical Society, the Museum of the City of New York, George Eastman House, and the Library of Congress. In December 1950, he sent letters to several maritime museums. HRT Austen Files.

16. Brinley's negotiation with the Library of Congress was the most extensive. Paul Vanderbilt, chief of the Prints and Photographs Division, asked Brinley to donate 1,000 negatives, and in exchange the Library would provide the Society with prints of any Staten Island subjects for a cost of one hundred dollars.

17. Grace Mayer, curator of prints at the Museum of the City of New York, asked for the "Street Types of New York," prints and negatives.

18. Invoice, May 25, 1951, HRT Austen Files. Brinley sent two negatives—"Pershing Square area 1906" and "Broadway and 10th Street 1896"—to the *Daily News* for a reproduction fee of ten dollars each. These appeared in the "Changing Scene" series on June 24 and July 1, 1951. The negatives were not returned and are lost. In a memo to the board of directors dated July 16, 1951 (HRT Austen Files), Brinley reported that he sold the rights to fifteen photographs of "character studies" to the *Daily News* for $150. Nine of these images appeared in "Looking Backward," February 28, 1965. In 1951 and in 1965, the credit line read, "Staten Island Historical Society" with no mention of Alice Austen.

19. Brinley's letters to maritime museums were signed: C. Coapes Brinley, Associate Curator of Photography.

20. Oliver Jensen, *The Revolt of American Women: A Pictorial History of the Century of Change from Bloomers to Bikinis—from Feminism to Freud* (New York: Harcourt, Brace, Jovanovich), 7.

21. Letter of Constance Foulk to Staten Island Historical Society, December 27, 1950, HRT Austen Files.

22. Ann Novotny, *Alice's World: The Life and Photography of an American Original: Alice Austen, 1866–1952* (Old Greenwich, CT: The Chatham Press, 1976), 11.

23. Letters between Oliver Jensen and C. Coapes Brinley, February–April 1951, HRT Austen Files.

24. *Pageant* was a small-format picture magazine for men which routinely ran photographs of scantily clad women. "Fun in the 80s," written by Jensen, contended that Alice's photographs dispelled "the present-day notion that grandpa's youth was a drab and joyless time." *Pageant* 9, no. 8 (February 1954): 94–101.

25. *LIFE* paid $2,000 for the prints and rights to publish Austen's photographs for a feature story. After deducting one hundred dollars for printing, the remainder was split between Picture Press and SIHS. To assure Alice's move from the Farm Colony, the Society agreed to contribute its entire share ($950) and Picture Press half its share ($475) for a total of $1,425.

26. Research memo, September 10, 1951, Jensen Papers.

27. Letter of Gertrude Tate to Oliver Jensen, November 13, 1951, Box 29, Jensen Papers. Gertrude happily reported that "Mrs. Park is certainly kindness itself. Patient with a capital P, but I tell Mrs. Park she is almost too indulgent."

28. *LIFE*, September 14, 1951. Some of the article's anecdotes are recorded in Jensen's research memos of July 12 and July 30, 1951.

29. In response to an angry letter from Austen's first cousin Patty Miller, *LIFE* replied: "We're sorry you thought LIFE's article on Alice Austen was unkindly written. Many former friends wrote to tell us how pleased they were to hear about Miss Austen and many of the letters with their warmth of feeling have undoubtedly given her pleasure." Letter of Helen M. Fleming to Mrs. Walter Miller, October 30, 1951, Courtesy of Martha Miller Cole.

30. *LIFE*, Letters to the Editor, October 29, 1951, 19.

31. Jensen sent Gertrude a print of "a picture Miss Austen made of you some 50 years ago; we thought you would like to have it as a souvenir." Gertrude always sent regards to Mrs. Jensen—

the novelist Jean Stafford—whom Alice and Gertrude had met when she visited the Farm Colony. Letter of Oliver Jenson to Gertrude Tate, November 8, 1951, Box 29, Jensen Papers.

32. Letter of Oliver Jensen to C. Coapes Brinley, July 17, 1951, Box 29, Jensen Papers.

33. Letter of Oliver Jensen to Gertrude Tate, November 8, 1951, Box 29, Jensen Papers. The live broadcast was not recorded.

34. Dorothy Doan, phone interview notes, n.d., Novotny Papers.

35. Letter of Gertrude Tate to Mr. and Mrs. McMillen, September 15, 1951, HRT Austen Files. Gertrude prepared a guest list of twenty-two people for Alice Austen Day.

36. "Remarks for Alice Austen Day," (handwritten notes), HRT Austen Files; "Alice Austen Day," *Staten Island Historian* 12, no. 4 (October–December 1951): 27.

37. "Sequel: Alice Austen Day, Old and new friends pay a long overdue tribute to the great woman photographer of Staten Island," *LIFE*, October 29, 1951, 67.

38. "To Note Alice Austen Day: Staten Island Museum to Show Her Photographs Tomorrow," *New York Times*, October 6, 1951, 12; "Old Friends Honor Miss Austen," *New York Times*, October 8, 1951, 19.

39. *LIFE,* October 29, 1951, 67–68.

40. Letter of Gertrude Tate to Oliver Jensen, October 10, 1951, Box 29, Jensen Papers.

41. Special Meeting of the Board of Directors of the Staten Island Historical Society, September 5, 1951, 1–5, HRT Austen Files.

42. Letter of Paul Maddaus to the Board of Directors, Staten Island Historical Society, September 12, 1951, HRT Austen Files.

43. Letter of Gertrude Tate to Oliver Jensen, undated; Jensen's response is dated November 8, 1951, Box 29, Jensen Papers.

44. Letter of Gertrude Tate to Loring McMillen, n.d. [January 1952], HRT Austen Files.

45. Letter of Gertrude Tate to Oliver Jensen, June 4, 1952, Box 29, Jensen Papers.

46. Letter of Arnold V. Schwartz to Harmon Funeral Home, October 5, 1954, HRT Austen Files.

47. "Alice Austen's America," *Holiday*, September 1952, 66–76. Jensen wrote Gertrude, "Mr. Angell . . . did write to say that he hopes to see you all soon." Letter of February 8, 1952, Box 29, Jensen Papers.

48. *Holiday*, 69, 71.

49. Jensen, *The Revolt of American Women*, 5.

50. Letter of Gertrude Tate to Oliver Jensen, November 10, 1952, Box 29, Jensen Papers.

51. Brinley wrote Jensen a three-page letter detailing his outreach to museums and newspapers which concluded: "In view of this we hold it unfair to say that the Alice Austen negatives were in storage at the Staten Island Historical Society until uncovered by Miss Foulk." Letter of C. Coapes Brinley to Oliver Jensen, December 12, 1952, HRT Austen Files.

52. Letter of C. Coapes Brinley to Oliver Jensen, April 20, 1956, HRT Austen Files.

53. Letter of Oliver Jensen to C. Coapes Brinley, May 10, 1956, HRT Austen Files.

54. Letter of C. Coapes Brinley to Oliver Jensen, June 1, 1956, HRT Austen Files.

55. Letter of Cass Canfield Jr., to C. Coapes Brinley, July 2, 1956, HRT Austen Files.

56. Letter of C. Coapes Brinley to Cass Canfield, July 12, 1956, HRT Austen Files.

57. Jensen sent the Society its share of $2,000 from *Holiday Magazine* and additional payments from *LIFE*. Letters of Oliver Jensen to Loring McMillen, February 8, 1952 and March 24, 1952, Box 44, Jensen Papers. The sale to *Pageant* paid only $120. Letter of Oliver Jensen to C. Coapes Brinley, December 7, 1953, HRT Austen Files. Jensen later recalled that Picture Press and the Society raised $5,000 for Alice. Foreword, Novotny, *Alice's World*, 12.

58. "Richmondtown, an important relic of the past years, will be preserved, restored and re-vitalized for the instruction, inspiration and pleasure of present and future generations." City of New York et al., *Fresh Kills Land Fill*, 1951, 12.

59. See Robert Moses, *Public Works: A Dangerous Trade* (New York: McGraw Hill, 1970), 245–46.

60. *Staten Island Advance*, April 23, 1964, HRT Austen Files.

61. On the eve of her eviction from Clear Comfort, Austen wrote her cousin: "You know the four portraits are here that you took for the money you were kind enough to help me out with when I was in such difficulty. What do you want to do with them now?" Letter of Alice Austen to Henry Rogers Winthrop, May 20, 1945, Novotny Papers. Winthrop explained to Jensen that the "sale" of the portraits was pretextual: "He let her sell her portraits of some mutual ancestors which he stored in a closet." Research memo, July 29, 1951, Jensen Papers. For two of the portraits, see Figures 1.7 and 1.8.

62. Adele Forsythe to Loring McMillen, 1964 (no month and day), Novotny Papers.

63. Archie Robertson, "The Island in the Bay," *American Heritage* 17, no. 581 (August 1966): 581.

64. Loring McMillen was one of the original twelve unpaid commissioners.

65. See Marjorie Pearson, "New York City Landmarks Preservation Commission (1962–1999): Paradigm for Changing Attitudes Toward Historic Preservation," Samuel H. Kress Mid-Career Grant Study, The James Marsden Fitch Charitable Foundation, 2010, www.nypap.org/wp-content/uploads/2017/11/320367933-Marjorie-Pearson-pdf.pdf.

66. See Jeffrey A. Kroessler, "Beyond the Bridge: The Unfinished Staten Island Parkways of Robert Moses and the Preservation of the Greenbelt," *New York History* 94, nos. 1–2 (Winter–Spring 2013): 111–29.

67. *Staten Island Advance*, November 19, 1966, HRT Austen Files.

68. The founding members of the Friends of the Alice Austen House included Edward Steichen, Berenice Abbott, Philip Johnson, Joseph Papp, and Cornelius Vanderbilt.

69. Letters of March 9 and 23, 1967, affirming the mayor's support for the Rosebank Esplanade project, Box 49, Jensen Papers.

70. Hugh Humphreys and Regina Benedict, "The Friends of Alice Austen," *Infinity* 16, no. 7 (July 1967): 4ff. Also see, Hugh C. Humphreys, "The Austen Family and Their Home and The Former New York Yacht Club," *Staten Island Historian* 28, no. 2 (April–June 1967): 9–16. Humphreys, a young lawyer, lived in the Austen House during the 1960s.

71. Brendan Gill, Talk of the Town, "Cottage," *New Yorker*, September 30, 1967, 36.

72. "The Proposal," *Gateway to America: The Alice Austen House and Esplanade*, n.p., 1967.

73. The brochure included maps drafted by Bradford M. Greene, an eminent landscape architect, who was a vice-chairman of the Friends and a founder of the Staten Island Greenbelt movement.

74. The Bevex Realty Corporation defended its plan to build high-rise apartments on the site by invoking McMillen's plan to move the Austen House to the Richmondtown Restoration site.

75. Invitation, SIHS Austen exhibition, 1967.

76. "The Park," *Gateway to America*, n.p.

77. The cost of the report was $15,000, half provided by the US Department of the Interior and half by the Friends' fundraising campaign.

78. Stuart Hersh, phone interview with the author, April 11, 2021.

79. The film aired only in New York; it is available on Amazon Prime Video.

80. The Austen House interview on April 12, 1976, was part of a series, "The Livable City," sponsored by the Municipal Art Society, https://www.wnyc.org/story/alice-austen/.

81. Letter of Ann Novotny to Oliver Jensen, February 29, 1976, Box 26, Jensen Papers.

82. Ann Novotny, *Strangers at the Door: Ellis Island, Castle Garden and the Great Migration to America* (Old Greenwich, CT: The Chatham Press, 1971).

83. Contract draft between Chatham Press and SIHS, October 28, 1971, Box 44, Jensen Papers.

84. "I will come back to talk to you with a tape recorder if I may." Letter of Ann Novotny to Oliver Jensen, April 4, 1974. Novotny Papers. There are no Jensen interview notes in Novotny's papers.

85. Novotny seems to have studied Austen's negatives, not her prints.

86. Novotny discovered Patty Miller and Winifred Tate Baker close to her deadline and convinced The Chatham Press to push back her publication date from early to late 1976.

87. Letter of Ann Novotny to Oliver Jensen, February 29, 1976, Box 26, Jensen Papers.

88. Letter of Oliver Jensen to Ann Novotny, August 16, 1976, Box 26, Jensen Papers.

89. Novotny, *Alice's World*, 162.

90. Rita Beschner Newell interview notes, October 28, 1975, Novotny Papers.

91. Letter of Ann Novotny to Oliver Jensen, February 29, 1976, Box 26, Jensen Papers.

92. Novotny was president of the Friends of the Alice Austen House from 1970 to 1982.

93. Letter of Ann Novotny to Margot Gayle, June 25, 1977, Box 26, Jensen Papers.

94. The Neikrug exhibition was a fundraiser for the Austen House renovation.

95. The show at the South Street Seaport Museum, on view from December 1979 through May 1980, included sixty-eight photographs. Jensen wrote an article for the museum's magazine, "The Seagoing World of Alice Austen," *Seaport* (Winter 1980): 18–22. Novotny published an article for the photography audience, "Alice Austen, Recognition of an American Pioneer," *Camera* 25, no. 5 (May 1980): 60–72.

96. The draft report was completed in August 1979, and the final report was filed in October 1981.

97. Letter of Ann Novotny to Bronson Binger, February 1, 1981, Box 26, Jensen Papers.

98. Novotny, *Alice's World*, 60.

99. Scholars have revealed the erotic dimension of many "Boston marriages." See for example, Lillian Faderman, *To Believe in Women: What Lesbians Have Done for America–A History* (New York: Houghton Mifflin, 1999), 222–28.

100. Winifred Tate Baker interview notes, August 26, 1976, Novotny Papers.

101. Pieter Vosburgh first met Alice at the Staten Island Cricket and Baseball Club when he was a child. His daughter married Gertrude's nephew. Gertrude died in a New Jersey nursing home; there were no newspaper obituaries.

102. "The red tape and expense of burying [Gertrude] next to Alice (as they both wished) proved to be too formidable for her sister Winifred to surmount." Novotny, *Alice's World*, 217.

103. Letter of Pieter Vosburgh to Ann Novotny, April 18, 1976, Novotny Papers. Only one of Vosburgh's three April 1976 letters to Novotny survive.

104. Letter of Ann Novotny to Pieter Vosburgh, April 22, 1976, Novotny Papers.

105. Stuart Hersh, phone interview with the author, April 11, 2021.

106. Novotny, *Alice's World,* 224.

107. Born Ann Peacock to British parents in Sweden, Novotny graduated from McGill University in 1957, completed a master's degree in English literature and married George Novotny,

a fellow graduate student, before coming to New York City in 1960. Five years later, she and Eakins, another McGill classmate, established Research Reports, a picture research agency. Shortly after the publication of *Alice's World*, Mary Miller (Patty Miller's grandchild) visited Novotny and Eakins in their New York City apartment.

108. Penny and Liza, "Alice Austen—Photographs," *Dyke, A Quarterly*, no. 3 (1976): 34–43.

109. [Editorial], *Lesbian Art and Artists: Heresies 3, A Feminist Publication on Art and Artists* (Fall 1977): 2.

110. Art historian Richard Meyer drew attention to Novotny's description of this photograph in a roundtable discussion at the Whitney Museum. "The Alice Austen House Presents: New Eyes on Alice Austen," March 31, 2016, https://whitney.org/events/alice-austen.

111. Ann Novotny, "Alice Austen's World," *Heresies 3* (1977): 28.

112. "Ann Novotny, 46, Founder of Editorial Research Service," *New York Times*, December 8, 1982.

113. Alice Austen House, *Commemorative Journal 1986*. The journal celebrated the christening of the new Staten Island commuter ferry named the *Alice Austen*. The dedication page reads: "In memory of another Remarkable Woman, Ann Novotny Our Daughter, Doris and Harold Peacock."

114. Dr. Rosemary L. Eakins, "Ann and Alice, Part III," *Friends of the Alice Austen House, Inc., Newsletter* 2, no. 1 (April 1984): 2.

115. Novotny, *Alice's World*, 148.

116. Novotny, *Alice's World*, 159.

117. Naomi Rosenblum, *A World History of Photography* (New York: Abbeville Press, 1984), 269–70; Sarah Greenough et al., *On the Art of Fixing a Shadow: One Hundred and Fifty Years of Photography* (Washington, D.C.: National Gallery of Art; and New York: Little Brown and Company, 1989), 175; Martha A. Sandweiss, ed., *Photography in Nineteenth Century America* (Fort Worth, TX: Amon Carter Museum; and New York: Harry A. Abrams, Inc., 1991), 282, 301; Rebecca Zurier et al., *Metropolitan Lives: The Ashcan Artists and Their New York* (Washington, D.C.: National Museum of American Art; and New York: W.W. Norton, 1995), 125, 127.

118. Peter Bacon Hales, *Silver Cities: The Photography of American Urbanization, 1839–1915* (Philadelphia: Temple University Press, 1984), 237–41.

119. Judith Schwarz, "Lesbian Photography, A Long Tradition," in *Photographs by JEB, Eye to Eye: Portraits of Lesbians* (New York: Anthology Editions, 2021 reprint), 13–17.

120. Emanuel Cooper, *The Sexual Perspective: Homosexuality and Art in the Last 100 Years in the West* (London and New York: Routledge & Kegal Paul, 1986), 87–90. Alice's name is misspelled "Austin."

121. Susan Butler, "So How Do I Look? Women Before and Behind the Camera," in *Staging the Self: Self-Portrait Photography 1840s–1980s* (London: National Portrait Gallery, 1986), 52–53.

122. www.ninalevitt.com/portfolio/submerged-for-alice-austen/.

123. Letter of Columbia University Press to Richmondtown Restoration, September 12, 1990, HRT Austen Files.

124. Letter of Richmondtown Restoration to Columbia University Press, September 18, 1990, HRT Austen Files. The photograph of Violet and an unidentified friend is at AAH (2017.38.002). Working against deadline, Novotny removed materials—including this vintage print—from HRT, which were never returned.

125. No catalog was produced for the 1994 exhibition, but "The Darned Club" was repro-

duced in the ten-page visitor's guide. HRT Austen Files. In the book based on the exhibition, "The Darned Club" was featured at the start of chapter 1. Molly McGarry and Fred Wasserman, *Becoming Visible: An Illustrated History of Lesbian and Gay Life in Twentieth-Century America* (New York: The New York Public Library and Penguin Studio, 1998), 46, 54–55.

126. Michael Fressola, "'We're here, we're queer, get used to it,'" *Staten Island Advance*, June 19, 1994, E1 and E3. "The Darned Club" was reproduced in the article.

127. James Thompson, "Contrary to Rumor, Alice Austen was not gay," *Staten Island Advance*, June 23, 1994, A22. On July 6, 1994, the *Advance* published opposing letters by Amy S. Khoudari and former board member Mel Hardin (A18).

128. Amy S. Khoudari, "Looking in the Shadows: The Life and Photography of Alice Austen," Master's thesis (Sarah Lawrence College, Bronxville, NY, 1993). She subsequently published *Looking in the Shadows: The Life of Alice Austen, A Novel* (New York: iUniverse, Inc., 2006).

129. See interviews by the New York Preservation Archive Project: Anne Maguire and Maxine Wolfe, founders of the Lesbian Avengers, November 5, 2017; and Mitchell Grubler, executive director of the Alice Austen House, 1991–1994, October 9, 2019.

130. Anne Maguire and Edward Rogowsky, *Alice Austen and Gertrude Tate House: A National Historic Lesbian Landmark*, [song sheet], July 1994, Lesbian Avengers file, Lesbian Herstory Archives, Brooklyn, NY.

131. See https://barbarahammer.com/films/the-female-closet/ available on Amazon Prime Video.

132. Elizabeth B. Waters, "Alice Austen House Museum, Phase I Strategic Planning Report," December 2001, courtesy of Amy Hufnagel.

133. Lillian Faderman and Phyllis Irwin, "Alice Austen and Gertrude Tate: A 'Boston Marriage' on Staten Island," introduction by Carl Rutberg, *Historic House Trust of New York City* (Fall 2010): 6.

Epilogue: Alice's Friends

1. Wendy L. Rouse, *Public Faces, Secret Lives: A Queer History of the Women's Suffrage Movement* (New York: New York University Press, 2022), 118.

2. C. Jane Gover, *The Positive Image: Women Photographers in Turn of the Century America* (Albany: State University of New York, 1988); and Trish Franzen, *Spinsters and Lesbians: Independent Womanhood in the United States* (New York: New York University Press, 1996), 4–5. Recent demographic data may challenge this claim.

3. Sue Ripley, who appears in "The Darned Club," is not included in this discussion. Although she and Alice were neighbors and knew each other since childhood, there are no letters from Sue, and they were not close friends. After her parents died, Sue lived alone in her family's large, waterfront home. She never installed gas or electricity and died in 1940 in a fire that started in an overheated coal stove. *New York Times*, November 30, 1940.

4. Figures 6.16 and 6.25 show Julie Lord at Clear Comfort in 1904 and the 1920s.

5. Ann Novotny, *Alice's World: The Life and Photography of an American Original: Alice Austen, 1866–1952* (Old Greenwich, CT: The Chatham Press, 1976), 70. Novotny's story, derived from conversation with John Morton, could not be independently corroborated.

6. Letter of Elisabeth Strong to Alice Austen, May 23, 1894, AAH Letters.

7. Letter of Kintzing Emmons to Alice Austen, August 25, 1894, AAH Letters.

8. Letter of Elisabeth Strong to Alice Austen, November 17, 1892, AAH Letters.

9. *Chicago Daily Tribune*, June 10, 1892.

10. Letter of Julia Bredt to Alice Austen, September 22, 1893, AAH Letters.

11. Letter of Julia T. Martin to Alice Austen, May 30, 1897, AAH Letters.

12. Letter of Julia T. Martin to Alice Austen, December 31, 1897, AAH Letters.

13. Case File 110, Box 1, Bloomingdale Asylum Patient Records, 1860–1932, Medical Center Archives of New York-Presbyterian / Weill Cornell Medicine, New York, New York (hereafter cited as Case File 110).

14. Case File 110, Note of September 15, 1919.

15. Letter of Violet Ward to Alice Austen, May 21, 1896, AAH Letters.

16. Letter of Violet Ward to Mr. C, May 20, 1922, HRT, Ward Family Papers, MS004, Box 4.

17. "Miss Ward Says Father Had her Wed at Age of 12," *New York Herald*, December 17, 1915, 1; "She's Sane Despite Twins and Lightning," *New York Tribune*, December 21, 1915, 3.

18. Anita Kershaw Jacobsen, "The Ward Family, Grymes Hill," *The Staten Island Historian* 6, no. 2 (April–June 1943): 11.

19. *Brooklyn Daily Eagle*, December 2, 1911.

INDEX

Bonnie Yochelson is a former Curator of Prints and Photographs at the Museum of the City of New York and an established historian of New York City's photographic history. Her notable works include *Jacob A. Riis: Revealing New York's Other Half*; *Alfred Stieglitz New York*; and *Berenice Abbott: Changing New York*.

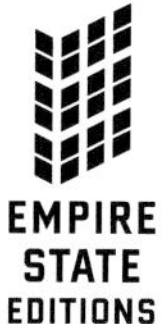

SELECT TITLES FROM EMPIRE STATE EDITIONS

William Seraile, *Angels of Mercy: White Women and the History of New York's Colored Orphan Asylum*

Andrew J. Sparberg, *From a Nickel to a Token: The Journey from Board of Transportation to MTA*

Daniel Campo, *The Accidental Playground: Brooklyn Waterfront Narratives of the Undesigned and Unplanned*

Joseph B. Raskin, *The Routes Not Taken: A Trip Through New York City's Unbuilt Subway System*

Phillip Deery, *Red Apple: Communism and McCarthyism in Cold War New York*

North Brother Island: The Last Unknown Place in New York City. Photographs by Christopher Payne, A History by Randall Mason, Essay by Robert Sullivan

Stephen Miller, *Walking New York: Reflections of American Writers from Walt Whitman to Teju Cole*

Tom Glynn, *Reading Publics: New York City's Public Libraries, 1754–1911*

Craig Saper, *The Amazing Adventures of Bob Brown: A Real-Life Zelig Who Wrote His Way Through the 20th Century*

R. Scott Hanson, *City of Gods: Religious Freedom, Immigration, and Pluralism in Flushing, Queens*. Foreword by Martin E. Marty

Dorothy Day and the Catholic Worker: The Miracle of Our Continuance. Edited, with an Introduction and Additional Text by Kate Hennessy, Photographs by Vivian Cherry, Text by Dorothy Day

Mark Naison and Bob Gumbs, *Before the Fires: An Oral History of African American Life in the Bronx from the 1930s to the 1960s*

Robert Weldon Whalen, *Murder, Inc., and the Moral Life: Gangsters and Gangbusters in La Guardia's New York*

Joanne Witty and Henrik Krogius, *Brooklyn Bridge Park: A Dying Waterfront Transformed*

Jean Arrington with Cynthia S. LaValle, *From Factories to Palaces: Architect Charles B. J. Snyder and the New York City Public Schools*. Foreword by Peg Breen

Boukary Sawadogo, *Africans in Harlem: An Untold New York Story*

Alvin Eng, *Our Laundry, Our Town: My Chinese American Life from Flushing to the Downtown Stage and Beyond*

Stephanie Azzarone, *Heaven on the Hudson: Mansions, Monuments, and Marvels of Riverside Park*

Ron Goldberg, *Boy with the Bullhorn: A Memoir and History of ACT UP New York*. Foreword by Dan Barry

Peter Quinn, *Cross Bronx: A Writing Life*

Mark Bulik, *Ambush at Central Park: When the IRA Came to New York*

Matt Dallos, *In the Adirondacks: Dispatches from the Largest Park in the Lower 48*

Brandon Dean Lamson, *Caged: A Teacher's Journey Through Rikers, or How I Beheaded the Minotaur*

Raj Tawney, *Colorful Palate: Savored Stories from a Mixed Life*

Edward Cahill, *Disorderly Men*

Joseph Heathcott, *Global Queens: An Urban Mosaic*

Francis R. Kowsky with Lucille Gordon, *Hell on Color, Sweet on Song: Jacob Wrey Mould and the Artful Beauty of Central Park*

Jill Jonnes, *South Bronx Rising: The Rise, Fall, and Resurrection of an American City, Third Edition*

Barbara G. Mensch, *A Falling-Off Place: The Transformation of Lower Manhattan*

David J. Goodwin, *Midnight Rambles: H. P. Lovecraft in Gotham*

Felipe Luciano, *Flesh and Spirit: Confessions of a Young Lord*

Maximo G. Martinez, *Sojourners in the Capital of the World: Garifuna Immigrants*

Jennifer Baum, *Just City: Growing Up on the Upper West Side When Housing Was a Human Right*

Davida Siwisa James, *Hamilton Heights and Sugar Hill: Alexander Hamilton's Old Harlem Neighborhood Through the Centuries*

Annik LaFarge, *On the High Line: The Definitive Guide, Third Edition*. Foreword by Rick Dark

Marie Carter, *Mortimer and the Witches: A History of Nineteenth-Century Fortune Tellers*

Alice Sparberg Alexiou, *Devil's Mile: The Rich, Gritty History of the Bowery.* Foreword by Peter Quinn

Carey Kasten and Brenna Moore, *Mutuality in El Barrio: Stories of the Little Sisters of the Assumption Family Health Service.* Foreword by Norma Benítez Sánchez

Kimberly A. Orcutt, *The American Art-Union: Utopia and Skepticism in the Antebellum Era*

Jonathan Butler, *Join the Conspiracy: How a Brooklyn Eccentric Got Lost on the Right, Infiltrated the Left, and Brought Down the Biggest Bombing Network in New York*

Nicole Gelinas, *Movement: New York's Long War to Take Back Its Streets from the Car*

Jack Hodgson, *Young Reds in the Big Apple: The New York Young Pioneers of America, 1923–1934*

Lynn Ellsworth, *Wonder City: How to Reclaim Human-Scale Urban Life*

Walter Zev Feldman, *From the Bronx to the Bosphorus: Klezmer and Other Displaced Musics of New York*

Larry Racioppo, *Here Down on Dark Earth: Loss and Remembrance in New York City*

For a complete list, visit www.fordhampress.com/empire-state-editions.